Great Outdoor Getaways

to the

Bay Area & Beyond

by Tom Stienstra

51695

9 780935 701524

Foghorn Press
BOOKS BUILDING COMMUNITY

Great Outdoor Getaways to the Bay Area and Beyond

Foghorn Press
555 De Haro Street—Suite 220
The Boiler Room
San Francisco, CA 94107
(415) 241-9550

For ordering information, call (800) 842-7477.

Library of Congress Catalog-in-Publication Data

Stienstra, Tom.

Great Outdoor Getaways to the Bay Area and Beyond,
by Tom Stienstra.
p. cm.

Includes index
ISBN 0-935701-52-4 : $16.95
1. Outdoor recreation—California—San Francisco Bay Region—Guidebooks
2. San Francisco Bay Region—Description and travel—Guidebooks
I. Title
GV191.42.c2s75 1993
790'.09794'6—dc20

91—2785
CIP

Printed in the United States of America

Great Outdoor Getaways

to the

Bay Area & Beyond

by Tom Stienstra

Foghorn Press
BOOKS BUILDING COMMUNITY

As a publisher of outdoor and recreation guidebooks, Foghorn Press is committed to protecting the environment. This book is printed on the California standard for recycled paper, which is 50% recycled paper and 10% post-consumer waste.

Book Credits

Managing Editor/Book Design—**Ann Marie Brown**
Assistant Editor—**Samantha Trautman**
Copy Editor—**Howard Rabinowitz**
Cover Illustration—**Ray Marshall**
Author Photo—**Michael Hodgson**

Special thanks to the *San Francisco Examiner,* Will Hearst, Jim Sevrens, Phil Bronstein, Glenn Schwarz, Dave Dayton, Larry Yant, Rick Nelson, Glenn Mayeda, Pete Cafone, Christine Barnes, Kevin Casey, Donald George, Judy Canter, and the rest of the *Examiner* staff.

For Mom and Dad

Introduction

Some critics are calling this book "Stienstra's Kiss and Tell." Maybe they're right. I am sharing my favorite adventure areas in the hope that the public will learn to love California as I do. In turn, that collective love will assure the future protection and wise use of the state's natural resources. It's also a way to have a lot of fun.

It's ironic that many Californians who love the outdoors complain about living here. They often dream of a vacation in some far-off paradise, thinking, "Someday I'm going to get out of here and start having a good time." Well, I wish I could show every person who has ever had these thoughts the Bay Area and Northern California from my airplane. They would discover that despite strips and pockets where people are jammed together and the roads are crowded, most of the state remains wild, unsettled and beautiful. The first time you see this land from the air, it can completely change your perspective.

The Bay Area, for instance, is circled by wildlands. There are 125 parks, 2,500 miles of trails, 44 lakes, a beautiful coast, mountains with lookouts, and a bay with islands. If you expand your adventures beyond the Bay Area, the state has 18 million acres of national forest, 185 streams, 373 lakes you can drive to and 483 lakes you can hike to. The land has no limits. Enjoy it. As a full-time outdoors writer, I can live anywhere I want, and I choose to live here. There is nowhere else that provides as much year-round adventure, diversity and quality as right here in California.

This book project started when Charles Cooper, at the time the sports editor of the *San Francisco Examiner*, asked me to write one "getaway" story per week. Nice job, eh? A weekly story evolved into hundreds of adventures, a 750-page manuscript and now this book. After I reviewed and checked each story, my research editor Robyn Schlueter confirmed every phone number, address, direction and fact to make the book as accurate as possible. Then my editor, Ann Marie Brown of Foghorn Press, completed an extremely detailed edit job to make the book as friendly and as readable as possible. Our mission is always to be as accurate and up-to-date as we can, and we welcome suggestions and comments from readers. Write to us at Foghorn Press, 555 DeHaro Street, Suite 220, San Francisco, CA 94107.

The outdoors is good for the soul. An adventure can refresh the spirit. So go for it—and don't be surprised if you run into me out there.

—Tom Stienstra

Contents

Chapter 8—Sonoma & Napa

Chapter 9—San Francisco Bay Area

How to Use This Book

This book is arranged geographically. The grid map below shows what regions of northern California are covered by each chapter (Chapters 1-14). For example, th San Francisco Bay Area is covered in Chapter 9, and Tahoe is covered in Chapter 13. See the beginning of eac chapter for a more detailed map of each region.

Chapters 15 and 16 are not arranged geographically, as they are compendiums of getaways, activities and adventures that are not single destinations.

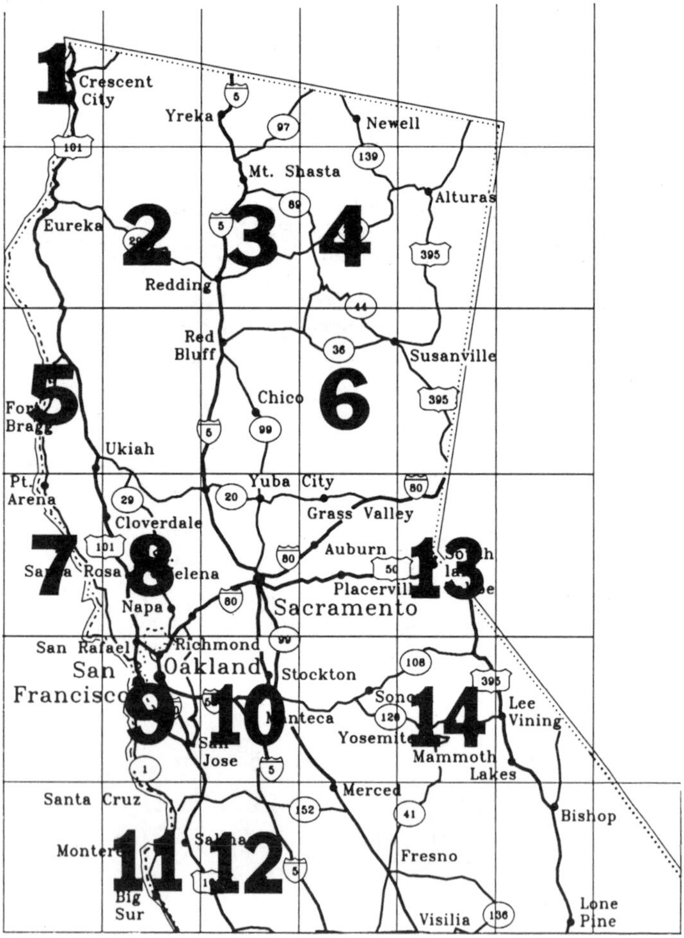

Chapter 1

Crescent City & Redwood Empire

1—Jedediah Smith State Park—p. 15
2—Patrick's Point State Park—p. 17
3—Prairie Creek Redwoods State Park—p. 19

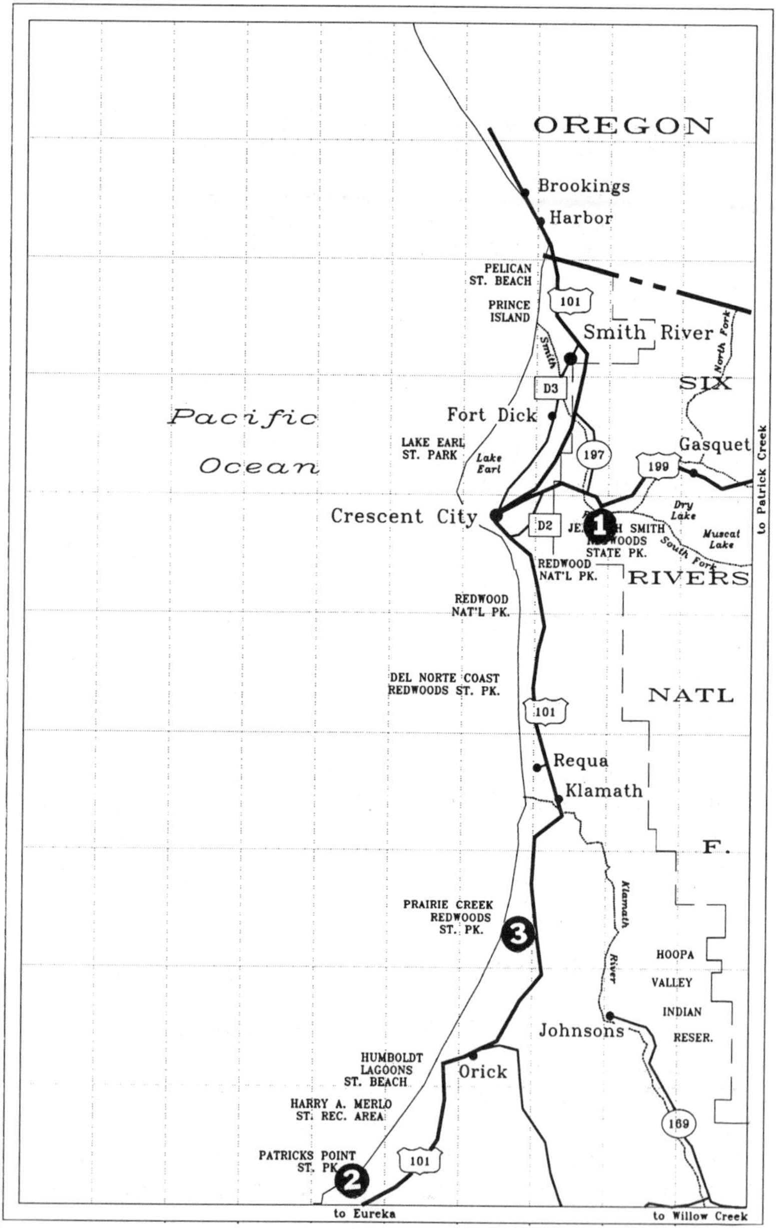

1

Jedediah Smith State Park

In the Redwood Empire near Crescent City

Disneyland, San Francisco and the North Coast redwoods are California's primary tourist draws, but it is only in the sanctuary of the redwoods that you can find peace as well as adventure.

Jedediah Smith State Park is the northernmost of 30 redwood state parks that are set along the coast from Monterey to the Oregon border. It is my favorite because of the variety of adventures that await explorers there. The kicker is that the summer climate is far warmer there than in most areas that harbor coastal redwoods.

The park is set in the northwestern corner of California off Highway 199, just on the edge of the Smith River, California's largest undammed river. In the spring and summer, the South Fork provides good fishing for rainbow and cutthroat trout. In the fall and winter, the main Smith River draws runs of giant salmon and steelhead, although they can prove quite elusive.

Jedediah Smith Park is an ideal base station for fishing adventures on the nearby river, and a good stopover for vacationers heading north as well. For hikers, the park has 23 miles of trails that wind through a countryside filled with giant redwoods, and is located on the edge of the vast Six Rivers National

Forest—which contains more than one million acres of wildlands.

The trails at Jedediah Smith State Park are varied enough so that you can match your hike to your physical condition. Of the 11 trails, six are rated "easy" and follow relatively flat terrain. A good example is the Stout Grove Trail, where you walk a half-mile to reach the awesome Stout Tree, which measures 340 feet tall and 20 feet in diameter. Ask the ranger for directions.

A good two-hour hike, rated "moderate," is the Hiouchi Trail, which takes you along the west bank of the Smith River and right through a hole in a giant burned-out redwood tree.

All the nearby diversity magnifies the appeal of the park, so even with 108 campsites, you can expect camping reservations to be necessary, particularly during the summer.

But for people who hear the call of giant trees, this place beats Disneyland by a mile.

Directions: From San Francisco, head north on Highway 101 and continue for approximately 370 miles, past Crescent City to the Highway 199 turnoff. Turn east and drive 13 miles to the park entrance on the right.

Fee or Free: A state park entrance fee is charged. Campsite fees vary depending on the season.

Campsites: Each campsite has a table, stove and cupboard. Restrooms with hot showers are nearby. No trailer hook-ups are available. If you want a more remote campsite, you should contact the Gasquet Ranger Station, (707) 457-3131, for camping areas in the Six Rivers National Forest. Camping reservations at Jedediah Smith State Park can be made through Mistix at (800) 444-7275.

Contact: Call Jedediah Smith State Park at (707) 464-9533 or (707) 458-3310, or write P.O. Drawer J, Crescent City, CA 95531.

2

Patrick's Point State Park

On the Humboldt coast north of Eureka

Patrick's Point State Park is a remarkable chunk of land on California's north coast. You get the best of two worlds: It's lush and green with a classic fern undergrowth, yet bordered by the rock-strewn Pacific, where you can go tidepool-hopping and whale watching.

But what makes Patrick's Point unique is its virtual wall-to-wall plant growth within the park's 625 acres. The trails are often nothing more than tunnels through vegetation. Hikers can become completely sheltered and isolated by the mammoth walls of ferns. The first time I stopped here was back in 1978, and like most folks, it was more by accident than intent. I just wanted a campsite for the night, but I got much more.

The park sits adjacent to Highway 101, and from the road, you have little idea of the beauty sheltered within. It's always a stunner for first-timers. It's like a rainforest jungle, where the dense undergrowth can only be experienced by foot. The Rim Trail, an easy two-miler, follows the edge of the bluff around three sides of the park. Short yet steep cutoffs can take walkers to the best vistas in the park—Wedding Rock, Palmer's Point, Patrick's Point and Agate Beach. From these lookouts, it is common to spot migrating gray whales.

It's nearly a year-long adventure here. Spring and fall are best for whale watching, however, because the air is crystal clear and the migration is peaking.

During the summer, dense fog can cover Patrick's Point, as well as the tourists within. Water droplets trickle from the ferns and tourist's noses, and many folks think it is raining. It isn't; it's just fogging. This drip-drip, low-visibility stuff almost never envelops Patrick's Point in spring and fall. The muggy days of Indian summer are the warmest days of the year here.

Four campgrounds offer 123 campsites, and like most state parks, they come with a sturdy table, barbecue stove and cupboard. Water faucets and restrooms with hot showers are provided just a short walking distance from each campground. Play it safe and get a reservation.

It is a good idea to plan your trip for when a low tide will roll back the Pacific and unveil the tidepools. Tiny marine organisms will conduct their little wars at your feet as you hop from one pool to another. Fishermen will discover good prospects for lingcod, cabezone and sea trout during low tides, because they can walk to the outer reaches of the tidal basin. During high tides, on the other hand, anglers will be casting into a shallow, rocky sea floor where a snag per cast is the likely result.

A side trip to Agate Beach is a necessity. Here you will find a shoreline loaded with semi-precious stones polished by centuries of sand and water.

Pick one up and put it in your pocket. Someday when you're enduring a day of frustration, the little rock in your pocket will provide you with a connection to a day of happiness.

Directions: Simply take Highway 101 straight up the coast. Patrick's Point is located about 40 minutes north of Eureka, about 10 miles beyond Trinidad.
Fee or Free: A state park entrance fee and camping fees are charged.
Reservations: Reserve campsites through Mistix at (800) 444-7275.
Contact: The park can be reached by phoning (707) 677-3570. The North Coast headquarters for state parks can be reached at (707) 937-5804.

3

Prairie Creek Redwoods

On the North Coast near Orick

The first time you stare at a giant animal eye-to-eye, it can make your backbone tingle. It doesn't have to be something that can eat you—it just has to be big. You have a sudden recognition that the critter standing before you is one huge fellow, and whether he knows it or not, he could do the Bigfoot Stomp all over your body. The funny thing is, though, he usually doesn't seem to know it.

This is how it is with the Roosevelt elk, a monstrous-sized animal that stands five feet at the shoulder. The bulls have long, pointed antlers that look like they could turn you into an instant shishkebab. But unless you try to pet one on the nose and say, "Nice elky," this animal is more likely to maintain an air of gentle indifference, rather than behave like a Doberman attack dog.

Visitors at Prairie Creek Redwoods State Park on California's northern coast get a quick understanding of this behavior, even after the initial shock of seeing something so huge, so close. The elk here are wild, not tame, but are domesticated to the point where they will allow various forms of humanoids, even Southern Californians, to view them from a certain distance.

When the big bulls look up and freeze you with a stare, that means "close enough, buddy." Most people

Directions: From San Francisco, drive approximately 330 miles north on US 101. The park is located about six miles north of Orick, and is divided by the highway.

Camping: Campsites in the park can be reserved through Mistix at (800) 444-7275. Other camping options outside the park include Gold Bluff near Fern Canyon and Del Norte State Redwoods north of Klamath: (707) 458-3115. Also Jedediah Smith Redwoods east of Crescent City at (707) 464-9533 and Six Rivers National Forest north

seem to understand this language.

If you have never seen a huge elk in its native habitat, Prairie Creek Redwoods is the spot. The park is located about 50 miles north of Eureka, where the two-lane Highway 101 cuts right through the park. Often the elk will herd up just beyond the old wooden rails that line each side of the road.

Sometimes all you have to do is pull over on the road's shoulder, which has been enlarged for parking, and you'll have what may be your first significant wildlife sighting not made in a zoo. As many as 50 to 75 elk will often mill around in the large meadow right along the highway. It can make for remarkable photographs.

One time while I was studying a big bull through a pair of binoculars, I saw a family of tourists in a motor home cruising by. The driver accidently turned his head and spotted all the elk in the adjacent meadow. He braked hard, jerked the RV over to the side of the road, and jumped out. "Look at that! Look at that!" he shouted to his family.

Ten minutes later, as he was calming down, he said to his wife, "Wendy, those are the biggest deer I've ever seen in my life. We sure don't have anything like that in Oklahoma. Did you get a picture? Howie back home won't believe this."

If you've never ventured up here, there are a lot of other things you and Howie won't believe—like the redwood forests, the secluded campgrounds, scenic drives and some of the prettiest day-hikes in the country. You've got Prairie Creek Redwoods as a good base camp with 75 campsites, one of the best day-hikes in California at nearby Fern

Canyon, and, of course, there are the elk—who will play hide-and-seek for as long as you want.

The redwoods here average more than 200 feet tall and 12 to 13 feet in diameter. They aren't as big around as the Sequoias in Yosemite's Mariposa Grove, but they are taller. Put thousands of them together, most of them 1,000 years old or older, and you get the feeling that this place has been here a long while without anybody fooling with it.

It's even more special in Fern Canyon. This canyon has 50-foot-high walls that are masses of ferns and flora, and the redwoods tower above. Most people have never seen anything like it.

The walks are not difficult, with little elevation gain or loss. There are many shorter options to the Fern Canyon Trail available right from the parking lot at Prairie Creek Redwoods. A good trail map is available at the park's headquarters.

Prairie Creek is one of four contiguous parklands on California's North Coast that stretches for miles and miles. That provides camping options and plenty of alternatives if you want to extend your stay. If the 75-site campground is full at Prairie Creek, you can camp at Gold Bluff Beach (27 campsites), Del Norte State Park (108 campsites), or in adjacent Six Rivers National Forest.

But if you want to see elk, Prairie Creek is the spot.

Two years ago, a fellow decided he wanted a special picture of an elk, that is, a close-up head shot. Well, the ambitious photographer did not have a zoom lens, so he innocently walked right up in front of an elk to take the picture.

and east of the park at (707) 442-1721.

Fee or Free: A state park access fee is charged. Campsite fees vary depending on the season.

Nearby Trips: Two are suggested; both are well signed. To get to the Fern Canyon Trail, take the Davison Road off Highway 101. To get to Lady Bird Johnson Redwood Grove, take the Bald Hill Road off Highway 101.

Contact: Call Prairie Creek Redwoods State Park at (707) 488-2171.

Well, Mr. Elk did not like that. In fact, Mr. Elk snorted and chased that fellow right up a tree. At last look, the fellow was perched on a limb, with the elk standing below, looking up at him.

As far as I know, he's still up there, and with pictures to be developed that are far more interesting than he first imagined.

Chapter 2

Weaverville & Trinity Country

1—Lewiston Lake—p. 25
2—Trinity Alps Wilderness—p. 28
3—Trinity River Rafting—p. 33

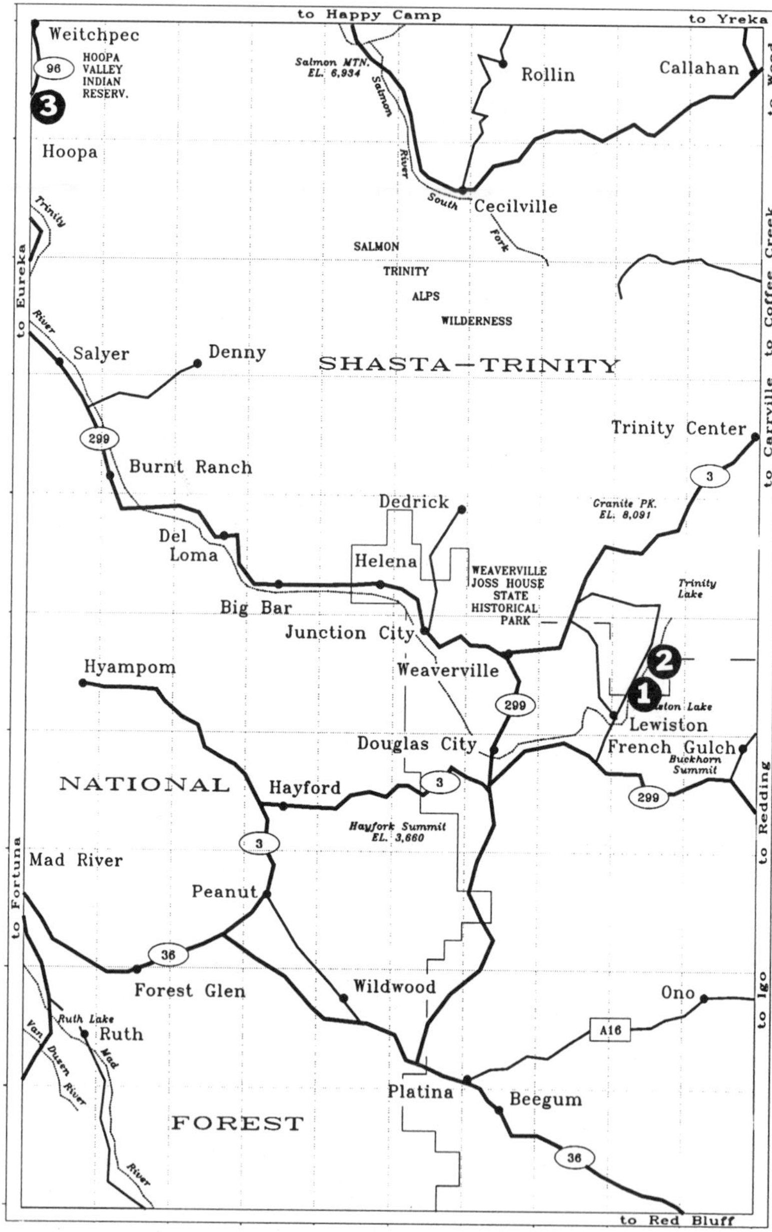

1

Lewiston Lake

At the foot of the Trinity Alps, west of Redding

When you roll out of your sleeping bag at your campsite alongside Lewiston Lake, you may rub your eyes a few extra times to make sure you're still on earth, not in heaven.

This jewel of a lake laps quietly at the bank, and a few trout rise to the surface just a few feet from your campsite. You rub your eyes some more. Thickly wooded mountains rise around you, and in the distance, the snow-covered peaks provide a backdrop. Is this Montana? Canada? Switzerland? Hardly. This is another adventure in our own California: Lewiston Lake, tucked away 30 miles west of Redding in Northern California, snuggled below the Trinity Alps.

It's a unique place that provides quality camping, fishing, boating and hiking, yet is just far enough away from the Bay Area—a five-hour drive—to keep it from becoming a zoo of summer vacationers.

Four campground facilities provide 100 campsites, and if tents are not for you, there's a private resort along the northwest end of the lake that offers cabins and hookups for motor homes. But a tent is all you need at Mary Smith Campground, a truly idyllic spot at the lake's edge. It has 18 campsites for tent camping and is the first campground you reach in your drive along the lake.

With 15 miles of shoreline, Lewiston Lake is just big enough so that it remains uncrowded both for camping and boating. A 10-mph speed limit on the lake

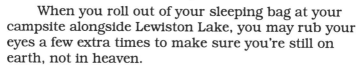

Directions: From the Bay Area, take Interstate 80 north to Interstate 505, then proceed north to Interstate 5. Drive approximately 125 miles north to Redding and take the Highway 299 West exit. Continue on Highway 299 for 23 miles, then turn on Lewiston Road. Proceed to the lake.

Camping: Campsites are operated on a first-come, first-served basis by the Shasta-Trinity National Forest. For information, phone (916) 623-2121. Motor home hookups are available as well; phone Pine Cove Resort at (916) 778-3838, or Lakeview

makes it ideal for canoes and small aluminum boats, and keeps high-powered boats out. You don't have to contend with waterskiers, only with the fish. And there are plenty of the latter.

As at any lake, the fishing runs in cycles, but you may find rainbow trout and a few giant but elusive brown trout here. A key is that Lewiston is actually the afterbay for Trinity Lake—and that means that water in this lake is cold year-round, since it comes from the bottom of Trinity Dam.

Some of the best fishing in the summer is just before sunset at the upper end of the lake, particularly upstream of Lakeview Terrace, just where you can start to see the current on the lake surface. This is the haunt for rainbow trout, most averaging 13 to 14 inches, sometimes bigger. By boat, you should anchor in this area and let a nightcrawler flutter in the current, testing different depths.

If you're without a boat, then bring chest waders, and from above the Lakeview Terrace area, wade outside the tules and either cast a threaded nightcrawler with splitshot for weight, or fly-cast. Spin fishermen might also try using a bubble-and-fly combination. Evening bites can be quite good.

Typical daytime fishing is not as good, but trollers using flashers and a needlefish lure or a nightcrawler can take rainbow trout in the 10 to 12-inch class, sometimes bigger. The exception is when the Trinity Dam powerhouse is running. Anchor in the current, and let a nightcrawler or Power Bait flutter near the bottom. That can be dynamite.

Boat and motor rentals are available at Pine Cove Marina in Lakeview Terrace for guests only.

A good option, especially for families, is to rent a boat for a half-day trip and fish the evening bite. Spend the morning and mid-day exploring a trail around neighboring Trinity Lake. A good suggestion is the three-mile trail that runs from Clark Springs Campground to Cedar Stock Resort.

If you're roughing it, and need supplies while you're here, there are small grocery stores at Lewiston (on the southern end of the lake) and at Pine Grove Trailer Park.

That leaves little to worry about here. You can just show up, kick back, and try to remember that you're not in some far corner of the world, but still in California. But then again maybe you don't even need to remember that.

❖

Terrace Resort at (916) 778-3803.

Boat Rentals: Boat and motor rentals are available from Pine Cove Marina at (916) 778-3770.

Cabins: Lakeview Terrace offers cabins of various sizes for rental. For information, phone (916) 778-3803.

Contact: For free maps, brochures, directions, and fishing tips, call Shasta Cascade Wonderland Association at (800) 326-6944, or write to 1250 Parkview, Redding, CA 96001.

2

Trinity Alps Wilderness

Northeast of Eureka and northwest of Redding

The rocky chute rose almost straight up, and from our perch on a narrow ledge, it seemed like we were trying to climb the backbone of a huge monster. Below was a 1,500-foot wall of rock, above was the Sawtooth Ridge of the Trinity Alps. Climbing off-trail as we were, in search of wonders, unknown lakes and big trout, meant accepting mystery and danger.

Rivers, lakes and oceans will attack you. Mountains are different. They wait for you to make a mistake.

I reached up and grabbed hold of a rock, and it gave way and went crashing down the talus slope like a bowling ball. My heart shook at the thought that it could be our bodies doing the same.

Then I remembered my old wilderness adage: Don't fight the mountain. Accept it, think it through and move forward. Deep inside of you, right in your chest, is a window, and when the window opens, the power of the universe will flow through you. Don't let the window shut and lock. Settle down and let it open, and you will move forward and achieve the greatness for which you are meant.

With that thought, and feeling more settled, I grabbed another rock. It held. I pulled myself up, a booted foot lodged in a crevice for support. A light breeze coming up the canyon made the sweat tingle on the back of my neck. The next foot came easier. Made it through a tough spot, just like that.

We scrambled to the mountain rim and peered from a ridge notch as if we were standing on the edge of the earth. Below us was the Trinity Alps Wilderness, northwest of Redding, immense wildlands with 585,000 acres, 82 lakes, 50 mountain peaks and 550 miles of trails.

The biggest mountain-bred rainbow trout of the West live here in remote, little-known lakes. But to reach them, you must leave the trail. One such lake, Little South Fork Lake, is said to have trout that average 15 to 18 inches and practically say, "Catch me." But in a guidebook for the area, author Wayne Moss called reaching this lake "a task for deranged souls."

Three likely candidates for such a title are Jeff Patty, Michael Furniss and myself. Over the years, we have gone off-trail in search of Bigfoot, hiked the entire John Muir Trail, and climbed Shasta, Whitney and Half Dome, among many other adventures. Patty, a wilderness explorer/photographer, and Furniss, a scientist, aren't quite over the edge, but they are a bit crazy. And the idea of giant rainbow trout in remote wildlands was enough to inspire another trip.

The Trinity Alps may be the prettiest land in the western United States. The granite chutes on the mountain rims make them look like the Swiss Alps. The lakes are set in classic granite bowls. Every deep canyon looks like a sea of conifers.

From the trailhead at Coffee Creek, we hiked in 12 miles to the Caribou Lakes Basin, spent the night, then stared hard at the map, studying the terrain and slope.

"There's no easy way in to Little South Fork Lake," Patty said. "No easy way out."

"Perfect for three deranged souls," answered Furniss.

There would be an altitude drop of 2,500 feet, then a climb of 3,500 feet without the benefit of a trail. In our way were two mountains, and we decided to lateral around them, taking bear paths and deer trails to do it. It wasn't long until we ran into a massive brush field, and one after the other, we three deranged souls disappeared into it.

We'd grapple with the branches, scramble for toeholds, fall down and curse the brush. After several hours, our forearms were scratched up like we'd been in a fight with a pack of bobcats and lost.

"Getting caught in that brush makes you feel like a bug in a spider web," Furniss said.

But there's no fighting it, I thought to myself. You lose every time. Remember the window in your chest. Let it open and you can move on.

Later, after dropping elevation and heading through a forest, Patty spotted what looked like a bear trail, and we were able to take one good step after another for the first time in hours. The air smelled of pines and you could faintly hear the sound of a small stream. I took a deep breath and felt like I was back in the 1830s when the first trailblazers came west.

Suddenly, right then, there was a terrible stinging sensation on my right hand. Then bang! Again, in my arm. And again right in the butt. I looked down at my stinging arm and hand and saw bees swarming around me.

I let out a howl, and in a flash, I unhitched my pack and went running through the forest, then stopped to see if I had outrun them. No such luck. Some 20 bees were clamped onto my pants, trying to sting my legs. Others were circling.

"They've marked you, they've marked you," shouted Furniss. "Run, run!"

In a panic-stricken rush, I swept them off my legs, and went running through brush and around trees. I would have given a million dollars for a lake to jump in. But there was no lake. A minute later, after being chased by a swarm, it was over.

Patty, certified for emergency medical treatment, immediately grabbed me.

"Do you have allergic reactions to bee stings?"

"No," I answered, and then he slid the stingers out, using care not to break the poison sack.

"You must have stepped on a hive," Furniss said. "You're lucky you didn't get stung a hundred times. One time they got me in the head, but they only got me three times."

"A lot of people get hurt when they're running from a swarm of bees," Patty added. "In panic, they don't watch where they're going and break an ankle or leg. Then, while laying there, the bees get them anyway."

Later, we dropped down the canyon stream, hoping to rock-hop straight up the river, eventually reaching the lake. The plan was working well until we ran head-on into a surprise, a 100-foot waterfall. We named it Crystal Falls, because the falling water droplets refracted by sunlight looked like crystals.

But as pretty as it was, that waterfall blocked our route. To get around it required backtracking, then scrambling up a 120-degree talus slope to gain altitude on the canyon wall, lateraling across thick brush, and climbing our way to a rock basin. It had taken us 10 hours to travel under two miles—but we could finally see it, Little South Fork Lake.

It was just before sunset. Little South Fork Lake is a particularly beautiful lake—small, but deep blue and surrounded by steep, glaciated granite. Even from a distance, we could see the insects hatching and the trout rising.

After a night of recovery, we made our first casts. In my first seven casts, I had five strikes and landed rainbow trout measuring 12, 13 and 16 inches. The biggest catch of the trip was 17.5 inches. I had another one that ripped off 20 feet of line in two seconds before splitting the hook.

Yes, the fish were as big as we'd been told. And there is a logical explanation for it.

Even though the Trinity Alps look like the top of the world, the elevations are 5,000 to 6,000 feet, much lower than the Sierra Nevadas or the Rocky Mountains.

"That's why there is more terrestrial productivity here than in the high Sierra," said Furniss, who is a soil and water scientist. "There is more soil, more trees, more algae in the bottom of lakes and more insect hatches."

In other words, there is more life in general, including fish. Big ones. There was no "evening rise," like at most lakes. The fish were feeding continuously. A gold Z-Ray and small Panther Martin spinner were the lures that enticed the most bites.

At night, there was a remarkable calm at this remote lake. Deer, sometimes 15 at a time, could be seen idling in the bright moonlight within 100 yards of the camp.

Patty pointed to the granite rim above the lake. "When it's time to get out of here, let's climb that," he said. "No way do we want to fight the brush, the bees and that waterfall again."

Patty smiled and started suggesting possible routes. Nearby, a big trout jumped and landed with a splash. Fifty yards away, a deer started at the surprise visitors, the three deranged souls.

Furniss sized up the ridge, bright in the moonlight, and smiled.

"It looks just about impossible to climb," he said with a laugh.

A minute later, he spoke again.

"Perfect."

For a map of the Trinity Alps Wilderness, send $2 to U.S. Forest Service, 630 Sansome Street, San Francisco, CA 94111. For information about trail conditions and wilderness permits, phone Shasta-Trinity National Forest headquarters at (916) 246-5222.

3

Trinity River Rafting

In the Hoopa Valley in Trinity County

The Trinity River is being turned into a stream of consciousness by the Native American nation whose land it runs through.

A rafting trip is the vehicle for a trek down a river and into the culture of the Hupa nation. There is nothing else like it in North America, where Native Americans are reaching out to their fellow countrymen of all races to share both a whitewater adventure and a history lesson.

This is taking place on the Hoopa Valley Indian Reservation in Northern California, the largest Native American settlement in the state with 4,000 people living on 90,000 acres of land. Suddenly, there is no such thing as an "outsider" anymore.

"What's important is that we're breaking down barriers through these trips," said Linc McCovey, a Hupa guide, pulling at the oars as our raft floated toward a bend in the river. "We welcome visitors. We're trying to show them respect, and hope that they, in turn, will have respect for what they see and hear here."

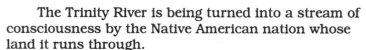

This new program has come about through the cooperation of the Hoopa Valley Tribal Council, Kimtu Outdoor Adventures, and tribal elders willing to share the tribe's history. The end result is an adventure that includes a visit to ancient village sites and the Hupa Museum, a rafting trip on the Trinity River, and a lunch complete with Native American smoked salmon and acorn soup, along with more mainstream fare.

"We've had decades of a defensive posture and now we're changing that," said Dale Risling, chairman of the Hoopa Valley Tribal Council. "The Hupa Tribe is reaching outside of the reservation for friendships that will be beneficial."

The rafting trip tours a mild piece of the Trinity River, about a five-mile trip from Tish Tang Camp downstream to the Hupa Village. Along the way, you pull up to the shore of an old Native American village called "Tsewenaldin," which means "the place of happy meetings." The stretch of water here is an easy float, nothing more formidable than Class II rapids. It is ideal for families or newcomers to the sport. In fact, many people spend much of the trip in the water, not in the raft, with their lifejackets on.

In the course of a few hours, Liam Furniss, 11, turned from a reluctant city slicker to a happy river otter. "I have to admit, before the trip, water scared me a bit," Liam said. "Not any more. I had the best time of my life."

A two-day trip is also available, which starts further upriver in the Trinity Canyon and covers more ambitious whitewater with inflatable kayaks.

The Trinity has always been the lifeblood of the Hupa tribe. It starts from drops of melting snow high in the Trinity Alps, joining to form trickles, brooks, creeks, and then pouring down the river canyon. It is very clear, being the product of a hard granite base, and in evening light, it glows like an emerald.

The Trinity's fertile banks led the Hupas to settle in the valley here. "We could always count on the salmon in the river, and the acorns from the oaks," said Jimmy Jackson, 82, the tribal elder. "We didn't have to move around searching for food, like tribes in other parts of the country."

Jackson and museum curator Bill Carpenter open the tour by guiding visitors through the museum and the sites of an ancient village, ceremonial dances and burial grounds.

"See that wood knob in the boat," said Jackson, pointing at the interior of a redwood dugout canoe. "That's the heart of the boat. The boat is alive, not dead."

He went on to explain how Hupas made baskets from willow roots and porcupine quills, and dip nets for salmon from the roots of wild irises. "It would take me a year to make a small dip net from wild irises," Jackson said. "Almost as long to make a rope out of horse hair."

Carpenter showed us a rare albino deer skin, used in a ceremonial dance—a dance that was performed 500 years ago, and is still honored by current tribe members.

An increasing number of younger Indian residents are taking an interest in their heritage. Some are learning the Hupa language. *The Hupa Encyclopedia*, written by Jackson and other tribe elders, is projected to be published next year and is awaited with great expectations on the reservation. It will be the first of its kind for a Native American nation.

Among the Hupas infused with the tribe's new energy is McCovey, the rafting guide, who once left the reservation, but has returned with a new-found sense of purpose.

"What I'm doing is coming back to the reservation and respecting what was here for me all along," McCovey said. "My favorite part of the trip are the areas of religious and ceremonial concerns. It's something I'm just now learning. When I go down the river, I want to be able to feel the same way my ancestors felt. They

Fee or Free:
Rafting trip rates include gear, lunch and a historical tour.

Contact:
For a free brochure, phone Kimtu Outdoor Adventures at (800)562-8475.

About the spelling:
The Indian tribe name is spelled "Hupa," whereas the town and the reservation are spelled "Hoopa."

made the same trip in their dugout canoes."

Rafting with the Hupas offers a unique mix of past culture and present adventuring. It works for visitors and Native Americans alike, shoulder to shoulder.

Chapter 3

Shasta & Cascade Area

Shasta/Cascade Area

1—Castle Crags State Park—p. 39
2—Lake Siskiyou—p. 41
3—Mount Shasta—p. 44
4—McCloud River Preserve—p. 47

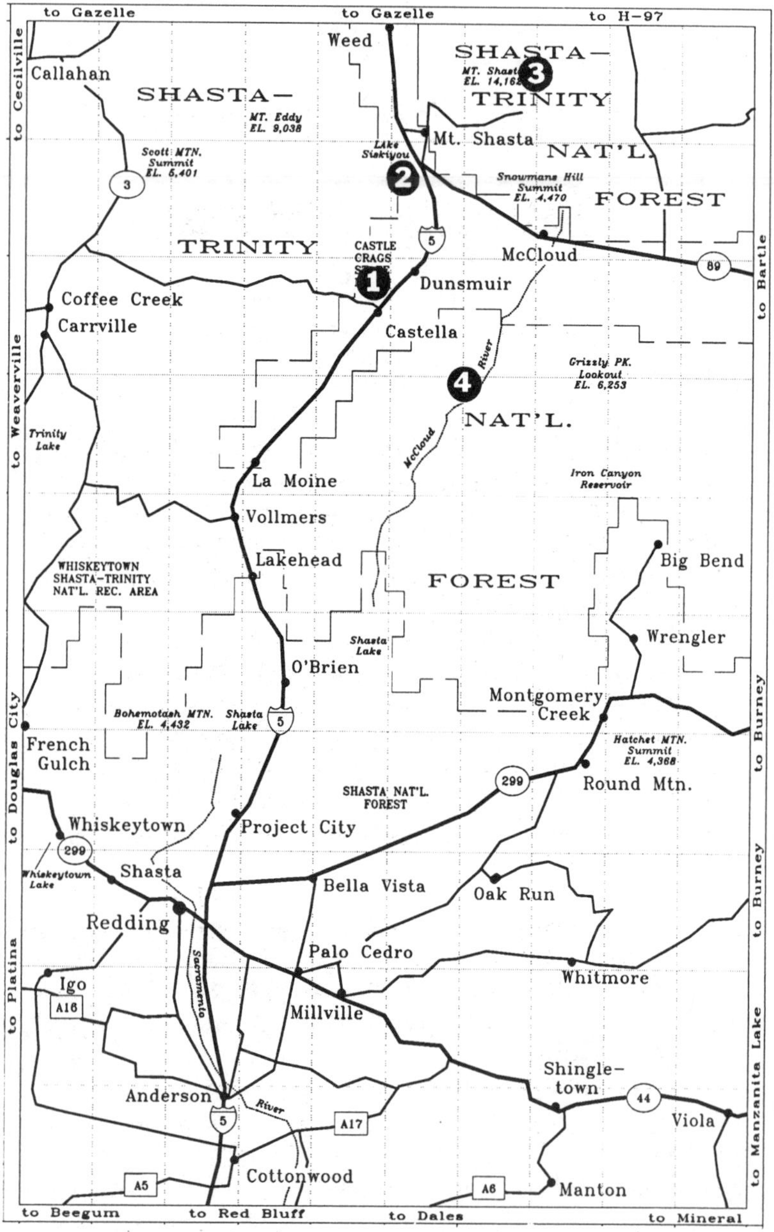

1

Castle Crags State Park

In Shasta County, north of Shasta Lake

One of the truly awe-inspiring views of the world can be seen at Castle Crags State Park, where soaring spires of ancient granite seem to lift above even giant Mount Shasta. At the base of the crags, Castle Creek tumbles, a classic babbling brook. The surroundings are miles of forested mountain wildlands, and it's just 25 miles north of Shasta Lake.

Many people have glimpsed Castle Crags while heading up Interstate 5; the ridge sits just west of the highway. But by driving on, they are missing one of California's geologic wonders, as well as a darn good place to spend a weekend. You can camp, hike and picnic—and the inspired can backpack into adjoining wild country to find a series of hidden lakes that provide even more trout fishing.

For car campers, there are 64 well-spaced campsites, with most of them large enough to accommodate trailers, although no hookups are provided. As at most state parks, each campsite comes with a table, barbecue stove and storage locker, with a nearby restroom/shower available.

Elevations range from 2,000 feet at the campsites to 6,000 feet at the top of the crags, so although it can be quite warm in the day, the temperature can get downright chilly at night, unexpectedly so in spring and autumn. Campers should come prepared for a range of temperatures.

The best hike at Castle Crags is a 3.7-mile climb from the Crags' lookout up to Castle Dome. It is well worth the effort, with great views of Mount Shasta and the Sacramento River Valley and many good picnic sites.

Castle Crags sits on the edge of wildlands filled with pines, firs and cedars, along with a number of alders, maples and oaks. Do not be surprised if you see wildlife, particularly if you come in the uncrowded off-peak season. The fewer tourists there are, the less apt deer and bear are to be spooked. Year-round, however, the park attracts squirrels, chipmunks, raccoons and countless lizards; all seem to be looking for a handout.

No matter where you go here, you are always in the shadow of the dramatic landscape. To the north, dominating the countryside for a hundred miles, is the 14,162-foot Mount Shasta, always huge, always covered with snow.

But the crags themselves provide a fascinating attraction. The giant rock chutes and clusters jut high for thousands of feet, looking like something out of a science fiction movie. But unlike a movie, Castle Crags is real, not make-believe.

❖

Directions: Take Interstate 80 north to the Interstate 505 cutoff, and continue north to Interstate 5. Drive approximately 170 miles north to the town of Castella, about 45 miles north of Redding. Take the Castle Crags Park exit and follow the signs to the park entrance.
Fee or Free: A state park access fee is charged. Campsite fees vary depending on the season.
Camping: Call Mistix for reservations at (800) 444-7275.
Lodging: If you do not wish to camp, write Shasta Cascade, 1250 Parkview Avenue, Redding, CA 96001, for a list of available lodgings, and for any information about or maps of Siskiyou, Shasta, Trinity, Lassen, Modoc, and Tehama Counties.
Contact: Castle Crags State Park can be reached by calling (916) 235-2684. The Shasta Cascade Wonderland Association can be reached at (800) 326-6944.

2

Lake Siskiyou

At the foot of Mount Shasta

Lake Siskiyou provides the classic camp setting. It's a small jewel of a lake with campsites along its shore, good fishing for both trout and bass, and located in the shadow of nearby Mount Shasta, a dominating sight with its 14,000-foot peak.

It is one of the best easy-to-reach camping/fishing lakes in Northern California and is bordered by wild, primitive country. At 3,400 feet, Siskiyou sits above the blowtorch heat of Redding, yet below the icebox cold of Mount Shasta.

A bonus is that the Siskiyou Campground is an ideal base camp for exploring a network of backcountry roads leading into wildlands. Nearby Gumboot Lake, for instance, is one of 35 alpine lakes in the Trinity and Shasta forests, and can provide excellent trout fishing, especially for anglers equipped with float tubes, prams or rafts.

Lake Siskiyou itself is one of the few reservoirs in the western United States created primarily as a recreation center. The lake level remains consistent year-round, and conditions are often optimal for fishing. A key is that a large stretch of the lake bottom has many tree stumps, which makes for an ideal habitat for big fish, both brown trout and black bass. It was here that I hooked the largest brown trout I've ever tangled with, a 15-pounder. Since crawdads are so abundant in the lake, plugging with diving crawdad lures is often the ticket for the bass.

Summer vacationers are often content to rent an aluminum boat and troll 20 to 40 feet deep for the stocked rainbow trout. Many fish are caught in this manner during the morning and evening bites.

Siskiyou Campground is the base camp for your adventure. There are 290 campsites, each with a fire pit, picnic table and food locker. You just drive right up. Most of the spots have RV hookups. It is so close to Highway 5 that the easy access causes the area's one drawback—people. Especially on hot weekends, there are too many of them, and it distracts from the outdoor experience.

For some folks, however, it is just what they want. There is a good swimming and beach area, along with volleyball and frisbee games. The area is very clean, the air has that fresh alpine taste to it, and of course, there is that awesome mountain always looming above.

Lake Siskiyou has many great features—it is easy to reach; has a beautiful setting, clean campsites, a good boat ramp and quality fishing; and it is almost always full of water. Sound good? It is good.

Directions: From the Bay Area, take Interstate 80 north to the Interstate 505 cutoff, then head north to Interstate 5. Drive approximately 190 miles north to the town of Mount Shasta. Take the Central Mount Shasta exit and turn left at the stop sign. Continue over the freeway to another stop sign at W.A. Barr Road. Turn left and drive one mile to the lake. You may turn right on North Shore Road to access the north shore, or continue straight and follow the signs to the beach, marina and campground.

Supplies: A small marina bait and tackle shop are available at the boat dock for supplies, the latter providing the latest tips. Call (916)926-2610.

Fee or Free: There is a small entrance fee to access the southwest side of the lake. Access to the north shore is free. There is a fee for camping.

Boating: Boats and motors are available for rent at the marina. A fee is charged to launch private boats for day-use visitors; if you're camping, it's free. Paddle boats and windsurfing lessons are also available.

Contact: Write or call Shasta Cascade at 1250 Parkview Avenue, Redding, CA 96001, (800) 326-6944, or Siskiyou Campground, P.O. Box 276, Mount Shasta City, CA 96067, (916) 926-2610.

3

Mount Shasta

In Siskiyou County

Indian legend has it that Mount Shasta was formed when the Great Spirit poked a hole in the sky and shaped a tepee with the fallen pieces. From afar, it's almost possible to believe it. The great snow-capped volcano is sometimes visible from as far as 150 miles away, rising 14,162 feet above the lowlands.

But Mount Shasta is more than just a colossus that casts its shadow over Interstate 5. It's also the centerpiece of one of the West's great lands of adventure. Name the activity, and the 25-square mile area that encircles Mount Shasta has it: quality stream and lake fishing, boating, hiking, rafting, camping, backpacking, and, in the winter, both alpine and cross-country skiing.

Whatever you want to do around Mount Shasta, one of the best places to begin is Castle Crags State Park. Located about fifteen miles from the base of the mountain, the park offers an awe-inspiring view of Shasta. (See the story on pages 39-40 for more details on this great state park and campground.)

But Castle Crags is only one of about 50 campgrounds that ring the Mount Shasta area, ranging from areas that offer full hookup facilities for motor homes to primitive sites in the Klamath and Shasta National Forests. If you carry a car-top boat or trailer, then head to Lake Siskiyou for a prime camping or fishing experience. Siskiyou glistens in the very shadow of Mount Shasta. The lake's western shore features both campsites and a swimming area, and it has plenty of trout and bass. You can rent boats and motors at the Lake Siskiyou Marina. (See the story on pages 41-43 for more information on Lake Siskiyou.)

If you'd simply rather commune with nature, consider spending a few days hiking, rafting or houseboating.

A network of trails crosses the mountain country. One of the best is the Pacific Crest Trail, which cuts across the southern slope of Mount Shasta, running past Castle Crags State Park, the Sacramento River and McCloud River. You can get is some great hiking in this area.

You say that vacations aren't meant for work? Then consider some whitewater excitement, riding a raft down the untamed stretches of the Sacramento or Klamath River, a wild but fun way to spend a day or two. Wilderness Adventures is one of the many companies in the area offering trips. For a complete directory of California river outfitters, phone (800) 552-3625.

The laziest vacation of all could be renting a houseboat on massive Shasta Lake, the largest reservoir in California. Though two million people venture to this lake every year, it has the space to handle them all. Figuring you'll need a week on a houseboat to do it right, you can rent one that sleeps 6 to 14 people for $900 to $2000. (For more information on houseboating vacations, see the story on page 345.)

In winter, skiing down the side of Mount Shasta can beat the heavily-used slopes of the Sierra Nevada. Because the skiing operation here was built in the

Hiking:
The Sisson-Callahan Trail is one of the best on the west side of Mount Shasta. For a map of trails on Forest Service land, write Shasta Cascade at 1250 Parkview, Redding, CA 96001.

Lodging:
In Mount Shasta, the Best Western Treehouse, (916) 926-3101, is a quality motel with all the amenities provided. For other lodging possibilities, phone the Mount Shasta Chamber of Commerce at (916) 926-4865.

Contact:
Call Shasta Cascade at (800) 326-6944 for information on the entire

1980s, the public has not yet discovered how good it is. You'll find short lines at the three lifts and lots of room on the slopes. For cross-country skiing, Bunny Flats is the top spot.

Whatever activity you love, whatever the season, Shasta could be your perfect outdoors getaway.

area, free maps and brochures.

Rafting: For a complete directory of California river outfitters, phone (800) 552-3625.

4
McCloud River Preserve

In Shasta-Trinty Forest, northeast of Redding

Sometimes you wish you could live in an earlier time, a time when deer roamed without fear, when old trees were left standing, and when wild rainbow trout were kings of the stream. At the McCloud River Preserve, Californians have the chance to return to such a time. You can experience the wild native wonder of California that trailblazers found in their first steps out West.

Hidden southeast of snow-capped Mount Shasta, the McCloud River remains in pristine condition. A person can walk among the woods, or fish hip deep for wild trout, and get the feeling that the area is much as it was 200 years ago, before humans had ever thought of dams and chainsaws. And it will always remain this way. The Nature Conservancy, a non-partisan, non-profit organization dedicated solely to purchasing and preserving unique wildlands, now manages more than six miles of the McCloud watershed. While fishing access is free, it is restricted to no more than 10 rods on the river at any one time. All trout hooked must be released, and anglers must use single barbless hooks or lures.

No hunting, tree cutting or wood gathering is allowed. When it comes to fishing, the ethic of the Nature Conservancy is clear: a wild trout is too valuable to be caught only once.

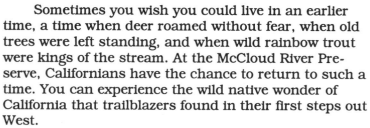

Directions: Take Highway 5 straight up the California Valley, past Redding toward Mount Shasta City, and turn east on Highway 89. Continue to the town of McCloud, turn right at the Shell gas station and drive 10 miles to Lake McCloud. Turn right and take the dirt road along the right side of the lake. At Battle Creek, turn right at the signed turnoff for Ah-Di-Na Campground.

Reservations: Only 10 rods are allowed on McCloud Preserve at a time. Reservations can be made by phoning the Nature Conservancy at (415) 777-0541.

The McCloud River is unique. Its source for thousands of years has been a huge 44-degree volcanic spring from the underground waterways of nearby Mount Shasta. The surrounding area has never lost its wild character either. Squirrels with giant tails play in the leaves; mountain lions hide in the woods. One morning, I saw a wild turkey running straight up the side of a mountain.

Another time, I came around a bend and saw what looked like two little kittens playing in the dust. They were baby bobcats, like nothing you've ever seen.

A few bald eagles, mink, wild turkeys and river otters may be seen on the McCloud River Preserve. A hundred years from now, their descendents will still be here. The chain of wildlife in the preserve will never be broken.

I remember my first morning on the McCloud. My waders were marked to the hip by river water, and I watched insects hatching on the river surface. "Caddis," I thought to myself.

My wrist twitched with my fly rod; I already had a fly patterned after a caddis tied on my fishing line. The late Ted Fay, a fly fishing legend, had tipped me off the previous day. Casting just 25 feet, I laid the fly in a riffle and watched the current take it downstream, the fly tumbling as if no line was attached. Then suddenly—got one! A red flash in the water was at the end of my line, and after a few minutes, it was brought to my side. It was a wild rainbow trout, about a 12-incher, not a giant by any means, but colored nature's most vivid red. Unhooked, it swam away to freedom.

Trout here are a special breed; they

are the Shasta Rainbow. According to the Nature Conservancy, it is from the McCloud strain that most hatchery trout in many parts of the world have descended. In 1872, an egg-taking station was situated at the mouth of the river, resulting in the introduction of the fish to places such as New Zealand, where it now provides a world-class fishery. Though the 10-pounders of New Zealand draw anglers from thousands of miles away, there are enough 15 to 30-inchers in the McCloud to entice Bay Area residents to make the 300-mile drive a few times each spring and summer.

However, don't get the false impression that just because they "know" they will be released, the fish are easy to catch. Many anglers are skunked. According to a logbook kept by the Nature Conservancy, the average catch during the morning or evening bite is four to five rainbow trout per fisherman. Experienced anglers do better, especially for larger trout.

A few key tips can aid your mission. For one, bring chest waders and a wading staff (an old ski pole is fine). The rocks here are coated with a light film of algae and are slippery, particularly the large flat ones. I once saw an outdoors writer fall in the water three times in a single morning. A good lesson for all. Take your steps with care, avoiding flat rocks and searching for gravel pockets between large rocks.

Another key here is the ability to detect the delicate bite of a trout. Rarely is there a distinct jerk. Usually all you see is a misdirection of your fly line as it drifts downstream with the current. If you

Guide:
Fishing guide Joe Kimsey can be reached at (916) 235-2969.

Camping:
A small camping fee at the primitive campsite Ah-Di-Na Campground is charged.

Hotel:
The nearest lodging is the Stoney Brook Inn in McCloud. They can be contacted at (916) 964-2300.

Contact:
For general information on fishing, hotels, directions and maps, call the Shasta Cascade Association at (800) 326-6944, or write to 1250 Parkview Avenue, Redding, CA 96001. The

Nature Conservancy can be contacted at 785 Market Street, San Francisco, CA 94013, (415) 777-0541.

see anything peculiar about your line as it drifts downstream, set your hook. Floating strike indicators can be a great help.

Anglers learning this craft usually have to pay their dues. The McCloud River is a little piece of heaven where making these payments comes easy.

Chapter 4

Burney & Lassen Forest

1—Burney's Trout Paradise—p. 53
2—Lassen Volcanic National Park—p. 60

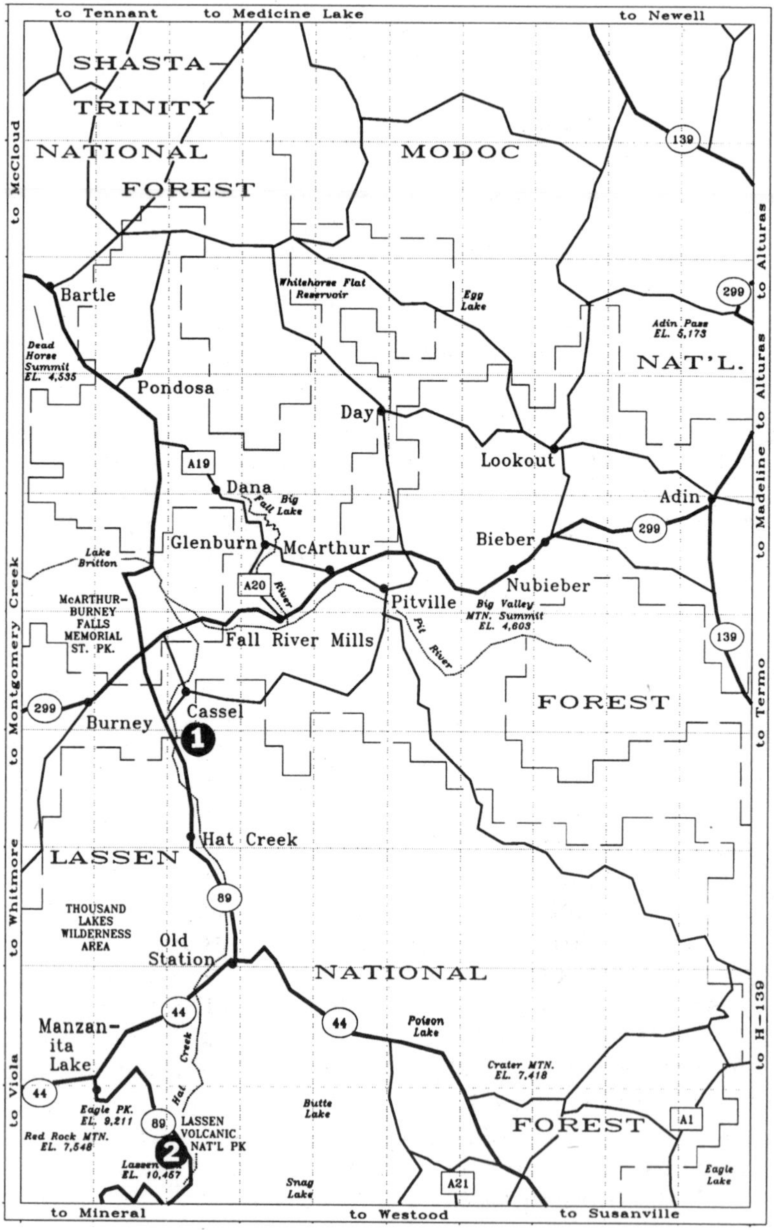

1

Burney's Trout Paradise

In Shasta County, east of Redding

In the northeastern corner of California is a valley where nature has carved two of the finest trout streams in the western United States. Hat Creek and Fall River are not filled by the many trickles of melting snow like most streams along the slopes of California's Sierra Nevada, or Oregon and Washington's Cascade ranges, but are spring-fed, each bubbling fresh out of the ground from the underground waterways of nearby Mount Lassen, a volcano that blew its top in 1914.

The area is tucked away near Burney, about 50 miles east of Redding via Highway 299, and is about a five-hour drive from the San Francisco Bay Area. It is a paradise for fly fishermen, but it also offers angling and camping opportunities for anybody who wants to set up a tent and plunk a bait in a nearby stream or lake. In addition to Hat Creek and Fall River, which have designated Wild Trout sections with special angling restrictions, the area has several prime trout streams and reservoirs that can provide action for all fishermen. Upper Hat Creek, Pit River, Burney Creek, Baum Lake and Lake Britton provide a network of trout fishing opportunities just minutes apart.

But the focal points here are the two spring-fed streams, Hat Creek and Fall River, where fly fishermen find contentment rolling out casts and watching the line settle quietly in the gentle flows.

Rather than being strewn with pebbles, the river bottoms of Fall River and Hat Creek are moss-covered, making them ideal homes for insect larvae. When the temperature reaches 60 degrees and warmer, the larvae emerge from the moss and hatch on the surface. At Fall River, the hatch can be so thick that it looks like San Francisco fog. Locals call it "Hatch Madness." The trout gorge themselves on the insects, with almost every summer day evolving into an all-you-can-eat smorgasbord. A native 14-inch rainbow trout can be considered an average specimen in this haven.

For either Hat Creek or Fall River, a good fly line is a No. 5. or No. 6. Figure on using about nine feet of leader when using nymphs and 12 feet when using dry flies.

Hat Creek

This is the most popular stream in the area because it offers both a pristine setting and good access. It is a classic chalk stream, and the lower three-and-a-half miles of river have been designated by California's Department of Fish and Game as a Wild Trout Stream—no hatchery fish have been planted in eons. The wild trout here average 10 to 16 inches, with an occasional rainbow trout in the 18-inch range. Some particularly elusive monster brown trout also roam here.

Highway 299, the two-laner that feeds into the Burney area from Redding, actually crosses Hat Creek, providing excellent access. Anglers can arrive from the drive, take a hard look at the river, and then choose whether to hike upstream or downstream. The farther you walk—to reach lesser fished areas—the better the angling can be. Typically, however, fishing is best on Hat Creek in the evening hours of summer, especially at dusk.

From Powerhouse No. 2 to Lake Britton, Lower Hat Creek is a designated Wild Trout Stream, where only flies and lures with a single barbless hook are allowed—and a two-fish, 18-inch minimum size limit applies. It is primarily a flyfishing stream, where anglers use small patterns and two and four-pound test tippets, very light lines, so the wild trout will not detect their presence. Although the fly patterns vary in size according to season and hatches, in the hot weather from mid-summer on, fishermen use very small flies, even as small as No. 20. Some of the best patterns are: Adams, Blue Dun, Dark Blue Upright, Quill Gordon, Jerry, Yellow Stone, and Pale Evening Dun.

This area is home to some of the wisest anglers in California. Just a few of the smartest of them are willing to provide up-to-the-minute information on Lower Hat Creek. One of them is Steve Vaughn, (916) 335-2381, at Vaughn's Sporting Goods, 1713 Main Street, Box AV, Burney, CA 96013. If you drop Steve a stamped, self-addressed envelope and $1, he will be happy to send you his "Fishing Guide Map" for the Burney Basin.

Four motels are available in Burney, with about a dozen set in the inter-mountain area. Reservations are strongly advised. A complete list, along with additional fishing information, can be requested from the Burney Chamber of Commerce by phoning (916) 335-2111 or by writing them at P.O. Box 36, Burney, CA 96013.

Campgrounds are abundant along Highway 89, which intersects Highway 299 about 10 miles east of Burney. The U.S. Forest Service operates eight campgrounds, with some specially tailored for recreational vehicles. For brochures, write the U.S. Forest Service, Hat Creek District, Fall River Mills, CA 96028. The Pacific Gas & Electric Company also provides campgrounds, with information available by writing PG&E, P.O. Box 340, Red Bluff, CA 96080, Attention: Land Department. The McArthur-Burney Falls State Park is exceptionally popular and reservations are necessary through Mistix, (800)444-7275.

Upper Hat Creek

A favorite campground here is the Big Pine Camp, operated by the U.S. Forest Service, which is nestled at streamside along Upper Hat Creek. It is an ideal alternative for fishermen who want to have a trout barbecue once the trip is completed, instead of releasing everything they hook, as is practiced at Lower Hat Creek and Fall River. The stream here is well stocked with hatchery fish, and baitfishing is not only allowed, but has become the favorite tactic to catch a trout dinner. The preferred bait are crickets, worms and salmon eggs. Most of the trout here are of the pan-size variety, in the 8 to 11-inch class.

Fall River

Snow-covered Mount Lassen sits above this trout paradise, watching quietly as it has done since its last violent eruption some 80 years ago. If you lose a few big trout on Fall River, you might blow your stack, too.

When the trout explode in a surface feed, there can be so many pools from rising fish that it can look as if it is raining. And these trout are big, with many measuring 16 to 20 inches, and a few five to eight-pounders. The water can be so clear during summer months that fly fishermen will sometimes even use leaders as long as 15 feet; otherwise the fish might detect the fly line. On some days, you can spot a dime at the bottom of 30 feet of water and reach in the stream with your hand thinking you can pick it up. Fall River is that clear.

This is a stream that flows so gently that it can be fished in a float tube. On the upper river near Glenburn, gasoline engines are prohibited and any form of fishing other than with flies is considered sacrilege. The only sound is that of your small craft, either aluminum boat or canoe, pushing water aside. Electric motors are popular.

The favored fly patterns are the paraduns—olive, tan or yellow—with a No. 16 as a good starting size. Nymphs such as the Zug Bug, Black AP, Black Leech, and Hare's Ear can also get the desired result. With the wild and varied hatches, this can be an entomologist's dream.

But here is where the problems start. The river is bordered by private land, primarily owned by ranchers, most of whom get their shotguns out at the slightest trace of "another Bay Area trespasser." As a result, access is severely restricted. While this keeps fishing pressure low so the river retains its wild identity, it can also be a source of irritation for anglers. But that factor can be overcome.

One private lodge and one public access point operated by the conservation organization California Trout are the access points an angler can choose from. Rick's Lodge at Glenburn is my favorite, providing the best access on the prime upper stretch of river. Anglers can gain fishing access by renting a room for $50 per night, $75 for double occupancy. Boats and electric motors ($40 per day, $30 per half day) are also available, as are advice and customized flies. Fishing classes and week-long package deals can be had. A free pickup service at the airport at nearby Fall River Mills is a bonus, along with a full bar and restaurant. Rick's Lodge can be reached by phoning (916) 336-5300, or by writing Star Route Glenburn, Fall River Mills, CA 96028.

The only public access point to the prime stretches of Fall River is at the Island Bridge, where a tiny parking lot has been constructed by California Trout. The lot will only hold about four or five vehicles, and no nearby areas are available for parking. On some summer days, a single recreational vehicle can take up all the available space. For information, phone California Trout at (415) 392-8887, or write to them at 870 Market Street, Suite 859, San Francisco, CA 94102.

Other Angling Opportunities

Cassel Forebay, Baum Lake, Lake Britton, Burney Creek and Pit River provide additional angling opportunities in a relatively small area near Burney. For more information, call Vaughn's Sporting Goods at (916) 335-2381, Shasta Cascade at (800) 326-6944 or the Burney Chamber of Commerce at (916) 335-2111. Here's a capsule summary:

Cassel Forebay—Located east of Burney, Cassel provides a well-stocked stretch of water with a 10-fish limit. Most anglers use traditional baits like red eggs or crickets, but flyfishing can be effective as well. A PG&E campground is available at Cassel Park.

Baum Lake—This is big fish country, where German and rainbow trout grow to surprising sizes. A 24-pounder was taken in the 1980s, but most trout average one to two pounds. Baum can be fished by boat or bank, but no motors are allowed on the lake. Most fishermen dunk worms or nightcrawlers; a few others cast flies under a bubble.

Lake Britton—This is a popular lake for vacationers, with campgrounds available on the north shore and also at McArthur-Burney Falls State Park. It's a take-your-pick fishery, with bass, crappie, bluegill and trout stocked in the lake.

Burney Creek—Burney Creek is a pretty setting, the river gurgling over rocks polished by centuries of rolling river water. Access is excellent and it is a well-stocked creek, although most fish are small.

Pit River—This is one of the West's most unheralded trout streams despite providing a quality fishing experience. The stretch of river below Pit River No. 3 Powerhouse can be particularly good. A problem here is a brushy shoreline, which may give access problems to first-timers. A phone call to Vaughn's Sporting Goods or the Chamber of Commerce (phone numbers on page 57) should be considered mandatory before heading out.

Contact: For maps and a list of campgrounds, motels and fishing guides for the entire area, call the Shasta Cascade Wonderland Association at (800) 326-6944 or write to them at 1250 Parkview Avenue, Redding, CA 96001

Lodging: For a list of motels in Burney and additional fishing information, call the Burney Chamber of Commerce at (916) 335-2111 or write to them at P.O. Box 36, Burney, CA 96013. In the Fall River area, contact Rick's Lodge at (916) 336-5300 or write at Star Route Glenburn, Fall River Mills, CA 96028.

Campgrounds: For information and brochures, contact the U.S. Forest Service, Hat Creek District, Fall River Mills, CA 96028 or Pacific Gas and Electric Company, P.O. Box 340, Red Bluff, CA 96080, Attention: Land Management. Reservations may be made for the McArthur-Burney Falls State Park through Mistix, (800) 444-7275.

Fall River Access: For information on the parking area, call California Trout at (415) 392-8887 or write to 870 Market Street, Suite 859, San Francisco, CA 94102.

Fishing Tips: Vaughn's Sporting Goods in Burney is an excellent source for current conditions and advice; write to 1713 Main Street, Box AV, Burney, CA 96013 or call (916) 335-2381.

2

Lassen Volcanic National Park

In the Cascades, east of Red Bluff

Lassen is the Northern California's spectacular national park that you have always intended to visit. Most folks never quite get around to it. Sound familiar? To many it does. Lassen has it all—great camping, fishing, hiking, lookouts and seclusion, in one of America's most beautiful parklands. Yet you've probably never gone.

During my visit, every campground in the park had vacancies. Weekdays are even more empty. Ask campers where home is and they're as apt to say "Cedar Rapids, Iowa" as they are "Bay Area."

You may have seen Lassen from a distance as you head north on Highway 5. As you get near Red Bluff, look east to the horizon, and spot the old extinct volcano, the one with its top blown off, that rises far above the other mountains. "Oh yeah, that's Lassen."

That's usually as much as the brain gears engage when you spot Lassen while cruising I-5. But you can get those gears turning, and open up a world of adventure at the same time, by turning east on Highway 36 at Red Bluff. In 50 miles, you'll rise above the rock-specked foothills and into a forest, come around a bend and suddenly enter one of the West's greatest parks.

The old volcano is the centerpiece, of course. Mount Lassen peaks out at 10,457 feet, which you can reach in a 2.5-mile zigzag of a hike. With a quart of water, you can make the climb in less than two hours. The view is remarkable, with Mount Shasta to the north, miles of forest and lakes to the east, and the Sacramento Valley plunging westward.

As you sit on the top of Lassen, you will see why the park is so special. For one thing, it doesn't even look like California, but more like Montana, with 80,000 acres of roadless wilderness. You will spot several lakes that look like jewels. And then there is the top itself, a crusty volcano flume with craters, spires, hardened lava flows and enough hidden trails to spend hours exploring.

The view from the top will likely inspire you to travel to what you can see. In Lassen Park, that includes 53 lakes. Of those, six can be reached by car, including Manzanita Lake and Summit Lake, where two of Lassen's prettiest campgrounds are located.

Manzanita Lake is set just inside the northwest entrance to the park on Highway 89. It's an idyllic setting and a perfect destination for trout fishermen. The lake has been converted to a natural fishery and a special program to protect the wild trout is now in effect. Rules mandate lures or flies only with a single, barbless hook, and a two-fish limit, none longer than 10 inches.

The campground at Manzanita Lake is the park's largest with 179 sites, although since it is set at the park entrance, you may want to push on farther. There are six other campgrounds, including three situated alongside lakes—Summit (94 sites), Juniper (18 sites) and Butte (98 sites). See the list on pages 63-64 for a detailed description.

To obtain a lakeside campsite, you might figure you have to book a reservation several months in advance, right? Wrong.

During our visit, we found a fairly secluded spot set on the edge of a meadow, not far from Summit Lake. At dusk, several deer suddenly walked out of the forest and into the meadow, grazing yet keeping ears raised as an alert for intruders. We snuck a bit closer,

Directions: From the Bay Area, take Interstate 80 north to Interstate 505, then proceed north to Interstate 5. Drive approximately 95 miles north to Red Bluff and take the Highway 36/ Lassen Park exit. Continue east for 47 miles to the Highway 89 cutoff, then turn north and proceed to the park entrance.

Fee or Free: A national park entrance fee is charged. Campsite fees are very reasonable.

Maps: A complete map of the park and the Lassen Trails map can be purchased at the park.

Contact: If you have

undetected, and saw a mother with a fawn that hadn't even lost its spots yet.

Along with deer, the park is loaded with ground squirrels, which are always hoping to find a surprise morsel. You'd best not leave anything out for them. That might attract a bear, the masters of the food-raiding business. There are enough bears in the park to cause rangers to advise campers to keep their food well protected.

The park can be toured by car to get an overview of the unique areas. There are signs of the area's latent volcanic underbase—boiling sulfur vents, huge, hardened mud flows, fields of volcanic lava balls. Lassen blew its top in 1914, then had other eruptions until 1921, so in geological time it's like it happened just yesterday.

You can get an even better look by taking a hike or two. Whether you want an easy stroll or a backpacking trip, there are enough trails to find a perfect match. The list on page 64 details the best. Lassen has more than 150 miles of trails, including 17 miles of the Pacific Crest Trail, which reaches from Mexico to Canada. (For more information on the Pacific Crest Trail, see page 360.) Habitat varies from forest to alpine tundra, and trails will take you to hidden lakes and streams.

However, no fishing is permitted at Emerald or Helen Lakes. Since the Park Service suspended trout plants, the fishing has gone to hell, especially in the backcountry lakes. Since no natural spawning occurs at these lakes, they are either planted or they have no fish. Manzanita, with its special wild trout program, provides the only hope. No power boats are permitted on any lake in the park, but canoes, rafts, row boats or float tubes work perfectly.

The best technique to catch the trout here is to offer what they feed on—insects. Fly patterns that imitate insects work the best: No. 14 Calibatis, No. 16 Haystack, No. 14/16 Loop Wing, No. 16 Hare's Ear Nymph, No. 6/8/10 olive or brown leach.

People from all over America touring California see the big park on the map and head straight for an entrance. At some point in your travels, so should you.

questions about the park, call Shasta Cascade at (800) 326-6944 which provides a free information service, or call the park at (916) 595-4444. You can also write to Lassen National Park at P.O. Box 100, Mineral, CA 96063.

Campgrounds

Lassen National Park operates six campgrounds with fees ranging from free to $6 per site, per night. All campsites are available on a first-come, first-served basis.

Summit Lake—There are actually two campgrounds here, one on each side of the lake. There are 94 campsites, all set near the water, where you can swim or fish for trout. Many trails begin at this area. The camps are set at 6,695 feet elevation.

Manzanita Lake—The park's largest campground (179 sites) is quite popular because of the good fishing and idyllic setting. Concession services are located nearby. It is located at 5,890 feet near the park's northern entrance on Highway 89.

Juniper Lake—This is a good spot for those wanting to "get away from it all." It is located on the east shore of Juniper Lake, one mile from a ranger station on a rough dirt road. There are 18 campsites, no charge for use, but no piped water is available. Set at 6,792 feet elevation.

Butte Lake—This is a popular lakeside campground, set at 6,1000 feet, with 98 campsites. There are many recreational options, with fishing, swimming and good hikes to nearby Cinder Cone and Snag Lake available.

Warner Valley—A little-used spot with 15 campsites, Warner Valley is located one mile from Warner Valley Ranger Station. This is the best choice for hikers who like to stream fish. The nearest supplies are in Chester, which is 17 miles away via a dirt road. It is set at 5,650 feet elevation.

Hiking

Lassen Park has 150 miles of trails across a great variety of terrain. Here are a few favorite hikes.

Crumbaugh Lake—This entails three miles of walking with little climb, taking you through meadows and forests to Cold Boiling Lake and on to Crumbaugh Lake.

Paradise Meadow—A three-mile round trip with a climb of 600 feet to a beautiful, glacier-carved meadow. Paradise Meadow contains a great wildflower display.

Mill Creek Falls—This is a four-mile round-trip that leads to Mill Creek Falls, which at 70 feet high is Lassen Park's highest waterfall.

Devastated Area—This is a one-hour breeze of a walk that tours through the site of a massive mudflow from the 1915 eruption of Lassen Park.

King's Creek Falls—A three-mile round trip with a 700-foot descent takes you to King's Creek Falls, just 30 feet high but worth seeing. The trail follows a mountain stream that cuts through both meadow and forest.

Sifford Lakes—This is for the adventurous—four miles round-trip, all of it cross-country style. This hike leaves the King's Creek Trail, explores a series of beautiful glacier-carved lakes, and has many great lookouts.

Chapter 5

Mendocino Coast

1—Mendocino Coast—p. 67

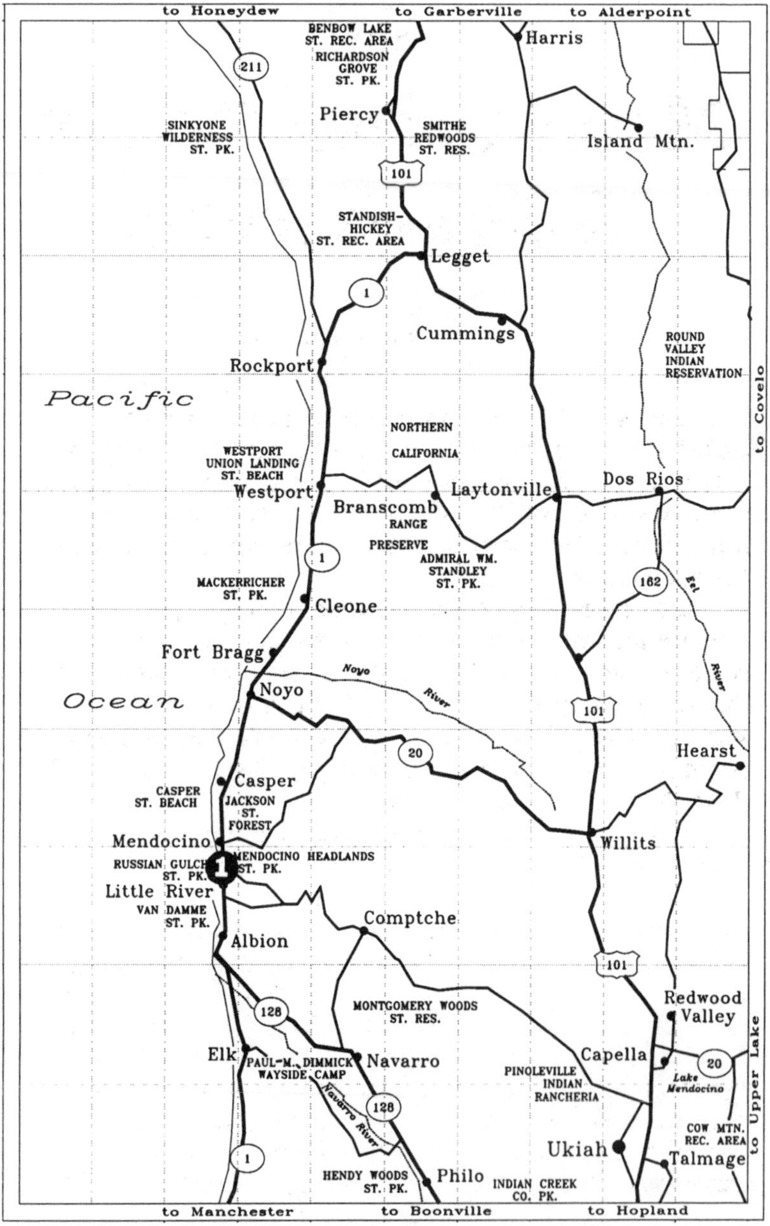

1

Mendocino Coast Adventures

Along the Mendocino coast

The Mendocino coast is so quiet you can practically hear the flowers bloom. Three hours up Highway 101 and over to the coast on Highway 128, and you've entered a new world. Instead of concrete and traffic jams, you get redwoods, wildflowers and miles of untouched Pacific Coast.

But more than anything else, you get quiet. It doesn't matter what you choose to do—walk the beaches, watch for whale spouts, hike the redwood forests or explore little towns like Elk or Mendocino—you get quiet. You can camp in a forest, rent a hotel room for a night or stay at an expensive coastal inn. It doesn't matter. You get quiet.

It's just what many Bay Area residents need and that makes the Mendocino coast an ideal retreat. Spring is a perfect time to visit because the whale migration is in full swing, all kinds of wildflowers are blooming in the nearby hills and the air is sparkling clean.

The coast has a different look to it here than in the south. In many areas, there are giant blocks of rock towering in the ocean shallows, rocks that look like they have been sculpted by an angry giant with a hammer and chisel, complete with tunnels and cutaways. They give the area a rugged, primitive feel.

Ocean and redwoods, you get it all on the Mendocino coast.

Van Damme State Park

One of the coast's best hikes is here. It's the Fern Canyon Trail, a gently sloping five-miler that cuts along the bottom of a lush creek. Because the park is located in a perfect setting for car campers heading up Highway 1, many people discover this hike by accident in the summer. You can beat the traffic, though, by going in the spring.

Contact: Call Mendocino Parks at (707) 937-5804.

Whale Watching

See what looks like a puff of smoke on the ocean surface? Look closer. It's more likely a whale spout, and watching the annual whale migration is one of the area's more popular events. In April, Fort Bragg hosts the Mendocino Whale Festival, which includes an arts and crafts show and a two-mile run. Big ocean-going boats run whale watching trips in April out of Fort Bragg.

Contact: Phone the Fort Bragg Chamber of Commerce at (707) 961-6300, or Sportsman's Dock at (707) 964-2619.

Fishing

Some of Northern California's best deep sea fishing is out of Noyo Harbor in Fort Bragg. Fishermen catch many species of rockfish, along with lingcod and cabezone. In summer, salmon is king. At times the area gets some of the best salmon fishing on the Pacific Coast. Because salmon from the Klamath River migrate as far south as Fort Bragg and salmon from the Sacramento River migrate as far north as Fort Bragg, it's like fishing two runs of fish at the same time.

Contact: Phone Sportsman's Dock at (707) 964-2619.

Hiking

Some 40 of the Mendocino coast's best walks are detailed in the book, *The Hiker's Guide to the Mendocino Coast.* Most of the walks suggested are two or three miles and set in Mendocino County's most beautiful coastal areas.

Contact: The book is available for $15 from Bored Feet, P.O. Box 1832, Mendocino, CA 95460. Phone (707) 964-6629.

Coastal Inns

On the more than 100 miles of coast from Westport to Gualala, there are 70 lodgings, including little countryside inns, more standard hotels in town, and vacation cottage rentals.

Contact: For more information, write Coast Chamber, P.O. Box 1141, Fort Bragg, CA 95437, or phone (707) 961-6300.

Camping

There are 25 public and private campgrounds along the Mendocino coast. The settings include redwood forests, such as Russian Gulch State Park, (707) 937-5804, near Point Cabrillo Lighthouse, and beach frontage, such as Wages Creek, (707) 964-2964, at Westport.

Contact: For a listing, write Coast Chamber, P.O. Box 1141, Fort Bragg, CA 95437. Or check out the book *California Camping* which describes 1,500 campgrounds throughout the state (Foghorn Press, San Francisco, (800) 842-7477).

Ocean Kayaking

Sound crazy to you? It's not. It's fun, exhilarating and anybody can do it.

Contact: Rentals are available at Big River Lodge. Call (707) 937-5615.

Horseback Riding

Trails lead either into the redwood forest or to the beach at Ricochet Ridge Ranch, which is located near Cleone. In addition, special horse pack-trips can be booked into the Mendocino mountain wildlands.

Contact: For more information, call Ricochet Ranch at (707) 964-PONY.

There are other activities, like visiting the wine country, photographing the coast and cruising the craft shops, but you get the idea.

After a few days here you will discover that quiet is an easy thing to get used to.

Chapter 6

Quincy & Plumas Forest

1—Plumas Wonderland—p. 73

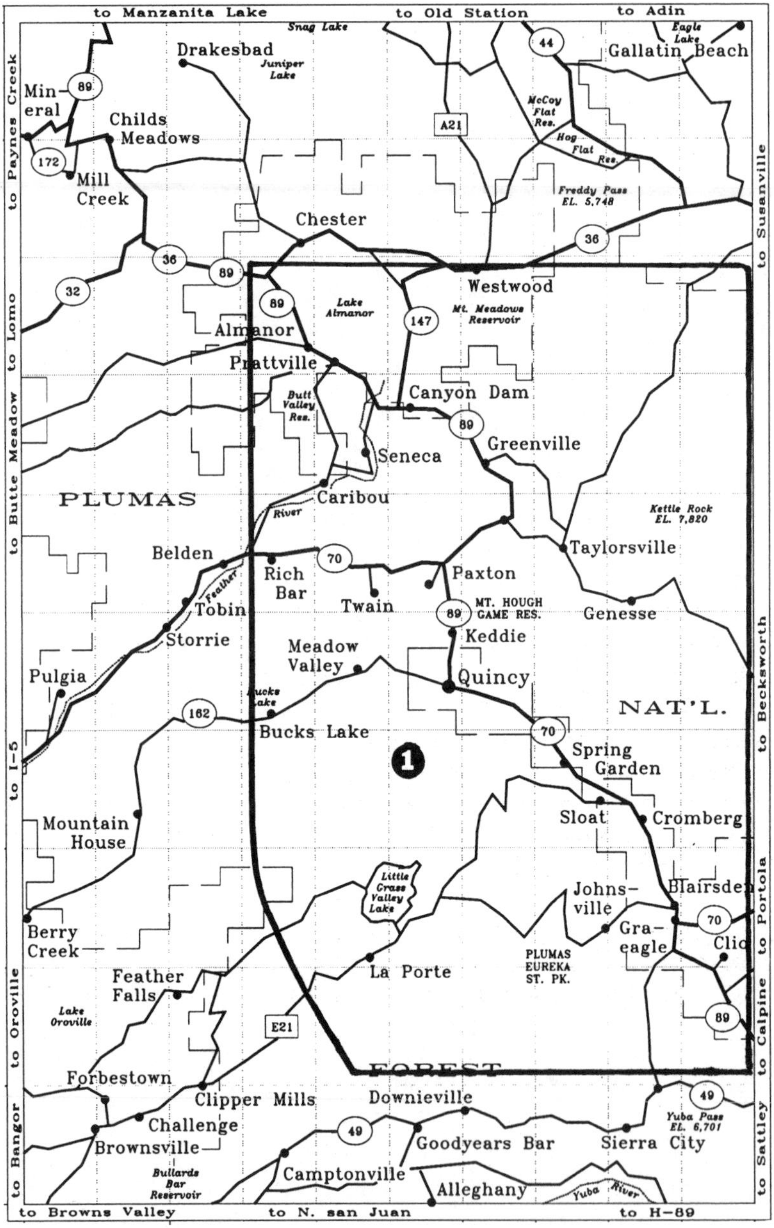

1

Plumas Wonderland

In Plumas Forest near Quincy

Every day can be a treasure hunt in Plumas Forest, the biggest chunk of undiscovered fortune in California.

The area is beautiful, much of it pristine, with one hundred lakes, one thousand miles of streams, and snow-crested mountains covered with pines and firs. There are nearly two thousand square miles of wildlands, room to wander and be free, whether you are driving or exploring on foot, fishing, hiking, or camping.

To put it in perspective, consider that there is not one single stoplight in the entire county. None. Zero. The thought of that could put someone from L.A. into paralysis. Even though California has nearly 31 million residents, only 20,000 of them live in Plumas County, despite it being one of America's most beautiful regions. If you get the idea that there is plenty of room, you are right. The deer far outnumber the people. Gold Lakes Basin, for instance, is very similar to the famous Desolation Wilderness near Tahoe, yet it gets one-tenth of the use.

It's not the 200-mile drive from the Bay Area that throws folks off, but rather the complicated route. There's just no direct way to do it. So while Tahoe, Reno, Clear Lake, Shasta, Yosemite and Kings Canyon are the state's recreation headquarters, Plumas remains detached from the rest of the world, and it's for the better.

Plumas County is located between Tahoe and Shasta, the top two vacation spots in the state. Those who take the in-between route will find a huge variety of lakes, streams, mountains and meadows to self-style virtually any kind of outdoor vacation. The best place for newcomers in search of solitude and good fishing is Plumas National Forest. You can reach 42 campgrounds by car, including many small, hidden spots accessible only by forest service roads. A map of Plumas National Forest can help you find your own secret camp. Forest service maps detail all backroads, lakes, streams and hiking trails.

The best camping spots are those adjacent to streams and lakes. The Middle Fork of the Feather River near Graegle has the best trout fishing, but getting there usually requires some hiking and scrambling down canyons. It is regarded by most outdoorsmen as one of the state's top five trout streams.

The North Fork of the Feather is more accessible, with Highway 70 running alongside much of it. The trout fishing is decent, primarily for 9 to 11-inch rainbow trout.

Other streams that provide good trout fishing include Indian Creek, Yellow Creek and Nelson Creek.

If you prefer lake fishing, Plumas offers many opportunities. The most famous are Lake Almanor and Davis Lake. Almanor, a big lake set near Chester, is the best for power boaters. Davis offers fishing for big rainbow trout.

But there are many other choices. Butte Lake, set a few miles from Almanor, has some of the largest rainbow trout in California. Bucks Lake, a short drive from Quincy, provides some of the most consistent trouting for 9 to 12-inchers in the country.

A good spot for a first trip is the Plumas Eureka State Park. It is set just west of the intersection of Highways 70 and 89 in the historic gold-mining area of Johnsville. You can either hunker down here, playing at Eureka Lake and taking day hikes in the forest, or set out for something more ambitious, which you can find in Gold Lakes Basin to the southeast. This is for backpackers only. For those who want to get off the beaten path, there are more than 50 lakes to choose from.

It is primarily a granite basin terrain, with a few stands of sugar pine and lakes like deep bowls of water. Since they are natural lakes, they are almost always full, unlike California's reservoirs that are being drained for agricultural use.

As a side trip, you can visit the state's second-highest waterfall, Feather Falls, at 640 feet. The streams here are in the heart of the gold country, and you could get lucky and pay for the trip with a few hours of panning. If you don't like to hike, you might consider renting a horse and visiting the back country.

One of my field scouts who knows every inch of this outdoor paradise in Al Bruzza. Bruzza has great enthusiasm and know-how, and has explored this area virtually since he took his first steps on the planet. He has fished 75 of the region's 100 lakes, every main artery of the stream systems in the Feather River country, and hoofed it across the mountains.

"Thank God I'm married to a woman who puts up with this stuff," Bruzza said. His wife, Robin, not only puts up with him, but caught an 11.5-pound trout one day at Bucks Lake.

Bruzza and I got together recently and ranked the region's current top fisheries. Here are our favorites:

Directions: From the Bay Area, take Interstate 80 east to Sacramento. There are two routes from Sacramento: Head north on Highway 99 for about 75 miles, then turn east on Highway 70 and continue up the Feather River Canyon. Or, continue east of Sacramento on Interstate 80 for approximately 105 miles, then turn north on Highway 89 and cruise through the forest country.

Maps: A map of Plumas National Forest can help you find your own secret camp. It can be obtained by writing to: Maps, U.S. Forest Service, 630 Sansome Street, San Francisco, CA 94111.

Contact: For a free map and brochure, write Plumas County Chamber of Commerce at Box 11018, Quincy, CA 95971, or phone (916) 283-2045 or (800) 326-2247.

Bucks Lake

This place has produced many big mackinaw trout and brown trout, more than any lake in the county. To do it right, you need to get 40 to 50 feet deep, trolling the old river channel coming out of Mill Creek, or the Rainbow Point area. Use a Macadoo lure, which looks like a crawdad, or a No. 2 J-Plug or No. 9 Rapala.

Gold Lake

This is the centerpiece for the Gold Lakes Basin. When the weather is warm, the brook trout can be on a great bite. If the wind comes up, no problem, just go over to nearby Sardine Lake, which also has brookies up to 16 inches. No fooling.

Antelope Lake

The nice campsites here add to a great experience, with a good chance at rainbow trout to 16 inches. The best bet is slow-trolling a No. 6 olive-green woolly bugger, giving the rod a jerk every 10 or 15 seconds. The key is getting down 20 feet, right along the underwater shelves.

Middle Fork Feather River

This is a premium trout stream, but requires hiking and scrambling to reach the best spots. In June, after the hatches start, flyfishing can be very good. A great trick here is to put a single salmon egg on a No. 14 or 16 egg hook with two-pound test line, and then drift it into holes. An insider's tip on mountain streams is to use the clear, oil-packed eggs made by Atlas, not the bright red ones.

Davis Lake

The damsel fly hatch at this lake can be the stuff of legends. When it's on, it inspires some of the best trout fishing in California. Catch-and-release is the way to go, with rainbow trout to 20 inches. Use a float tube, bring waders, or troll using woolly buggers. The west side of the lake is the prime area, especially from Eagle Point down to Freeman Creek.

Lake Almanor

This is a pretty lake circled by conifers, where the fish come big, although not always easy. Underwater springs and a large population of pond smelt help salmon, rainbow trout, brown trout and smallmouth bass get big and frisky. The best time of year to fish is from late April to early June, from dawn to about 9 a.m. Beware of north winds and rough water.

Chapter 7

Marin & Sonoma Coasts

1—Armstrong Redwoods—p. 81
2—Lake Sonoma—p. 83
3—Point Reyes—p. 86
4—Tomales Bay—p. 89
5—Bodega Bay—p. 91

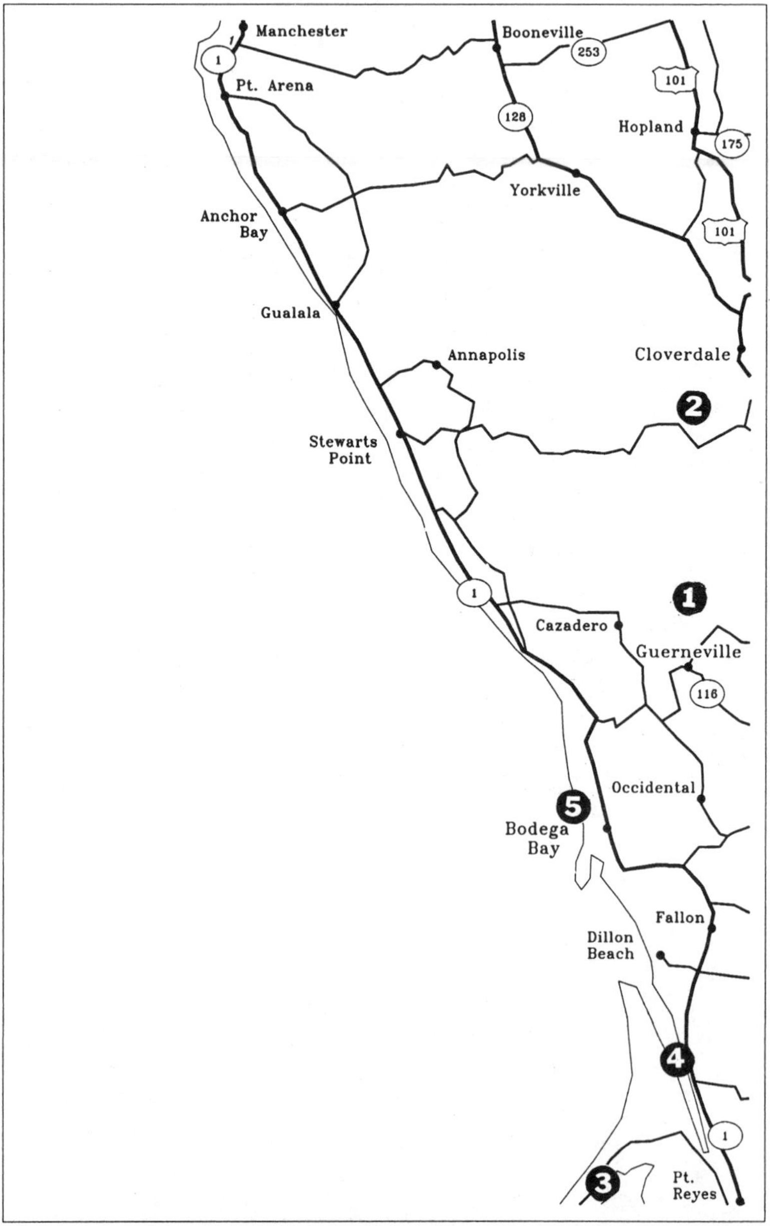

1

Armstrong Redwoods

Northwest of Santa Rosa near the Russian River

Ever wish you were seated in the middle of a cool redwood forest, away from city madness? If you're willing to make a 90-minute drive north of San Francisco, you can get exactly that.

Armstrong Redwoods State Reserve is the answer, a jungle of some of the tallest trees remaining in California, including several that have lived for more than a thousand years. The reserve sits adjacent to the Austin Creek Recreation Area, so you can turn your sojourn into a full-scale camping and hiking expedition.

This area is tucked away just northwest of Santa Rosa, a relatively short distance from the Bay Area. Yet despite the relative ease of getting here, you can still capture the sense of total privacy that comes in the midst of giant redwood trees. Some 5,000 acres of wildland, studded primarily with redwoods, tan oaks and madrone, provide just that.

The area was designated as a redwood reserve way back in the 1890s by a logger, of all people. While other timber interests were cutting wide swaths through California's giant redwoods, logger James Armstrong set this area aside. Armstrong was one of the few loggers who recognized the beauty and natural value of the forests, as well as the lumber value, and that is why this reserve bears his name.

Campers will find two choices: 24 drive-in sites at tiny Redwood Lake, or three prime hike-in areas. The drive-in family campground near the lake sits at the end of a steep, winding two-laner that climbs to a thousand feet and cannot be negotiated by trailers or motor homes. The other alternative is to head to the primitive campsites at Gilliam Creek, Mannings Flat and Tom King Campground, short hikes on the park's trail system.

A bonus is that the trails follow the streams that cut through the park. Austin Creek, Gilliam Creek, Schoolhouse Creek and Fife Creek provide water sources for backpackers (boil or filter all water before drinking). In addition, horses are allowed on the trails so equestrians can share in the redwood beauty with their steeds doing all the puffing. Austin Creek, a tributary to the Russian River, is home to a wide variety of animals and birds. In the fall, when water is a bit scarce, deer, raccoons and squirrels are likely to be seen near the watersheds. On rare occasions, bobcats and wild pigs have been spotted.

Tiny Redwood Lake, which can be reached by car and has an adjacent campground, provides bass and bluegill fishing, but the fish tend to be runts.

Not the trees. You can drive all over the world and never see taller trees than those that grow in the Armstrong Reserve.

❖

Directions: The easiest route from San Francisco is to head north on Highway 101, exiting on River Road (located five miles north of Santa Rosa). Head west on River Road for 20 miles to Guerneville, and take a right on Armstrong Woods Road.
Fee or Free: An access fee is charged per vehicle. Walk-in access is free. There is no charge for camping.
Dogs: Dogs are permitted in Armstrong Redwoods, and must be on a leash.
Supplies: Last-minute shopping can be done in Guerneville.
Contact: Call Armstrong Redwoods State Reserve at (707)869-2015 or write to 17000 Armstrong Woods Road, Guerneville, CA 95446.

2

Lake Sonoma

North of Santa Rosa

Lake Sonoma is California's mystery spot, but soon the only mystery is going to be why people haven't visited it yet. Sonoma is California's newest lake, created with the construction of Warm Springs Dam, located north of Santa Rosa.

The creation of this lake provided the government with a chance to do something right, and they have succeeded. It is a perfect lake for camping, fishing, waterskiing (in designated areas), canoeing and sailing—but it has some other key elements that make it particularly special: boat-in camping, 40 miles of hiking and horseback riding trails, and an 8,000-acre wildlife area.

It takes less than a two-hour drive to reach the lake from San Francisco, and the first stop should be the Sonoma Overlook at the south end of the lake. From there, you get an ideal picture of the adventure ahead of you. The big lake is set in rich foothill country with thousands of hidden coves to be explored by boat or trail.

From the dam, the lake extends nine miles north on the Dry Creek arm, four miles to the east on Warm Springs Creek. Each of the lake arms has several fingers and miles of quiet and secluded shore. The public boat launch is located near the junction of the lake arms.

If you don't own a boat, rentals are are available from the marina. If you don't want to rent one, but still

Directions:
From San Francisco, drive approximately 75 miles north on US 101 to Geyserville. Turn left on Canyon Road and drive five miles west to the lake. Anglers should take the Dry Creek exit at Healdsburg, about eight miles south of Geyserville, which will route them past the Dry Creek Store, which has live minnows for sale.

Marina:
Boats with motors, canoes and paddleboats are available for rental. For information, phone (707) 433-2200 or (707) 526-7273.

Trip Tip:
A special access point for car-top boats is provided at the quiet north end of the lake from Hot Springs Road.

Camping:
Camping is on a first-come, first-served basis,

want a secluded lakeside campsite, there are eight that can be reached by trail.

At some lakes, such as Berryessa and Shasta, for instance, waterskiers and fishermen are in constant conflict. At Sonoma, that problem has been solved by providing a large area for waterskiing and jet skis, and outlawing skiing elsewhere. Two miles of the Warm Springs Creek arm are off-limits to skiing, along with almost five miles on the Dry Creek arm.

As a result, waterskiers can "hit the coves" without worrying about running over fishermen, and fishermen can sneak up on quiet shoreline spots and not get plowed under by skiers. Each group has large areas to do their own thing.

As the word gets out, the fishing here is going to attract some excitement. Right now, the bass fishing is quite good, both for anglers casting lures such as the Countdown Rapala, and those using live minnows for bait. Minnows are available from the Dry Creek Store, located on the approach road south of the lake.

If you are interested in a visit, you should obtain the Lake Sonoma brochure, which details campgrounds, trails and posted areas for boating.

The key for good fishing is habitat. When Lake Sonoma was created, trees were left on the upper stretches of both lake arms. The submerged trees provide an ideal underwater habitat for bass and red-ear sunfish.

The centerpiece for campers is the Liberty Glen Campground, with 113 developed sites. Each campsite has a tent pad, barbecue grill, picnic table and developed restrooms, which include hot running water and showers. Water spigots are spaced about every four or five sites. No electrical hookups for motor homes are provided.

There are no reservations for individual campsites. They are available on a first-come, first-served basis, with a maximum 14-day stay. Two large group camps are also available, and reservations are required for these.

If you want a more secluded, lakeside option, 15 primitive shoreline camps are available. Seven can be reached only by boat, while eight are accessible by boat or trail. All are detailed on the Lake Sonoma map.

For hikers, there are 40 miles of trails, located on the Warm Springs arm of the lake. In addition, there is an 8,000-acre reserve set aside as a wildlife management area. Limited hunting for wild boar is permitted here, but only during special hunts offered by the Department of Fish and Game.

When visitors first see Lake Sonoma, the comparison they make will likely be to Lake Berryessa, which is in a similar setting. But when it comes to solving the waterskier/fisherman conflict, and offering opportunities for secluded camping, boating and hiking, Sonoma kicks booty on Berryessa.

❖

with a maximum stay of 14 days. The Liberty Glen Camp has 118 developed campsites and opens April 13. There are 15 boat-in sites, eight of which can also be reached by trail. Two large group camps are available, each holding 40 to 100 people. Reservations are required for the group camps, Call (707) 433-9483.

Fee or Free:
An entrance fee is charged. Boat-in campsites are free; there is a nightly charge for developed sites.

Maps:
Maps and brochures detailing posted lake areas, campgrounds and trails are available for free from Corps of Engineers, Lake Sonoma, 3333 Skaggs Springs Road, Geyserville, CA 95441; (707) 433-9483.

3

Point Reyes

On the Marin coast

Some places project a special aura, and some places do not. Mount Shasta has it, for instance, but Mount Whitney does not. Lake Tahoe has it; Lake Berryessa does not. In the Bay Area, Point Reyes definitely has it. Sure, the area offers more recreation potential than anywhere else within 150 miles, but that is not what you remember when you leave the place. What you remember is the feeling you get when you're there.

For one thing, there is a sense of total separation from the Bay Area, even though it's actually very close. For another, there are hundreds of little hideaways to be explored. After awhile, some of them start to feel like your own secret spots.

It is a gigantic area, bordered by the wide open ocean to the west, with a unique and varied terrain inland. The coast itself has miles of untouched beach just north of the lighthouse, and to the south, it offers miles of little bays, inlets and sea tunnels.

Inland, there is even more diversity. The coastal bluffs are sprinkled with wildflowers and chaparral, the rolling hills with wild grasses and poppies, and the mountain interior is heavily wooded, with little creeks following the earth's fissures. With that kind of diversity, weekenders are given a huge number of recreation choices. And Point Reyes is one of the few popular areas able to handle the weekend traffic.

You can pick an easy walk or a rugged stomper,

look for a migrating whale or a resident tule elk, stay just a few hours or overnight. You can go canoeing or kayaking, study the geology or simply enjoy the ocean lookouts.

Two things don't fit in, though. The mountain bicycles on the trails seem out of place because any form of mechanization is intrusive in a park preserved in its natural state. I've done some biking myself, but Wild America and Machine America just don't mix. The other thing that strikes you are the cows, the good ol' bovines. They're nice enough creatures, but there are just too many of them. In some areas, you have to remain alert to keep from planting your Vibram soles in the middle of a fresh meadow muffin.

Aside from that, the area is among the best in California for day-hikes. There are some 30 trails covering 65,000 acres of wildlands. The easier hikes are on the northern end of the parkland, where easy, rolling hills lead to the ocean.

The more rugged trails are in the southern end of the park, in the coastal mountains. The Bear Valley Trail, which extends along much of Coast Creek all the way to the ocean, is one of the better hikes in the park. If you want something more rugged and remote, four other trails intersect the Bear Valley route, all of them with steep climbs. You know the old adage: If you want to be alone, just start walking up.

If a day-hike isn't your game, there are a number of very short walks that can provide excitement. My favor-

Directions:
There are two possible routes from San Francisco. The shortest is to drive north on US 101 to San Rafael and take the Sir Francis Drake Boulevard exit. Turn west on Sir Francis Drake Boulevard and drive about 35 miles to the tiny town of Olema. You will see a red flashing light; turn left and drive a short distance to the Point Reyes National Seashore entrance on the right. A longer, more scenic route is to drive north of San Francisco on US 101 and take the Highway 1 cutoff. Turn west and continue to Point Reyes. The park is located on the left side of the highway, along the western shore of Tomales Bay.

Fee or Free:
Access, maps and camping are free.

Camping:
There are four primitive, hike-in campsites. Permits are required but available without charge at Bear Valley Visitor Center.

Contact:
Call park headquarters at (415) 663-1092. For free maps, write to the Superintendent, Point Reyes National Seashore, Point Reyes, CA 94956.

ite is at the tip of Point Reyes, where a five to ten-minute walk from the parking lot will take you right to the lighthouse. This is the best shoreline lookout on the Pacific Coast for spotting migrating whales. Because Point Reyes extends so far west into the sea, the whales often pass within a few hundred yards of the lookout. They can be identified by their telltale spouts. Because it is easy to reach, however, the lookout is often crowded.

The Tomales Peninsula is just as easy to reach, yet far less crowded. It is here that Point Reyes' herd of tule elk roams. The herd, several dozen strong, often hangs out near the parking lot. You can take short walks from here, or go for a three-miler to Tomales Point.

At Tomales Point, there is an area that slid more than 16 feet during the 1906 earthquake, providing a fascinating look into the area's unique geology. The entire Point Reyes Peninsula is a dislocated land, set just west of the San Andreas Fault. It's a rift zone that is steadily moving north at an average of three inches per year. The rocks of Point Reyes match those from the Tehachapi Mountains, more than 300 miles to the south.

The area has natural history and a special feel to it. When you leave, that's what you will remember. The place just feels good.

4

Tomales Bay

On the Marin coast

Tomales Bay State Park is an ideal example of a quiet, secluded area within close range of millions of Bay Area residents. While thousands of weekenders might descend on Point Reyes, Muir Woods or Stinson Beach, nearby Tomales Bay sits relatively undisturbed by anything except the small waves lapping against the shore.

The wide sandy beaches are a prime attraction for family picnics, and during minus tides, clamming is often outstanding. Hiking, surf fishing for perch and cross-country running are also popular. Car-top boats can be launched in the quiet surf.

This state park sits on the Point Reyes Peninsula on the west side of Tomales Bay, with more than 1,000 acres within park boundaries. It seems as if the retreat is much larger, however, since it is bordered by the Point Reyes National Seashore.

A unique element here is that Inverness Ridge acts as a blockade to much of the wind and fog that hammers away at the Pacific coast. When Point Reyes is buried in a rolling, 10-mile-per-hour fog, Tomales Bay can be warm and sunny. It is a good secret to know.

The best hike here is on the Jepson Trail, a six-and-a-half-mile trek which crosses through one of the largest remaining virgin stands of Bishop pines in California. About 70 percent of the park is filled with pines, oaks and madrone. In this habitat, you can see foxes, raccoons, badgers, weasels and mule deer.

Directions:
From San Francisco, drive north on US 101 to San Rafael. Take the Sir Francis Drake Boulevard exit and head west. Continue on Sir Francis Drake Boulevard three miles past Inverness to Pierce Point Road. Turn right to enter the park.

Trip Tip:
If you want to fish or clam, check tides carefully, with high and incoming tides best for perch, and minus tides best for clamming. Dogs are not allowed on the beach or the trails.

Fee or Free:
A state park access fee is charged.

Contact:
Call (415)669-1140, (415)456-1286, or (707) 576-2185 or write to Tomales Bay State Park, Star Route, Inverness, CA 94937.

Clamming is an option here. Bring a shovel and pick a good minus tide. When the tide goes out, you will see acres of prime clam beds loaded with cockles. Two of the best spots are south of Heart's Desire Beach and north of Indian Beach. Be certain to have a fishing license and a measuring device, and adhere to the limit of 50 cockles. Wardens commonly cite clammers here for not having licenses, which usually turns out to be a $50 to $300 fine; the exact amount depends on the mood of the Marin County judge. You can get a fishing license at the fishing department of sporting goods stores and at most tackle shops.

On high and incoming tides, perch fishing can spice up an otherwise lazy day at the beach. Because of the relatively calm surf in the bay, giant surf rods are not necessary, although long, medium-weight rods can certainly help in attaining long casts.

If you choose to launch a car-top boat from the beach, it is not advisable to head out to the mouth of Tomales Bay. Just south of the black buoy there, the water is very shallow, and can become very choppy with just a 15-knot wind.

Most folks, however, are content to explore the wooded areas or soak up the sun in relative isolation. That's how it is when you discover a place that seems to be one of the Bay Area's best kept secrets.

5

Bodega Bay

On the southern Sonoma Coast

One of the best ways I know to refresh your spirit is to take the nice, easy drive out to Bodega Bay, then spend a day exploring, just kind of dawdling around with a friend, finding special little places to share. It's a beautiful area, clearly unique and separate from the Bay Area, and it's close enough to do in a day.

Bodega Bay is set on the southern Sonoma coast, about 100 miles from the Bay Area, far enough away so it has formed a singular personality. From Petaluma, you meander westward on a country-style two-laner, the kind of ride where you enjoy slowing down a bit. You drive along through pretty rolling hills, past dairy farms and eventually over a hill, when suddenly the blue expanse of the Pacific Ocean looms in front of you.

It is quite a greeting, and it seems to welcome visitors onward. And on you will go, enjoying great lookouts, quiet walks, perhaps a picnic or dinner in town. Bodega Bay has also become one of the state's true quality ports. It has an exceptional boat ramp, and there is often very good fishing nearby.

For newcomers, an excellent first destination is Bodega Head, that massive rock that guards the entrance to the harbor. To get there, you drive along Bay Flat Road, which curls around the Bay and then climbs to the top of the Head, where there are good parking areas and lookouts.

From there, you can look westward over the top of Bodega Head for a sweeping view of the ocean and the Sonoma coast. In the winter, this is one of the better spots to see the little puff-of-smoke spouts from passing whales. Then you can turn the other direction, and have a perfect vantage point of Bodega Bay and the rolling hills of Sonoma County beyond. The scene is like a painting you might hang on your wall.

As you scan that landscape, you can start to see the possibilities here for adventure. Though you won't be in any big rush. What's the hurry? After all, you're at Bodega Bay.

The best hikes start right here at Bodega Head. One is a five-mile round trip that begins at the west parking lot and is routed down to Salmon Creek Beach, traversing the Bodega Marine Reserve. This is a real pretty walk with ocean views, ending along a beach with great sand dunes.

The other hike is a shorter loop that takes only an hour and just about circles Bodega Head. It starts at the east parking lot, and in a mile and a half, will take you into wonderland, with views of cliffs, untouched beaches, and southward to the sea and beyond. A side trip is also available on this hike, a short tromp on a side trail up to the tip-top of Bodega Head for 360-degree views.

Several other adventures are available, of course. A favorite destination is the Spud Point Marina and nearby boat ramp on the west side of Bodega Bay. The harbor is quite beautiful, and the boat ramp is wide and well protected from ocean surge, one of the best on the coast.

In the afternoon, when the boats return from the day's fishing, many anglers are happy to display their catch to onlookers. If you like what you see, you can arrange a trip of your own quite easily. Nearly a half-dozen party boats venture out early every morning, fishing for either salmon or rockfish, and the catches are often the best along the California coast.

If you own your own boat, Bodega Bay is very attractive. The six-lane boat ramp makes launching quite fast and easy, and in addition, in summer the salmon are usually quite nearby. That means no long boat rides are required to reach the fish. Three of the better spots here for salmon, for instance, are just a few miles off shore of Bodega Head at the Whistle Buoy, north at the mouth of Salmon Creek, and south just offshore of Tomales Point.

❖

Directions: From Highway 101 at Petaluma, take the East Washington exit, and from there take Bodega Avenue west through Petaluma and on for 26 miles to Bodega Bay (the road will turn into Highway 1). At Bodega Bay, turn left on East Shore Road and drive less than a half-mile. At the stop sign, turn right on Bay Flat Road and continue around Bodega Bay. The road turn into West Side Road, and continues past Spud Point Marina and leads to Bodega Head. The route is well signed.

Fishing boats: Phone Bodega Bay Sportfishing (707) 875-3344 or the *New Sea Angler/Jaws* at (707) 875-3495.

Free travel packet: Write Jennifer Sauter, Bodega Bay Chamber of Commerce, P.O. Box 146, Bodega Bay, CA 94923, or phone (707) 875-3422.

Chapter 8

Sonoma & Napa

1—Annadel State Park—p. 97
2—Bothe-Napa State Park—p. 99
3—Cache Creek Rafting—p. 101
4—Calistoga Mud Baths—p. 104
5—Clear Lake—p. 107

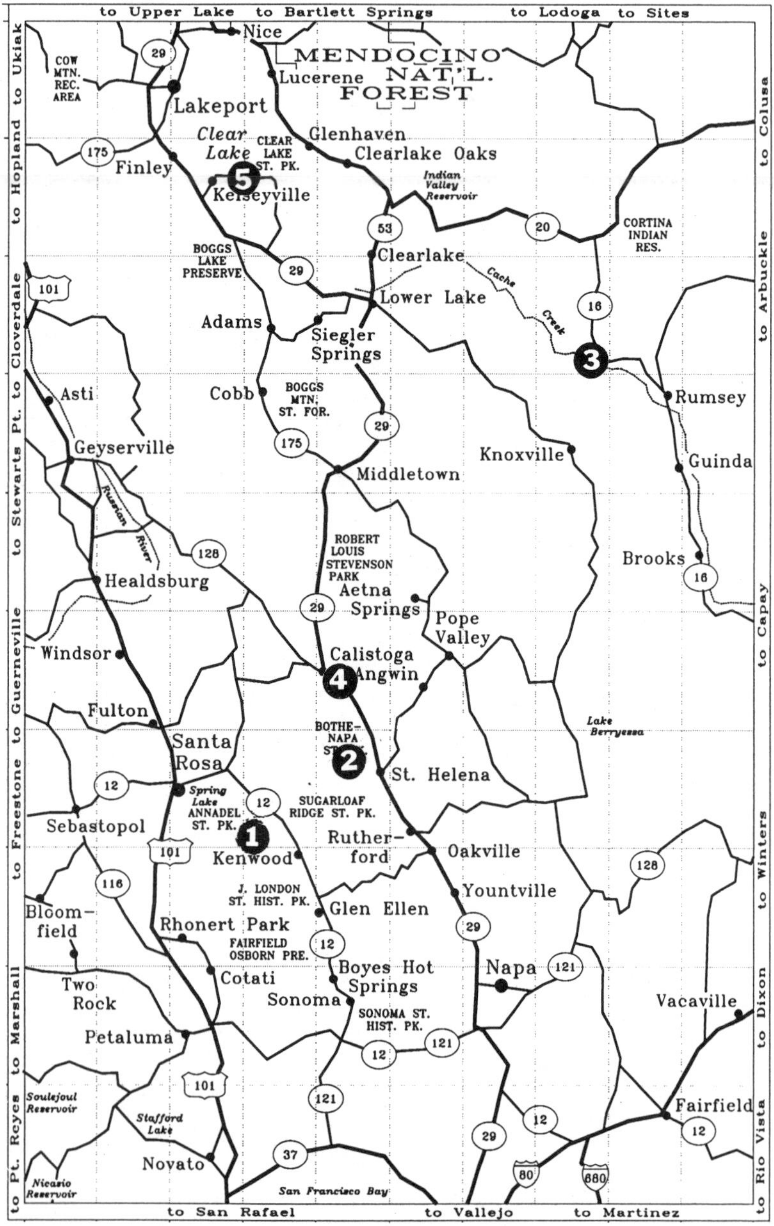

1

Annadel State Park

In the Sonoma foothills east of Santa Rosa

An example of an ideal spot rarely visited by the masses, especially in the fall, is Annadel State Park. It offers a 35-mile network of trails for hikers or equestrians and good black bass fishing, yet it's just an hour's drive north of San Francisco, just east of Santa Rosa.

The park spans almost 5,000 acres of rolling hills, meadows and woodlands, and is cut by several creeks. A secret is that two miles inside the park border is Lake Ilsanjo, a good bass and bluegill fishing lake that will always remain that way because you have to hike for an hour to reach it. Most people are not willing to hike to fish, and that's just fine for those who are. They know that the lake record here for bass is a nine-pounder, and that every spring, anglers tangle with other bass of similar proportions.

If you like to explore by foot or horseback, then Annadel Park is for you. My favorite hike here is the Lake Trail to Lake Ilsanjo (two-and-a-half miles), where I stop to fish, then return via steep Steve's Trail (three miles). Horses are allowed on the trails, and although the creeks do not flow year-round, there is usually plenty of water available for the animals. For yourself, be sure to carry a canteen.

While camping is not allowed in Annadel State Park, if you want to make a weekend out of your trip, there are some nearby campgrounds available. The western edge of Annadel is bordered by Spring Lake (which is stocked with trout) and its 31-site campground.

The rangers at Annadel say that a few herds of wild pigs run loose at the park, rooting, snorting and doing what wild pigs do. Their reputation as fighters is overblown; I've been face to face with several wild boars, and given a choice, they always run. Just don't box them in. This wild country is also home to deer and fox, although sightings are infrequent.

The terrain varies, so use care in selecting a hike. How much sun each respective area receives determines the kind of plant and tree growth it can sustain, so in just a few hours, you can hike through forests of Douglas fir to meadows and chaparral areas. A dozen different plant communities thrive here, as do the bass in the lake. Arriving at Ilsanjo after an early-morning hike seems like a perfect way to start a day.

❖

Directions: Drive north on US 101 to Santa Rosa, and take the Highway 12 exit. Head east on Highway 12, which eventually becomes Farmers Lane, until you reach Montgomery Drive. Turn right on Montgomery Drive and continue southeast. Stay on Montgomery when it merges with Mission Drive. Drive past the Spring Lake Dam to Channel Drive. Turn right and proceed to the park.

Fee or Free: A state park access fee is charged. Maps are available for a nominal fee from a machine at the park.

Pets: Horses are allowed on trails but dogs are not.

Fishing Tip: Purple plastic worms are tops for the bass at Lake Ilsanjo, and bluegill prefer small baits like meal worms or red worms.

Hours: Annadel is open from sunrise to sunset.

Camping: Campsites are available at adjacent Spring Lake Park Campground on a first-come, first-served basis. For information, phone (707) 539-8092.

Contact: Call Annadel State Park at (707) 539-3911 or (707) 938-1519, or write to 6201 Channel Drive, Santa Rosa, CA 95409.

2

Bothe-Napa State Park

In the Napa Valley

Most people think of the Napa Valley as a 20-mile stretch of wineries and tourists, but nearby Bothe-Napa State Park offers a spot for camping and picnicking, as wells as hiking trails that wind their way through the most easterly stands of coastal redwoods in California.

Now wait a minute. Redwoods in the Napa Valley, you say? That's right, and that's not all that will surprise Bay Area residents who are more accustomed to driving past this area rather than walking through it. Bothe-Napa State Park is cut by Ritchey Creek at the bottom of a canyon, and is bordered by mountains that climb from 300 to 2,000 feet. It provides a habitat for squirrels, foxes, deer, raccoons and coyote.

One critical tip is to be sure to get a reservation if you plan on camping, because the park has just 50 campsites, including 10 walk-in sites. Reservations can be made through Mistix, and rangers advise allowing a minimum of four weeks lead time. Each campsite offers a table, cupboard and barbecue stove. Rangers ask that no downed wood be used for fires. They often sell firewood at the park entrance. Barbecue chips are advised for cooking.

Many of the park's visitors are folks who have just taken a tour at one of the Napa Valley wineries. They're just looking for the shade of a tree to sit down and sample the contents of a recent purchase, and usually find the park by accident. However, on the return trip, most return, and it is no chance occurrence. Not with walks available that range from an easy stroll on the Loop Trail to a rugged hike that takes you up to ridges for panoramic views. The best moderate hike is the Coyote Peak Trail, an hour-long jaunt that climbs to a lookout offering views of the park's back canyon and glimpses of the Napa Valley.

One of the most popular hikes at Bothe-Napa Park is the Ritchey Canyon Trail, an easy walk that borders Ritchey Creek and is hidden by redwoods, firs and ferns. This cool spot is a special refuge during the summer, when temperatures elsewhere often reach 90 to 100 degrees.

One key tip is to stay on the trail. The park is loaded with poison oak. Remember that poison oak always grows in clumps of three leaves, and turns from a shiny green in the spring to rich orange and red in the summer and fall.

Directions: From San Francisco, take Interstate 80 north to the Highway 29 cutoff to Napa. Turn north and continue on Highway 29, past St. Helena. Turn left at the park entrance, just past Bale Lane.

Fee or free: A small park access fee is charged. Campsite fees vary depending on season. A small fee is charged for pets, as well as for access to the swimming pool at park headquarters.

Reservations: Camping reservations can be made through Mistix; phone (800) 444-7275.

Pets: Dogs must be kept on a leash and have proof of rabies vaccinations. While dogs are allowed in the park, they are not allowed on the trails.

Contact: Call the Bothe-Napa State Park at (707) 942-4575, or write to 3801 St. Helena Highway North, Calistoga, CA 94515.

3

Cache Creek Rafting

South of Clear Lake, near Rumsey

Mad Mike is waiting for you. Regardless of where you are reading this—at home, on a bus, on a train—Mad Mike is waiting. If you make a mistake, he'll get you. And if you don't watch it, Big Mother will get you, too. Mad Mike? Big Mother? That's right, these are the names of two pulse-pounding rapids on Cache Creek, which is the closest river to the Bay Area to provide a classic whitewater experience. For beginners and experienced paddlers alike, Mad Mike is a fellow worth tangling with.

"I've dumped three times at Mad Mike," rafting guide Mark Gholson told me. But as rafting goes, if there isn't the chance at dumping, you miss the excitement. The idea is to get out there on the edge, and sometimes, when you go over the edge, you find it's an amazing and exhilarating place to be.

Cache Creek is located north of the Bay Area, below Clear Lake. It is 110 miles from San Francisco, about a two-and-a-half hour drive. For North Bay residents, it's only 65 miles from Napa.

Upper Cache and American River Rafting Trips offers a two-day trip for around $100, complete with a New York steak dinner, which is priced as reasonably as any weekend rafting excursion in California.

For one-day trips, a good put-in spot is about 10

Directions: Take Interstate 80 north to Interstate 505. Continue north to Highway 16, then head northwest. Highway 16 runs adjacent to Cache Creek.

Camping: If you own your own raft, a campground is available at Cache Creek Canyon Regional Park; phone (916) 666-8115.

Trip Tip: Remember to bring a change of clothes, primary camping equipment such as a sleeping bag, and a stuff sack to pack your clothes.

Fee or Free: Upper Cache and American River Rafting Trips offers reasonably-

miles north of Rumsey. You can cover about eight miles of river, including shooting three Class III rapids (on a scale of I through VI), and use the adjacent Highway 16 as your shuttle road. A beginner can float it safely, while still getting the excitement of a quality run. For two-day trips, the rafting company will take you on a remote four-wheel-drive road off Highway 16 that climbs to 3,000 feet. On a clear day, you can see Mount Shasta and Mount Lassen to the northeast, and the Coast Range to the west. You camp at stream's edge at Buck Island, where rafting techniques are reviewed, and you can also watch for wildlife or go fishing. Turtles, tule elk and even eagles are common sights, and for fishermen, catfish seem to come in one size—big. A 30-pounder is on display in a little tackle shop in the town of Guinda.

On the two-day trip, you'll cover about 15 miles of river, spending about four hours on the water the first day, and about six hours the second. You go through many rapids, but the highlights are Mad Mike, Big Mother and Mario Andretti Bank.

The only things in your boat, which looks something like an inflatable kayak, are yourself, your paddle, and your lunch and drinks in a waterproof bag. Two-person inflatable kayaks are also available. Don't worry about getting wet; it's welcome in the typical 90-degree summer temperatures.

"This trip is unique, compared to most other river runs in California, because you do not paddle with a guide, but with a buddy," said river guide Gholson.

"That means you can control your own destiny, as well as take a break when you want. Novices start out scared and tense, but by the end of the first day, they have a great feeling of accomplishment, because they have done it themselves. The next day, they're ready for anything."

And it's a good thing, because Mad Mike is waiting.

priced rafting packages.

Contact:
For a brochure, phone Upper Cache and American River Rafting Trips at (707) 255-0761.

4

Calistoga Mud Baths

In the northern Napa Valley

The first time you imagine taking a mud bath, you are apt to get all kinds of crazy ideas about what it's like. Then when you do it, you will find out that most of them are true. As you slowly sink into the hot black ooze, you feel like you are being enveloped by a giant sponge. Your body submerges deeper, and then an attendant covers you right up to your Adam's apple. There are several immediate sensations: the 100-degree heat, the weight of 100 pounds of muck, the smell of peat, and a general sort of strange euphoria.

After five minutes, your body has a strange glow from the heat and you might start to feel light-headed. Two minutes later, you might become a little short of breath as the toxins begin leaving your body, and sweat pours from your forehead. Ten minutes into the process, you start thinking you can't take it anymore—you need to escape. Your breathing is short; the heat is all-encompassing.

Finally, you surrender. Then you find out this strange journey has only begun.

After the mud bath, the rejuvenating treatment called "The Works" comes with ten minutes in a tub full of 106 to 108-degree mineral water, a sit in the steam room, a towel wrap and a massage. At that point, what you will probably need is somebody to cart you away in a wheelbarrow, because after all of this, you will feel like a happy, amorphous blob.

This is the treatment at Dr. Wilkinson's Hot Springs, one of the oldest mineral spas in Calistoga. Your first visit here might be out of curiosity, relief for stress, or a search for a cure for rheumatism. Regardless of what gets you here, you leave feeling like you are starting a whole new life, and the glow stays with you for days.

"People originally came here looking for relief from rheumatic ailments," said Dr. John Wilkinson, founder and owner of the spa. "Nowadays the main reason they come here is because of stress." They come back because they find the treatment works pretty well.

Calistoga, located in the north end of the Napa wine valley, is the nation's headquarters for mud baths and hot springs. Why here? Because submerged in the earth under this small town are several boiling cauldrons of mineral water. The mineral spas tap it, and in turn, are able to offer its unique powers to the public.

"It's like a giant tea kettle under this building," Wilkinson said. "Imagine a boiling pool of 250-degree water. That's what it's like down there. Our biggest problem is cooling it down before we use it."

A large mineral spa with bubbling 103 or 104-degree mineral water is available. But when you sign up for "The Works," the water goes into the tub much hotter, like 107 or 108 degrees. Two larger pools are also available at Wilkinson's, one that feels like soaking in a big bathtub, the other set at swimming pool temperature.

At the least, just soaking in mineral water will take the fight out of you. At the most, it will make you feel like a new person. Most folks walk out feeling somewhere in between.

According to Wilkinson, soaking in hot mineral water helps rid your skin of toxins. The effect is compounded in the mud bath, in which the "mud" is actually composed of Canadian peat and Calistoga volcanic ash mixed with hot mineral water. Topping it off with a session in the steam room seems to purify your entire body. Although you sweat out fluids profusely during the experience, cold carbonated mineral water is provided so you do not get dehydrated.

"The Works" has become so popular that a reservation is usually required, even on weekdays.

Ironically, sometimes it is not the mud bath or mineral spa that ends up as the most memorable moment. It is the towel wrap. What happens is that you are wrapped in a towel and blankets, with an ice cold towel on your forehead—just after having finished the mud bath, mineral spa and steam room. As you lie there, you feel as if you are in the midst of some phenomenal sensory experience. It's because you are.

The mud bath itself is a relatively small, square tub filled with dark, bubbling goo. As you first start sinking into the stuff, it feels kind of like wallowing in warm, shallow quicksand. Then, when submerged to your neck, you feel a sense of weightlessness, as if there are no sides or bottom to the tub and you are floating in space, suspended in hot mud.

If you think it might be a strange experience to find yourself sitting in the stuff, well, you are right. But if you want to feel like a "whole new person," this is one of the best ways there is to do it.

❖

Directions: Take Interstate 80 north to the Highway 29 cutoff to Napa. Turn north on Highway 29 and continue past St. Helena to Calistoga.

Fee or Free: Packages typically include a mud bath, mineral whirlpool bath, mineral steam room and blanket wrap. Massages can be added for an extra charge. Phone individual spas for price lists. Mud bath packages range between $30-$100.

Contact: Call the Calistoga Chamber of Commerce at (707) 924-6333. If you have time (allow three weeks), ask for them to send you the free visitor's guide to Calistoga. Or call Dr. Wilkinson's at (707)942-4102, International Spa at (707)942-6122, Roman Spa at (707)942-4441, Calistoga Spa and Hot Springs at (707)942-6269, Village Inn and Spa at (707)942-0991, Pine Street Inn and Spa at (707)942-6829, Golden Haven Hot Springs at (707)942-6793, Indian Springs at (707)942-4913, Nance's Hot Springs at (707)942-6211, Lincoln Avenue Spa at (707)942-5298, and Mountain View Hotel and Spa at (707)942-6877.

5

Clear Lake

In Lake County

One of the most beautiful sights in America in the spring is Clear Lake in Northern California, the big lake full to the brim, ringed by lush, green foothills, with an occasional puffy cumulus cloud dotting an azure blue sky.

Clear Lake is becoming one of the great vacation destinations anywhere in the West. In the spring, the great natural beauty of Clear Lake approaches that of Lake Tahoe, and it's warm, not cold. Like Tahoe, Clear Lake is a natural lake, not a reservoir, so it is not drained in the summer to provide water for agriculture. As a result, it has a completely different look and feel than most other lakes in California, and with old Mount Konocti set near the western shoreline, it also has a sense of history.

State park camps are set at lakeside, and the fishing can be so good that it is rated the Number One bass lake in America, with prospects best from April through June. It is also one of the few lakes in California where there are shoreline cabins, campsites and boat rentals.

If you haven't visited Clear Lake for a while, recent changes have significantly improved the quality of the place. New entertainment possibilities, an improved information service and much better fishing make it a first-class destination.

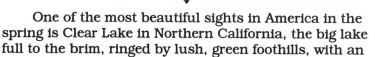

The centerpiece of the renovation is Konocti Harbor Resort, set in a big cove just below Mount Konocti. The change started when Greg Bennett, who used to book music acts in Southern California, took over Konocti Resort and started a music program. Featured performers are often legends, such as B.B. King and Waylon Jennings. At capacity, the concert hall holds 400.

"I really liked playing here," Waylon told me after one show. "With the big crowds at football stadiums and giant auditoriums, the music can get lost. Here you feel real close to the crowd, and sense them more into the music, and not just the event. I like to pick out individuals in the crowd, look right at them, and play for them. You can do that here."

Another part of the renovation of Clear Lake is the quality of lodging. At one time, it seemed like many of the places were run-down. There has been enough new money invested here in the past few years that the general level of quality is up, though a few down-and-out holes-in-the-wall still exist. Virtually all the resorts have lake views.

The fishing, boating and waterskiing provide outstanding recreation. Catch rates for bass are very high, among the top five lakes in California, and the chance of catching a four- or five-pounder over a weekend is very good. In addition, there are probably more big catfish and crappie here than in any lake in the state.

Comparing the fishing to Lake Tahoe, Clear Lake has the edge. The reason is because Tahoe is a pristine, clear water habitat with few nutrients, with 95 percent of the fish in only five percent of the lake. Clear Lake, on the other hand, is loaded with nutrients, which start the aquatic food chain. The final result is an abundant fishery throughout the lake.

Clear Lake is located 132 miles from San Francisco, 96 miles from Sacramento, and is the largest natural freshwater lake within state borders, covering nearly 45,000 acres. It is surrounded by wildlands, including the vast Mendocino National Forest to the north, with mountain peaks to 7,000 feet. There are a dozen free boat ramps.

The best time to visit is from April through June,

when the average high temperature is in the 80s. In the summer, it really bakes here, with typical daily highs running 95 degrees, which makes it great for waterskiing. Until Memorial Day weekend, there just aren't many folks here. The campgrounds are almost empty, resorts have only a light sprinkling of visitors, and only a few boats are leaving their fresh white wakes in the emerald green waters.

During the summer, Clear Lake State Park is among the most popular campgrounds in the state, with reservations required virtually every day of the vacation season.

There are many routes to the lake, the most popular being Highway 29 from the south and Highway 20 from the west or east. If you don't mind the narrow, twisty road, the two-laner from Hopland is a great trip. After topping the summit, you look down and at the center of the panorama is Clear Lake, aqua blue from that distance, a beautiful sight amid the green hills. It is one of the great natural treasures of Northern California.

It is no accident that Clear Lake provides some of the best fishing in America. In fact, about the only accidents that happen here are when you catch fish without even trying.

That's what happened to me. Dave Zimmer and I were paddling our canoe into position to make a few casts along the shoreline near the state park, while our ignored, unattended lures were just bobbing a little on the surface right next to the boat. Wham! A bass hammered that lure, and I dropped my paddle and managed to grab the rod just in time to keep it from being pulled into the lake.

These kinds of things have a way of happening at Clear Lake. There can be 50-fish days in April and May, catching and releasing, of course, but you get the picture: you catch fish. Fishing at Clear Lake is not an act of faith, a scientific expedition, or a matter of having a charmed life. It's a matter of being there. And the results are no accident.

You see, the fisheries at Clear Lake are not funded

Directions: From the Bay Area, take Interstate 80 north over the Carquinez Bridge, then turn north on Highway 29, continue through Vallejo and Napa (jogging left just after Napa College), and proceed on Highway 29 through Napa Valley, past Middletown to the town of Lower Lake.

From Sacramento or Interstate 5, take 5 north to Williams, then turn west on Highway 20 and continue to the town of Nice.

From the North Coast, take US 101 to Calpella (17 miles south of Willits), then turn south on Highway 20 and continue to Nice.

or managed by the troubled Department of Fish and Game. Rather, a unique program is directed by the county, which understands the value of a quality fishery and how many recreation dollars it can bring to the local economy.

The program is funded by a hotel and homeowners' tax, and is called "Lakebed Management." Some 50,000 Florida bass and 17,500 black crappie are stocked each spring, and in addition, rules are enforced to protect the aquatic habitat from lakeside homeowners. When a newcomer from L.A. removed the tules along the shore near his lakefront home in Lucerne in order to create a beach, the county immediately made him replant the tules. Tules, of course, provide breeding and nursery habitat for bass, crappie and bluegill, as well as nesting areas for ducks and other birds.

"We rely on the Department of Fish and Game for advice, but not for money or decisions," said guide Terry Knight, a member of the management group. "We're not involved in any way with the state bureaucracy. That allows us to get things done that need to be done, and get them done quickly. This is clearly the best-managed lake in California."

The results are in the catches. To document it, Knight directed a local program where he honored anglers who caught large fish. In a year, he awarded 200 certificates for bass over eight pounds, 100 certificates for crappie over two and a half pounds, and 400 certificates for catfish over 15 pounds. That is more big fish documented than at any other lake in California.

Last year, professional bass fishermen across America voted Clear Lake the Number One lake in America. The reasons are many—catch rates are good; about one out of four bass is a four-pounder; and the fish tend to be in the top three to four feet of water, not down deep like at reservoirs. Because it is a natural lake, the water level is always near the brim, and with Mount Konocti looming overhead, the area has great beauty.

In addition, the success here is a testimonial to catch-and-release fishing, providing perpetual benefits for anglers. At all bass tournaments, fishermen keep their fish in a live well on their boat, then after weigh-in, release them. At Clear Lake, however, they go one step further. The fish are placed in a special "bass truck" before release. The bass truck is actually a pick-up truck with an oxygen-flooded water tank, where the bass are resuscitated before release.

"We haven't lost a fish in two years," said Skip Simkins, who helps run the truck.

Keys to success here are the high nutrient and algae levels, which create an abundant aquatic food chain from minnows to bass. Another key is that in the past 10 years, the county has phased out northern largemouth bass and white crappie, which rarely grow to large sizes. Florida bass and black crappie have been stocked instead, causing the sudden boom in giant fish in the past few years here.

Fishing here makes for a wonderful experience. From a boat, you move along, making casts along the shore as you go. Tules are abundant, as are old docks,

Fee or free: Access to the lake is free. Campsites, cabins and room rentals are available at reasonable rates.

Free boat ramps: Public boat ramps are available at no charge at the following locations: in Clearlake, at Rosebud County Park; in Kelseyville, at Lakeside County Park; in Lakeport, at First Street, Third Street, Fifth Street, Clear Lake Avenue, and at the junction of Lakeshore Boulevard and Crystal Lake Way; in Lucerne, at Lucerne Harbor County Park; in Nice, at H.V. Keeling County Park, Nice Community Park and Hudson Avenue.

Contact:
For general information and a free travel packet, write to the Lake County Visitor Information Center, 875 Lakeport Boulevard, Lakeport, CA 95453, or phone (800) 525-3743 (toll free in California), or (707) 263-9544. For fishing conditions or lodging information, phone Konocti Harbor Inn, (707) 279-4291. Guide Terry Knight can be reached at (707) 263-1699.

pilings and rockpiles, making for an ideal fish habitat. It's almost impossible not to catch a bass or crappie.

At Clear Lake, fishing is kind of like riding a bicycle. The only way you fall down is if you stop pedaling.

Chapter 9

San Francisco Bay Area

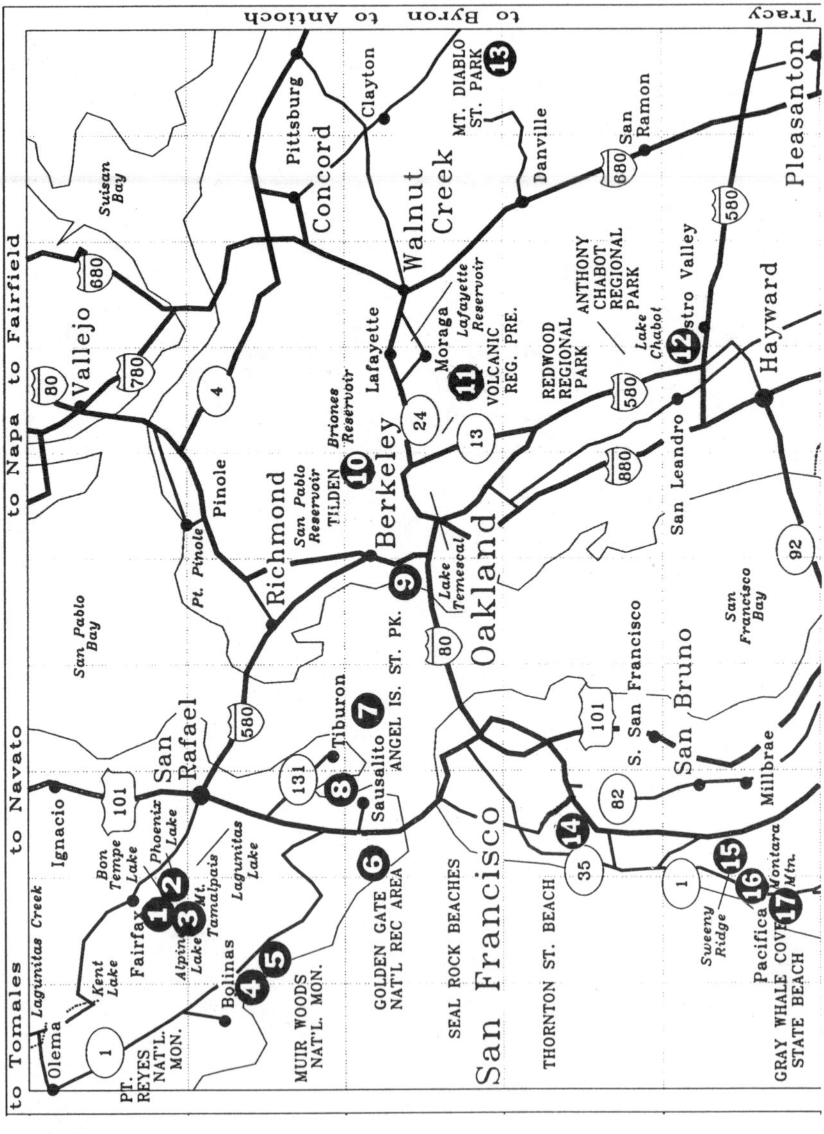
to Tomales
to Navato
to Napa to Fairfield
to Byron to Antioch
Tracy
Olema
Lagunitas Creek
Kent Lake
PT. REYES NAT'L. MON.
Bolinas
Fairfax
Ignacio
Bon Tempe Lake
Phoenix Lake
Alpine Lake
Mt. Tamalpais
Lagunitas Lake
MUIR WOODS NAT'L. MON.
San Rafael
San Pablo Bay
Pt. Pinole
Pinole
Vallejo
Suisan Bay
Richmond
San Pablo Reservoir
TILDEN
Briones Reservoir
Berkeley
Lafayette
Moraga
Lafayette Reservoir
Walnut Creek
Concord
Pittsburg
Clayton
MT. DIABLO ST. PARK
Danville
San Ramon
Pleasanton
ANTHONY CHABOT REGIONAL PARK
Lake Chabot
Castro Valley
VOLCANIC REG. PRE.
REDWOOD REGIONAL PARK
Hayward
San Leandro
Oakland
Lake Temescal
ANGEL IS. ST. PK.
Tiburon
Sausalito
GOLDEN GATE NAT'L REC AREA
SEAL ROCK BEACHES
San Francisco
THORNTON ST. BEACH
S. San Francisco
San Bruno
San Francisco Bay
Millbrae
Sweeny Ridge
Montara Mtn.
Pacifica
GRAY WHALE COVE STATE BEACH
1 2 3 4 5 6 7 8 9 10 11 12 13 14 15 16 17
1 4 13 24 35 80 82 92 101 131 580 680 780 880

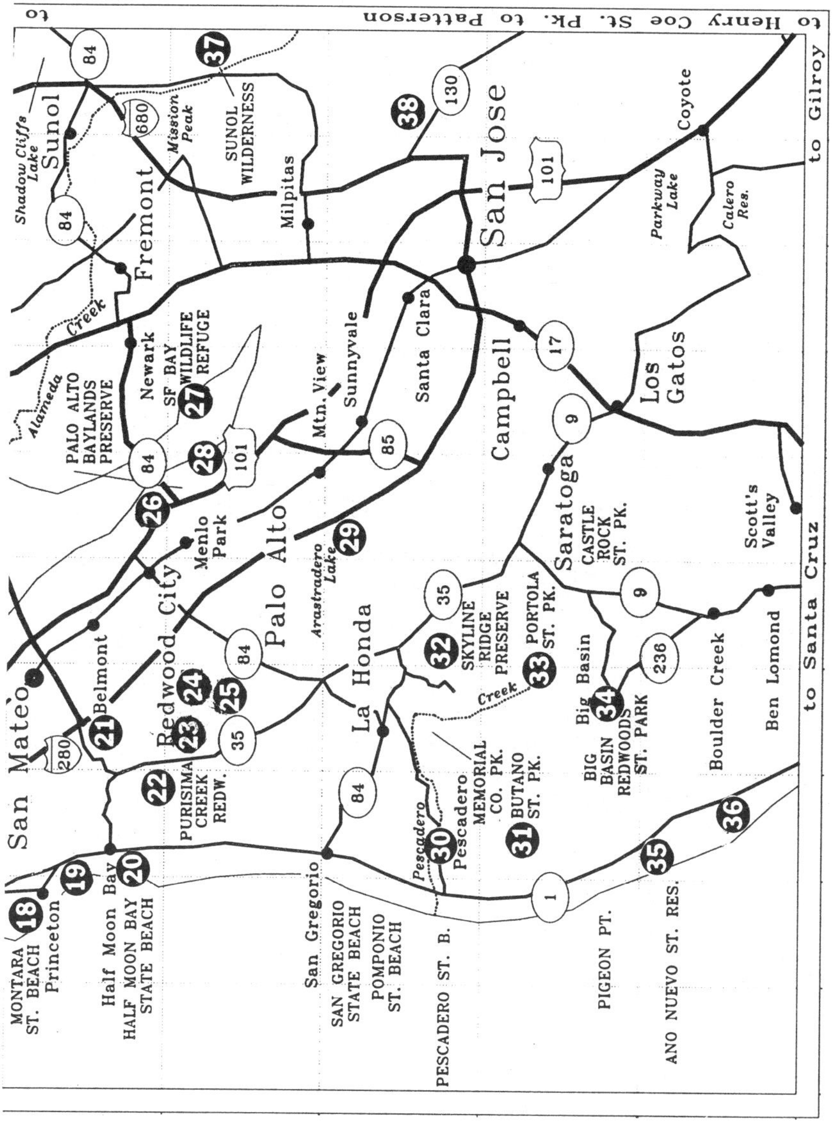
to Henry Coe St. Pk. to Patterson
to
to Gilroy
to Santa Cruz
San Mateo
Redwood City
Palo Alto
La Honda
Menlo Park
Belmont
Fremont
Sunol
Shadow Cliffs Lake
Mission Peak
SUNOL WILDERNESS
Milpitas
San Jose
Coyote
Parkway Lake
Calero Res.
Newark
SF BAY WILDLIFE REFUGE
PALO ALTO BAYLANDS PRESERVE
Alameda Creek
Mtn. View
Sunnyvale
Santa Clara
Campbell
Los Gatos
Saratoga
CASTLE ROCK ST. PK.
Scott's Valley
Arastradero Lake
SKYLINE RIDGE PRESERVE
PORTOLA ST. PK.
Big Basin
BIG BASIN REDWOODS ST. PARK
Boulder Creek
Ben Lomond
Creek
PURISIMA CREEK REDW.
Pescadero
Pescadero
MEMORIAL CO. PK.
BUTANO ST. PK.
MONTARA ST. BEACH
Princeton
Half Moon Bay
HALF MOON BAY STATE BEACH
San Gregorio
SAN GREGORIO STATE BEACH
POMPONIO ST. BEACH
PESCADERO ST. B.
PIGEON PT.
ANO NUEVO ST. RES.
18
19
20
21
22
23
24
25
26
27
28
29
30
31
32
33
34
35
36
37
38
84
680
130
101
17
9
85
280
35
236
1

1

Marin's Hidden Road to the Outdoors

From Fairfax to Bolinas

The Bay Area has plenty of unique, hidden backroads, but the best might just be a little winding two-laner in Marin County, west of San Rafael. It's Marin's hidden road to the outdoors—we're talking about a road that provides access to three lakes, 15 trailheads for secluded hikes and even a golf course.

The route is called Bolinas-Fairfax Road. It's pretty enough to enjoy just for a Saturday evening drive or a Sunday morning bike cruise, but you can take it one giant step forward by using it as a jump-off for hiking or fishing trips.

To get there is simple enough: From Highway 101, take Sir Francis Drake Boulevard west into Fairfax, then just turn left onto Bolinas-Fairfax Road.

That is where your journey starts. After leaving Fairfax and passing the Meadow Club Golf Course two miles later, the road twists its way up to a 600-foot elevation. Another mile and you will start seeing little turnouts dotting the side of the road. Look closer. Each of those turnouts marks a hiking trail, with the trailhead nearby.

Between Fairfax and Bolinas, there are 15 trails.

You can just head down the trail for a little in-and-outer, or manufacture a longer trip by hooking up with the network of trails that are linked in the Marin backcountry.

It can make for very quiet and secluded hiking. If there are no other cars parked at the turnouts, you will know that there is no one on the trail but you.

Your mission, should you decide to accept it, can be made easier by obtaining a detailed map of the area.

Two of the best hikes in the late summer and fall months start on either side of Alpine Lake, which is about a five-mile drive west of Fairfax. You should park at the dam, then take your pick.

The easier hike heads north and follows a gentle grade downhill along the section of Lagunitas Creek that connects Alpine Lake to Kent Lake. Having a picnic at creekside, amidst the big oaks, you might feel like you're in Tennessee wilderness, not just five miles from the Marin suburbs.

If you want more of a challenge and some good views of Alpine Lake, cross the dam, and right where the road takes a hairpin turn, look for the trailhead for the Cataract Trail. You can put together a loop hike that zigzags its way to almost 1,700 feet, then drops back down along the southeast shore of Alpine Lake.

In the fall and spring, after the rains come, another good hike can take you to a little-known series of waterfalls. The trail starts about a mile past the golf course at the first large parking area on the left side of the road. Cross the road from the parking area, and with map in hand to help you make the proper turns, you can arrive at Carson Falls in an hour's walk.

If hiking is not for you, there are three lakes along Bolinas-Fairfax Road. The most impressive is Alpine Lake, a long, deep lake bordered by forest. Fishing, however, is often poor. No boats are allowed, either.

The other lakes, which are reached by taking the Sky Oaks Road turnoff, are Bon Tempe and Lagunitas. Bon Tempe is stocked with rainbow trout in the fall and winter, and Lagunitas has been converted to a special wild trout lake.

No boats, rafts, float tubes or water contact of any kind are permitted at the lakes, which is something of a rip-off. Marin Water District officials have told fishermen that they fear the spread of a water plant called hydrilla, but that is absolute nonsense.

Hydrilla can only be spread by boats if it is somehow stuck on the bottom of somebody's raft or boat, then comes off and starts growing in a lake. It's a potential problem at every lake, but the chances are so infinitesimal that other water districts virtually ignore it. At Contra Loma Reservoir near Antioch, which is part of the State Water Project, a sign has simply been posted asking boaters to please clear their boats and propellers of any weeds. That warning has been sufficient since Contra Loma was constructed in 1969. Enough said.

The Marin lakes are all pretty, primarily because they are hidden among forested hillsides. The entire area is like that, hidden and secluded. Driving along the Bolinas-Fairfax Road helps unveil these secrets.

Directions:
From Highway 101, take Sir Francis Drake Boulevard west into Fairfax, then just turn left on Bolinas-Fairfax Road.

Maps:
The best available map of the area can be purchased from the Olmsted Brothers Map Company. It details all roads, trails, creeks and lakes, and includes contour lines. It is available by phoning (510) 658-6534, or writing P.O. Box 5351, Berkeley, CA 94705.

2

Marin Lakes

In Marin County

Marin County has eight hidden lakes, but most people don't even know of one. They are ideal for fishing, picnics and hikes. They vary widely, from little Phoenix Lake and its spring trout fishing to hidden Soulejule Reservoir, where each evening crappie fishing can provide the spark for anglers of all ages.

The lakes are ideal for a family adventure, or for just going solo. Several of the lakes are perfect for an evening picnic, especially Lagunitas, Bon Tempe and Stafford lakes. Just bring your fried chicken. A number of the lakes also provide ideal jump-off points for hikes. One of the best is Bon Tempe, with trails that connect to several other lakes. One of my favorite areas is the far side of beautiful Alpine Lake which has an extensive trail system. The hikes here are steep, remote and provide stunning overlooks.

For more information on any of the lakes, call Western Boat in San Rafael at (415) 454-4177, the Marin Water District at (415) 924-4600 or the North Marin Water District at (415) 897-4133.

Here's a capsule look at each of the lakes.

Alpine Lake

Alpine is the most well-known of the Marin lakes. It's a big reservoir set in a tree-bordered canyon along Bolinas-Fairfax Road. It is larger and prettier than any first-timer would expect. Trailheads for several excellent hikes can be found here, which can lead you back into pristine woodlands. The best trailhead is near the dam. This lake has a few large rainbow trout and largemouth bass. It's not stocked, and the fish can be elusive.

Directions: Drive north on US 101 to San Rafael and take the Sir Francis Drake Boulevard exit. Head west and drive to Fairfax, then turn left on Pacheco and travel less than a block to Broadway. Turn right and drive past the Fairfax Theatre. Turn left on Bolinas Road and continue for five miles; the road borders the lake.

Bon Tempe Lake

This is headquarters for hikers, picnickers and shore fishermen. A network of outstanding hiking trails start at Bon Tempe, a pretty lake that is probably the most popular of all the Marin lakes. Why? It seems to get more sun than the others. It is stocked with rainbow trout by the Department of Fish and Game. From early winter through late spring, shorefishing can be excellent. There's no secret to it: just bait fish with salmon eggs and marshmallows along the shoreline. It's a good way to spend a pleasant evening.

Directions: Drive north on US 101 to San Rafael and take the Sir Francis Drake Boulevard exit. Head west and drive to Fairfax, then turn left on Pacheco and travel less thana block to Braodway. Turn right and drive past the Fairfax Theatre. Turn left on Bolinas-Fairfax Road and continue for 1.5 miles, then turn left at Sky Oaks Road and continue to the lake.

Lagunitas Lake

This lake has a picnic area along the west side of the lake, just below the dam. It is located right next to Bon Tempe, and the same hikes are available. This little lake gained national attention because the organization California Trout is attempting a program here where the lake supports a self-sustaining wild trout fishery with no future stocks. To do that requires a special slot limit, with all 10 to 16-inch fish being released, and a new law mandating the use of artificials with single barbless hooks.

The anglers having the most fun are using dry flies and a Cast-A-Bubble, catching and releasing during the evening rise.

Directions: Drive north on US 101 to San Rafael and take the Sir Francis Drake Boulevard exit. Head west and drive to Fairfax, then turn left on Pacheco and travel less than a block to Broadway. Turn right and drive past the Fairfax Theatre. Turn left on Bolinas-Fairfax Road and continue for 1.5 miles, then turn left at Sky Oaks Road and continue to the lake (located directly above Bon Tempe Lake).

❖

Phoenix Lake

This lake is less accessible than Alpine, Bon Tempe or Lagunitas, and requires a half-mile hike. That's just far enough to keep a lot of people away—and to ensure good fishing for those willing to hoof it. The shore is undeveloped for picnickers, but for hikers it's one of Marin's jewels. A network of trails connects Phoenix Lake to Bon Tempe, Lagunitas and Alpine lakes.

This is a good trout lake from February through May. Try baitfishing from the shore on the southern side of the lake. A fly-fisherman can have some fun here fishing the mouth of the feeder stream.

Directions: Drive north on US 101 to San Rafael and take the Sir Francis Drake Boulevard exit, heading west. Turn left on Lagunitas Road and continue for a few miles into Natalie Coffin Green Park. You can't see the lake from your car. After parking, hike a quarter of a mile on the signed trail.

❖

Kent Lake

The only way in is to hike, and when you first see the lake, its immense size will surprise you. Space for parking is poor along Sir Francis Drake Boulevard, and after you've found a spot, it's another half-hour walk before you reach the lake. The area is undeveloped for recreation. It's primitive, with just one trail that loops the lake. And the fishing is not easy (no stocks are made). The resident trout and bass have taken plenty of smart lessons. One good strategy is to bring a minnow trap to the lake, catch your own minnows (taking foreign minnows to the lake is illegal), then use the live bait with a sliding sinker rigging. The best prospects are to the left of the dam, along the back side.

Directions: Drive north on US 101 to San Rafael and take the Sir Francis Drake Boulevard exit and head west for about 10 miles. Go through the town of Lagunitas and park off Sir Francis Drake Boulevard just before reaching Samuel P. Taylor Park. A small sign is on the gate on the left side of the road—a ranch road that is the trail to the lake, about a one-mile hike.

Nicasio Lake

You can drive right to this lake because three-quarters of it is accessible by road. There are no picnic tables, so you have to improvise, and that is just how some people like it. It is only fair hiking, since the area isn't wooded. This lake has been a surprise, providing good bass and crappie fishing during the evening in spring and early summer.

Directions: Drive north on US 101 to San Rafael and take the Sir Francis Drake Boulevard exit and head west for about seven miles. Turn right on Nicasio Valley Road. Follow that for another five miles and it will take you directly to the lake.

Stafford Lake

The lake is open for hiking, which is only fair since the hillsides here are sparsely wooded. There is a picnic area on the west side of the lake.

This little lake was the site of a local project to improve the fishing for bass and red-ear sunfish. It was drained to repair the dam, than volunteers completeed a habitat-improvement project. It is now full of water and bass, and bluegill have been stocked and are becoming re-established.

Directions: Drive north on US 101 to Novato. Take the San Marin exit and continue west to Novato Boulevard. Turn right and drive about five miles to the lake.

Soulejule Reservoir

This is a little-known, hike-in lake in northern Marin. You can drive to the base of the dam; a short hike will get you to the lake's edge. It is a small, hidden spot where crappie and small largemouth bass are abundant. It provides the country's best crappie fishing, with shoreliners using chartreuse and yellow crappie jigs.

Directions: Drive north on US 101 to Novato. Take the San Marin exit and continue west to Novato Boulevard. Turn right and continue nine miles to Petaluma/Point Reyes Road. Turn right, continue for a quarter of a mile, then turn left on Wilson Hill Road. Continue for three miles and turn left on Marshall/Petaluma Road. Continue for five miles to the lake entrance on the left side of the road. You can drive to the base of the dam.

3

Mount Tamalpais

In Marin County

The best place to hike in the Bay Area is on the slopes of Mount Tamalpais. Trails peek in and out of redwoods and tan oaks, at times providing the seclusion of forest, at other times guiding you to lookout points with astounding views of the Bay Area and the Pacific Ocean.

Mount Tamalpais, of course, is that big mountain you see in Marin County. When John Muir spent his winters in the Bay Area, it was his favorite place to hike. It doesn't take much time here to find out why.

Mount Tam is one of the few places in the Bay Area that projects a genuine "feel" to it, kind of like sitting in your favorite chair. You might try it on for size and find it fits pretty well. You don't even have to hike here to sense this. You can drive to the East Peak Lookout, for instance, which at 2,571 feet provides one of the world's truly spectacular vistas. I've traveled all over the Western Hemisphere and the view from this spot can match just about anything you can drive to, anywhere. It is a reminder that the beauty of the Bay Area is timeless and special.

I found a clipping dated 1909, author unknown, that described the view here. It reads: "Mount Tamalpais—where 100 points of scenic interest, with San Francisco in the background, unveil to you the diversified lands of sunlit charm beyond the Golden Gate."

You can take it a step further by parking your car, picking a trail and taking a nice walk. Some folks will

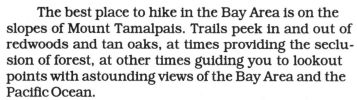

Directions: From San Francisco, take US 101 north.
To get to the **Pantoll Ranger Station**, take the Stinson Beach exit and drive about four miles to the Panoramic Highway. Turn right and continue uphill for four miles. Enter at the Pantoll Ranger Station on the left.

To get to the **Rock Springs Picnic Area** from San Francisco, take US 101 north. Take the Stinson Beach exit, drive about four miles to the Panoramic Highway. Turn right and continue uphill for 3.5 miles. Turn right on Pantoll Road and drive about one mile, where a

bring their mountain bikes up here on weekends and cruise the fire roads. Bikes are prohibited on hiking trails, but there are enough fire roads to make it the most popular bike area in the Bay Area.

But you lose much of the intimacy of the adventure on a bike—or in a car. Try strolling down one of the trails here with a friend. That's when you really begin to connect with the surroundings.

There are hundreds of miles of hiking trails in the area, crossing land managed by Mount Tamalpais State Park, the Marin Water District, Golden Gate National Recreation Area and Muir Woods National Monument. There are several maps and books available as well that detail the area.

With map in hand, you can design your day, whether you want a short stroll, a hike with a picnic or an all-day thumper. Here are some of the better hikes available:

Start at the Rock Springs Picnic Area, where four trailheads are located. If you just want to take a 10-minute stroll, the walk to Mountain Theatre is ideal. After parking your car, walk (northeast) up the road for about 100 yards, then take the trail on the right side of the road. Mountain Theatre is a large amphitheater with terraced rows of rocks for seats. At 2,100 feet, you get a good lookout of San Francisco Bay from here.

For a longer walk with more diversity, continue on Rock Springs Trail past the Mountain Theatre for the 2.5-mile hike to the West Point Inn. The trail provides lookouts, and in some spots cuts a tunnel through a thick forest canopy. The West Point Inn is a small picnic area that has a limited menu, but the place had a good feel to it. It can also be reached by bicycle via fire roads. On Sundays, it is a major destination point for mountain bikers.

There are two other alternate hikes from the Rock Springs Picnic Area. One leads southwest, past a grove of big trees to the hilly grasslands that overlook the Pacific Ocean. This is a popular jump-off point for hang gliders. Another possibility is the Cataract Trail, which heads north into state parkland. You can continue on the Cataract Trail, an easy walk that laterals the west slope of Mount Tam at 1,850 feet, or take the cutoff on the Simmons Trail. The latter climbs as high as 2,200 feet, then descends into an open area called Barth's Retreat.

If you are seeking a more rigorous hike that will reward you with views of woods, water and gem-like lakes, head to the northern flank of Mount Tamalpais.

The "Three Lakes Trail" is one of the Bay Area's best loop hikes. It starts at Lagunitas Lake and is routed west along the shorelines of Bon Tempe Lake and Alpine Lake, then up the mountain (only a 400-foot climb), and back down (east) to Lagunitas. In winter and spring, there is a prize opportunity for a hike-to sidetrip to see a small, but memorable set of waterfalls.

Lakes are the focus of the adventure. The trailhead is at little Lagunitas Lake, the smallest of the eight lakes in Marin County. Start at the Lagunitas Picnic Area and walk west along the Bon Tempe Shadyside Trail. It borders the western side of Bon Tempe Lake, and beyond that, connects to the Kent Trail,

parking area is located at the "T" intersection.

To get to the north side of Mt. Tamalpais and the **Three Lakes Trail,** drive north on US 101 to Sir Francis Drake Boulevard. Take Sir Francis Drake to the town of Fairfax. In Fairfax, take a left at the BP gas station, then an immediate right onto Broadway. Within a block, at the stop sign take a left on Bolinas Road. Continue one and a half miles to 700 Bolinas Road, and take a left on Sky Oaks Road (look for the Lagunitas Lake sign) and continue to the park entrance.

which follows the pristine, southern edge of Alpine Lake.

Alpine Lake, a good-sized lake at 224 acres, is one of the prettiest of the Bay Area's 44 public lakes. The only one prettier may be Loch Lomond Reservoir near Ben Lomond, a gem-like blue pool in a canyon bordered by redwoods in the Santa Cruz Mountains.

For two miles, Kent Trail tracks the southern outline of Alpine Lake, then arrives at a junction. To make the loop trail back to Lagunitas, you make a left turn, and with it start a 400-foot, one-mile climb up Mount Tam. At the junction with Stocking Trail, turn left, and then loop back (with a short jog on the way) to Lagunitas Lake. A map is very helpful, of course, and is provided at the park entry station.

In all, the hike covers about five-and-a-half miles, as close as I could estimate it. That makes it an ideal weekend walk with a stop along the way for a picnic lunch.

If you are more ambitious, a sidetrip to see Cataract Falls is worth the climb. For the most direct route here, take the nearby drive over Alpine Dam on Bolinas-Fairfax Road and then park at the hairpin turn, which is set adjacent to the Cataract Trail.

The trail climbs 720 feet in one-and-a-third miles to the falls, including one short gut-wrenching ascent. But in return, you get to see beautiful Cataract Creek, which boasts a small set of waterfalls.

As previously mentioned, bikes are not allowed on these trails. However, other nearby routes are available for

Maps:
Maps are available at the Pantoll Ranger Station in the park, or by sending a stamped, self-addressed envelope to Sky Oaks Ranger Station, P.O. Box 865, Fairfax, CA 94978. A premium color trail map can be purchased from the Olmsted Brothers Map Company. Phone (510) 658-6534, or write P.O. Box 5351, Berkeley, CA 94705.

Trip Tip:
To get to the East Peak lookout from Rock Springs Picnic Area, turn right on Ridgecrest Road—the road dead-ends at the East Peak lookout. To see spectacular sunsets,

bikers. Ride on either Rocky Ridge, an old ranch road with a 500-foot elevation drop in two miles, then along Bolinas-Fairfax Road, which borders much of the north side of Alpine Lake. At the Alpine Dam, head north on the ranch road to Kent Lake.

Mount Tamalpais is not the highest mountain in the Bay Area (Mount Hamilton and Mount Diablo are taller), but it does have the most profound sense of place. That is why I keep returning here. Every trip will leave the weekend visitor with a sense of enchantment.

start from Rock Springs Picnic Area, then turn left on Ridgecrest Road, which provides lookouts to the Pacific Ocean.

Fee or Free: Entry is free. A parking fee is charged if parking in the state park, but you can park alongside the road for free.

Contact: Call Mount Tamalpais State Park at (415) 388-2070 or Golden Gate National Recreation Area at (415) 331-1540 for free maps and brochures. Or phone the Sky Oaks Ranger Station at (415)459-5267.

4

Audubon Canyon Ranch

On the Marin Coast

Audubon Canyon Ranch on the Marin coast is a little niche of paradise for the people who know of it. It's the premier place on the Pacific Coast to view herons and egrets, those large, graceful seabirds, as they court, nest, mate and rear their young. Hatchlings can be seen discovering the world, some flying for the first time. The ranch also has eight miles of nature trails, routed up the canyon, along streams, and through redwoods, which include lookouts where you can see Bolinas Lagoon and the Pacific Ocean. There are 90 species of birds at the ranch, in addition to deer, fox, lots of bunny rabbits, and even bobcats.

But the herons are the feature attraction. They have wingspans approaching six feet and build nests on the tops of redwood trees about 100 feet off the ground. From an overlook, you can use spotting scopes (which are provided by the ranch) to get a unique glimpse of life in a nest. Watch Junior eat. Watch Mom Heron whack Junior in the head. Watch Junior fly. There isn't anything else quite like this anywhere.

Access is free, but Audubon Canyon Ranch is open on weekends and holidays only, 10 a.m. to 4 p.m., spring through mid-summer. Donations are welcome, and are used to bus school children to the preserve who otherwise wouldn't have the opportunity to visit. Typically there are enough donations to pay for more than 5,000 youngsters to make the trip each year.

The adventure begins with the drive to the Marin coast, a rural woodland where birds outnumber people. The drive is quite pretty (as long as you don't get stuck behind a Winnebago), taking Highway 1 three miles north of Stinson Beach. A natural history display and book store are available at the ranch headquarters.

From headquarters, you take a short, steep hike, about 20 minutes long with rest benches available on the way, to the canyon overlook. There, you can use spotting scopes to peer across the valley and zero in on the giant nests atop the redwoods. In May, the eggs start hatching, and by June, there can be as many as 200 hatchlings in the nests. You can see the adult herons flying away—a spectacular sight with their slow, gentle wingbeats powering them off to nearby Bolinas Lagoon—then returning shortly thereafter with goodies. The feeding process is unique, with Mom and Dad Heron allowing their beaks to be seized by Junior, which causes them to throw up undigested food all over the nest. It is then happily gobbled up by Junior and his brothers and sisters. By the way, what's for lunch?

In late June and early July, one of the highlights of the year occurs when the juveniles decide to find out what this flying thing is all about. You will see the youngsters standing in the nest, practicing wing strokes. Sometimes they hop out on a branch, practicing, getting their courage up. Eventually, if

Directions:
From San Francisco, take Highway 1 north. The ranch is located 3.5 miles north of Stinson Beach.

Fee or Free:
Entrance is free, but donations are requested.

Contact:
Phone Audubon Canyon Ranch at (415) 868-9244.

they don't take the big plunge, Mom Heron might give them the heave anyway. Since the nests are 100 feet in the air, Junior has about 10 seconds to figure out how his wings work before the ground suddenly arrives.

The three primary species of birds nesting here are the great blue heron, great egrets and snowy egrets. When silhouetted, the great blue heron looks something like a pterodactyl, with its long thin body and massive wing span. The great egrets are pure white, quite thin, and about four feet tall. Snowy egrets are also pure white, but smaller than the great egrets, about two feet tall.

Early in the spring, viewers have the opportunity to see the birds' courtship ritual. It consists of the birds offering sticks to each other. If the stick is accepted, the birds will then work together to build a nest, and from there, great things happen.

Volunteer docents are available to answer questions at the overlook area and the parking lots. Maps of the ranch are provided.

During the week, the ranch is closed to the general public, but reserved as an outdoor classroom for groups of school children. For some, it is their first time hiking or seeing nature up close. On one recent visit, a youngster refused to hike into the forest.

"I ain't goin' up in them woods," the boy told Skip Schwartz, executive director of the ranch. "Are there tigers up in them woods?"

"No tigers up there," answered Schwartz with a smile. Having worked here since 1975, he is familiar with the fears of youngsters from the city. "The animals we might see are more afraid of you than you are of them."

Eventually, the boy decided to trust Schwartz, take a chance, and take the hike.

He was later eaten by a tiger. Heh, heh, heh.

"People are afraid of things they aren't familiar with," Schwartz said later. "Audubon Canyon Ranch offers a chance for people to learn to love and respect nature."

One of the volunteer guides is Clerin Zumwalt of Greenbrae, who has been involved with the area for 31 years.

"There's a real warmth to this place," he said. "The joy of the kids is very exciting to see. There is an excitement with all these birds out there on the tops of the trees. It's a down home experience."

5

Muir Woods

On Mount Tamalpais

There are two Muir Woods and they are about as far apart as the North and South Poles. One of them seems to have more people than trees. The trail is so heavily used that it is paved with asphalt—and your chance of seeing a deer is about as good as sighting Bigfoot. The whole place seems about as peaceful as a bowling alley.

The other Muir Woods, however, is a sanctuary, a cathedral of redwoods and ferns. It is a place where people are few and the only sound is that of the light breeze brushing through tree limbs. By the time you leave, the world feels fresh and clean again.

Both of these Muir Woods are in Marin County, set in a canyon on the slopes of Mount Tamalpais. Your approach to the park determines which one you visit.

For example, consider a typical visit on a summer day. When I arrived at noon, the two parking lots were jammed full, including four tour buses that were shooting people out like a popcorn machine. The information stand and small store were crowded with visitors. The Bootjack Trail, the paved loop hike that travels along Redwood Creek on the valley floor, was more of a parade than a nature walk.

But then I turned right, taking the Panoramic Trail, and in less than a minute, I had entered a different world. This is the Muir Woods where you can find peace and serenity.

The Panoramic Trail is one of the best-kept secrets in what is one of the West's most popular parklands. It can provide solitude and a good hike. From the valley floor of Muir Woods, the trail veers right and heads up the east side of the canyon. It is a steady grade, just enough to get most hikers puffing in a natural rhythm as they make the climb.

It is three miles before you clear the treetops and get a lookout over the entire valley—a sea of conifers—and glimpses of the Pacific Ocean to the southwest. In the meantime, you walk a trail that gets little traffic. Your worries begin to fall away, and no matter what your problems, all seems simple and pure.

There is another attraction as well. When you reach the canyon rim, you can take a quarter-mile detour to the town of Mountain Home, or turn right on the connecting trail that leads to the German House. Both serve ice cold drinks, and nothing tastes better after the three-mile climb to the lookout. The German House is a premium destination because it has a redwood deck and offers a great view of Marin's wildlands.

The other trail option that provides a degree of solitude in Muir Woods is the Dipsea Trail, although it is a famous route among Bay Area hikers. This trail runs all the way to Stinson Beach, about four miles. The hiker follows a series of "ups and downs," passing a network of connecting trails on Mount Tamalpais.

August often seems the coldest month of the year here. When the Central Valley burns in 100-degree temperatures, nature's built-in air conditioner fogs in the coast and sends chilly breezes eastward.

A unique feature about Muir Woods is that headquarters can be something of

Directions: From San Francisco, drive north on US 101 to the Highway 1 exit. Continue to the stoplight and turn left on Shoreline Highway (Highway 1). Continue for a few miles and take the right fork on Panoramic Highway. From there, drive one mile and take the left lower road. Drive one mile to Muir Woods Parking Area. All turns are well signed.

Trip Tip: Hikers only. No mountain bikes, motorcycles, horses or dogs are allowed, except for seeing-eye dogs.

Fee or Free: Access is free. Maps are available for

a nominal fee.

Contact: The Muir Woods Ranger Station can be reached at (415) 388-2596, or by writing Muir Woods National Monument, Mill Valley, CA 94941.

a United Nations. People from all over the world touring the Bay Area find the old-growth redwoods a special attraction.

There are two Muir Woods. You decide which one you want to visit.

6

Marin Headlands

In Marin County, overlooking the Golden Gate

Somewhere in the course of time, you see this amazing film clip or photograph—an overhead view of the Golden Gate Bridge with a backdrop of the San Francisco skyline. It makes the Bay Area look like a world apart, and as you stare at the picture, you eventually figure out the photographer could only be standing in one place: the Marin Headlands.

That makes you curious, and from there comes your inspiration for the first trip—the desire to stand in the same place as the photographer who snapped that picture. Then it takes only a few hours to discover that the Marin Headlands is an easy-to-reach destination where there are so many ways to spend an afternoon that you'll find yourself coming back again and again.

Most of these adventures are available year-round: hawk watching on hilltops; hiking along pristine bluffs, valleys and beaches; exploring former missile-launching sites; fishing for free at a pier where no license is required; visiting a museum with hands-on exhibits for children; watching sea lions and harbor seals play tag at Point Bonita; picnicking at a wheelchair accessible picnic site; camping with a spectacular ocean sunset as the backdrop—and there are many other options.

You can always just tromp up to a lookout, maybe that famous one, and bring your camera along to record the event.

To make your trip easier, the Park Service has completed a new Headlands Visitor Center at Fort Barry Chapel. Hiking maps, field guides and event

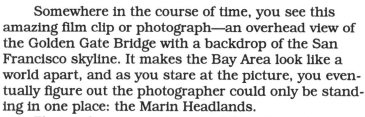

Directions: From U.S. 101, take the Alexander Avenue exit, loop underneath the highway, heading west, and take the wide paved road to the right (look for the sign that says Marin Headlands). Continue for one mile, take a right on the downhill fork, and follow the direction signs for two miles to the Marin Headlands Visitor Center.

Fee or free: Entrance and use of all facilities is free.

Contact: Phone the Marin Headlands Visitor Center at (415) 331-1540.

Maps: Write for maps to the Golden Gate

schedules are available, as well as rangers who will answer questions or help provide directions to your chosen venture.

Here is a guide to the best of them:

Missile Site

During the Cold War, the Marin Headlands was chosen as a missile-launching site because of its strategic defensive position at the entrance of San Francisco Bay. Now it is a popular visitor attraction, with two underground concrete pits, missile assembly buildings, and guard dog kennels. On the annual Headlands Day each year, park volunteers and Army veterans conduct simulated missile raisings each hour.

Birds Of Prey

Each fall, Hawk Hill is one of California's top viewing areas for raptors, as thousands of hawks and other raptors pass here as they migrate.

Harbor Seals and Sea Lions

Harbor seals play games at Point Bonita, jumping in the water and jumping out. In the coves, such as those just east of Point Bonita, sea lions will sometimes swim about the shallows and play peek-a-boo with beach strollers.

Horses and Horseshoes

Mi-Wok Stables are open for self-guided tours. Any stray horseshoes can be kept as good luck charms, and if you want to take a ride, guided trail rides are available from the private concessionaire there.

Great Hike

The walk to the Point Bonita Lighthouse is easy, yet has great views of the mouth of the Bay and adjacent ocean. It is spectacular at night under a full moon.

Family Museum

Hands-on exhibits are ideal for children, including a demonstration on marine life in San Francisco Bay and a crawl-through underbay tunnel.

Weekend Picnic

A picnic area is available near what is called Battery Wallace. The views of the Golden Gate Bridge and passing ships are fantastic. The picnic area includes a windbreak and tables designed so visitors in wheelchairs can fit right up to the table.

Sunset Camping

Hawk Camp is a primitive setting located just above Gerbode Valley. It is surrounded by a small stand of trees, yet there are views of both San Francisco and ocean sunsets.

Free Fishing and Boating

Both a free fishing pier and a free boat ramp are available at Fort Baker. In fall months, salmon are sometimes caught from the pier as they migrate past on the journey from the ocean to points upstream.

National Recreation Area, Marin Headlands, Building 1056, Fort Cronkite, Sausalito, CA 94965.

Horseback riding: Phone the concessionaire at (415) 383-8048.

Camping: Camping at Hawk Camp is free, but reservations are required. Phone (415) 331-1540.

7

Islands of the San Francisco Bay

In San Francisco Bay

If you ever forget how special the Bay Area is, all you have to do to remember is take a trip to one of the islands in San Francisco Bay.

Alcatraz, Angel Island, Treasure Island and the East Brothers Islands all offer unique adventures and great views. From start to finish, these trips are just plain fun, and in some cases, unforgettable and spectacular.

Each island offers something special. On Alcatraz, rub shoulders with Al Capone's ghost. On Angel Island, take the most scenic hike in the Bay Area. On the East Brothers, stay at the most secluded, romantic inn imaginable. On Treasure Island, find a view of San Francisco that makes it look like Oz.

Just getting to these islands makes the trip an adventure. Except for Treasure Island, which can be reached by car, each requires taking a boat—a ferry to Angel Island, a cruise ship to Alcatraz and a private yacht to the Brothers.

Here's a synopsis:

Alcatraz

A trip to Alcatraz Island can provide an eerie walk through history. The old prison is the feature attraction, of course, with the ghost of Al Capone casting a spell over visitors. The trip starts with a ride on a cruise ship of the Red and White Fleet from San Francisco, includes a tour of the prison and the opportunity to walk around the island. If you act nice, they might even take you back. You get great views of the Bay and an excellent nature walk. There is an abundance of bird life here, with a large population of night herons, friendly fellows that look like their heads are sitting on their shoulders.

Fee or Free: $8.50 adults, $4 children and includes ferry boat ride and tour of the prison.
Audio tour: For an extra $3, you are provided with a Walkman headset and cassette tape that provides an audio tour of island.
Charge by phone: Tickets can be charged by phone with all major credit cards by phoning (415) 546-2700.
Ferry departure: From Pier 41 in San Francisco with the Red and White Fleet, departing daily at 9:30 a.m. and every half hour thereafter till 2:45 p.m.
Contact: Red and White Fleet, (415) 546-2628; National Park Service, (415) 556-0560 or (415) 776-0693.

Angel Island

The top of Mount Livermore, the highest point on Angel Island, is probably the best lookout in the Bay Area. You are at the virtual center of the Bay, surrounded by dramatic scenery in every direction—the Golden Gate Bridge, the Sausalito waterfront, the San Francisco skyline . . . you need a swivel on your neck to see it all.

The trip starts with a ferry ride from Tiburon or San Francisco, and from the dock in Ayala Cove, you're on your own. The five-mile perimeter trail is most popular, but the climb to the summit is the choicest adventure. A small campground is also available, with reservations available through Mistix at (800) 444-7275.

Trip cost: $5 adults, $3 for youngsters, $1 extra for bicycles.
Ferry departures: The Angel Island Ferry departs from Tiburon at the top of every hour from 10 a.m. to 4 p.m. For the return trips, the ferry

departs the Angel Island dock at 20 minutes past each hour, from 10:20 a.m. to 4:20 p.m. Trips also depart at 10:40 a.m. on weekends from Pier 43 1/2 in San Francisco.

Contact: Tiburon Ferry, (415)435-2131; Red and White Fleet (San Francisco), (415)546-2628; Angel Island State Park, (415)435-1235.

Treasure Island

Few views match the one from the western shore of Treasure Island, especially at night, when the glow of lights makes San Francisco look like it is glistening with emeralds. It is easy to reach, just a short ride on the Bay Bridge. Right in front of the gate is a turn-around area—that is where the views are best.

At the present time, a military facility is still based here, leaving most of the island off-limits. In addition to the view, the other attractions are a fine restaurant called the Fogwatch (reservations advised), and a museum located in Building 1, just inside the gate.

Contact: Public Affairs, Naval Station, (415)395-5012.

East Brothers Islands

This is the least known of the islands in the Bay, one of a set of big rocks located just off of Point Richmond, north of the Richmond Bridge. On the east island, there is a Victorian-style inn that provides one of the most unique bed-and-breakfast lodges anywhere. There are three rooms for individual couples, and dining is family style. You get a tour of the old foghorn, and on rare occasions the hosts will even sound it off for you.

This is an unusual trip from start to finish, starting with a private boat ride from Point San Pablo Harbor in Richmond out to the island's docking area.

Contact: East Point Light Inn, (510) 233-2385.

8

Sausalito Bay Kayaking

In Richardson Bay

Kayaking on the Bay for the first time is the oddest feeling. It's like you're sitting right in the water, but you don't need to sprout a set of gills. Then with a few easy strokes with a plastic double-ended paddle, you launch forward 25 feet, and the quiet, smoothness and excitement envelops you all at once.

The first time you push off the shore of Sausalito, kayaking headquarters for the Bay, you feel a profound sensation of freedom. Some people just start laughing, or whooping like wild hyenas, because they're just too thrilled for words. They find that kayaking is easy and stable, that they are in total control (for the first time in their life), and they feel a complete release from their daily pressure cooker.

Fall is the best time of the year to kayak in the Bay. The spring and summer winds are long gone, leaving serene waters in protected Richardson Bay near Sausalito. Your companions include diving terns, harbor seals and flocks of passing migratory seabirds. Sometimes, a surprise submarine may even pop up in the main channel. No fooling.

Now get this: You can try it on for size—free! Unbelievable, eh? The first Sunday of every month is called Demo Day, and anybody can just show up, hop in a kayak, and try paddling around for awhile. (Of course, always call ahead to make sure the event will be staged.) This is an ideal time to bring youngsters with you under the guise of introducing them to the sport, when actually it's you who wants to do it all along.

The biggest fear that everybody has in a kayak is the same: you are going to tip over, and then while floating around, get eaten by Great White sharks. First off, you don't tip over. Sea kayaks are not constructed like tippy river kayaks, but are longer, wider and more stable than a canoe. In addition, the water is calm, so if you don't want to tip over, you don't.

But what if you do? Well, you fall out of the boat and then hold on to it. What about the sharks? There are none, of course. In fact, there has never been a shark attack inside the Golden Gate in the history of the Bay.

Thousands of people a year are now taking advantage of sea kayaking on the Bay, and it is turning out to be one of the safest outdoor activities available. Watching sunsets may be a little bit safer. But from a kayak, you can do both, or better yet, paddle off to dinner (at Sam's at Tiburon) under a full moon.

The experience in the little boat is unique. Just floating around can give you a charge. You can feel the power of the water, the tides and the wind. Just a few hundred yards offshore, you can feel completely alone, even though just over yonder are the homes of millions of people.

That is why so many people are deciding to buy into the sport, getting fully outfitted with a kayak, paddle, life jacket, car rack, and a waterproof paddling jacket. To go all the way will cost you about $800 with a used boat, watching your pennies. If you want the best of everything and want it new, the cost will be in the $2,000 range.

The one-person sea kayak typically is about 16 feet long and weighs 45 pounds. That means with a good car rack with a kayak saddle (Yakima makes the best), anybody can pick the boat up and put it on their car for transport. Stowing a kayak at home is not difficult, since the boat does not require a trailer, and can be set on end along a wall to take up minimal space.

Who goes? "It is almost 50-50, men and women," Diane Christiansen, co-founder of Sea Trek in Sausalito, told me. "It's really a great singles sport, and many couples have met in a double kayak on the water, either on a guided trip or in a class."

Special trips are offered throughout the year and include exploring Richardson Bay and the Sausalito waterfront, paddling to Angel Island, moonlight kayaking to Tiburon for dinner, and for the advanced, trips to Alcatraz, San Francisco and even right around the Golden Gate Bridge (don't look up). One trip that is a lot of fun is just following the current, paddling a bit, but letting the tidal flows take you wherever. It's a great sensation, one that you will not soon forget.

Typically, this is how the progression works: 1—You show up on a Demo Day and take a test paddle. 2—You like it and decide to take an introductory class. 3—You like it and rent a kayak, heading off wherever your little heart desires and your skills can take you.

This is a sport you may never have considered. That's how it is for most folks. All it takes, however, is to sit in one of these little boats one time on the Bay. It may forever change the way you look at the world.

Contact: For a free brochure or more information, including dates and directions for Demo Days, phone Sea Trek in Sausalito at (800) 934-2252 or (415) 488-1000.

Fee or Free: Demo Days are free, but a fee is charged for subsequent introductory classes, and includes equipment and seven hours of instruction.

9

Berkeley Pier

On the East Bay shoreline

Some Bay Area folks complain of feeling like a hamster on a treadmill after a few years of the daily commute and the grind at work. One way to snap out of that mood is to take a slow stroll down Berkeley Pier, with or without a fishing rod.

At Berkeley Pier, you discover that waiting, the thing people hate most about city life, is the very heart of pier fishing, and it's a medicine that should be taken in regular doses. Tension has a way of eating at you, but out here, you find yourself unworried, and that tight spring within begins to slowly uncoil. This historic structure extends 3,000 feet into San Francisco Bay, in the midst of some awesome landmarks that people travel around the world to see. You haven't looked lately? You're not alone.

Straight to the west is the Golden Gate Bridge, a classic panoramic view. During the next few hours, you will see giant tankers come and go through the Gate. If you watch a sunset here, you will discover how the Gate got its name. It looks different out here than when you're burning up the road—especially if you bring along a loaf of French bread and some cheese, plus something to wash it down with, and maybe a fishing rod as well.

Hanging out at Berkeley Pier has become one of the favorite ways to spend a day in the Bay Area since 1937, when Berkeley Pier was converted to a fishing pier. Since then, the pier has provided a place to spend a day on the Bay for everyone from old pros who want some peace and quiet to young anglers out for excitement.

Perch, jacksmelt, founder, sharks, sting rays and bat rays are the most common catch here. Even the grand prizes of bay fishing—striped bass, halibut and salmon—are occasionally caught here during their respective migrations, in spring, early summer and fall. For decking the larger fish, it is essential to bring along a crab net, which can be dropped by a rope and then scooped under the fish. Anglers attempting to land a fish by hoisting it up by fishing line have lost some beauties in the past few years.

A fishing shop for bait, tackle, and most importantly, advice, sits at the foot of Berkeley Pier. Even if you don't need any tackle, you should always check here first for the latest information.

Don't get the idea that this is a complicated adventure. Berkeley Pier is 3,000 feet long, so walking to the end takes an average of about 20 minutes. Many of the best perch fishing spots require just a short walk, however. Most folks just hook on their bait—either grass shrimp, pileworm, or a chunk of anchovy—flip it in the water, take a seat and watch their line trailing out into the Bay in little curls. Sometimes they get a bite, sometimes they don't. Somehow, it doesn't always seem to matter.

❖

Directions: From Interstate 80 in Berkeley, take the University Avenue exit and follow the signs to the Berkeley Marina. The pier is at the foot of University Avenue, just past the bait shop and marina.

Trip Tip: A Department of Fish and Game regulation allows anglers to fish with two lines here—either two fishing rods, or a fishing rod and a crab trap simultaneously.

Contact: Call Berkeley Marina Sports at (510) 849-2727.

Fee or Free: Free. Since Berkeley Pier is a municipal pier, no fishing license is necessary.

10

Tilden Park

In the Berkeley hills

When you're perched atop Inspiration Point in the East Bay hills during the early evening, the beautiful views can sweep away any of your daily gripes.

This quiet spot is roosted above Berkeley in Tilden Regional Park. The best thing about this park is that it offers a number of different activities, including hiking, bicycling, horseback riding, weekend backpacking, cross-country jogging, and even a scenic trail for those who do their walking in a wheelchair. And you can bring your dog along to join in the adventure, a bonus most state parks don't allow.

One of the Bay Area's most dramatic lookouts is on the western border of Tilden Park, where the entire Bay and its skyline unfold before you.

For impressive vistas to the east, take Nimitz Way, a four-and-a-half-mile trail that winds its way from Inspiration Point to Wildcat Peak, overlooking San Pablo and Briones reservoirs. To the west, you get views of wooded parklands and beyond to San Francisco Bay. Since this stretch of trail is gentle terrain and also paved, it is well-suited for wheelchairs, bicycles, and even baby strollers.

Most of the East Bay Regional Park System is joined by the Skyline National Trail, a 31-mile hike for backpackers. To the north from Inspiration Point, hikers can extend their walks either into Wildcat Canyon Regional Park, where a gorge has been cut by Wildcat Creek and is lined by riparian vegetation. To the south, you can hike onward through Sibley Volcanic Preserve, Redwood Park, and ultimately to Lake Chabot just east of San Leandro, all connected by the Skyline Trail.

Within Tilden Park are two of the highest points in the East Bay hills—Volmer Peak (1,913 feet) at the southern tip of the park and Wildcat Peak (1,250 feet) at the northern end of Tilden. Wildcat Peak is tucked away in a stand of trees, and is a popular two-hour hike from Inspiration Point.

❖

Directions: From Interstate 580 to the west or Interstate 680 to the east, drive to Highway 24. Proceed to just east of the Caldecott Tunnel and take the Fish Ranch Road exit west to Grizzly Peak Boulevard. This leads to the southern entrance of Tilden Park.

Best Times: Evenings are prime, especially to cool off after a hot day. Expect company on weekends, although long trails still provide seclusion.

Contact: For free tips, maps, or brochures, call the East Bay Regional Park District at (510) 635-0135.

11

Volcanic Regional Preserve

In the East Bay hills

Have you ever wanted to walk on the side of a volcano? Well, you don't have to go to Mount Saint Helens in Washington to do so, not with ol' Mount Round Top sitting above Oakland. And you don't have to worry about getting your toes fried either. Round Top is extinct, and is now named the "Volcanic Regional Preserve." It's a unique part of the East Bay Regional Park District.

It's an ideal half-day hike or evening jaunt for explorers and geologists alike. From the old quarry site at the eastern border of the park, hikers can get a first-class view of the East Bay hills and Mount Diablo.

Spring is the best time to go because the area is fresh with newly sprouted grass and wildflowers, and the park is cooled by northwesterly breezes off San Francisco Bay. Avoid the summer, particularly September, when it can get so hot here that you'll think you could fry an egg on a rock. You'd swear a cauldron of lava was getting ready to blast out of Round Top.

But a close look at the mountain allays those fears. Round Top has already shot its steam. In fact, after it blasted out its lava contents, the interior of the mountain collapsed into the void left by the outburst. Blocks of volcanic stone are scattered everywhere around the flanks of the peak.

Some of these have been dated at almost 10 million years old. When you pick up a rock that is 10 million years old, it has a way of making your stay on earth seem a little bit short.

About a half mile northwest of Round Top, a quarry operation has made a large cut into the side of the extinct volcano. This allows hikers to view the roots of the volcano, as well as a major volcanic vent. If you want to explore the unusual geology of the mountain, a self-guided tour brochure that marks the key spots is provided free at the East Bay Regional Park district office. One sector, located on the northern edge of the park, shows one of the most spectacular volcanic outcrops in the Bay Area.

If geology is not your game, no problem. The park still provides a good half-day hike, especially if you want to bring your dog. Park rules allow you to let your dog run free in open space and undeveloped areas of parkland, provided he or she remains under your control. Considering that state parks do not even allow leashed dogs on trails, this is quite a bonus for dog owners.

A section of the East Bay Skyline National Recreation Trail cuts across the western border of the park and connects to a road that circles the park. It makes for a few hours of puffing. For the ambitious, the Skyline Trail can connect you to the town of El Sobrante, 12 miles by trail to the north, or to Castro Valley, 17 miles to the south.

Other volcanic areas in California include the Pinnacles near Hollister, the Sutter Buttes in the Sacramento Valley, and Mount Lassen in the Shasta area.

Directions:
From Interstate 580 to the west or Interstate 680 to the east, drive to Highway 24. Proceed to just east of the Caldecott Tunnel and take the Fish Ranch Road exit west to Grizzly Peak Boulevard. Continue south to the park entrance.

Trip Tip:
If long hikes are not for you, you can drive within a quarter mile of the peak of Mount Round Top for spectacular views of the Bay Area.

Pets:
Your dog is allowed to run free in open spaces and undeveloped areas, but must be under control at all times.

Fee or Free:
Access and brochures are free.

Contact:
For more information, phone East Bay Regional Parks District at (510) 635-0135.

Mount Round Top is right in the back-yards of a million East Bay residents, yet is known by only a few.

❖

12

Chabot Regional Park

In the East Bay hills, above Castro Valley

Okay, so you don't have anything to do this weekend? If you venture over to Chabot Regional Park, you'll find something better to do than watching *Bonanza* reruns.

This park covers 5,000 acres, with 31 miles of hiking trails, and a fish-filled lake with nine miles of shoreline. Want more? There is also horseback riding, boating, camping, a marksmanship range for target practice, bicycling and picnic activities such as horseshoes and volleyball.

Chabot is in the East Bay hills above Castro Valley, a few miles east of Highway 580. Some folks pronounce Chabot so it rhymes with "habit," but the right way is "Shuh-Bowe," after Anthony Chabot. He was a pioneer California philanthropist who created Lake Chabot in the 1890s by building a dam across San Leandro Creek. Almost 100 years later, the lake is still the centerpiece of the park. It provides a close-to-home fishing hole, and receives special stocks of rainbow trout.

You can rent an aluminum boat with an electric motor, and head over to Vasco, Indian Point or Coot Landing, the best fishing spots in the area. Honker Bay is another good spot, especially for crappie.

If you just want to paddle around the lake, row boats and canoes are available for rent at the marina. If that isn't enough for you, there are lots of other options.

One of the better deals is the Lakeside Trail, which starts at the marina and traces much of the lake's shoreline. It is paved, so it is accessible for bicyclists and wheelchairs.

If your idea of hiking isn't walking on pavement, then take a look at the Chabot map that details 31 miles of hiking trails. The park is distinguished by a long, grassy valley, bordered both to the east and west by ridges. Select one of the 16 trails, head off up a ridge, and you'll get a workout and some seclusion. If you want to do some real tromping, the Skyline Trail runs the length of the park and connects northward to a network of six other regional parks. Up along the ridge line, the cities in the East Bay flats seem quite distant.

If you want to get the feeling of isolation without doing all the legwork yourself, horse rentals are available. If you're new to the saddle, don't worry about it. Inexperienced riders will find that most of the rental horses are real tame and seem to go on automatic pilot. When the hour is almost up, an inner alarm clock goes off and back they go to the barn. They know where the hay is, and it sure as heck isn't out there on the trail.

Most people who go to Chabot Park do so for an afternoon or evening picnic and parlay fishing, hiking or horseback riding into the trip. But you can do it one better, because Chabot has a nice campground with 75 spacious sites that provide plenty of elbow room, even when they are filled.

At the campground, 62 of the sites are for tents and 12 have full hookups for motor homes. Piped water, fireplaces and tables are provided at each site, and toilets and showers are available. It's one of the few Bay Area campgrounds that has a lake nearby.

Unexpectedly pleasant things happen at this park. A few years ago, for instance, a 17-pound, two-ounce bass was caughthere. It was the biggest bass in Northern California history.

Directions: Take Interstate 580 to San Leandro, then head east on Fairmont Drive, which goes over a ridge and merges with Lake Chabot Road.

Fee or Free: A parking fee is charged. There are access fees for fishing and the marksmanship range. Campsite fees vary depending on the type of site.

Fishing: A California fishing license is required, along with a one-day Chabot fishing pass, which is used entirely for future fish stocks. Kids under 16 don't need either.

Boat Rentals: Aluminum boats with electric motors are available for rental. Phone Lake Chabot Marina, (510) 881-1833, for more information.

Hiking: Maps are available at the Lake Chabot Marina Coffee Shop, or you can phone Regional Park Headquarters at (510) 635-0135.

Camping: Reservations can be made through the park; phone (510) 562-2267.

Horseback Riding: Horse rentals are available for ages 13 and up. Phone the Chabot Equestrian Center, (510) 569-4428.

Marksmanship Range: Access for shooting sports is available for ages 17 and up. Phone the Chabot Gun Club, (510) 569-0213.

Contact: For general information, call the East Bay Regional Park District, (510) 635-0135.

13

Mount Diablo State Park

East of Walnut Creek

One of the best lookouts in the world is at the top of Mount Diablo. It's the kind of place you can go in any mood and come away refreshed, seeing the world in a new perspective. No matter how fouled up things get, you can't foul up the view from Mount Diablo.

Compared to the mountains in the Sierra Nevada, Diablo may not seem so tall at 3,849 feet. But it is the highest in the Bay Area, and since it is surrounded by so much land at sea level, it provides a dramatic panorama.

The lookout is the centerpiece of Mount Diablo State Park and you can drive right to the top, but the park also has some excellent hiking trails, 12 in all, spanning from one that is less than a mile in length to a thumper of a nine-miler. This is also an excellent destination for birdwatching and wildflower observation in the spring, and incredible sunsets in the fall. The only downtime is in peak summer, when it just gets too hot out here.

Regardless of your interests, you always come back to the view from the top. I can tell you about it, but it is something that has to be experienced. Looking west, you can see across the Bay to the Golden Gate, the Pacific Ocean, and 25 miles out to sea, the Farallon Islands. Northward, you can see far up the Central

Valley and spot Mount Lassen east of Red Bluff. To the east, the frosted Sierra crest is in view. With a telescope, high-power binoculars and a perfect day, I'm told you can see a piece of Half Dome sticking out from Yosemite.

The park itself covers about 10,000 acres, primarily a habitat of oak and grasslands. However, there are hidden canyons, pines, deer and other wildlife as well.

At the park entrance stations, the first thing you should do is buy the trail map, which costs about $5. It details 12 hikes, all do-able in a day, a few in less than an hour, as well as the extensive network of single-track state park trails, abandoned ranch roads, and regional park trails that link into the park. With that map, you can cross and connect trails to set up your own routes.

The most ambitious hike is called the Giant Loop, covering 8.6 miles and requiring about five hours of hiking time. The trailhead is located at the end of Mitchell Canyon Road near the town of Clayton, where an automatic gate called an "iron ranger" will take your admission fee, a $5 bill. To get in, you must have a $5 bill.

This is a difficult hike, but it will give you a real feel for the mountain. It is set on the east side of Diablo and includes an 1,800-foot climb up to Murchio Gap, then a steep descent into Donner Canyon. On the way you will pass flower-strewn scenery and endless views of Northern California.

Note that if you want to try this hike, the usual entrances to the park will not work. The North Gate and South Gate

Directions: From the Bay Area, take one of several routes to Danville at Interstate 680. Take the Diablo Road exit and drive a short distance, then turn east on Black Hawk Road until you come to South Gate Road. Turn left and proceed to the park.

Trip Cost: A state park access fee is charged. Campsite fees vary.

Reservations: During the summer, camping reservations are on a first-come, first-served basis. During the winter months, reservations can be made through Mistix at (800) 444-7275.

entrance stations do not access the Giant Loop, but rather go to the Mitchell Canyon Trailhead. To reach it, take the Ignacio Valley Road out of Clayton, then turn on Mitchell Canyon Road toward Mount Diablo. The road descends at the gated trailhead.

The best-known trail at Diablo State Park is the Briones/Diablo Regional Trail, one of the East Bay's hallmark hikes. It covers 13 miles, connecting Briones Regional Park to Diablo State Park, including crossing past Walnut Creek.

But when you get right down to it, it is not the walks you will remember at Diablo. It is the view. Nothing else compares.

Campfires: Fire use is often prohibited in July and August. At any time, gas burning stoves are recommended.

Contact: For park information, write Mount Diablo State Park at P.O. Box 250, Diablo, CA 94528, or call (510) 837-2525.

14

Lake Merced

On the San Francisco coast

The trout program at San Francisco's Lake Merced is one of the nation's top urban fishing programs. Merced is stocked every week, year-round, with nearly 250,000 trout in all. Those fish include 400 to 500 trout per week that range 3 to 15 pounds. The program works because both the Department of Fish and Game and a private concessionaire make regular plants. Add it up and San Francisco anglers have a chance at quality close-to-home fishing.

Anglers at Lake Merced pay a $2.50 per-day fee, with 70 percent of the money turned back to purchase more and larger rainbow trout—a higher percentage than at any time in the lake's 100-year-plus history.

Dave Lyons of San Francisco, 74, a veteran Lake Merced fisherman, can tell you firsthand about the lake's revival. On 46 of 50 trips, he caught his legal limit (five fish per day), often catching and releasing 10 to 15 trout per visit.

"My best went about 22 inches," Lyons said. "I only fish a few hours during the evening, yet they tell me the fishing here is going to get even better."

The lake has some other unique advantages, particularly during the winter/spring transition. Because the lake is spring-fed, it is often clean in the late winter, even when most other lakes in California are turbid from heavy storm runoff. In addition, it provides a good spring alternative to fishing in the Bay and the Pacific, which have the roughest water conditions of the year from February through May. Then in the summer, the region's coastal breezes and fog keep the waters cool enough to sustain a top trout fishery.

Although Merced sits within a few miles of San Francisco's 700,000 residents, it seems to have carved out its own niche far removed from the city's concrete and skyscrapers. The lake is located just a half-mile from the Pacific Ocean, adjacent to the Harding Golf Course and the San Francisco Zoo. It's a pretty place with the water surrounded by tules and set amid rolling green hills.

Lake Merced is actually two lakes separated by a sliver of land, along with a third body of water, a pond named the Impoundment. The lakes cover 386 surface acres, and are surprisingly rich in marine life. In 1956, aquatic biologist Bill Johnson of the California Fish and Game Commission called Merced "the richest trout lake in the state." More than 35 years later, it is much the same. The lakes are filled with freshwater shrimp, a natural feed for the trout, along with perch, bullheads, catfish and largemouth bass.

As a result, survival rates of stocked fish are high, and they often seem stronger than trout stocked at more barren reservoirs. The trends at Merced have become clear: fishermen using boats out-catch shore fishermen by as much as three-to-one; the North Lake produces larger rainbow trout than the South Lake, but results are sporadic; and the South Lake has a steady catch rate for trout, usually averaging two to three per rod, but the fish are smaller—rarely longer than 20 inches. The South Lake also has some big largemouth bass hiding along the tules, but they are difficult to catch.

If you want the closest thing to a guarantee at Merced, or want to get a kid turned on to fishing, then rent a boat and fish the South Lake. If you want a chance at catching a trophy-sized rainbow trout, like one of those 10-pounders, then the North Lake is your best bet.

Either way, all anglers over age 16 are required to have a California sportfishing license in their possession.

Boat ramps are available for both lakes, but no gas engines or boats with gas motors are permitted. Canoes, prams and small boats set up for rowing or rigged with electric motors are ideal. There is a small launch fee.

Some anglers prefer to fish from shore. The favorite spots are the beach on the North Lake and the bridge on the South Lake.

Best results, however, come to boat fishermen who are willing to explore Merced's tule-lined shore. Dave Lyons suggests tying up your boat along the tules, then casting 10 to 30 feet from the tules.

Since the trout here have so much natural forage at their disposal, they often are reluctant to strike spoons, spinners or plugs. Instead, bring a variety of baits, including Power Bait, nightcrawlers, salmon eggs, cheese and marshmallows. Over the course of a few hours, Lyons will use them all, often in combination, such as salmon eggs with power bait on one hook, a nightcrawler with a small marshmallow on another.

A light-duty spinning rod is the best outfit for Merced fishing. The simplest and most effective setup is a two-hook rigging. On the bottom hook, thread half of a nightcrawler partially on the hook so it will lay straight and have a natural appearance in the water.

Another strategy is to inflate the worm like a little balloon by using a worm inflater (a small, plastic bottle with a hollow needle). With an inflated worm, the bait will float off the bottom of the lake, just where the big trout swim. The same effect can be achieved by topping off the nightcrawler with a small marshmallow.

After you cast out and let the bait sink to the bottom, you must be alert for even the most subtle signs of a nibble. On a windless day, simply watch where the line enters the water—if it twitches even an inch, you're getting a pickup. A technique Lyons suggests is just to lay down your rod, leave the bail of your spinning reel open, and place the line under a light plastic lid of a worm tub.

"There's virtually no resistance, so it doesn't spook the fish," Lyon said. "But when the line gets pulled out

Rigging for Big Trout: The simplest way to rig your outfit for big trout is to slide a small barrel sinker over your line, then tie on a snap swivel. From there, tie on three feet of leader and a No. 8 or 10 hook. But you can take it a step further. Midway up your leader, tie a small dropper loop, then add a second hook. This gives you the ability to double your chances; after a hungry trout has stolen the bait off one hook, you still have a shot at catching it on the other. For an advanced lesson, use no weight at all. A night-crawler for bait will

from under the lid, I know darn well what's going on down there."

What's going on most likely is a rainbow trout on the prowl—a premium stocking program has made sure of it. Merced receives approximately 250,000 trout per year, a tremendous number when compared to most other lakes. Bon Tempe Lake in Marin County, for instance, receives about 15,000 trout per year. The difference is that in addition to stocks from Department of Fish and Game, special trout plants are made with the funds accrued from the sale of Lake Merced fishing permits. So as more fishermen try their luck, the trout stocks improve at the same rate.

In a typical year, 80,000 fishermen will average one-and-a-half fish per rod at Merced. The largest fish documented was a 17-pound rainbow trout landed in the North Lake by Will Rose of San Francisco, and an eight-pound, 10-ounce largemouth bass caught in the South Lake by Mike Rainey of San Francisco in 1987.

Since Merced was converted to a reservoir in 1877, a number of fishing programs have been attempted. Many have failed. In 1891, carp were stocked, but the water roiled up so much that 19 sea lions were trapped and put in the lake to clean them out. Two years later, 90,000 muskies were stocked and never heard from again. Officials next tried largemouth bass, but few anglers could figure out how to catch them. It wasn't until 1944 that trout were planted, but because of the lake's infestations of carp, hitch and squawfish, sport fishing didn't have much of a chance to get established. Finally in 1949, the lake was poisoned with rotenone to clear out the trash fish, then restocked with rainbow trout and re-opened to fishing in 1950.

But it hasn't been until the past few years that anything like the present trout fishing program has been attempted. So before you head to some far-off place in search of quality rainbow trout fishing, first try San Francisco's backyard hole, Lake Merced.

Directions: From Interstate 280 west of Daly City, take John Daly Boulevard west. Turn right at Skyline Boulevard and continue to the lake.

Fishing Permit:
A special daily permit is required for all anglers over age 16, with separate prices for North Lake and South Lake. An annual pass can be purchased for South Lake fishing access. Kids under 16 do not need a permit to fish at South Lake, and at North Lake, they are allowed to share a permit with another angler. Permits can be obtained at Merced Bait Shop.

California State Fishing License: Anglers age 16 and over must have a state fishing license in their possession. Annual licenses and one-day permits are available; for information, contact the California Department of Fish and Game at (916) 227-2244.

Boat Rentals: Rowboats, canoes, motor boats, rods and reels are available for rental at the lake. There is a fee for boat launching.

Limits: A five-fish limit is in effect for trout or bass, 10 for catfish.

Whopper Club: Any trout or bass over three pounds wins a free whopper button from the Merced Bait Shop. The largest trout caught each month wins a quality spinning rod-and-reel combination.

Contact: Contact the Merced Bait Shop, 1 Harding Road, San Francisco, CA 94123; (415) 753-1101.

provide enough casting weight. Hungry trout are easily spooked by the sensation of any unnatural weight attached to a baited hook. Dave Lyons, Merced's fishing master, is happy to show people how to rig their lines. He's available at the Merced Bait Shop.

15

Sweeney Ridge

Near San Bruno

You practically need a 360-degree rotating head when perched atop Sweeney Ridge, one of the most spectacular vistas in the Bay Area. Way back in 1769, explorer Gaspar de Portola first viewed the San Francisco Bay from this spot, and they say his neck still hurts. Millions of people have since moved to the Peninsula, yet just a few can tell first-hand of the sights from Sweeney Ridge. They're the one with the neck braces.

It is just a 40-minute walk from the trailhead at the Skyline College campus, located on the ridge which splits San Bruno and Pacifica atop the San Francisco Peninsula. A bonus is that the trail is easily accessible using mass transit, with SamTrans buses providing the connecting link at the Daly City BART Station.

On clear mornings, the entire Bay Area seems to be at your feet. With a pair of binoculars or a spotting scope, even the most distant sights will seem within your grasp.

Sweeney Ridge provides remarkable glimpses of three of the largest mountains in the Bay Area. To the north is Mount Tamalpais in Marin County, to the east is Mount Diablo, and to the south is Mount Montara. You get the proper sense of perspective when you realize how long the mountains have been here—compared to your own lifespan.

Just below is Pacifica, from Mussel Rock to Pedro Point, where the ocean appears like a giant lake lapping at the beach. To the west, the Farallon Islands jut out from the Pacific Ocean, and look as if you could reach them with a short swim. They are actually 25 miles away. That expanse of curved blue horizon spanning hundreds of miles will remind you that the earth isn't flat after all.

To reach Sweeney Ridge, you hike up a moderate grade that takes you through coastal grasslands, which sprout with green after the first rains of fall. In the spring, there are lots of wildflowers.

The ideal time for a hike here is the morning after a good rain, which leaves the air sparkling fresh and clear. Summer evenings can often be the worst times, because thick fog powered by 25-mile-per-hour winds can reduce the visibility to zero and make your hike about as cold as an expedition to the Arctic.

Directions: From points south, take Highway 280 to Hickey Boulevard, and head west. Turn left on Highway 35 (Skyline Boulevard), then turn right on College Drive. From the north, take Highway 280 to the Skyline Boulevard exit, and turn left on College Drive.

Mass Transit: SamTrans offers buses that will take you to the Skyline College campus. For route information, phone (800) 660-4BUS.

Trailhead Location: The trail starts on the southeast end of the Skyline College campus, near Lot 2. Walk east up past the maintenance yard, and then right to the service road—a sign marks the trail.

Trail Time: From the San Bruno entrance, figure about an hour for a round-trip hike, not including viewing and picnic time.

Fee or Free: Access is free.

16

San Pedro Park

In Pacifica

What you put in is an hour-and-a-half of hiking time, most of it on a calculated, easy grade. What you get out are ocean views, access to true isolated wildlands, and that good feeling that comes with a special walk.

It's close—and you can get there even if you don't own a car. Rangers call it the Big Canyon Trail, overlooking San Pedro Valley in Pacifica, a 15-mile ride from San Francisco by car or by BART and a SamTrans bus. It is a four-and-a-half-mile loop hike that is the feature hike for San Pedro Valley County Park.

There are still places of beauty in the Bay Area and this is one of them. The first thing you notice in the park is that it is one of the quietest places in the Bay Area. Then you notice the miles and miles of surrounding wildlands that give it this quiet.

The area seems to have a friendly, relaxed atmosphere. There is no litter; the park is sunny and warm compared to the cool, fogged-in coast, and it doesn't take long until you start feeling pretty darn good.

After parking, you should head along the trail in San Pedro Valley, which opens up into a green meadow bordered by blooming wildflowers. After a mile, it connects to Big Canyon Trail, which rises for two miles along the northern slopes of Montara Mountain to a series of 1,000-foot-high lookouts.

On a clear day looking out to sea, you can spot the Farallon Islands, Point Reyes and some memorable sunsets. But even when the coast is fogged in, the views are still prime—because San Pedro Mountain to the west often diverts the ocean fog. As a result, views of Sweeney Ridge and the surrounding mountains and canyons remain panoramic.

And because of some forethought on the part of rangers, you can enjoy the views without feeling completely exhausted from the trip. The trail up is not steep, but a gentle 10 percent grade for two miles.

"We used a device called a clinometer to keep the slope of the trail at about 10 percent," ranger Don Curran told me. "That shouldn't be confused with 10 degrees, which is real steep. Ten percent means it rises one foot every 10 feet of trail."

Because of the grade, the park attracts hikers of all ages, from kids to seniors, rather than just hard-core foot stompers.

The hike down, returning to park headquarters, is a steep one, having been constructed many years ago. Good gripping boots are advised. This means that which direction you choose to route your trip is critical to the kind of hike you'll have.

"For hikers, we advise walking down the valley, then heading up the Big Canyon Trail," Curran said. "You get the gentle slope up, a flat spot on the top, and a fast trip down." Going the opposite direction would involve a very steep climb.

A highlight to the park is the frequency of wildlife sightings. The park is bordered to the south by land owned by the San Francisco Water District, which in turn adjoins a state wildlife refuge. It is

Directions:
From San Francisco, take Highway 1 south into Pacifica. Turn east on Linda Mar Boulevard and continue until it deadends at Oddstad Boulevard. Turn right; the park entrance is located about 50 yards west on the left-hand side.

Mass Transit:
Transportation is available through SamTrans. Phone (800) 660-4BUS for schedule and route information.

Pets:
Dogs are not allowed.

Fee or Free:
A small entry fee is charged.

Groups:
Reservations are required for the Group Picnic Area.

Call the County Park Center at (415)363-4020.

Contact: Call San Pedro County Park at (415)355-8289, where an answering machine will take messages. For more direct information, call the San Mateo County Parks and Recreation Department at (415)363-4020 or write to Parks, County Government Center, 590 Hamilton Street, Redwood City, CA 94063.

common, especially during summer evenings, for animals to venture into the meadow on the valley floor to graze or get water in San Pedro Creek.

"We see rabbits and deer all the time," Curran said. "I've seen bobcats and coyotes too."

Because of the number of wild animals that move in and out of the park, dogs are prohibited.

The flora varies from chaparral sprinkled with hemlock, nettle and gooseberry to a few thick groves of eucalyptus and occasional oaks, willows and dogwoods.

17

McNee Ranch State Park

On Montara Mountain

Let's get right to the point: You've never heard of McNee Ranch State Park, right? That's one of the best reasons why this is the place you should visit this weekend. Nobody else seems to know about it either.

McNee is one of California's newest parks, is only 25 miles away from San Francisco, and can provide one of the Bay Area's best lookouts from the top of Montara Mountain. It's a primitive setting, with no camping or piped water, but it's perfect for short walks or gut-thumpers to the ridge—and you can bring your leashed dog.

McNee Park is located on the San Mateo County coast between Montara and Pacifica.

You'll find it is a remarkably peaceful place with many good walks or hikes, and with them come some of the best coastal views anywhere. Most of the trails are actually long-abandoned ranch or country roads. They connect to enough footpaths to provide endless options for weekend walks.

But no matter how many different routes you take, eventually you will want to head to the top, the peak of Montara Mountain.

It's not far, but it's a challenge, climbing from sea level to about 2,000 feet. From the entrance gate at the park to the summit is 3.8 miles. A round trip requires nearly four hours. But in that short time, you can experience many of the elements of a wilderness mountain trip.

The trail follows the ridgeline of San Pedro Mountain until it connects to the Montara Coastal Range, and has three "serious ups." One of the serious ups is three-quarters of a mile, and can get you puffing like a locomotive for two minutes.

Then suddenly, the trail nearly flattens on a mountain saddle, and a 30-yard cutoff to the left provides a perch for a dazzling view of the Pacifica coast, and on clear days, Point Reyes. My dad, Robert G. Stienstra, Sr., made the hike to this great lookout when he was in his sixties. You can make it, too.

Another 45 minutes of "steady up" will take you all the way to the top. You'll look around as if you have just discovered the Bay Area for what it is—miles of open range and mountains, with only the flatlands jammed with people.

On a clear day, the Farallon Islands—30 miles away—can look close enough to reach out and pluck right out of the ocean, and Mount Diablo to the east can seem like you could take a giant leap, cross the Bay and land on its peak. Some 10 miles to the north and south is nothing but mountain wilderness connecting to Sweeney Ridge and an off-limits Fish and Game Refuge.

More than 150,000 people jam into Half Moon Bay for the annual Pumpkin Festival. Virtually all of them drive right past McNee Park. This weekend if you'd like a nice quiet walk, stop at McNee and go for it.

❖

Directions: From San Francisco, drive south on Highway 1 for about 17 miles, going past Pacifica. Continue up through Devil's Slide and down to the base of the hill. Look for a small pullout area on the left. There is a small yellow gate with a state park property sign; that is the access point. There is only enough room to accommodate a few cars, so if there is no room, continue down Highway 1 a short distance and park at the lot for Montara State Beach.

Trip Tips: Strap on a small daypack in which you carry lunch and drinks. If you plan to reach the top, it's a good idea to bring a change of shirts so you can stay dry and warm as you enjoy the views. A small stream in the valley is a good watering hole for dogs and horses, but there is no water available at higher elevations—so bring a quart of water and a small drinking dish for your dog, as well as plenty of water for yourself.

Fee or Free: Access is free, including access for leashed dogs.

Contact: For information, phone the ranger station at Half Moon Bay, (415) 726-8819; or the State Park Regional Office, (415) 726-8800.

18

Fitzgerald Marine Reserve

In Moss Beach, on the San Mateo County coast

The closer you look, the better it gets. The problem is that most people don't look close enough. When you go tidepool-hopping, you either look close enough to see all the little sea critters, or you see nothing.

There is no better place to do that than at Fitzgerald Marine Reserve in Moss Beach, although there are rocky tidal basins all along the Northern California Coast.

At this special reserve, you can explore 30 acres of tidal reef during the minus low tides that arrive every late fall and winter. In almost every pool, there is all manner of life, from little warring hermit crabs to bright blue sea anemones and little sculpins swimming about.

During winter, the minus low tides will cycle in and out of phase on a two-week basis, so arrange for your visit with the tides in mind. During a minus tide at Fitzgerald Marine Reserve, the Pacific Ocean rolls back, leaving pools, cuts and crevices filled with a few feet of sea water. You can walk on the exposed rock, probing the tide waters below as you go.

You don't have to worry about a sudden, giant wave hammering you from behind. On the outside edge of the tidal area, about 50 yards from the beach, there is a natural rock terrace that blunts attacks from waves. So you and the critters that live here are all protected from a heavy ocean surge.

This is one of the most abundant and diverse marine life regions in California. The ranger here says there are 200 species of marine animals, 150 of plants and 125 of gastropods, or mollusks. Just take a close look.

You don't need to be an oceanographer to enjoy it. The easiest critters to recognize are starfish, hermit crabs, rock crabs, sea anemones, sea urchins and zillions of different kinds of snails. For instance, in one pool, we saw two hermit crabs trying to pick food from a giant aqua-colored sea anemone. The anemone just flinched its rubbery tentacles, sending the hermit crabs on their way. It's all a lesson in observing detail, seeing the world as a connection of many small living things.

That's why 20,000 kids visit the marine reserve every year. It's become the most popular outdoor classroom in the Bay Area.

One lesson the rangers teach quickly here is to look, but don't touch. That's hard for kids, particularly when they find a large starfish. The problem is that an adult starfish is on average 15 to 25 years old, and when one is taken, another one doesn't magically replace it. Rangers now have the option to cite people (including kids) if they get caught with a starfish or any other marine creature.

But hook-and-line fishing is permitted here because studies have demonstrated that sportfishing has no impact on fish populations in this area. Part of the reason is because of the difficulty of the sport. However, there always seems to be someone attempting to close down Fitzgerald to fishing, so check before you go.

If you show up with your fishing rod and cast out a bait, you will inevitably find yourself snagging on the reef with every single cast, losing your gear and wanting to quit the sport forever.

A better technique is called "poke-poling." You use a long Calcutta pole or its equivalent, like a worn-out CB antenna, and tie a three-inch piece of wire and a 2/0 hook on the end. Then place a small piece of squid bait on the hook, and poke the pole in crevices, under ledges and in any deep holes on the outer edge of the tidal basin.

While other people are snagging, you can catch sea trout, cabezone, lingcod and eels with this unique method. As with tidepooling, the best fishing is during the minus low tides.

This area is also a favorite for scuba divers, abalone pickers and plain ol' beach walkers. Just remember to look close—you don't want to miss it.

❖

Directions: From the north, take Highway 280 or Highway 101 to Highway 1, and continue through Pacifica over Devil's Slide and into Moss Beach. The turnoff is well signed. From the East Bay, Peninsula and south, take Highway 92 into Half Moon Bay, then head north on Highway 1 seven miles to Moss Beach.

Fee or Free: Entry is free.

Best Times: Prime times are during the minus low tides in late fall and winter.

Tips: Dogs are prohibited. Wear good-gripping rubber-soled shoes.

Contact: For information, call the Fitzgerald Marine Reserve at (415) 728-3584, or contact the San Mateo County Parks and Recreation Department at (415) 363-4020.

19

Half Moon Bay Horseback Ride

On the San Mateo County coast

If you dream of the days of roaming the open rangeland and watching sunsets from a saddle, there's still a place for you, and a horse waiting as well in the coastside town of Half Moon Bay. You can put a cowboy boot in a stirrup, saddle up and literally ride off into the sunset.

You don't have to be John Wayne, and even if you have never ridden before, the cowboys at Sea Horse and Friendly Acres Ranch will find a horse to match your ability. For small children, the ranch provides a special pony corral, where youngsters can get 15 minutes with Old Paint. Should your child start to get visions of the Grand National, a few bucks more will get him or her 15 more minutes.

Horseback riding is popular in Half Moon Bay, where dirt streets, hometown post offices and vast farms give the coast its special brand of country. One way to share in this experience is to hop in the saddle and go trotting down to the beach. With 200 horses and ponies to pick from, the hired hands here will be able to find you a relatively fresh and well-mannered horse to match your size and experience.

One Sunday afternoon, I climbed aboard Moon, a big strong horse. Ol' Moon and me trotted on out to the beach and watched the sun sink clean into the Pacific Ocean, the light refracting for miles across the water.

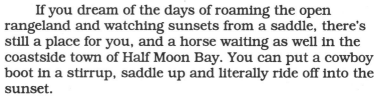

Behind us, an orange hue was cast across Montara Mountain, and any moment I expected Waylon Jennings to come by singing, "Mama, don't let your babies grow up to be cowboys." Well I've always felt you shouldn't let your cowboys grow up to be babies. Then Moon suddenly decided that with the sun down, it was time to head for the barn. Over yonder, a buddy of mine, Gus Zimmer, was experiencing a similar phenomenon, his horse heading hell-bent for leather for the barn. "Slow doooown," he yelled at his horse. Gus was hanging onto the big saddle horn with both hands, the reins flapping loosely. "I'm outta control," he shouted, disappearing around the bend.

Up until this point, the relationship between Moon and me had been something like the Lone Ranger and Silver. I mean, whenever Moon would pull his ears back and snort, I would pat him on the neck and say, "Good horsey," and he would behave.

But after the sun went down and my buddy disappeared, no amount of saying "Good horsey" did any good. With a snort, Moon had decided the hour was up and he was heading for the barn as well. He knew there was some hay waiting for him, and that it was time for me to get a little shut-eye.

Directions: From the north, take Highway 1 past Princeton Harbor. From the east, take Highway 92 to Half Moon Bay, then head north on Highway 1 for three miles. Friendly Acres Ranch is on the west side of Highway 1, between the city of Half Moon Bay and the town of Miramar.

Fee or Free: Horses and ponies can be rented at reasonable rates.

Trip Tip: Get a horse that matches your riding ability, and remember always to treat the animals with respect.

Contact: For information, call Sea Horse and Friendly Acres Ranch at (415) 726-2362, (415) 726-9903 or (415) 726-9916.

20

Half Moon Bay

On the San Mateo County coast

Depending on which eye you look out of, the San Mateo County coast can provide something you might be searching for. Out of one eye, you might see the Half Moon Bay coast as something of an anachronism, with its small town, dirt streets, cowboys on horseback and sprawling fields of brussels sprouts. It may seem like you've stepped into an earlier time. In a 10-mile area, quality fishing, horseback riding, hiking and camping are also available.

But out of the other eye, you might see quite a different picture: expensive seaside restaurants, crowded roads, and on sunny days, beaches packed with folks for whom life's desires seem to end with a suntan and a cool drink.

Because Half Moon Bay can satisfy people with opposite interests, it has become one of the most popular places for a weekend visit.

Is it close? Via Highway 92, it's only 12 miles from San Mateo, and 27 miles from Hayward. Taking Highway 1, Half Moon Bay sits 13 miles from Daly City, and from San Francisco at Highway 280, it's about 20 miles away. But there's a catch, of course. Because the highways are two-laners with no passing, one slow vehicle will jam up traffic for miles and the road will look like a parade of frustrated gerbils.

The centerpiece of the area is Pillar Point Harbor at Princeton. Salmon and deep sea fishing trips on sportfishing vessels are offered here, a new beautiful boat ramp is available, and several fine restaurants ring the harbor. Many folks like to walk down Princeton Pier to look at the boats, and in the afternoon, they can watch fishermen return with the day's catch.

But if it's walking that you like, then head to the Fitzgerald Marine Reserve in Moss Beach, or to the northern end of Montara at McNee State Park. If you want someone else's feet to do the work, horse rentals are available just north of Half Moon Bay, on the west side of Highway 1. (Details on the Fitzgerald Marine Reserve, McNee State Park and horseback rides in Half Moon Bay can all be found in preceding stories in this chapter.)

Camping at Half Moon Bay State Beach often seems to be taken advantage of by out-of-towners touring Highway 1, but overlooked by Bay Area folks who have it in their own backyard. It's one of the closest campgrounds to the San Francisco Peninsula. The beaches along the coast here can be really packed on warm sunny days. If you're heading to the beach, wear some kind of footwear to protect yourself from broken glass hidden in the sand.

In most cases, however, the problems are few, and the adventures and scenic backdrop outstanding. In many ways, Half Moon Bay can seem the perfect place to be.

Directions: From San Francisco, drive south on Highway 1 for approximately 20 miles. From the Peninsula, take Highway 92 west to Half Moon Bay.

Contact: For information, phone Half Moon Bay State Park at (415) 726-8819.

Fishing: Deep sea and salmon fishing trips are offered at Pillar Point Harbor by Huck Finn Sportfishing, (415) 726-7133, and Capt. John's Sportfishing, (415) 726-2913. Most trips cost in the $35 range.

Marine Reserve: The Fitzgerald Marine Reserve is located in Moss Beach, with a well-signed turnoff on Highway 1. Access is free. For information, call (415) 728-3584.

Horseback Riding: Horse rentals are available at Sea Horse Ranch and Friendly Acres, (415) 726-2362 or (415) 726-9903.

Camping: Campsites are available through Half Moon Bay State Park. Reservations are recommended on weekends; phone Mistix at (800) 444-7275.

21

San Andreas Trail

In the Millbrae foothills, along Skyline Boulevard

The San Andreas Trail overlooks Crystal Springs Reservoir and winds its way through wooded foothills. It is minutes away by car for Peninsula residents, can be reached by bus, and provides access to the edge of a special fish and game refuge where eagles still fly. The air is fresh and clean up here, and the wide trail is suitable for jogging, hiking and bicycling.

The trail sits on the eastern edge of Crystal Springs Reservoir, just off Skyline Boulevard (Highway 35) in Millbrae. All you have to do is show up, park your car and go for it. The only irritation is that a few miles of the trail run fairly adjacent to the road, within earshot of cars. A wall of trees provides refuge in some areas, and south of the access point at Hillcrest Boulevard, the trail meanders away from the road and cuts along the edge of the south end of the lake.

Whether you run, walk or bike, at some point you will come to a complete halt, and just gaze at the wonder of this country. The western slope of Montara Mountain is true wilderness, untouched by mankind, and the sparkling lake below might trigger visions of giant fish. But don't get any ideas about bringing a fishing rod. Fishing or trespassing on the lake or wooded refuge to the west is illegal and doing so will quickly land you in the pokey. The area is patrolled around the clock.

The San Andreas Trail starts near the northern end of the lake, where a signed trailhead marker sits on Skyline Boulevard, which runs parallel to the trail. It goes about three miles and is fairly level until the next access point at Hillcrest Boulevard.

A good option for well-conditioned runners is to start their trip at the Hillcrest Boulevard access point, then head south. The trail connects to Sawyer Camp Trail, which cuts six miles along the lake, away from the road. It provides the quiet that you might miss on the San Andreas Trail, but with the serenity you get a longer distance and a steeper grade (a drop of 400 feet). You can plan on some huffing and puffing on your return trip.

If you plan on bicycling here, then plan on going slow. Street speed limits are enforced by rangers, sometimes with radar.

During the winter, this area is remarkably cool, green and fresh. On summer evenings, you can witness the spectacle of rolling fogbanks cresting Montara Mountain to the west. Regardless of whether you hike, run or bike, this is a great spot to bust loose.

❖

Directions: From the north, take Highway 280 to the Skyline Boulevard (Highway 35) exit. A signed trail entrance is on the west side of the road. From the south, take Highway 280 to the Millbrae Avenue exit, and head north on what appears to be a frontage road (Skyline Boulevard) to Hillcrest Boulevard at the trailhead.

Mass Transit: SamTrans offers a bus that stops at Hillcrest Drive and Skyline Boulevard. For route information, phone SamTrans at (800) 660-4BUS.

Trip Tip: If you plan to run, bring a friend along so you can car shuttle rather than having to double back on the trail.

22

Purisima Creek Redwoods

In the Half Moon Bay foothills, on Skyline Boulevard

Purisima Creek Redwoods is the kind of place many people in the Bay Area constantly yearn for—but don't even know exists. This is one of the truly great secret spots that the Bay Area has to offer. A giant preserve with redwood forests, creeks and glens, and fantastic lookouts, this spot seems as if it is in a secluded Northern California forest, 350 miles away.

But it isn't. It is located on the western slopes of the San Francisco's Peninsula ridgeline, about a 30-minute drive from San Francisco or Hayward, even closer for Peninsula residents.

There are three access points, with two on Skyline (Highway 35) about four miles south of the Highway 92 junction. The other is off Higgins Canyon Road, a four-mile drive from Main Street in Half Moon Bay. The southern Skyline entrance (located near road marker SM 16.65) is accessible to wheelchairs.

Between those three points is a vast area—some 2,500 acres—that will be preserved forever by the Midpeninsula Regional Open Space District. Because it is a newer parkland, having opened in 1988, not many people know about it.

The centerpiece of the preserve is Purisima Creek Canyon and its classic redwood forests, bedded with ferns, wild berries and wildflowers. But the area also offers great views of the Pacific Ocean and Half Moon

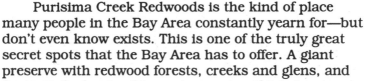

Bay to the west, and, from the ridgetop on Skyline, of San Francisco Bay to the east. That combination of woods and ocean views makes it feel like Big Sur, Mount Tamalpais and the Humboldt Coast all in one.

This is a do-it-yourself trip. There is no ranger station, park kiosk or information center. If you have a good memory, there are permanent wood trail maps mounted at the trailheads.

A better bet is to obtain the one-page trail map of the park by writing to headquarters. The map details 10 miles of trails for hikers, along with fire roads for mountain bikes. The southern side of the park is more heavily wooded than the northern side. So if you want views, start from the northern access point on Skyline Boulevard, located near road marker SM 18.36. If you want woods, start at the southern access point near Skyline road marker SM 16.65.

The ideal walk here is to start at the southern Skyline Ridge access point. You can make the beautiful four-mile walk downhill to the western end of the park at Higgins Canyon Road. With a companion, you can park another vehicle at the trail's end to use as a shuttle. That way you can get a one-way hike with almost no uphill walking, perfect for people planning their first walk of the summer.

The trail is a beauty, following along much of Purisima Creek. At times it is a lush watershed, heavy with redwoods and ferns. In some of the more open areas, you can spot all kinds of wildflowers including large patches of blue forget-me-nots.

Like other lands managed by the

Directions: From San Francisco, drive south on Interstate 280 for about 15 miles to the Highway 92 cutoff. Head west toward Half Moon Bay, then turn south on Highway 35 (Skyline Boulevard). There are two access points off Skyline. The northern access point is a 4.5-mile drive at road marker SM 18.36, the other a 6.5-mile drive at road marker SM 16.65. Parking areas are provided.

Access from Half Moon Bay—From Main Street in Half Moon Bay, drive south through town and turn east on Higgins Canyon Road. Continue on the winding

Midpeninsula Regional Open Space District, this is an open space preserve, not a developed park. That means there are no barbecues, ball fields, campsites or developed recreation areas.

What you have instead is a big chunk of Bay Area land protected in its natural environment. It is one of the best secrets you might uncover this year.

❖

road for four miles to the park. A small parking lot is on the left side of the road.

Fee or Free: Access and parking are free.

Maps: A trail map of Purisima Creek Redwoods is available by calling (415) 691-1200.

Contact: Phone the Midpeninsula Regional Open Space District at (415) 691-1200.

23

Woodside's Huddart Park

In the Woodside foothills

Huddart Park is a perfect example of an attractive, hidden woodland, located near thousands of residents, that goes almost unused from October to May. A lot of folks just don't seem to know it's here, even on the crackling fresh weekends of spring.

But it is here—some 1,000 acres of redwoods, tan oak and madrones cut by miles of trails that can take you on an easy walk, a picnic, or a good puffer of a hike that rises to the 2,000-foot Skyline Ridge.

A bonus is that the Skyline Trail connects Huddart Park to Wunderlich Park, which sits just below the town of Sky Londa. The resulting 20-mile hike provides a good close-to-home weekend backpacking trip for Bay Area hikers who don't want to wait until summer for the Sierra Nevada icebox to defrost. Combined with Wunderlich Park, hikers have access to nearly 2,000 acres of mountain vistas. In all, there are about 45 miles of trails, enough to keep you coming back for more.

Every time you return to Huddart, you see something different. This makes Huddart probably the best hiking park on the Peninsula, and a worthwhile trip for people from all over the Bay Area.

During the summer, Huddart Park is quite popular, especially for family picnics. There are a variety of short, loop trails well-suited for little kids that make for

Directions: From Highway 280, take the Woodside Road exit west, then turn right on King's Mountain Road and drive two miles to the main entrance.

Fee or Free: An entrance fee is charged.

Camping: Backpack camping is permitted by reservation only; phone the park headquarters at (415)851-0326. No drive-in camping is allowed.

Contact: Park headquarters can be reached at (415) 851-0326. At times, the phone is unattended.

a good family trip. One of the best is the Redwood Trail, little more than a half-mile long, that starts from the Redwood Picnic Area. However, because much of it is such an easy walk set amid redwoods, this trail gets heavy use, and by mid-summer it's what backpackers call a "highway." For hikers who yearn for solitude, there are several excellent options, all good half-day hikes.

My favorite is a route that circles the park, about a five-mile trip that takes you through redwood forests, along stream-bedded canyons to skyline ridges, and eventually back to your starting point. With map in hand, you should start on the Dean Trail from the Werder Picnic Area, and eventually connect to Richard Road's Trail, Summit Springs Trail and Archery Fire Trail to complete the circuit. Because several trails intersect at Huddart Park, you can tailor your hike to your level of ambition.

Woodside was originally given its name for the stands of native redwoods on the nearby mountain slopes. However, little more than 100 years ago, there was hardly a redwood tree left. Loggers went wild here after the 1849 gold rush, cutting down practically anything in sight. The giant stumps you see here beckon back to that era—but the present second-growth forest, now thick and lush, is a testimonial to how man's best work with nature is often just to do nothing.

24

Woodside's Phleger Estate

In the Woodside foothills

Imagine this scene: a bobcat stalking a cottontail creeps through the high grass. In a nearby meadow, a dozen deer graze in silence, the only sound in the air being the chattering of squirrels playing tag nearby on a 150-year-old oak. A red-tailed hawk circles overhead, using rising thermals to stay aloft without a wingbeat. Along an adjacent dirt path, little birds hiding under bushes make crunch-crunch sounds as they hop around on old leaves.

A small stream pours crystal-pure water down the center of a densely-wooded canyon, with refracted sunlight sifting through the branches of madrones, oaks and redwoods. You take a deep breath and taste the pureness, you smell the scent of woods and water, and before long, every cell in your body starts to feel alive.

This portrait is a recollection of an early summer day I spent exploring in some beautiful off-limits Peninsula wildlands, to which I was given access. It turns out, however, that this area will be opened to the public sometime in late winter 1993 or early 1994, as a new part of the Golden Gate National Recreation Area.

It is called the "Phleger Estate," and is located in the Woodside foothills on the San Francisco Peninsula, just a minute's drive from Highway 280 near Edgewood and Canada roads. The land covers 1,257 acres of forest and watershed from Skyline to 280, long considered a forbidden paradise for travelers scanning it from the nearby highway.

Its addition as parkland will complete the missing link of unbroken Peninsula greenbelt from South San Francisco to San Jose. Hiking north to south, it will be possible to walk from Sweeney Ridge above San Bruno all the way to Portola Valley, or hiking east to west, from Edgewood Park in Redwood City all the way to the outskirts of Half Moon Bay at Purisima Creek Redwoods.

In the process, a small group of conservationists is proving once and for all how to protect unique natural areas like this: buy them. That has been the strategy of the Peninsula Open Space Trust, an organization with about 3,000 members. It is headed by Audrey Rust, a persistent woman who understands the financial realities of conservation.

When Mary Phleger died in December of 1991, she left behind this vast wonderland. You don't need to be a developer with a cash register for a brain to figure out that subdividing it into 50 25-acre parcels, then building homes worth $4 million on each one, could offer a developer the chance to clear $100 million or so in a few years. But before she died, Mary Phleger and her family asked the Peninsula Open Space Trust to make a competitive bid against three commercial real estate outfits, and a little while later, the Phleger family selected a bid of $25 million from the Trust. Key cooperation has come from private donations, the Trusts' revolving land acquisition fund, a grant from the Save The Redwoods League, the sale of the property's mansion, and funding by U.S. Congress. The result is the property can be added to the Golden Gate National Recreation Area as public parkland.

For most of this century, this piece of property has been kept secret and protected behind a massive stone gate. While a secret no longer, it appears it will always remain protected.

"Keeping the western hillsides and coastal plains

in open space is not just for human enjoyment," Rust told me. "We are also meeting the very real needs of the wild inhabitants who share this special place with us. The purchase of the Phleger property will accomplish two missions. It will create a corridor for people trails, and it will increase the total number of protected wild acres that support a myriad of creatures."

"We are only a few of us, but we try hard to do what we do," she said. "It is very satisfying to know we are protecting beautiful, wild places forever. You can go out and kick the dirt and know you had something to do with protecting it."

Anyone who has driven Highway 280 in the Peninsula foothills has likely gazed at this piece of land and wondered what it is like. In the summer, you can watch from a distance as wisps of fog slip down the slopes, working their way across the miles of treetops. It is impressive from an airplane, where the solid band of humanity on the Bay Area flatlands gives way to less populated foothills, then to virtual wilderness, with woodlands, creeks and lakes hidden in canyons.

It is by foot, though, that you really start to feel the magic of the place. A redwood forest has a feel to it like no other; it's a place for old souls who like old things. Below the giant forest canopy are cradles of ferns, beds of crunchy, old redwood leaves, three-leaf clovers, mushrooms, and banana slugs. It is a cool, quiet place, where you can find pleasure in just sitting against the trunk of a tree and letting nature's artistry sink in while your cares drift away.

Out here there are no winners and

Directions: From San Francisco, take Interstate 280 south and turn off at Edgewood Road. Turn west and continue to the end of the road.

Contact: For a brochure, write Peninsula Open Space Trust, 3000 Sand Hill Road, Building 4, Suite 135, Menlo Park, CA 94025, or phone (415)854-7696.

no losers, no heroes and no bums, only visitors who share a pristine environment, then leave it as they found it.

Note: The Phleger Estate will be open to the public in late 1993 or early 1994.

25

Wunderlich Park

In the Woodside foothills

What most people want from a park is a sense of remoteness, without actually being far from home. Wunderlich Park offers just that, with 25 miles of secluded trails that cut quiet pathways through forest and meadow, located on the nearby San Francisco Peninsula above Woodside.

Wunderlich Park is one of the best areas for cleaning out the cobwebs in your brain, offering a variety of trails from short strolls to all-day treks. Take your pick. I hiked here all day with a companion and did not see a single other hiker. That's called solitude. The trail cuts through lush ravines to mountainsides strewn with redwoods. That's called beauty. It's the combination you may be looking for.

First get a map of the park which details all of the trails. You will discover that because the network of trails intersect at several points, you can tailor your hike to fit the amount of time you have as well as your level of ambition. A good hike for first-timers is a loop trip from the main park entrance to "The Meadows," or to Alambique Creek and Redwood Flat. If you don't want to spend all day hiking, this is a good compromise.

But if you want to extend yourself, your goal should be the Skyline Ridge at 2,200 feet. A ten-mile, five-hour round-trip to the ridge can be a highlight. You gain almost 2,000 feet, which can get you puffing like a locomotive, but most of the grade is a gentle, steady climb, and in the process you cross through a wide variety of plant and tree communities—and also reach some classic vistas of San Francisco Bay and the East Bay hills.

It's at these lookouts where the rewards of hiking become clear. Here you are on the edge of the Bay Area, on the outside looking in.

A few notes, however. Poison oak can be prevalent in some areas. If you're vulnerable, wear long-sleeved shirts, wash your clothes right after your hike, and of course, stay on the trails. The latter can do more than anything to protect you. In addition, no drinking water is available on the trails, so bring a small day pack with a lunch and drinks, or at least a canteen.

Directions: The most direct route from Highway 280 is to take the Sand Hill Road exit, then head west to Portola Road. Turn right and continue just past the junction with Highway 84. The park entrance is on the left, where a large sign is posted.

Maps: For a free map, send a stamped, self-addressed envelope to the San Mateo County Parks and Recreation Department, 590 Hamilton Street, Redwood City, CA 94063.

Pets: No pets are allowed.

Fee or Free: No fee.

Contact: Call San Mateo County Parks and Recreation Department at (415) 363-4020, or Wunderlich Park at (415) 851-7570.

26

Redwood City's Discovery Voyages

In Redwood City on the Bay

What might start as nothing more than a boat ride can end by changing your perspective on life. Providing, that is, the name of the boat is the *Inland Seas* and your ride is a four-hour tour of San Francisco Bay—with the chance to see, touch and experience all the little critters that make the Bay environment click.

The ride is called Discovery Voyages and it is one of the most unique adventures available anywhere in the West. From the outside, it appears to be a fun, four-hour cruise exploring south San Francisco Bay. From the inside, it is like a Jacques Cousteau expedition with a chance to view the Bay in a way you may have never imagined.

The *Inland Seas,* an 85-foot cruiser, departs from Redwood City and heads out to the Bay between the San Mateo and Dumbarton bridges. You don't need seasickness pills. In fact, the Bay is often so calm out here that the skipper calls it "San Francisco Lake."

Out on the water, the crew takes charge—with a net trawl for fish, and samples of plankton water and mud from the Bay bottom. You see, this boat is a floating marine laboratory and the public is invited along for a special science lesson.

By itself, the boat ride is lots of fun, but the chance to explore, question and observe the inner workings of San Francisco Bay will make you feel different about the area as your home.

"Five million people live and work around the Bay," said Bob Rutherford, president of Discovery Voyages. "Few of them realize their quality of life is greatly influenced by the Bay.

"We don't pull any punches and we're not pointing any fingers. We are analyzing the Bay with students. It doesn't matter who is aboard. Whether it is someone from an oil company or the Leslie Salt Company, we do the same thing."

Since the first voyage, Rutherford estimates more than 150,000 people have taken the trip. Some go for the boat ride, some to supplement their science education, others to get in touch with the vast body of water that is the center of the Bay Area.

You start with a simple water sample. It is like looking into a crystal ball, because it can tell you the future. In that water you will find plankton, the basis of the marine food chain. A net with tiny openings just 80 microns across is dragged through the water, and after it is retrieved, you follow a scientist to a room inside the boat. Using a specially designed microscope/projector, the image of the plankton is projected on a screen, where everyone can view it at once.

You see tiny copepods, diatoms, dinoflagellates, and small protozoa, all of them squiggling around. Without them, there would be no other life in the Bay.

"This is the beginning of the marine food chain," said Peter Olds, one of the scientists aboard. "We explain how everything starts with plankton on the bottom of the food chain. And we emphasize the possible effects that man might have on it.

"If there's too much sewage going into the Bay, for instance, there can be an algae bloom. The plankton and algae will rot, and then the decomposition of the plant matter uses up the oxygen in the water. Without enough oxygen, fish cannot survive."

The mud samples are especially fascinating to

kids. They seem to like the idea of a scientist getting all mucked up.

But then they discover that all kinds of little critters are living in the mud as the scientist finds and identifies them: tubeworms, oysters, mussels, clams, sponges, little crustaceans and snails. They find out that there is more to the muck than just muck.

The fish trawl experiment is often the most exciting. The small net is called an otter trawl, and it is dragged behind the boat, allowing a wide sampling.

Perch—seen in many species—are the most abundant. You are likely to see leopard sharks, brown smooth-hound sharks and bay rays. Anchovies, sole, halibut, kingfish, jacksmelt, mudsuckers, bullheads, shiners, and sometimes, although rarely, striped bass and sturgeon also are captured. After inspection, the fish are returned unharmed.

You end up with a unique look at the Bay in the midst of a fun adventure. You also begin to understand the chain of life in Bay waters, and how people affect it.

❖

Directions: From Highway 101, take the Port of Redwood City exit. Continue past the harbor, eastward. The Discovery Voyage headquarters is located across from the giant salt pile of the Leslie Salt Company.

Tour Schedule: Charters are available year-round. Public trips are scheduled, but individuals can often join private charters too.

Fee or Free: Boarding pass prices vary for students aged 10 to 18 and adults.

Contact: For a brochure or information, write Discovery Voyages, 500 Discovery Parkway, Redwood City, 94063-4715, or phone (415) 364-2760.

27

San Francisco Bay Wildlife Refuge

At the eastern foot of the Dumbarton Bridge

How many times have you sped in your car along the shores of San Francisco on Highway 101, 17 or 237, dodging traffic like Mario Andretti at the Indy 500?

If you hatch out of that metal cocoon, rub your eyes to a new day, and look just over yonder, you might see a far different world. The shores of our Bay offer a perfect environment for a diverse population of little critters, from tiny crabs to rabbits. And the marshlands also act as one of the major rest stops for millions of birds traveling on the Pacific Flyway.

This all adds up to the San Francisco Bay National Wildlife Refuge, headquartered along the eastern foot of the Dumbarton Bridge. You can't beat the price, with access, brochures and regularly scheduled guided walks all free. It's an ideal adventure, especially for families or groups. It can be explored by trail or boat—but not by car, motorcycle or bicycle. That means you can go it alone, on land or on water, and get that special quiet you deserve.

The diversity of wildlife here is spectacular. Even a handful of Bay mud can contain 20,000 tiny living creatures, the primary levels of the marine food chain. There are as many different kinds of birds in this area as almost anywhere else in Northern California. In a given year, more than 250 bird species will find food, resting space and nesting sites here. Birdlife, particularly waterfowl, is most abundant in the fall when snowstorms across Canada, Montana and parts of Washington send migratory birds to their wintering sanctuaries by the Bay.

After just 15 minutes and before I lost track, I scoped six different kinds of ducks, along with a pelican, egret, sandpiper, and another species I could not readily identify. No problem. A check at the ranger station later provided the answer. It was a willet, which gets its name from its oft-repeated call during the breeding season, "pill-will-willet."

During low tides, the Bay will roll back to reveal miles of tidal flats, filled with mussels, clams and oysters. Pollution control since the "Save Our Bay" campaign of the 1960s has been so successful that the water is cleaner than it has been in 25 years, and shellfish digging is now permitted in a few areas.

Fishing and hunting (in specified areas) are permitted, and actually can be quite good if you hit the right place at the right time. For fishing, the right time is during a high incoming tide. The right place is at the Dumbarton Pier along the main channel of the Bay, a natural fishway. Sharks, rays, perch, and occasional striped bass, jacksmelt, and flounder can be caught, according to season.

Most folks, however, go just for the walk, an easy hike along the Bay shoreline. If you follow in their footsteps, you'll find a close-to-home spot that you may have driven past thousands of times on a

Directions: From San Francisco, drive south on US 101 to the Willow Road-Dumbarton Bridge exit. Continue east, and take the first exit (Thornton Avenue) after the toll plaza. At the bottom of the offramp, turn right and drive 1.5 miles to the refuge entrance on the right.

Mass Transit: It's not convenient at the present time. The Alameda County bus system schedules a stop about a mile away. For information, call AC Transit at (510) 839-2882.

Trip Tip: Bring good walking shoes and binoculars. Leashed dogs are allowed only on the Tidelands Trail.

Fee or free: Access, brochures and scheduled guided tours are free.

Contact: Write to the San Francisco Bay National Wildlife Refuge, P.O. Box 524, Newark, CA 94560, or phone (510) 792-0222.

highway, without ever having taken a good look at it.

❖

28

Baylands Trail

In Palo Alto, along the South Bay

If you get a flat tire on the Baylands Bicycle Trail, it might actually help you enjoy your trip. The slower you go, the better it is. This sprawling acreage of wild marshlands is tucked away near the edge of South San Francisco Bay. There is no charge to visit and it is just minutes from Highway 101, yet it still retains a spirit independent of the nearby metropolis.

The best place to start the trip is right behind the grandstand of the Baylands baseball park.

The opening part of the trail is built from flat and hard crushed rock. It is bordered by a creek on the left and a golf course on the right. Judging by the golfing ability displayed by the hackers, a football helmet and a coat of armor might be suitable apparel. Soon enough the trail turns from rock to hard-packed dirt, and you will wind your way past the golf course, past the Palo Alto Airport, and to the marshlands.

Even on a bike, you'll find yourself intentionally slowing the pace. The air was so clear on our visit that it looked like you could take a running start, leap and clear the Bay, and land on the East Bay hills.

We parked and locked our bikes and decided to hoof it. The tidal marsh here is cut by sloughs and filled with diverse bird and marine life, as well as the plants that support them. The food chain that starts in the marshland supports almost all the fish and wildlife in San Francisco Bay and its tidelands. Some 250 species of birds use San Francisco Bay as either a resting spot or home, including birds only rarely seen elsewhere. We counted some 15 snowy egrets. There are also lots of fast little ground squirrels.

If you want to extend your visit, you should continue to the Baylands Interpretive Center, where an old wooden walkway lifts you just above the soggy marsh. It leads to the edge of the Bay. During low tides, the water will roll back and expose bare mudflats for miles. The walkway is accessible to wheelchairs, and for that matter, so is the rock-built portion of the bike trail. The entire trail is not wheelchair accessible because storms soften the dirt portion.

The marshlands are filled with plants such as pickleweed and cord grass, and to the developer, may look like a good spot to pave over with concrete and condominiums. However, this is actually one of the most productive ecosystems on earth.

When the plants decay, little bits of the decomposed material are carried into the Bay by tidal action and are fed upon by small animals such as clams, crabs, snails and pile worms. The food web is completed when these are eaten by seals, birds, large fish and other animals. The richness of the area is reflected in the diversity of birdlife and the abundance of ground squirrels.

You can also follow the bike path across a bridge, then head down the trail behind Palo Alto. It goes practically to the Dumbarton Bridge.

By foot, one to three hours is plenty of time to see the Palo Alto Baylands area. Regardless of your physical conditioning or age, it can be enjoyable, be-

Directions: Take Highway 101 to Palo Alto, then take the Embarcadero east exit. At the second light, across from Ming's Restaurant, turn left at Geng Street and continue to its end. The trail begins directly behind the baseball field and is signed.

Mass Transit: SamTrans, (415) 965-3100, doesn't make trips east of Highway 101 on Embarcadero. It's about a 15-minute walk from the trailhead.

Trip Tip: Your best chance of seeing the maximum number of birds and wildlife is in the early morning,

cause there are no hills at all.

Sure, the rubber on a wheel is faster than the rubber on a heel, but at the Baylands Bike Trail, you can take your pick.

---

when people numbers are lowest.

Pets:
Dogs must be leashed.

Fee or Free:
Free.

Contact:
Call the Baylands Interpretive Center at (415) 329-2506, either Wednesday through Friday (2 p.m. to 5 p.m.) or on weekends (1 p.m. to 5 p.m.) The Palo Alto Recreation Department can be reached at (415) 329-2261.

29

Arastradero Lake

In the Palo Alto foothills

A truly hidden lake on the Peninsula offers an opportunity for hiking, fishing, birdwatching and picnicking. It is called Arastradero Lake. Open since 1987, it is the only lake that allows public access between San Francisco and San Jose. It is set in the foothill country above Palo Alto as part of a 600-acre nature preserve.

There are some 60 lakes around the Bay Area, but Peninsula residents have long been frustrated by "No Trespassing" signs set up by public agencies that are supposed to serve them. The Peninsula has several magnificent lakes—Crystal Springs, Pilarcitos, Felt, Searsville, Boronda—but they are all off-limits to the public at large.

Belmont has a tiny, squarish reservoir that is open to the public, but it provides few recreational opportunities and can't be called a lake by any definition.

Park rangers are stretching it a bit, too, calling Arastradero a lake, but the recreational opportunities here make for a worthwhile visit anyway. The best time to visit is on a warm summer evening, when the birds are feeding and the fish are jumping.

The lake looks more like a farm pond, circled by tules and set in the foothill country. It was created by a small earth dam built across the canyon, then is filled with water from the winter runoff from a small creek.

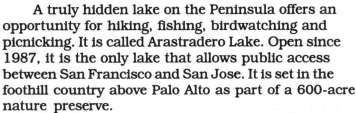

It's a 10-minute walk from the parking area to the lake, and even though you know the lake is there, it is still a surprise when you top the rise and see it for the first time. It is prettier than you might anticipate. The birdlife is abundant, and on a quiet evening, it makes an idyllic setting.

The area is a good one for a short walk, say just to the lake and back. If you have kids, it's short enough to keep their attention, and long enough to get the ants out of their pants.

But the area is worth exploring on a longer trip. The Perimeter Trail connects to both the Acorn Trail and Corte Madera Trail, and from those you can visit most of the preserve. It is mostly flat; the highest rise is 300 feet, so it is comfortable for hikers of all ages.

My favorite piece of trail is the Corte Madera Trail above the lake, where it borders the Arastradero Creek watershed. A map that shows all the trails is available for free in a box at the parking lot.

The birds and wildflowers provide a good sideshow. In the foothill country, there are a lot of hawks circling around, looking for prey. As you near the lake, there is more diversity, with both songbirds and waterfowl. In less than an hour, I spotted more than a dozen species of birds.

The area is exceptionally pretty as spring gives way to summer. The hills are still green, though fading, and there are blooms of lupine, blue-eyed grass and California poppies to give the hillsides some close-up color.

If there is a frustrating aspect to the trip, it is that fishing should be great at Arastradero Lake. It isn't. Why? Because of over-regulation and poor management by the Palo Alto Department of Recreation. The lake is set in an area where climate, food production and cover make for abundant populations of largemouth bass and bluegill. The lake is creek fed, so it is full (another plus). The fish are in there, including some big ones—I know, because I have seen them. But fishing for them is virtually impossible, which is a shame, especially for the kids in the area who have no other place to try.

The fishing problems are shoreline access, weed growth, and a rule that makes fishing from a raft or float tube illegal. There are just a few breaks in the tules along the shoreline where a kid could try to fish. But even if you are lucky enough to get a spot which isn't taken, the heavy weed growth in the shallows makes every retrieve a frustrating experience.

The solution would be to fish from a raft or float tube, as is so much fun at farm ponds in the Central Valley. But, alas, the city of Palo Alto has deemed that illegal. As a result, they have screwed up the one public freshwater fishing spot between San Francisco and San Jose. What's left is a chance to catch a small bluegill or two, that is, if you can get them through the weeds.

Regardless, the Arastradero Preserve provides a good adventure for visitors. It is hidden away, known only by a few local residents and is pretty, warm and peaceful.

And you won't find any signs that proclaim "No Trespassing." That's the best news of all.

Directions: From San Francisco, drive south on Interstate 280, about 30 miles. Take the Page Mill Road exit and turn west. Turn right on Arastradero Road. A signed parking lot is on the right side of the road.

Fee or Free: Admission and parking are free. A trail map is available for free in a box at the parking lot.

Pets: Dogs are permitted Monday through Friday and must be leashed at all times.

Restrictions: No boats, flotation devices or swimming at Arastradero Lake. No camping and no bicycles on the Perimeter Trail.

Contact: Call headquarters at Foothills Park at (415) 329-2423.

30

Pescadero Marsh

Along the southern San Mateo County coast

Sitting just east of Highway 1 near Pescadero is a natural marsh area, 600 acres in all, which has a quiet trail winding its way through it. It is called Pescadero Marsh, and it may provide the best area in Northern California to see the great blue heron. It is hikable by almost anybody, and it is one of the most overlooked wildlife areas in the Bay Area. The kicker is that after your walk, you can have a meal at Duarte's Restaurant, which offers great artichoke soup (a unique concoction), and homemade bread .

Pescadero Marsh is one of the few remaining natural marsh areas on the entire central California coast. For that reason, it is critical that you not wander off the trail and unknowingly let your feet destroy any of this habitat. The trail is almost flat, which makes it an easy walk for almost anyone of any age. It routes you amid pampas grass, pickleweed and bogs. It is the main stopover for birds on the Pacific Flyway, as well as home for a good population of year-round residents. You will see a surprising variety of birds.

You do not need to be a birdwatcher to enjoy the scene. However, if you have binoculars, bring them. During the year some 250 different species of birds use the marsh. The most impressive is the blue heron, a magnificent creature that stands almost four feet tall with a wingspan of seven feet. The sight of one of them lifting off is a classic picture. They fly with labored wing beats, which makes them appear even bigger. Pescadero Marsh is a prime nesting ground for the blue heron.

Other unique birds sighted here include the snowy egret, a pure white, frail-looking fellow that seems to spook easily, and the night heron, a bird that seems to have all its feathers squeezed together, as well as having a short neck, short legs and a short bill. The distinct appearances of these coastal birds seems to give each of them a personable character, especially in the case of the night heron. After awhile, they seem like old friends.

The marsh is bordered by the Pacific Ocean on one side, and Pescadero Creek on the other, so the result is a unique setting that can attract birds that live in both saltwater and freshwater environments.

After your walk, there is no reason to get back on the Highway 1 treadmill. Not when you can go to Pescadero's historic Duarte's Restaurant, a place ingrained with a coastal tradition. Reservations are a must. It all makes for a memorable outing.

Directions: From Highways 280, 92 or 84, head west to Highway 1, then turn south and continue past Half Moon Bay. Pescadero Marsh is located just northeast of the Pescadero turnoff, 18 miles south of Half Moon Bay.

Fee or Free: Access is free.

Duarte's: For reservations to Duarte's Restaurant in Pescadero, call (415) 879-0464.

Contact: For general information, call the state park office in Half Moon Bay at (415) 726-8819, or the State Park Regional Office at (415)726-8800.

31

Butano State Park

In the coastal foothills, south of Pescadero

This park sits just 10 miles south of Pescadero amid redwood trees. It's a year-round facility ideal for either an after-work picnic or a weekend hike—and you can also camp, backpack, run cross-country, or just sit down and commune with a redwood tree. Many days, the park is uncrowded.

One of the highlights here is the 11-mile Loop Trail, which is one of my favorite all-day hikes in the Bay Area. The trail takes you across a broad spectrum of terrain and back to where you started, without forcing you to backtrack.

Butano (pronounced "bute-uh-no") provides an alternative for campers who love redwoods and ferns, but don't have the time for long drives. All of the campsites here are fairly secluded, including 21 with parking spaces for a vehicle, and 19 walk-in sites. For the adventurous, six campsites for backpackers are set on the Loop Trail. Reservations and permits for these few spots are required through park headquarters.

About 80 percent of the park is forested with conifers, with the rest speckled with chaparral, especially along the upper ridges, and wildflowers such as golden poppies and trillium. In the canyon, there are all kinds of heavy vegetation, including rare wild orchids.

If you bring your own food to Butano, you will likely find yourself surrounded by many new friends, especially Steller's jays, looking for a handout. They are among more than a hundred species of birds here. Hawks are common sightings, and if you're lucky, you might spot an owl at sunset. Squirrels, raccoons, coyotes, foxes, deer and even bobcats make their home on the range at Butano, and on the Loop Trail, it is fairly common to suddenly find yourself practically nose-to-nose with a deer.

That's how it can be when you find a special hide-away—something that is practically guaranteed at Butano State Park.

Directions: From the intersection of Highways 1 and 92 in Half Moon Bay, drive 18 miles south on Highway 1 to the Pescadero Road exit. Turn east on Pescadero Road and drive past the town of Pescadero. Turn right (south) on Cloverdale Road and drive until you see the signed park entrance turnoff on the left side of the road.

Pets: Dogs are allowed on leashes in campgrounds, but are not permitted on trails.

Fee of Free: A state park access fee is charged. Campsite fees vary. A small fee is charged for pets.

Reservations: Camping reservations can be made through Mistix; phone (800) 444-7275.

Contact: Call the Butano State Park at (415) 879-0173, or write P.O. Box 9, Pescadero, CA 94060.

32

Skyline Ridge Preserve

On Skyline Ridge above Palo Alto

Skyline Ridge Preserve is a quiet place that offers classic ridgetop vistas from secluded trails routed near both a lake and a pond. The preserve is perched above Palo Alto on Skyline Boulevard, nearby for thousands of Peninsula residents. This is a good place to go if you want some peace and quiet.

December is one of the best times to visit, since a good Christmas tree farm, Skyline Ranch Tree Farm, borders an edge of the preserve. You can take in the view, and then take home a tree you cut down yourself, a good two-for-one offer.

Skyline spans about 1,100 acres and is bordered by open space. Horseshoe Lake is the focal point for the preserve, located in the southeastern region. It can be reached by a number of trails that connect and border the western edge of the lake.

Another hike can take you to the highest point in the preserve at 2,493 feet. When you look down from here, the canyon seems to plunge thousands of feet below you.

Most of the trails are actually more like old dirt roads, but they provide a good walking surface. Combined with a network of old paths, they can take you to a wide variety of scenic spots. The trails cut through woodlands filled primarily with Douglas fir, madrone and oak, as well as prairie-like grasslands.

In December, you can drive right up to the Christmas tree farm on Skyline Boulevard, cut your tree, and then continue your day by exploring the Skyline Ridge Preserve. In fact, the trail that can take you most quickly to Horseshoe Lake starts at the Christmas tree farm.

The other access point is just south of the intersection of Skyline Boulevard and Page Mill Road. Access is free.

One note: the preserve could become one of the best in the Bay Area if fishing was allowed in both Horseshoe Lake and in the nearby pond. But the Midpeninsula Regional Open Space District currently prohibits fishing here, and that seems like a crime by a public agency against the public. Horseshoe Lake ranges to 40 feet deep and is lined with tules. It could support an excellent largemouth bass fishery. What a shame! The people that run the Open Space District are smart folks, so perhaps they will be persuaded by common sense in the near future.

❖

Directions: From San Francisco, drive south on Interstate 280 approximately 30 miles. Take the Page Mill Road exit and turn west; continue until you reach the intersection with Skyline Boulevard.

Access Points: You can gain access to the preserve at the southeast corner of the Page Mill Road/Skyline Boulevard intersection, or through the Christmas tree farm located two miles south of the intersection.

Fee or free: Access is free.

Contact: For maps and information, phone the Midpeninsula Regional Open Space District at (415) 691-1200.

33

Portola State Park

In the Peninsula foothills near La Honda

If explorer Don Gaspar de Portola saw the suburbia of the San Francisco Peninsula today, he'd probably do exactly what thousands of Bay Area residents do every year: seek the refuge of Portola State Park.

The area from San Francisco to Morgan Hill can seem like one long chain of houses and cars, but just over Skyline Ridge, behind the outskirts of Palo Alto, you can still find an asylum of peace. It looks much as it did when Portola first set foot in the area in 1769. Peters and Pescadero Creeks wind through rugged country studded with redwoods, Douglas firs and oak. It's an ideal spot for the weekender who is ready to escape the grip of city life, but who doesn't want to drive far.

Portola State Park is best known for its natural beauty; hiking, camping and communing with the quiet are the prime attractions. Some 14 miles of hiking trails lead through varied terrain. Some hikers head up the ridge through redwoods and into chaparral, while others follow the streams and the forest floor of azaleas and ferns.

Campers have 52 campsites to pick from at Portola, each with a picnic table, barbecue pit and wood food locker to protect your eats from raccoons during their nightly raids. All of the camping spots are "drive-in" sites, which means a parking space is adjacent to each spot. Always phone ahead for campground site availability.

In the spring, a special bonus awaits streamside explorers. Steelhead can be seen spawning in the gravel riverbeds after a long journey from the ocean to the high reaches of the streams. But don't bring your fishing rod. All fishing is illegal year-round here, and has been for years. In the winter, the big steelhead are protected so they can spawn, and in the summer, so are the steelhead smolt. In the past, kids catching those "little trout" in the summer were actually killing baby steelhead, which were trying to grow large enough to head out to sea.

Portola Park is a good destination for a family outing on a weekend or for a place of quiet during the week.

❖

Directions: From Highway 280 near Redwood City, take Highway 84 east to Highway 35 (Skyline Boulevard). Turn south and drive about seven miles, then turn west on Alpine Road and continue to the park. The turns are well signed. An alternate route is to start at Palo Alto, taking the twisting Page Mill Road southwest to the park.

Pets: Dogs must be licensed, kept on a leash, and are not allowed on the trails.

Fee or Free: A state park access fee is charged. Camping fees vary.

Camping: Reservations can be made through Mistix at (800) 444-7275.

Contact: Write Portola State Park, Star Route 2, La Honda, CA 94020, or call (415) 948-9098 for information.

34

Big Basin State Park

In the Santa Cruz Mountains

Imagine a short Sunday morning drive from the Bay Area, a two-hour walk, mostly downhill, then lunch beside a magnificent 70-foot waterfall in a canyon lined with ferns. It's a scene that looks like a picture out of Yosemite.

When you visit Big Basin State Park in the Santa Cruz Mountains, you will discover that this image is not a product of your imagination. Big Basin became California's first state park in 1902, and after you hike it, you will understand why. It is a place of special calm, with thousands of acres of redwoods, ferns, moss-lined canyons and a series of waterfalls that make prime destinations for hikers.

Spending time in the mountains here can give you a fresh perspective. A few drops of water caught by a spider web look like crystals in mid-air. A blooming trillium alone in a bed of ferns catches your eye as you stroll amid huge redwoods, some more than 2,000 years old. When you return, you'll feel as if your batteries have been recharged.

Big Basin is an ideal place for a one-day hike, with some 80 miles of trails to choose from. But you may choose to visit the park for week-long camping trips, since then you won't squander your time driving long distances. Some 145 drive-in campsites, 43 walk-in

Directions: From San Francisco, take Highway 1 south to Santa Cruz, turn east on Highway 9, then turn left on Highway 236 and continue to the park.

From the San Francisco Peninsula, take Highway 9 from Los Gatos over the ridge, then turn right on Highway 236 and continue to the park. Signs to the park are posted.

Fee or Free: A parking fee is charged for day-use. Campsite fees vary depending on the season.

Camping: Reservations for drive-in campsites can be made through

sites, and 38 tent cabins are available. Each camp is in a redwood setting, and includes a tent site, picnic table and food locker.

Big Basin also offers unique options for backpackers either in training for a Sierra expedition, or just in need of a good two-day pull. You'll find one of the best weekend hikes in the Bay Area here. It's part of the Skyline-to-Sea Trail, a 12-miler from headquarters at Big Basin to the Pacific Ocean. I have always enjoyed this hike. However, this is not a loop trail, so you will need to arrange for shuttle service with a friend in order to return to your car.

If you have a little of the adventuring spirit in you, then consider the entire Skyline-to-Sea Trail, a 38-mile foot-stomper. It starts at Castle Rock State Park in Highway 35, set at 2,700 feet just south of the Highway 9 junction. It's a good three-day jaunt, most of it downhill as the trail descends to the shores of the Pacific. Several backcountry camps are available for overnights. In order to be certain that wildlife and the forest habitat are not damaged, park rules mandate no fires (use a camp stove), and bedding down is allowed only in designated sites.

The strict rules have left most of the native animals undisturbed. Gone are the grizzly bears (one killed logger William Waddell in 1875) and the eagles, but deer, coyotes, raccoons, bobcats, possum and the like remain. Also more than 250 species of birds have been observed in Waddell Valley. The most common is the Steller's jay, mistakenly called a blue jay by most; the Steller's jay has a crested head while the blue jay does not. These birds arrive promptly when you start eating lunch, hoping for a handout, and leave just as quickly when you are finished.

The centerpiece of Big Basin is Berry Creek Falls. The entire loop from park headquarters requires five to six hours hiking time. If you take the direct route on your return trip, you can cut it to about four-and-a-half hours. If you have never seen it, then a Sunday drive and hike should be at the top of your priority list.

Mistix; phone (800)444-7275. Reservations for backpacker campsites must be obtained through park headquarters at (408)338-6132.

Maps: Park maps can be obtained for a small fee through the Santa Cruz Mountains Natural History Association; write them at 525 North Big Trees Parks Road, Selton, CA 95018, or phone park headquarters at (408) 338-6132.

35

Ano Nuevo State Reserve

On the southern San Mateo County coast

One of the more curious adventures in the Bay Area has become one of the most popular—touring Ano Nuevo Reserve to see the giant elephant seals.

It is curious because the elephant seals are such peculiar comrades. They spend most of their time sprawled out on the sand dunes, basking in the sun. But every so often, they will surprise you. At the least, they are capable of some fast, jerky movements, or even a mini-charge. When the male elephant seals challenge each other, they will rear up and cut loose with a clucking-type roar, then slam their open jaws into their opponent's blubbery neck. It's a ritual out here, and the scars on the necks prove it.

It has also become a ritual to watch, a ritual so popular that reservations are required to join a tour group. Crowds are not a problem, however, because rangers keep groups small so the elephant seals will not feel threatened.

It's a pretty ride to the reserve, located about 10 miles south of Pescadero, just west of Highway 1. Actually, Ano Nuevo is the name of the island here, where elephant seals have been breeding since practically the beginning of time. There are now so many elephant seals that there isn't enough room for all of them on the island, hence hundreds have taken up residence on the mainland, providing the chance for close-up viewing.

In your tour group, you walk along roped-off trails, winding your way amid the animals. You'll be surprised at the creatures' size and their complete lack of interest in you.

Size? Yeah, they come big. Most elephant seals range in the 2,000 to 3,000-pound class, but the old boars can reach nearly 20 feet long and 5,000 pounds. Definitely heavyweights, they are, and they are born that way. At birth, the pups often weigh about 75 pounds, and within four weeks, will approach 300.

The creatures look like giant slugs, and seem content to put up with being viewed from a distance, usually at least 50 feet or more. If you plan on taking photographs, don't plan on a mug shot without a telephoto lens. A 200mm lens is a good choice. The beasts are soft-hearted enough, but they don't like posing for tourists with an Instamatic at point-blank range.

In fact, after people get accustomed to walking among the sunbaked blobs, they start thinking, "Hey, I can walk right up to one." That is exactly why each tour group is led by an experienced leader with a careful eye. Mr. Elephant Seal needs his space, and if you get within his squirming range, well, how would you like to be squished?

The elephant seals start arriving every year in mid-November, with tours offered daily from December through March. In January, hundreds of pups are born, which is quite a phenomenon to see. While elephant seals don't reproduce

Directions: From San Francisco, drive south on Highway 1 to Half Moon Bay. Continue south for about 30 miles. The park entrance is located just off the highway, and is well marked.

Mass Transit: SamTrans offers three tour packages per day on Saturday and Sunday. Advance reservations are required. For information, phone (800) 660-4BUS or (415) 508-6200.

Fee or Free: Fees are charged for guided tours and parking.

Reservations: Reservations are required through Mistix outlets at (800) 444-7275. No self-guided tours are permitted until May, when most of the elephant seals have departed.

Length of Walk:
The tour is about three miles long. A shorter route is wheelchair accessible.

Contact:
For information, call Ano Nuevo State Reserve at (415) 879-2025.

at a rabbit-like pace, they are doing quite a job of repopulating the Pacific Coast, with well over 70,000 elephant seals now ranging south to Baja, living primarily on islands.

At the turn of the century, the species was nearly extinct. Whalers turned their sharp harpoons toward them for oil, and just about wiped them out. Great fellows, those whalers. But sanity won out and elephant seals have long been a protected species, along with other marine mammals. Their comeback is a testimonial that shows how just leaving something alone is often the best wildlife management of all.

The reward for this policy today is a chance to go for a walk among the elephant seals, where they are willing to share all their idiosyncrasies with visitors. All they ask is that you share their world from a respectable distance. Fair enough.

36

Waddell Creek

On the northern Santa Cruz County coast

If the only time you see wildlife is on television, there is an easy walk on the outskirts of the Bay Area that can change that. In the course of an evening stroll, I saw seven deer, three rabbits, several squirrels, five quail, a pair of grouse, ten ducks, a blue heron, and baby steelhead feeding on an insect hatch, all in just two hours.

Birds and fish are the centerpiece of this beautiful streamside walk that can take you from a lagoon to meadows to redwood forest.

Most hikers call it the Waddell Creek Walk. The trailhead is located on Highway 1 just inside the Santa Cruz County line, about 20 miles south of Half Moon Bay. It starts at the Rancho del Oso outpost, the western border for Big Basin State Park. Technically, the trail is the lower portion of the Skyline-to-Sea Trail.

It is an ideal spot to view wildlife and birds in their native habitat. But it is also just a good place to walk, a near-flat trail that plays peek-a-boo with forest and meadow. The trail is popular with horseback riders and bicyclists. If you choose to ride, please go slowly and quietly, and show courtesy to walkers.

You can also stay here overnight. There are secluded hike-in campsites available as close as 1.2 miles from the trailhead, with two others within another two miles. Reservations are required. No open fires or barbecues are permitted, so bring a backpacking stove. Camping is permitted at designated sites only.

You start the trip with a nice cruise on Highway 1,

Directions:
Drive south on Highway 1 about 20 miles past Half Moon Bay, just inside the Santa Cruz County line. After passing Ano Nuevo, look for the signs marking Big Basin State Park/ Rancho del Oso.

Maps:
For maps of Big Basin, contact the Sempervirens Fund, P.O. Drawer BE, Los Altos, CA 94023; or call (415) 968-4509.

Camping:
For reservations to hike-in campsites, phone park headquarters at (408)338-6132.

Contact:
For information on Waddell Creek, phone the Rancho del Oso

which provides continual views of the Pacific Ocean. After passing Ano Nuevo and entering Santa Cruz County heading south, be on the lookout for the large sign announcing Big Basin State Park and Rancho del Oso. That's your calling. Park at the sign for Rancho del Oso.

The first half-mile of the trail loops around the Waddell Creek Lagoon to the park's outpost headquarters. Maps are available here, along with information about the park.

In the next four miles, you can see a lot of wildlife. There are huge meadows on each side of the trail that attract grazing deer, especially during the late afternoon and evening. Photographers with long-range lenses can get classic shots.

In the wooded areas, keep alert for any chattering sound. If you hear one, stop and look around you. Somewhere, likely hopping down the side of a tree and scurrying off to another, will be a gray squirrel.

In areas where the trail is lined with dense bush, walk quietly and keep your eyes focused far ahead. You are apt to see a little brown bush bunny hopping across the trail or playing in the dirt. Often, when they first spot you, the rabbits freeze in their tracks for five or ten seconds, rather than immediately disappearing into the bush. This allows you to watch the little critters closely, and can teach children the merits of being quiet in the woods. Unlike the rabbits, the deer seem almost acclimated to passing hikers.

You can see a surprising diversity of birds here. Because it is close to a fresh-water lagoon, ducks and blue heron nest in the watershed. The most common waterfowl seem to be mallard. The coastal fields between ocean and forest are perfect for nesting quail. I saw a nice covey of them, which included some females that were so close to nesting that they were as round as grapefruits.

Waddell Creek itself is a pleasant stream that attracts steelhead in the winter. No fishing is permitted, but you can occasionally spot an adult. It is more common to see the newly hatched smolts, the three to five-inch steelhead darting to the surface for insects during the evening rise. They look like little trout.

The trail is like an old ranch road and is easy on the feet. It continues level for four-and-a-half miles, until it enters the redwood interior of Big Basin State Park. No bicycles are allowed past this point. Here, the trail starts to climb. If you have the spirit for it, you can continue up to Berry Creek Falls, and on (and up) farther to the Cascade Falls.

outpost at (408) 425-1218. If the ranger is on patrol, phone headquarters at (408) 338-6132.

37

Sunol Regional Preserve

In the East Bay hills east of Fremont

There are unique, hidden places in the Bay Area that can make you feel like you have your own secret spots. That's how Little Yosemite is. Now wait a minute. Little Yosemite? Isn't that the park where four million campers a year look at Half Dome and get their food raided by Smokey the Bear? No, that's big Yosemite.

It has a little brother situated east of Fremont near Highway 680. There is no El Capitan or Cathedral Rocks here, but there is also no Curry Village. In other words, there is usually nobody here. Little Yosemite is part of the Sunol Regional Preserve, a 6,500-acre wilderness area in the East Bay hills. You say you've never been there? Join the club.

The centerpiece of the park is this hidden canyon, named Little Yosemite. It is edged by craggy rock outcrops and cut by a nice little trout stream, which is just a trickle in late summer. When the rains come, the river forms a nice waterfall around a giant boulder.

Visiting here makes for a prime half-day adventure. The park is only a short drive away for most Bay Area residents, and if you have a dog, by all means bring him along because this is one of the few places where dogs are allowed on the trails.

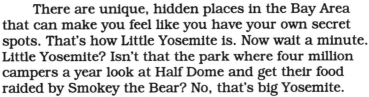

There are six trails in the Sunol Regional Preserve. For your first trip, the best choice is the Canyon View Trail, about a three-and-a-half-mile round-trip that sweeps above the valley to the canyon rim above Little Yosemite. It offers a fine view from the top of the cliffs. (A wide, flat trail in the bot-tom of the valley makes Little Yosemite wheelchair accessible.)

For a good loop hike from the parking area, take the Canyon Rim Trail to the Yosemite Valley Overlook. From there, you will spot a gated cutoff trail that drops down to the floor of Little Yosemite.

Like much of the East Bay hills, Little Yosemite is owned by the San Francisco Water District. The East Bay Regional Parks District has taken the lead in working out a few special deals for the Water District land—opening not only Little Yosemite, but the 28-mile Ohlone Wilderness Trail as well. In the process, it has proved that recreational access can be provided to the public without environmental impact of any kind.

In fact, the biggest impact to this area is not from the few people visiting, but from the numerous wild boar who live here. You can see evidence of their rooting and digging, and if you're lucky, you might even spot one deep in a shaded canyon.

Little Yosemite is also an ideal habitat for a variety of birds. In a morning, you might spot 20 different species. It's a result of the riparian habitat of the Alameda Creek setting, which has alder, willow and sycamore trees.

Out here, you can see red-tailed hawks cruising for their next meal. In addition to boar, deer sightings are common. There are also a few skunks in the hills, so if you bring a dog, keep him on a leash—or it might chase the "black and

Directions: From Highway 680, take the Calaveras Road turnoff just south of the town of Sunol. Turn left at Calaveras Road and continue to Geary Road. Turn left on Geary and follow it to the park entrance.

Special Law: No alcohol permitted in the park.

Fee or Free: Fees are charged for parking and camping.

Camping: There are a few campsites near the parking area, as well as backcountry hike-in camping. A backpack camping permit is required in advance. For information, phone (510) 562-2267.

white cat with the big tail" and end up getting a skunk blast.

Regardless of whether you're there for an overnighter, or just to take the short half-day loop through Little Yosemite, you'll remember this park as a hidden spot—one that you wished you knew about years ago.

Contact: For maps or general information, phone the East Bay Regional Parks District at (510) 635-0135. For trail information, phone the park headquarters at (510) 862-2244.

38

Grant Ranch Park

In the foothills east of San Jose

Sometimes you just can't figure it. Grant Ranch is a park that provides exactly what so many people yearn for, yet it gets less use than any other large park in the Bay Area. To figure out why, I decided to visit for myself, but after a day there, I'm just as confounded as when I'd started.

Grant Ranch County Park, you see, is the Bay Area's suburban wilderness, covering a vast area, 9,000 acres, in the foothills of Mount Hamilton in rural Santa Clara County. The land is perfect for hiking, biking, fishing and even offers a campground that is open on weekends, spring through fall. Yet there's just about nobody here.

And it isn't all that hard to reach either, with a parking area and entrance right along the road to Mount Hamilton, about 10 miles east of San Jose. You pull up, park, put a couple of dollars in a little envelope, deposit it in a metal receptor and you're on your way. And what a way to go.

There are about 50 miles of old abandoned ranch roads and hiking trails, the former perfect for mountain bikes. Hikers can create their own routes, heading off the trail, down canyons and over rims into unpeopled valleys. There is also a 40-acre lake, Grant Lake, which has bass and catfish.

It is a classic oak woodland habitat, and with no pressure from any nearby development, wildlife thrives here. My buddy and I walked less than 10 minutes when we spotted a bobcat near the trail. There are flocks of wild turkeys, 25 to 30 in all, that are commonly seen, and more rarely, herds of wild pigs for those adventuring into the canyons. By the way, there are also some bovines in the area, and if you come across them, the bulls should be given plenty of leeway.

The hills turn lush green from the first good rains of fall and stay that way well into May. In summer, the warm evenings seem perfect for a walk or bike ride. My favorite time is spring, when the lake is full and several Canadian geese are nested down. The creeks pour down the center of canyons, creating many beautiful little waterfalls.

Many parks are not well suited for both mountain biking and hiking, but Grant Ranch is an exception. The abandoned ranch roads are ideal for bikes, with the roads wide enough, hard, and routed well into the backcountry. Meanwhile, hikers can either share the ranch roads (not many bikes out here), or head off on their own across the countryside.

We chose the latter, hiking past the lake, then down into Hall's Valley. We reached a creek at the bottom of the valley, and then headed upstream in search of little waterfalls. We found a procession of them, all flowing strong.

There are many good lookout points, too. For a view, we clambered up to a craggy point at the canyon rim where we could see clear to the South Bay, with miles of wildlands in between. People? What people?

Other prime destinations at the park are Deer Valley, which is huge and tranquil; the crest (2,956 feet) on Washburn Trail above Hall's Valley; and in the spring, the remote habitat around Eagle Lake in the southern reaches of the park.

Grant Lake has some promise for anglers, too. The lake is much larger than you might first expect, and has good cover for bass and catfish. The fishing is just fair, but with the recovery from the drought and the chance for some stocks to jumpstart the fishery, the prospects could be decent in the near future. The park has four other ponds—McCreery, Bass, Rattlesnake, and Eagle Lakes—all nice picnic settings during the cool months.

If all this sounds like a place where you can have a good time, you should give it a go. As for why there is almost nobody else here, well, after completing my research, I still just can't figure it.

❖

Directions: Drive south on Highway 101 to San Jose, then turn east on Highway 680. From there, take the Alum Rock exit, and head east on Alum Rock Avenue. Turn right on Mount Hamilton Road and drive eight miles to the park entrance.

Fee or Free: A nominal entry fee is charged per vehicle on an honor system.

Contact: Phone park headquarters at (408)274-6121.

Chapter 10

The Delta & Stockton/ Modesto

1—The Delta—p. 231
2—Henry W. Coe State Park—p. 236
3—Ohlone Wilderness Trail—p. 243

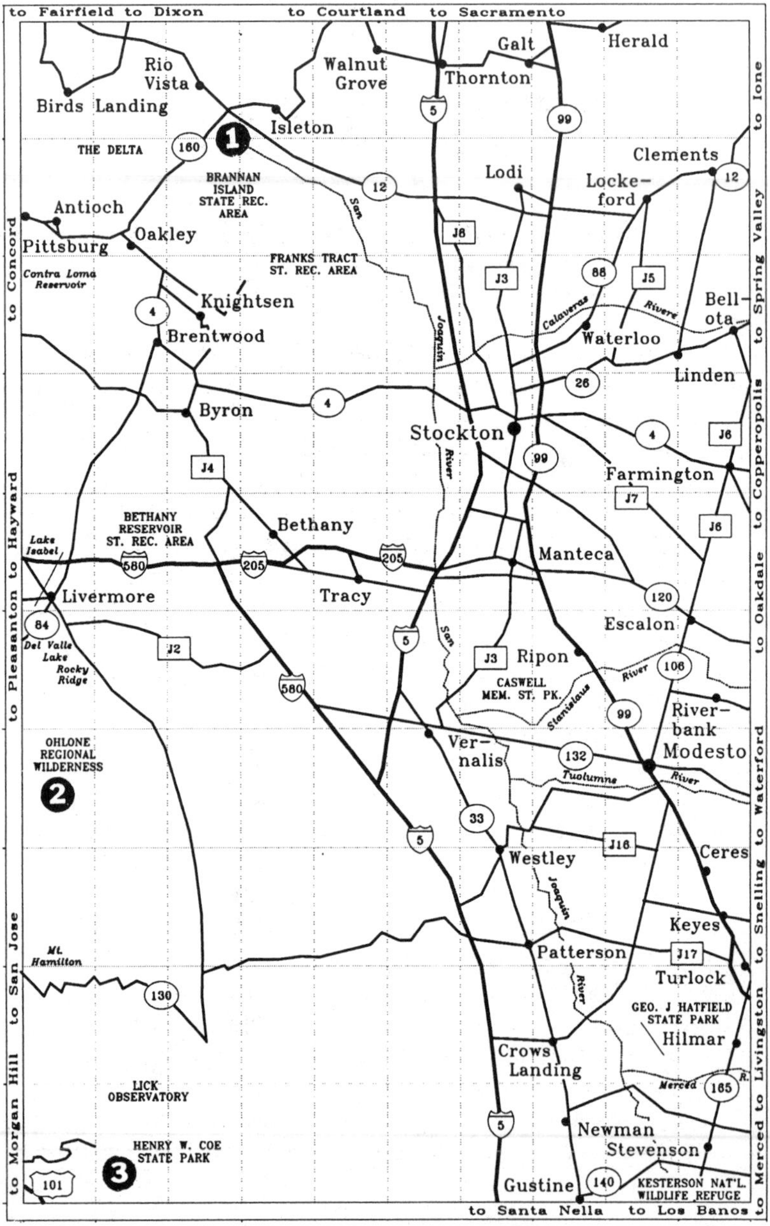

1

The Delta

Bordering Antioch, Rio Vista, Stockton and Byron

If you are losing your zest for life, some doctors prescribe "looking at everything as if you were seeing it for the first time." The Delta is the perfect place to take the cure. Because there is so much to explore, everything you see can literally be for the first time, every day, for the rest of your life. All you need is a boat.

"I've been exploring this son-of-a-gun Delta my whole life and I still haven't seen all of it," Tony Addimando of Livermore told me. "I'm 60 and I'm going to keep at it the next 60 years just to see how much I can see. But you know, we'll never see it all. There's just too much out there."

The Delta is one of America's largest recreation areas for all kinds of activities, and for boaters, it's likely the best. The only comparable waterway is the Okefenokee Swamp that runs over the state line between Georgia and Florida, a tangled bayou web where the public is barred without a guide and a permit.

The public is welcomed to the Delta, on the other hand, and there is room to play for pleasure boaters, fishermen, waterskiers and houseboaters alike. It seems to have no end, with 1,000 miles of navigable waters, 46 boat launches, and 44 public and private campgrounds.

If you don't own a boat, there are many options. Houseboat rentals are available at 16 locations, skiff

Directions: The Delta is crossed by Highways 4, 12 and 160, all of which are accessible from the Bay Area via Interstate 80. A detailed map of the Delta can be obtained for a small fee from any area tackle shop or by mail; write to Hal Schell, Delta Map, P.O. Box 9140, Stockton, CA 95208; (209) 951-7821.

Boat Rentals: Available at Paradise Park Marina at King Island at (209) 952-1000; Rainbow Resort at Brannan Island at (916) 777-6172; and Kourth's Pirate Lair on the Mokelumne River at (916) 777-6464.

rentals can be had at five marinas, and one and two-day trips on tour boats are available out of Stockton, Brentwood, Isleton, Sacramento and Oakland.

The Delta is located about 60 miles from San Francisco, but when you are on the water, it can feel like you're a million miles away from any city. Access routes by car include Highways 4, 12 and 160, which gives you an idea of the Delta's vast size. It is fed by two of the West's largest rivers, the Sacramento and the San Joaquin, along with many big feeder rivers—the Mokelumne, Stanislaus, Tuolumne, Merced and Kings. All of them start as little trickles from melting snow high in the mountains, but eventually join at the Delta, and then rumble as one to San Francisco Bay.

When viewed from the air, the mosaic of smaller connecting rivers, sloughs and islands make the Delta look like the product of intricate masonry work. By boat, it can look like paradise.

The first thing you notice is that no matter where you go, you are shadowed by that big mountain, Mount Diablo. At 3,849 feet, it isn't so tall when compared to peaks in the Sierra Nevada, but since it is surrounded by the Bay Area and Delta virtually at sea level, it can be seen for hundreds of miles.

On the water, old Diablo gives you a reference point, a connection to something familiar, something strong and still amid stirring waters. It also provides a backdrop for spectacular sunsets in the fall, when orange sunlight refracts through cumulus clouds and across the slopes of Diablo and the Delta's waterways.

"I love this old Delta," said Jay Sorensen, of Stockton. I've lived here since I was 10 months old, and in the past 40 years, I've been on the water five days a week. One time I was out 30 straight days, just on my own.

"I just plain love being on the water. We catch a lot of fish, but a few days you just don't get 'em. A lot of people don't mind, because they're out here on the Delta. There's a special feeling to this place."

Musician David Crosby even recorded a song called "The Delta" on a Crosby, Stills & Nash album, an album which was awarded a gold record for sales.

The gold for boaters and anglers, however, is the variety of fisheries the Delta supports.

The biggest attraction is the striped bass, which arrive in their annual fall run. Also in the fall, salmon migrate through the Delta, headed upriver to spawning grounds on the upstream rivers. Resident fish that live here year-round include catfish, black bass, bluegill, and of course, the giant sturgeon.

How big do the sturgeon get? Well, consider the tale of Bill Stratton, who was fishing for striped bass in the lower Delta one November day. It was a warm day, but when "something huge" took his bait, a cold tingle went down his spine. Several hours later, when the fish was finally brought alongside the boat, it looked like some kind of whale.

Boat Launches: Available at Collinsville, Rio Vista, Brannan Island, Antioch Bridge, west tip of Sherman Island, Bethel Island, Walnut Grove, Terminous, and Del's near Clifton Court Forebay, West Stockton.

Camping: Brannan Island State Park is the most popular public area with 32 tent sites, 15 sites for motor homes, 102 sites for tents or motor homes, and a boat launch. For information, phone (916) 777-6671. Private campgrounds are shown on Delta maps, and are detailed in my book *California Camping* (also published by Foghorn Press).

Fishing: Phone Hap's Bait in Rio Vista at (707) 374-2372; Panfili's in Antioch at (510) 757-4970; Delta Harbor in Bethel Island at (510) 684-2260; and Tony's Tackle in Livermore at (510) 443-9191.

Fishing Guides: Two excellent fishing guides are Barry Canevaro at (916) 777-6498, and Jay Sorensen at (209) 478-6645.

House boating: There are 16 Delta houseboat agencies that can be

That's because it was over eight feet long and weighed 390 pounds. It was a world record for 30-pound test line. (A six-foot maximum size limit is now the law.) He had been fishing for stripers, like most of the others who are attracted to the Delta during fall and winter. Stripers have been severely impacted by state and federal water projects, but still number about 750,000, according to Fish and Game estimates. It is a viable fishery.

Sometimes it is better than "viable." In one recent winter season, guide Barry Canevaro and his customers caught 1,300 stripers, releasing many—remarkable numbers by any standards. Some years are not as productive. Weather, water flows, and fishing skills are key determinants.

During November, the first sprinkling of striped bass arrives to the Delta. The big school locates in San Pablo Bay, where it awaits rain and freshened-up waters before heading home. From fall to spring, several traditional spots attract fish: Big Break, San Andreas Shoals, the Mouth of False River, and the Mouth of the Mokelumne on the San Joaquin River; Sherman Lake, the southern tip of Decker Island, just up river of the Rio Vista Bridge, and the shoal at the river bend between Rio Vista and Isleton, on the Sacramento River.

You don't have to fish to have a good time on the Delta. You can go houseboating for a week, or take a two-day tour boat ride from Sacramento to San Francisco's Fisherman's Wharf. Or just show up on a hot Indian Summer weekend and waterski all your willies away.

Or maybe you could just pick out your own spot and watch the water go by. No extra pushing needed.

❖

reached through the Chambers of Commerce for Antioch (510) 757-1800 and Stockton (209) 547-2770.

Tour Boats: One and two-day deluxe tours on large double-decker boats are available out of Oakland by calling (510) 834-3052.

2

Henry W. Coe State Park

In the Gavilan Mountains, southeast of San Jose

Great solitary spots are like $100 bills—the supply never seems to equal the demand. But just a short drive from the San Francisco Bay Area is such a place, a hidden wildland that you can use as your personal fishing reserve.

Imagine catching and releasing dozens of black bass in a weekend, chasing scads of bluegills, and locating fat crappies and sunfish.

That's what you'll find at Henry W. Coe State Park, which sits on the edge of the Bay Area southeast of San Jose in the Gavilan Mountains. Coe Park contains more than 100 square miles of wildlands, some 68,000 acres, with 74 lakes and ponds, more than half of which support fisheries. The prime fishing areas can be found on the 150 miles of trails and long-abandoned ranch roads. It is a place for the person who wants solitude and quality fishing in the same package and who isn't adverse to rugged hiking or mountain biking to find it. If there's a catch, that's it—the lakes and ponds can be reached only by trail, not by car, and the routes in are long and rugged.

For starters, you should obtain a map of the park. With the map in hand, you can plan your route. Without a map, you can wander around to many of the lakes and risk missing much of the quality fishing.

The best bets for bass are Coit Lake, Hoover Lake, Kelly Lake, and the ponds in the Orestimba and Red Creek drainages.

"In the spring, there are times when you can catch and release 200 bass in a weekend at Coit Lake," said ranger Barry Breckling. "I told this one guy that he could catch a bass per cast here. He came back from his trip a few days later and said he did even better than that—he caught two bass at once on the same lure." That guy was me.

Most of the largemouth bass at Coit Lake are in the 10 to 13-inch range, with an occasional larger fish. Hoover, Kelly and Paradise Lakes have bass ranging to larger sizes, and Kelly has the bonus of some big crappies as well, including some in the 14-inch class.

The lakes are virtually untouched, and in some cases the fish are even stunted in size from overpopulation. How is it that few people take advantage of the fishing here? The answer lies in the history of the park. Much of the land was once owned by rancher Marvin Coit, who built most of the ponds and reservoirs 35 to 60 years ago, then stocked them with fish for his personal use. This property was added to Coe Park in the late 1980s; thus, some of the lakes have been fished very lightly in the last 50 years.

One of the park's prettiest settings is Mississippi Lake, an 11-mile hike from headquarters and a haven for the few who know of it. The lake is home to a small number of wild trout with a remarkable growth rate—reaching 16 inches in as little as two years. All should be released, given that there are so few.

The park is about an hour's drive from San Jose. If you're planning on taking advantage of the fishing ahead, I suggest calling or stopping at Coyote Discount Bait and Tackle located five miles south of San Jose off Highway 101. Owner Denise Bradford is a good source for up-to-date information on fishing tips in the area. Another good idea is to call Coe Park for angling and camping conditions.

Once you reach the park, you should get a wilderness permit for overnight backpacking from the rangers. For drive-in campers, there are only 20 campsites at headquarters, each with a picnic table and barbecue. It's on a first-come, first-served basis, with no reservations allowed. A more appealing plan is to obtain a backpack permit from park headquarters, then hike or mountain bike into one of the many wilderness camps. They are spaced apart so that you can hike for five days without having to camp twice in the same area, and in the process, you can sample the wide variety of fishing the park provides.

Since open fires are not permitted in the park, a lightweight backpacking stove should be taken along. A water purification system is a necessity; dehydration can be a problem for some hikers on California's warm spring days. Since thoughts of outstanding fishing can set off ambitious plans, you should be sure to wear a quality pair of hiking boots.

Most hikers travel light, and that includes fishing equipment. Five or six-piece backpack rods, micro spinning or lightweight fly reels, and tiny boxes that will fit into your shirt pocket are the most practical equipment. I use a six-piece, graphite pack rod—which can be used for spin or fly fishing—along with a spinning reel filled with four-pound-test line, and a Plano "macromagnum" tackle box. The latter will fit into a shirt pocket, yet it holds many lures and flies.

What to use? The wise angler would do well to listen to scientist Jerry Smith of San Jose State, who has studied the feeding patterns of trout at Mississippi Lake.

According to Smith, the major source of food for trout there is the water flea, a

Directions:
From San Jose, drive south on US Highway 101 for seven miles to Morgan Hill. Take the East Dunne Avenue exit and drive east, past Morgan Hill, over Lake Anderson for 15 miles to the park entrance.

Maps:
A free map of the park is available from Henry W. Coe State Park, P.O. Box 846, Morgan Hill, CA 95038. Hikers may be interested in a newer, more detailed map, which shows elevation gains and losses, and is for sale at park headquarters.

Fishing:
All anglers should possess a

tiny swimming crustacean. Fly fishermen casting small dart patterns, particularly nymphs, can do quite well in the spring months. Small midge, mosquito, and gnat patterns should be included in your box. At times, it can be necessary to use fly patterns as small as a No. 16 in order to match the size of insects the trout like to eat. Pinch down the barb on your hooks to make it easier to release your catch without injury.

The bass are less picky about what they strike. Some of the lakes have golden shiners as forage fish, and anglers should take a tip from that. In the spring, shad-type plugs in the one to three-inch range are the most effective. I use the floating Rapala in blue/silver, Countdown Rapala in black/silver, and the black/silver Shad Rebel Shorty. For fly fishermen, small bass poppers gently laid along lines of tules with floating fly lines can inspire strikes from bass and bluegills alike. Crappies hit best on small white jigs.

In addition to the fishing, springtime at Coe Park is highlighted by its explosions of wildflowers. In some areas, entire hillsides change color when the Shooting Star blooms. Your hike can take you to summits of 3,000 feet and along hillsides studded with oak, madrone, buckeye and pine. The valleys are bright green from the crackling fresh grasslands.

Blacktail deer and ground squirrels are common sightings; you will likely see far more of them than people. If you spend enough time exploring, you may see wild pig, coyote (or at least hear one), or a golden eagle. Mountain lions and bobcats are widespread, but their cautious natures make sightings rare. Often,

valid California fishing license. They are available at most tackle shops. Call Coe Park at (408) 779-2728 for angling and camping conditions.

Camping: For drive-in campers, there are only 20 campsites at headquarters, each with a picnic table and barbecue. It's on a first-come, first-served basis, with no reservations allowed. With a backpacking permit, you can hike into one of the many wilderness camps.

Camping fees: A state park access fee is charged. Campsite fees vary depending on type of site.

footprints from many of these species can be found in the mud at the edge of lakes.

"This is one of the best parks in California, yet few know of it," said Harry Battlin, District Superintendent of the Gavilan Mountain District. "It offers solitude, yet is close to an urban area. People who spend all week cooped up in an office can set out for Coe Park when they get off work on Friday, camp at headquarters, then head for the hills Saturday morning."

The best time to visit Coe State Park is from February to May, before the arrival of the furnace-like heat of summer. In the spring, the lakes are full to the brim, and the fish are awakening from their annual winter slowdown. They are hungry and will do their best to prove it to you. It won't take much proving before you'll draw the conclusion this place is your own private fishing wonderland.

Wilderness Permits: As soon as you reach the park, you should go to headquarters to acquire a wilderness permit for overnight backpacking.

Contact: Call Coe Park at (408) 779-2728.

Henry W. Coe Park's Top 10 Fishing Spots

With 74 lakes and several streams at Coe State Park, you could spend more time searching for the perfect spot than fishing here. Some 35 to 45 of the lakes and ponds in the park provide fisheries, according to biologist Tom Taylor. Here's a guide to the top prospects, in order of hiking distance:

Frog Lake—Since it is just a 1.5-mile hike from park headquarters, this pond gets more fishing pressure than many of the others. It has bass that top out at 18 inches, although most are smaller, along with bluegills and some catfish.

Bass Pond—Golden shiners provide an excellent forage fish for the bass and bluegill in this lake. Two miles out, it's a good resting stop on your way to the outback.

Mahoney Park—This tiny pond (you can cast across it) was originally stocked with just six bass and two bluegill. It now provides an abundant fishery, although most of the fish are stunted. Figure about a six-mile hike.

Middle Fork of Coyote Creek—The upper stretches of the stream are quite good for rainbow trout. Eight- inchers are common, with a few 12 to 14-inchers. The largest trout are in the 16-inch range.

Hoover Lake—Eager bass fishermen often stop to hit Hoover en route to Colt Lake. Eight miles out, you can't blame them, with largemouth bass in the 12 to 14-inch range.

Colt Lake—A long hike, 11 miles with an elevation climb of 1,600 feet, will bring you to a lake where a bass-per-cast is possible on spring evenings. Most of the fish are in the 10 to 12-inch range, with some larger. A bonus at this lake are large green sunfish that hit bass plugs.

Mississippi Lake—This is the promised land for many. Rainbow trout grow fast here, to 16 inches in just two years, and fish ranging to 26 inches have been caught. A one-fish, 18-inch minimum size limit is in effect. Expect a rugged hike, almost 12 miles from headquarters with a 2,000-foot elevation gain.

Kelly Lake—A good dose of large crappies in this lake makes it a winner, although at a distance of 13 miles from headquarters, it is rarely fished. Bass and green sunfish are also present.

Paradise Lake—Like most lakes in the Orestimba drainage of Coe Park, Paradise provides larger bass than elsewhere in the park. It is best in the spring, and should usually be avoided after mid-May, when it takes a long, hot hike to get there.

Hartman Reservoir—Close to Paradise Lake and quite similar in the fishery it provides. You'll find larger bass than at Colt Lake, which is the benchmark for bass fishing in the park.

3

Ohlone Wilderness Trail

In the East Bay hills from Del Valle to Sunol Parks

Some of the East Bay's most unspoiled back-country is accessible to hikers along a spectacular 28-mile trail. The trail is set in the wilderness between Fremont and Livermore, cutting a path through fields of wildflowers and forests of oak, and rising to 3,000-foot summits. Among the latter is Rose Peak, one of the highest spots in the Bay Area at 3,817 feet.

This hike is called the Ohlone Wilderness Trail and links four parklands in the East Bay Regional Park District. It offers Bay Area hikers a superb close-to-home alternative to mountain backpacking, as well as shorter day hikes that can be taken year-round.

A special bonus here is your chance to see rare birds and wildlife. This region is home to bald and golden eagles, as well as a herd of wild goats near the top of Mission Peak. Tule elk are occasionally spotted along the trail as well.

The Ohlone Wilderness Trail can be an ideal three-day backpack trip, with hikers able to make their trail camps at Sunol and Ohlone Regional Parks. Both are spaced perfectly for a three-day expedition. The opening of the Ohlone Camp solves what was previously a logistics problem. You can now break the distances down to a 12-mile trip the first day, followed by two days at about eight miles each.

Because of the design of the Ohlone Wilderness Trail, portions of it can provide a one-day hike, or what I call an "in-and-outer."

If you want to feel a real sense of accomplishment here on a weekend, plan on a gut-thumping hike, traveling 12 miles the first day, and 16 the second. It might be a little crazy, but you have to have a little of that in you anyway to be a backpacker.

The steepest section of the trail, located near Del Valle Park, has an elevation change of 1,600 feet in just one-and-a-half miles. If you plan on going up, we're talking serious business, but why kill yourself in the process? By traveling west to east, from Mission Peak Regional Preserve to Del Valle Park, you will be going down, not up, in this steep section of trail.

However, don't expect anything easy. From the western trailhead in Fremont, you will climb from 400 feet to Mission Peak at 2,517-feet elevation in 3.5 miles. If you are not in good physical condition, you will find out quickly here. In the spring, this trail is one of the best hikes in the Bay Area. With panoramic views of San Francisco, the Santa Cruz Mountains, and on crystal clear days, even the Sierra Nevada, it won't stay a secret for long.

Directions: To reach the trailhead at the western end of the Ohlone Wilderness Trail from Highway 680, take the Mission Boulevard exit, near Fremont, and turn east on Stanford Avenue. At the end of Stanford Avenue, there is a parking lot, information panel and the trailhead.

Permits/Maps: Since the trail passes through land leased from the San Francisco Water District, a trail permit is required. It can be purchased by mail from the East Bay Regional Park District. Maps and brochures are available as well. For information, phone (510) 635-0135.

Camping: Camping is permitted by reservation only at the Sunol backpack loop and at Del Valle Park; you can book your spot by calling (510) 636-1684.

Day Hikes: For information on one-day hikes, call Sunol Regional Wilderness, (510) 862-2244 or Del Valle Park, (510) 443-4110.

Contact: For general information, phone the East Bay Regional Park District at (510) 635-0135.

Chapter 11

Monterey & Big Sur

1—Big Sur—p. 247
2—Capitola Wharf—p. 250
3—Monterey Bay—p. 252
4—Mount Madonna Park—p. 255
5—Santa Cruz Steam Train—p. 258

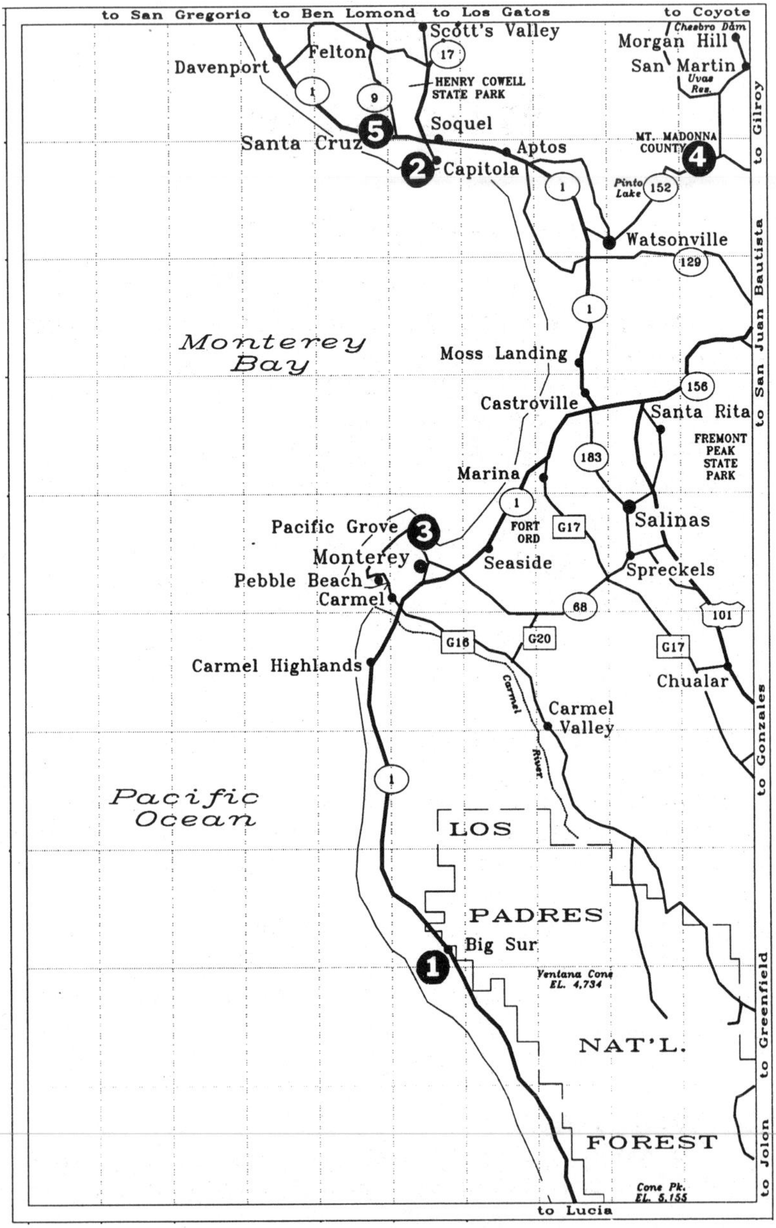

1

Big Sur

On the coast south of Monterey

Visitors to Big Sur, the magnificent stretch of coast south of Monterey, are rewarded with a magical world.

Heading south on Highway 1, you pass by Carmel, crest a hill, and Big Sur opens up before you—an awesome rocky coast bordered by plunging mountains, pockets of redwoods, lush green valleys, and a quiet sense that all is right.

You can travel throughout the hemisphere and not find anything that matches it—a waterfall that runs off a cliff and into the ocean, a beach where sea otters play peek-a-boo in a nearby kelp bed, the best winter backpacking in the West in the adjacent Ventana Wilderness, and lodgings that range from inexpensive rental cabins set in redwoods to $600-a-night suites with ocean views from a hot tub on a deck.

You can just drive on down and take it all in, perhaps stopping at an ocean bluff to watch the spouts from the migrating whales passing by. It seems like just about anything is possible here. While eating at Nepenthe's one evening, the sun set into the ocean while a full moon rose over the hills to the east at exactly the same moment. I've never seen anything like it anywhere.

In Big Sur, the choices are many:

Driving tour

The drive on Highway 1 from the Carmel Highlands south to Lucia is one of the prettiest cruises anywhere.

The route passes ocean bluffs, rocky lookouts, redwood forests, wide open and untouched hillsides, and then plunges down into deep valleys and across bridged canyons. All the time, the ocean spans as far as you can see to the west, often appearing much calmer and more serene than at points north.

Coastal waterfalls

You get redwoods and waterfalls at Julia Pfeiffer-Burns State Park, set right along Highway 1. The biggest waterfall pours over a cliff and onto the beach below, then runs into the ocean. A series of smaller waterfalls are found in the park, up a canyon and surrounded by redwoods, requiring a short hike with a moderate climb.

Friendly sea otters

Just park at the sign for Andrew Molera State Beach, then take the pleasant walk to the untouched beach, about a 30-minute trip. At nearby kelp beds, just beyond a very mild surf, you can often see sea otters playing hide-and-seek. They're friendly little fellows. The rangers at the park will provide visitors with a one-page handout detailing the best places to see sea otters.

Wilderness hiking

The Ventana Wilderness and Los Padres National Forest borders Big Sur to the immediate east, providing the best off-season backpacking in California. Several campgrounds are set at trailheads.

Camping

The easiest-to-reach campground in Big Sur is Ventana Campground, set 29 miles south of Carmel along Highway 1. It is located near the center of Big Sur, making adventuring in the area easy. A nearby grocery store is a plus.

Restaurants

Of the local dining options, Nepenthe's is a favorite, with an ocean view, decent prices and good grub. If "price is no object," a dinner at the Ventana Inn can easily cost you a Ben Franklin, as in the picture that is on a $100 bill, maybe a lot more. Hey, one Caesar salad goes for $16.50. But it's great food.

Monterey side trip

If you want to get back into the hustle and bustle, nearby Monterey to the north has the Monterey Aquarium, Cannery Row, shopping at Carmel, whale watching and fishing trips, and a wide array of restaurants.

Information

For a free Big Sur travel packet, call the Big Sur Chamber of Commerce at (408) 667-2100 or write Monterey County Chamber of Commerce, P.O. Box 1770, Monterey, CA 93942; (408) 648-5350.

2

Capitola Wharf

Near Santa Cruz on Monterey Bay

Time has a way of changing every day, and truth has a way of changing all the time. But when it comes to fishing at Monterey Bay, more than 30 years seem to have flashed by in a day or two. Little appears to have changed here.

It was back in 1962 when my Dad first took my brother and me to Capitola. While fishing, we'd listen to the Giants game; Willie Mays was hitting the left field wall, Billy Pierce was hitting the corners, and we were having the time of our lives, catching rockfish like crazy on the quiet waters of Monterey Bay.

More than 30 years later, Willie Mays is long gone, but Barry Bonds now patrols Candlestick Point, and at Capitola, the good times remain for the few people who know of the angling attractions here.

Capitola Wharf is one of the few places on the West Coast where you can rent a small boat for a day of fishing. Hence, an adventure is waiting here for any angler yearning for it. It is the perfect place for a father and son fishing trip. Just ask my Dad.

At 7 a.m. or so, we'd arrive at Capitola, which is a relatively short drive (under two hours) from San Francisco. After hopping aboard a rental skiff, it is just a five-minute ride to the prime fishing grounds, situated at the edge of the nearby kelp beds. Spots such as

Adams Reef, Surfers Reef, and South Rock all produce outstanding fishing.

With rod in hand, you allow your bait to descend to the shallow sea bottom. Squid-baited shrimpflies, strips of mackerel, or cut anchovy chunks entice a surprising variety of rockfish. A bonus is that very little weight is required to reach the bottom here, often just a few ounces.

Most folks use light saltwater rods, with line rated at 12 to 20-pound test. Rod rentals are available at Capitola Pier for a few dollars.

In the fall, Monterey Bay gets its quietest water of the year, as well as its best rockfishing.If you'd like to tussle with some heavyweights, autumn also brings with it a good number of blue sharks. For folks with even bigger plans, long-range trips are made this time of year in search of albacore and tuna. If you just want to stick to the pier, crabbing and fishing for mackerel can be productive.

Finding a common ground for a father and son can be difficult, but a fishing trip from Capitola can provide that rare space, and in the process, some special memories.

Maybe time doesn't have to change every day after all.

Directions: From San Francisco, take either Highway 17 or Highway 1 south to Santa Cruz. Continue south to Capitola and take the 41st Avenue exit. Turn left on Capitola Road and go through three stop signs. Continue west to the wharf; parking areas are available nearby.

Fee or Free: Access to the wharf is free, but fees are charged for the rental of skiffs, rods and reels.

Contact: For tips on fishing, weather and sea conditions, call the Capitola Wharf at (408) 462-2208.

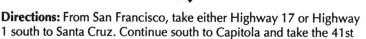

3

Monterey Bay

Along the Monterey coast

Monterey stands apart from the rest of California, both north and south. It combines the best of both worlds—Southern California's weather and Northern California's rural beauty, and it offers the ideal short vacation spot for Bay Area residents.

The area became famous in the early 1940s due to Steinbeck's novel *Cannery Row*. But after the sardine industry was wiped out by overkill in 1948, Monterey became better known as a hangout for the rich. For other folks, it has taken the spectacular Monterey Aquarium to bring them back to the area.

And people like what they see. There is as much variety in outdoor recreation here as at any place in the state. Spring is the best time to visit, when the salmon are swimming along inshore areas, the hills are green, and the fields of wildflowers are in full bloom.

The Monterey Aquarium can be the focus of a multi-day trip to the area. The giant tanks are like glass houses, where people get an inside view of all the levels of marine life in Monterey Bay. Re-creations of a kelp forest, deep reefs and a sea otter playpen are the big attractions. But the sideshows are just as fascinating. For example, you can dip your hands in the water and touch a stingray, or look through a microscope at tiny sea creatures.

A three-hour aquarium tour can inspire you to go on other mini-adventures in the area. You can take what you've learned at the aquarium and extend it to the wild outdoors. You can go fishing, hiking, whale watching, scuba diving, ocean kayaking, or camping on a beach or in a forest. Take your pick.

Monterey Bay is cut by a deep underwater canyon that extends west from Moss Landing. For years fishermen have had great success here, and exhibits at the aquarium explain why. The 5,000-foot-deep canyon generates nutrient-rich water that sets off one of the West Coast's most diverse marine systems.

In Monterey Bay, good runs of salmon arrive every spring from the north, and by mid-summer, schools of albacore come from the south. It's the best of both worlds.

Because the Monterey Peninsula juts out into the Pacific Ocean, it is a prime area for whale watching, by boat or on shore. Point Pinos, Cypress Point, Point Lobos and the Asilomar State Beach in Pacific Grove all provide lookouts for whales. Sightings usually remain good through April.

Monterey is known for its first-class, expensive lodging and restaurants, but during the warm days of spring and summer, a campout is a good alternative.

You have your pick of parks set on ocean frontage or in pine trees. Coastal state parks on Monterey Bay's shoreline include Sunset, Seacliff and New Brighton State Beach. If you want trees, Big Sur State Park is located south of Monterey on Highway 1. If you want solitude, you can head for the outback in Los Padres National Forest.

Monterey Bay is a remarkable area, and you can feel it just by watching the waves roll in. The water seems a deeper blue than anywhere along the California coast. It has a tranquilizing effect.

You can search the Pacific Coast and find few places that come close to matching it.

Directions: The Monterey Bay area is located approximately 115 miles south of San Francisco on Highway 1.

Monterey Aquarium: Located at the north end of Cannery Row, the aquarium is open from 10 a.m. to 6 p.m. daily. For more information, call (408) 375-3333 or (408) 649-1770.

Fishing: Salmon and rockfishing trips are available on the *Point Sur Clipper*. For information, call Sam's Sportfishing at (408) 372-0577.

Whale Watching: Chris' Charters, (408) 375-5951, makes whale-watching trips. By shoreline, Point Pinos and Asilomar State Beach are prime lookouts.

Scuba Diving: Reefs and the underwater trench are rich marine regions that are top areas to explore. For information, call Bamboo Reef at (408) 372-1685, or Aquarius Dive Shop at (408) 375-6605.

Ocean Kayaking: You might have a sea otter as your partner. Instructions and rentals are available from Monterey Bay Kayaks. For information, call them at (408) 373-5357.

Big Sur State Park: One of California's top state parks, it's located off Highway 1 just south of Monterey. For information, call (408) 667-2316.

Beach Camping: Camping by the Bay is available at Marine Dunes, Sunset, Seacliff, and New Brighton State Beaches. For information, call the California Department of Parks at (408) 649-2840.

Hiking/Backpacking: Hundreds of miles of trails cut through Los Padres National Forest, which is located just inland from Big Sur State Park. For information, call (805) 683-6711.

Lodging/Restaurants: For a list of Monterey's accommodations, call the Monterey Chamber of Commerce at (408) 648-5350.

4

Mount Madonna Park

West of Gilroy in the Santa Cruz Mountains

Mount Madonna Park provides great scenic beauty, good hiking, camping and horseback riding. It is located between Gilroy and Watsonville, and set around the highest peak in the southern range of the Santa Cruz Mountains. A three or four-hour visit here, capped by dinner at one of nearby Monterey Bay's fine restaurants, can make for a classic day.

In late summer, this area can be like a hot volcano, but the temperate days of spring and early summer provide ideal weather for hikes and picnics. In spring the grasslands bloom in color from brilliant wildflower displays.

The park covers more then 3,000 acres, and if you take the time to hike and explore it, you will find surprising diversity. Imagine redwoods near Gilroy. No way? Look closer. The park's major canyons not only shelter redwoods and tan oaks, but are also cut by streams gurgling over rocks and submerged limbs. Redwoods up to 100 feet tall can be found at the top of Mount Madonna, as well as on the west slopes. There are also some rare white deer in a pen accessible only to hikers.

Mount Madonna Park includes a network of 18 miles of trails, which intersect in several spots, allowing you to custom tailor your hike. Be sure to obtain a trail map from park headquarters, since the best hikes are combinations of different trails. My favorites are the Redwood and Blackhawk Canyon Trails. At 1,897 feet, the elevation of the peak of Mount Madonna may not seem like much, but since most of the surrounding land is near sea level, the peak can provide a lookout with impressive views. To the west, you can see the Salinas Valley unfold to Monterey Bay, and to the east, the vast Santa Clara basin.

Some of the better vistas can be seen without even leaving your car. Pole Line Road and Summit Road lead to near the summit. But don't be content with that. This park has many secrets, none of which can be discovered by car. The most unusual find is the pen rangers built in 1993, home for a few rare white deer. If you have never seen white deer, this is a must-do hike.

If Mount Madonna Park sounds like the kind of place where you'd like to spend more than an afternoon, there are some 115 campsites available on a first-come, first-served basis. Unlike state parks, reservations are not necessary. Why? Because most folks have never even heard of this place. It is a well-kept secret.

Directions: From the Bay Area, take US 101 south to Gilroy. Turn west on Highway 152 and proceed to Pole Line Road. Turn north and continue to the park. For the slow, winding, scenic route from Gilroy or Watsonville, take the Old Mount Madonna Road to the Summit Road entrance.

Maps: A good map detailing 18 miles of trails can be obtained at park headquarters for free.

Pets: Your dog can be brought along for the ride, but is not permitted on trails.

Fee or Free: An entrance fee is charged. There is a fee for camping.

Camping: Campsites are taken on a first-come, first-served basis. Group camping reservations can be obtained by phoning (408) 358-3751.

Contact: Park headquarters can be reached at (408) 842-2341, though the phone line is sometimes not attended.

5

Santa Cruz Steam Train

From Santa Cruz to Felton

Spending a day touring the Santa Cruz Mountain redwoods by train and by foot is like venturing back into history.

Roaring Camp Train Rides offers two unique trips, one that putts from Felton to Santa Cruz, another that meanders up to Bear Mountain. Potential sidetrips include the Santa Cruz Boardwalk and Henry Cowell Redwood State Park near Felton, both of which are within short walking distance of the train's two staging areas. The adventure is based near Felton in the Santa Cruz Mountains. This region has the Bay Area's largest stand of redwoods, a pretty stream called the San Lorenzo River, and several little restaurants in the area where the motto is still "good grub—cheap."

An old steam train set on a narrow gauge track attracts most of the publicity to this area. It should. The old mare huffs and puffs, then leads you on a unique scenic tour of Bear Mountain. We're not talking about the Silver Bullet here. This train just kind of goes, pretzeling its way through the redwoods, with the six-mile round-trip taking about an hour and 15 minutes. There are both open and closed passenger cars, including a special observation car that is open on the sides and closed on top. Riding in that car adds a nice dimension to the experience, allowing you to smell the redwoods, hear the old steam belcher, and feel in close touch with your surroundings.

The other train ride is routed between Felton and Santa Cruz. The route roughly parallels Highway 9, running along the San Lorenzo River, over a trestlework bridge, through a tunnel, and into Santa Cruz. The train features open-air and old-fashioned parlor cars, with seating both inside and outside.

This train, too, is no speed demon. It runs on a broad gauge track and is powered by an old diesel. Perfect, eh? It takes an hour and 15 minutes for the trip to Santa Cruz, one way, traveling just under five miles-per-hour. The train meanders. It moseys. It ambles. But it gets there.

Depending on where you start from on this train, the destination is either the Santa Cruz Boardwalk or Henry Cowell Redwoods State Park in Felton. The staging area in Santa Cruz is adjacent to the Boardwalk, and the staging area in Felton is about 30 steps from the entrance to the state park. Both destinations provide quality side trips. The city of Santa Cruz deserves some credit for cleaning up the Boardwalk. A while back, it was getting run down, but the place has been spruced up and it's once again great for a family outing.

The other option is Henry Cowell State Park. The park has 20 miles of hiking trails. You can route trips to a lookout where you can see the Pacific Ocean (when the fog isn't in), or through redwoods and to the San Lorenzo River. If you want to stay overnight, a campground is available, though reservations

Directions: From the Peninsula, take Highway 280 south to Highway 17. Take Highway 17 west toward Santa Cruz, then take the second Scotts Valley exit, Glen Canyon/ Mount Hermon Road. Take Mount Hermon Road through Scotts Valley and continue until it deadends at Graham Hill Road. Turn left, drive a half mile, and Roaring Camp will be on the right.

From the coast, take Highway 1 south to Santa Cruz, then turn east on Highway 17. Take the Scotts Valley/ Big Basin turnoff, which will lead you to Mount Hermon

Road. Continue until it deadends at Graham Hill Road, then turn left, drive a half mile, and Roaring Camp will be on the right.

Fee or free: Reasonable rates for adults and children 3 through 15, with prices slightly higher for the Santa Cruz tour.

Contact: For a brochure and schedule information, phone Roaring Camp Train Rides at (408) 335-4484.

are necessary during the summer.

When you add it all up—an old-style train ride, a hike through redwoods, maybe a tour of the boardwalk, topped off by dinner at a good restaurant—this is one of the top single-day destinations in this part of the state.

Chapter 12

Hollister & Pinnacles

1—Pinnacles National Monument—p. 263

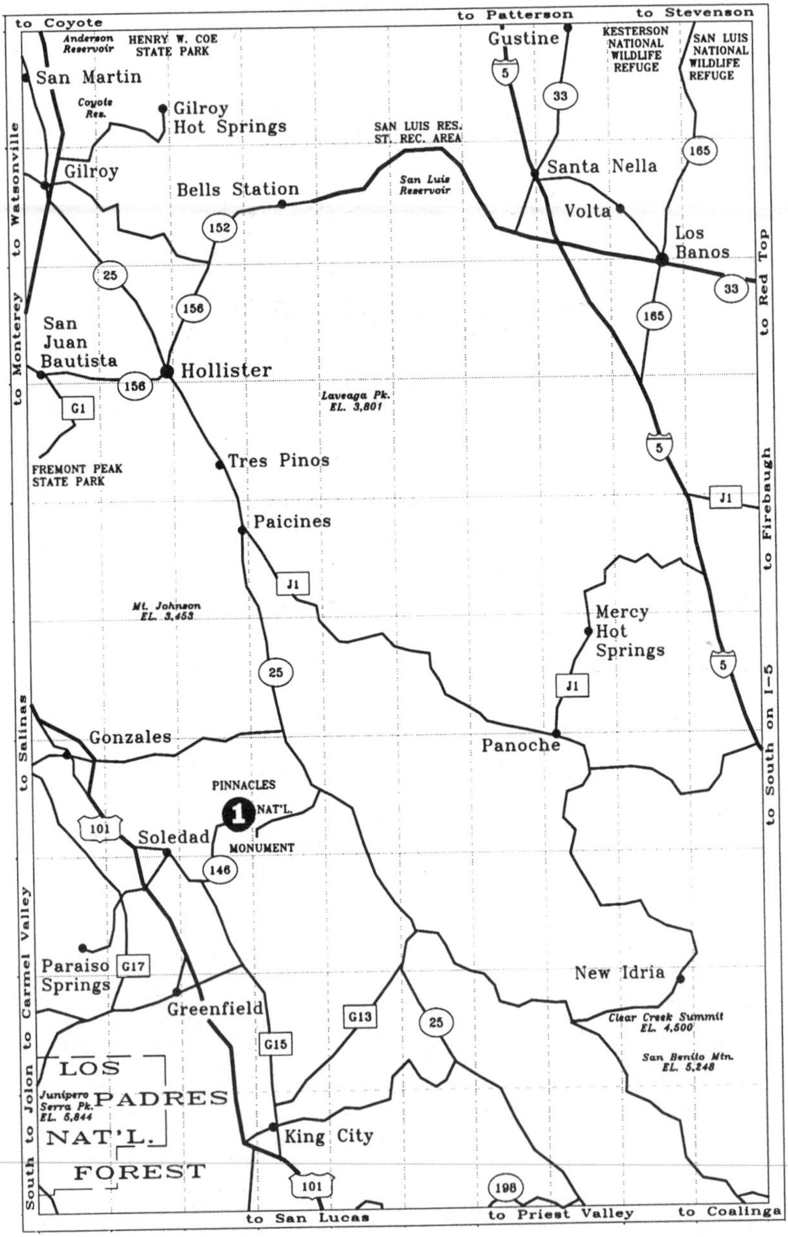

1

Pinnacles National Monument

South of Hollister

If you've ever wanted to stop the world and jump off, Pinnacles National Monument is a good place to do it, at least for a weekend. For one thing, it looks like a different planet. For another, it is a completely out-of-the-way place, located in obscure San Benito County, about an hour's drive south of Hollister. Nobody comes here by accident.

Add those factors together and Pinnacles provides an ideal hideaway for an overnight trip, whether you just want to get away from it all or want the chance to explore the strange caves and huge volcanic clusters that cover much of the 16,000-acre park.

Winter and early spring are the only times to make the trip. In the summer and fall, it's hot, dry and sticky down here. You might as well plan a trip to Mercury. It can get extremely hot, like in the 90s and 100s, just about every day of the summer. Spring is the time to come.

This is a place of secrets, and the two extensive cave systems hold many of them. The Bear Gulch Cave is approximately four-tenths of a mile long and the Balconies Cave extends about three-tenths of a mile.

They are not subterranean tunnels, like the old gold mines of the Sierra Nevada, but talus caves. They were created over time in canyons and crevices where rocks have slipped or fallen, and storm runoff has removed the softer volcanic material. The result is a unique series of connected spaces under a rocky canopy.

Once you enter the cave system, you feel like you are entering a new world. If you turn your flashlight off, it gets as dark as the sockets of a skull. You wave your hand in front of your face and you can't see it.

As you probe on, you need to keep the light roaming the darkness, not just where you're walking. Do the latter and you are liable to ram your head into a stalactite, which is a different way of adjusting your thought patterns than you originally planned with this trip.

All the cave walks are self-guided, which adds a lot to the adventure. (At the Oregon Caves, only guided group tours are permitted.) If you forget your flashlight, rangers sell them. If you remember to bring you own, be certain your bulb and batteries are fresh.

The caves are subject to closure if there are earthquakes or heavy rains, either of which can loosen material. What the heck, finding it closed is better than having a five-ton volcanic block fall on your big toe. However, when rain is light, the caves can be open all winter without closure.

The rest of the park is as unique as the cave system. The Pinnacles consist of a huge rock mass that suddenly rises in chutes from the valley floor. It was cre-

Directions: To enter from the east side from the Bay Area, drive south on US 101 to Gilroy and east to Highway 156. Turn south and drive to Hollister. Continue south on Highway 25 for about 30 miles, then turn west on Highway 146 and proceed to the park.

To enter from the west, drive south on US 101 to Soledad. Turn east on Highway 146 (a winding, narrow road) and continue to the primitive camp.

Camping: Pinnacles Campground Inc. is a privately-operated campground with full facilities,

ated from a volcanic blast, similar to the one that formed the Sutter Buttes north of Sacramento. Hawkins Peak, a vertical barren spire at 2,720 feet, is what remains of the volcano's flume.

The trails can take you to the canyon ridges, which provide great lookouts onto the surrounding valley. The High Peaks Trail is one of the best. Because this is a primitive area with no piped water, be certain to bring a filled canteen or day pack with your favorite liquid refreshment.

Two campgrounds are available, one primitive and isolated (located on the west side of the park), the other privately developed with full facilities (located on the east side of the park). Because no road extends through the park, you can't just hop over to the other if your first choice is filled. It is strongly advised that you phone ahead for space availability. Weekends can be crowded on the east side.

The primitive camp is located on the western side of Pinnacles National Monument. You reach it by driving south on Highway 101, then turning east on Highway 146. The road narrows and leads to a small campground with 23 sites, with water and toilet facilities available nearby.

The east side gets more visitation because it has a better access road and full facilities, and is closer to the Bear Gulch Caves. The camp here is called Pinnacles Campground Inc. and is privately operated. It includes 125 sites, including space for motor homes, but even so, it can fill up on weekends. To assist with the growing number of visi-

located on the east side. It is often full on winter and spring weekends. For more information: (408) 389-4462. The primitive camp is located on the west side and has 23 campsites, with water and toilet facilities available. Rangers can be reached at (408) 389-4526.

Fee or free: An entrance fee is charged, along with fees for camping.

Note: The privately-owned, developed campground has slightly lower rates than the primitive campground inside the park.

Contact:
Phone the headquarters at (408) 389-4485.

tors, rangers have arranged a shuttle system to carry day visitors from a parking area to the caves.

A good time to plan a trip is during March or early April. That is when the valley's wildflowers begin to bloom, and with the greened-up hills as a backdrop, you can see the most colorful scenes of the year here.

Chapter 13

Tahoe Area

1—Hope Valley—p. 269
2—Lake Tahoe—p. 271
3—Sierra Nevada Lakes—p. 274

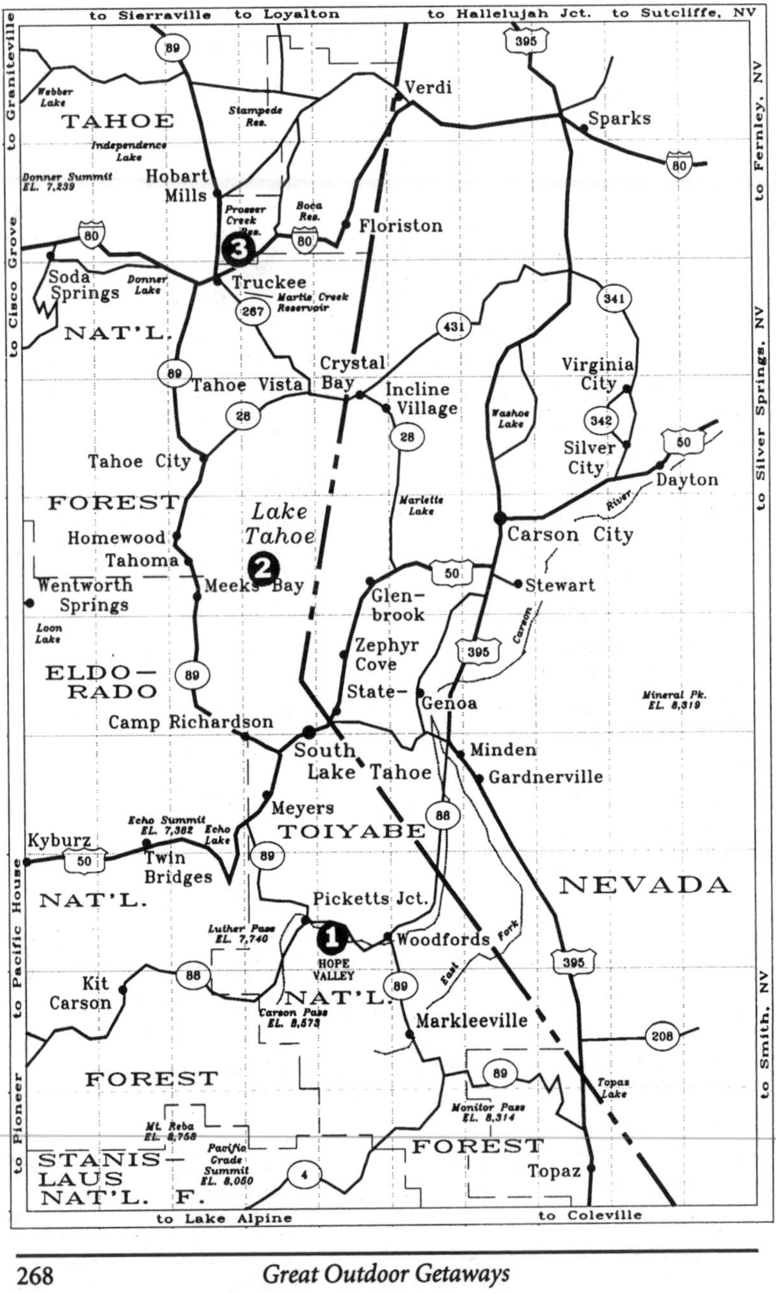

1

Hope Valley

Near Carson Pass

The early pioneers traveled more than 2,000 miles to face the Sierra Nevada, their last barrier to the land of golden dreams in the Sacramento Valley. In the 1990s, "pioneers" from the Bay Area head to South Tahoe with golden dreams of casinos. As with the 49ers, a day or two here in nearby Hope Valley can add a degree of reality to your trip.

The remnants and scars of the westward migration of gold seekers can still be seen in Hope Valley, a territory known for its natural beauty, historic character, hiking and trout fishing. Campgrounds set alongside the Carson River, along with cabins at Sorensen's Resort, can provide a temporary home, and many folks venture to this area for the hot springs in nearby Markleeville.

Hope Valley is located about 20 miles south of Lake Tahoe. The valley is divided by Highway 88, a quiet two-laner. Access to the campgrounds and the river is easy.

A good day-hike, which most people will find quite easy, is to retrace some of the same steps taken by the pioneers on the Emigrant Trail. Sorensen's Resort, which is more an assemblage of cabins than a resort, offers a guided tour of this trail. Much of this route, which continues over Carson Pass, was used by the Pony Express.

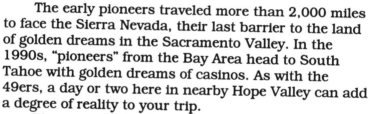

Come evening and it's time to pull out your fishing rod. The trout fishing on the Carson River provides the classic "babbling brook" setting that armchair fishermen like to imagine. Because access to the river is so easy, the fish can be spooked by folks who approach without care. The trout should be stalked. Regardless of your experience, you should move to a new spot after just a few casts. The best fishing here in late summer is usually in the last hour of light, with carefully presented fly patterns. The mosquito, abundant here, is a favorite. Stocks are made at the bridges and campgrounds along the stream.

Summer is the most popular time to visit, but my favorite period is in the fall, after Labor Day weekend has passed. Most of the summer vacationers are back home, the road is no longer clogged up with Winnebagos, and you can see the remarkable change in seasons, from summer to fall. In the Sierra Nevada, the aspens explode in color, and being here in the center of it can make you feel much as the pioneers did 130 years ago.

❖

Directions: From the Bay Area, take Interstate 80 to Sacramento. Turn east on US 50 and drive 90 miles to the Highway 89 turnoff. Turn south and continue for about 15 miles to Hope Valley.

Log Cabins: Log cabins are available through Sorensen's Resort; they include two beds and a kitchen. Sorensen's also offers a special package: two nights of lodging, four meals and a tour guide for the Emigrant Trail.

Camping: Campsites are free on a first-come, first-served basis. Campgrounds operated by the Forest Service sit at river's edge and are quite popular during the summer.

Contact: For information regarding fishing tips, tour guides or cabin reservations, contact Sorensen's at (916) 694-2203. For camping information, contact the Forest Service at (916) 694-2911. For a brochure on the Emigrant Trail tour and cabin rentals, write Sorensen's, Hope Valley, CA 96120.

2

Lake Tahoe

The natural laws of gravity don't seem to apply at the casinos at Lake Tahoe. Although the gaming tables are perfectly level, your money seems always to slip out of your hands and into the grasp of a blackjack dealer. Those wary of this phenomenon know that the best bet you can make at Tahoe is to minimize your time at the casinos and instead take your chances with the fishing, boating and hiking.

Tahoe's excitement, adventures and remarkable natural beauty make it the number one weekend vacation area for Californians. Just make sure you come home with your shirt; a lot of people don't.

Tahoe is "The Lake in the Sky," as Mark Twain called it, a natural wonder set amid miles of national forest. It is colored the deepest blue of any lake in California, a true gem situated at 6,000 feet. A definite tinge of mystery surrounds it. Just how deep is Lake Tahoe? Some scientists claim Tahoe is 1,648 feet deep, yet some old-timers say it is bottomless. The fact that boats and airplanes have disappeared in the lake, never to be seen again, seems to support the latter.

When it comes to the fishing, there is a lot less mystery. Big mackinaw, rainbow and brown trout, along with kokanee salmon, attract anglers from throughout the Pacific Northwest. However, newcomers to Tahoe are usually quite surprised at the techniques used to catch these monsters.

The big fish, the mackinaw trout, are deep at Tahoe, and sportfishing boat skippers use downriggers to troll 180 to 260 feet deep. Your fishing line is clipped to a separate reel of wire line and a 10-pound weight, and both lines descend to the trolling depth. When you get a strike, your line pops free of the release clip on the weighted line and you fight the fish free of any lead weight. Skippers troll just off the edge of the underwater shelf, using lures such as J plugs. Be on the water at first light, because the bite is often kaput by 10 a.m., or fish when the moon is in its dark cycles.

Some locals in small boats score with rainbow and brown trout by trolling near the surface in coves. They use Rapala minnows or a flasher/night-crawler combination. But for the big trout, you have to go deep, way deep.

Timber Cove Marina, which is closer to the Stateline area, offers boat tours and scuba diving, in addition to fishing trips.

A tremendous number of camp-grounds, motels and resorts ring the lake, but reservations are still a must in the summer.

If you want to break free from the crowds here, a good alternative is to visit Tahoe National Forest, which borders the north shore of the lake. It provides good backpacking trails, as well as access to wilderness. And out here you don't have to worry about unfriendly dealers either.

Trout fishermen have two good rivers in the area. To the north is the Truckee River, a fine trout stream with excellent access, and to the south is the Carson River. If your idea of breaking free is not camping, well, some fine motels can be found in the Tahoe Basin. If you want to

Camp-grounds: Five camp-grounds are operated by the California State Park System, two by the U.S. Forest Service. Campsite reservations are available through Mistix; phone (800) 444-7275. For information on privately-operated camp-grounds, contact the Tahoe Chamber of Commerce or refer to *California Camping: The Complete Guide* (Foghorn Press, San Francisco).

Tahoe National Forest: For information or permits (for Desolation Wilderness), call the U.S. Forest Service at (916) 587-3558.

stick to your car instead of hoofing it on a trail, it takes about three hours to complete the loop drive around the entire lake, about 70 miles on a two-laner.

Just don't spend too much time at the casinos. Never forget that the blackjack tables have their own special laws of gravity.

Boat Tours: A wide variety of cruises are available. For the *M.S. Dixie,* call (702) 588-3508; for the *Tahoe Queen,* call (916) 541-3364. Rentals of small boats are available at many marinas around the lake.

Lodging: Call the Tahoe Visitor's Bureau at (800) 288-2463.

Contacts: Contact the Tahoe Chamber of Commerce at (916) 541-5255, or by writing P.O. Box 15090, South Lake Tahoe, CA 95702.

3

Sierra Nevada Lakes

Near Truckee

Interstate 80 is the route to zip you up to one of six prime camping, fishing and hiking areas near Truckee, taking about four hours driving time from the Bay Area. You don't need a four-wheeler, just four wheels and an engine, and you can discover Donner Lake, Martis Lake, and Boca, Stampede and Prosser Reservoirs. The air has the crackling fresh scent of pines up here on a pure mountain morning.

Donner Lake

This can be a good choice for family camping. Since the lake sits directly adjacent to Highway 80, all facilities are provided, and the area is well developed with cabins and roads. However, it is for those same reasons that many serious anglers skip Donner. Donner State Memorial Park at the east end of the lake is for weekend campers, and reservations are advised. A public boat ramp is available at Donner Village Resort, where trout fishing is good in the summer. But if you hope to tangle with something big here, like a 15-pound mackinaw or brown trout, then you'd better be on the water at daybreak in a boat, trolling a Countdown Rapala or J plug near the northern shoreline.

Martis Creek Reservoir

This is a small lake that has been set aside by the Department of Fish and Game as a special fishing refuge. There are wild trout, but all fish are released, and only the use of artificial lures or flies with a single barbless hook is allowed. It's definitely not for family campers. But for proficient fly fishermen, there is no better place to tangle with 18 to 24-inch wild trout, brown or lahontan cutthroat. Boat motors are not permitted on the lake, so fishing from a float tube or small raft is ideal. The Sierra View Campground has hookups for motor homes, and provides fair sites for tent camping.

To get to Martis Lake, turn south on Highway 267 at Truckee, then after six miles, turn east on the first turnoff to the lake.

Boca Reservoir

Boca Camp, on the far side of the lake, is the best spot to camp, and has a boat ramp nearby. Motor home hookups are available nearby. A few giant, elusive brown trout and a good sampling of stocked rainbow trout make Boca a good lake for trollers.

Boca can be reached by turning north on Stampede Meadow Road, six miles past Truckee.

Prosser Reservoir

Prosser is tucked away just five miles from Truckee, so supplies can be obtained with a very short drive. A 10 mile-per-hour speed limit on the lake keeps skiers off, and with steady trout fishing, makes the lake a favorite for local anglers. Prosser Campground is perched on a wooded lake overlook and is a great spot. However, many campers don't discover it, since they usually stop at the first campground they see here, Lakeside Camp.

Stampede Reservoir

If you want the classic Sierra experience, this is a good choice. It offers some 250 postcard-type campsites and consistent trout fishing year-round. A bonus is a chance at big brown trout; troll a large Rapala directly across from the boat launch along the northern shoreline, and be on the water at dawn.

Stampede is tucked away at 6,000 feet, 14 miles from Truckee, and eight miles off Highway 80 from the Stampede Road turnoff.

Maps: The U.S. Forest Service has published a map that details all fishing waters, campsites, Forest Service roads and backpack trails. Ask for the map of Tahoe National Forest from the Office of Information, U.S. Forest Service, 630 Sansome Street, San Francisco, CA 94111.

Fishing Tips: Call either Tahoe Truckee Sports at (916) 587-9000, Mountain Hardware at (916) 587-4844, or Tourist Liquor & Sporting Goods at (916) 587-3081.

Camping/Lodging: Phone the Truckee Chamber of Commerce at (916) 587-2757, or write P.O. Box 2757, Truckee, CA 96160.

Contact: For more information, call U.S. Forest Service headquarters at (415) 705-2874.

Chapter 14

Yosemite & Mammoth Area

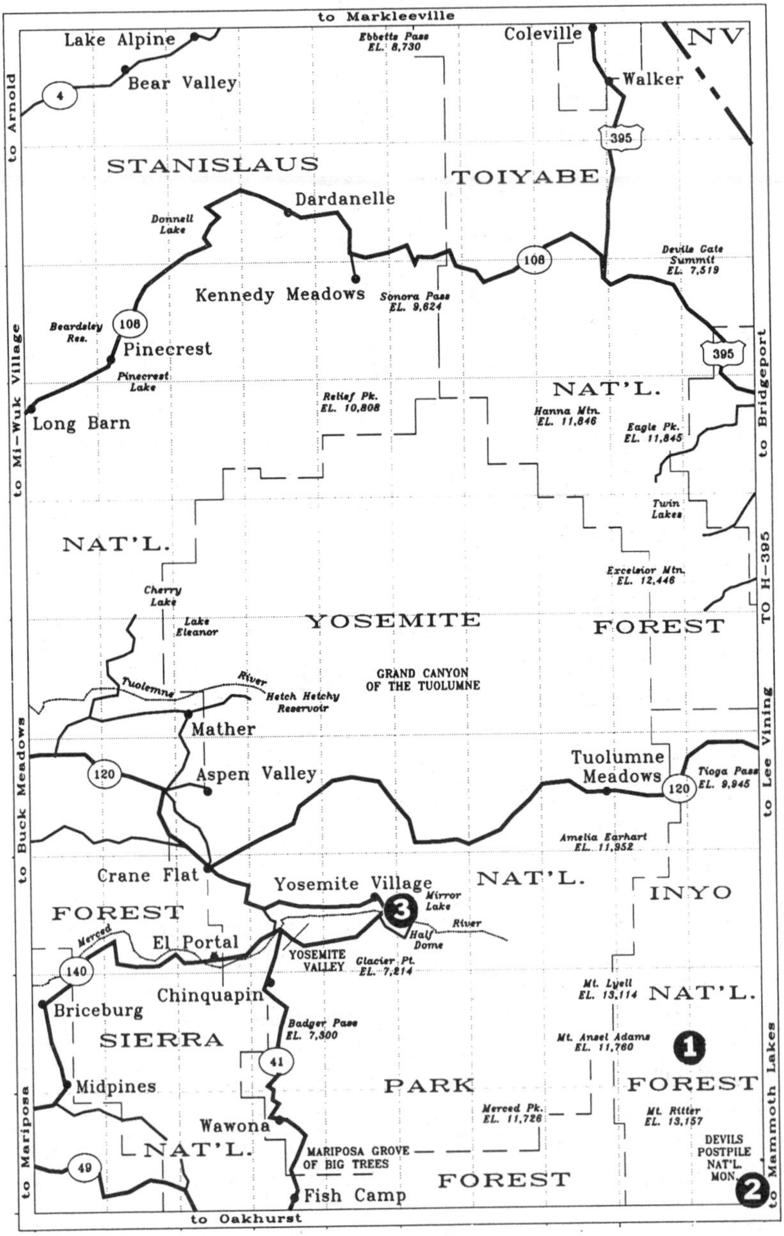
to Markleeville
Lake Alpine
Bear Valley
Ebbetts Pass EL. 8,730
Coleville
Walker
NV
to Arnold
STANISLAUS
TOIYABE
Dardanelle
Donnell Lake
Kennedy Meadows
Sonora Pass EL. 9,624
Devils Gate Summit EL. 7,519
Beardsley Res.
Pinecrest
Pinecrest Lake
Long Barn
to Mi-Wuk Village
Relief Pk. EL. 10,808
NAT'L.
Hanna Mtn. EL. 11,846
Eagle Pk. EL. 11,845
to Bridgeport
Twin Lakes
NAT'L.
Excelsior Mtn. EL. 12,446
TO H-395
Cherry Lake
Lake Eleanor
YOSEMITE
FOREST
GRAND CANYON OF THE TUOLUMNE
Tuolumne River
Hetch Hetchy Reservoir
Mather
Aspen Valley
Tuolumne Meadows
Tioga Pass EL. 9,945
to Lee Vining
to Buck Meadows
Amelia Earhart EL. 11,952
Crane Flat
Yosemite Village
Mirror Lake
NAT'L.
INYO
FOREST
Merced River
El Portal
Half Dome
YOSEMITE VALLEY
Glacier Pt. EL. 7,214
Briceburg
Chinquapin
Mt. Lyell EL. 13,114
NAT'L.
SIERRA
Badger Pass EL. 7,300
Mt. Ansel Adams EL. 11,760
Midpines
PARK
FOREST
Merced Pk. EL. 11,726
Mt. Ritter EL. 13,157
Wawona
NAT'L.
MARIPOSA GROVE OF BIG TREES
DEVILS POSTPILE NAT'L. MON.
to Mariposa
Fish Camp
FOREST
to Mammoth Lakes
to Oakhurst
4
108
395
120
140
41
49
1
2
3

1

High Sierra Hiking

In the Southeast Sierra, west of Mammoth

You walk in the footsteps of legends in the high Sierra. With each step, you feel the shadows of ghosts, of Muir, Walker, Adams, Carson and Bridger. These shadows from the past always seem to be there, along with the beauty of the present—the untouched, pure crystal mountain streams, forests and vibrant meadows filled with wildlflowers.

My favorite piece of wilderness is in the high country of the southern Sierra, in and around the Ansel Adams Wilderness west of Mammoth and the nearby John Muir Wilderness to the south. These are among the prettiest backpacking areas in the world, where John Muir and Ansel Adams got much of their inspiration, with the Minaret Mountains providing the backdrop for some of nature's finest architecture.

The trail system is extensive in the Ansel Adams Wilderness, with 250 miles in the Minarets alone, and links to more than a hundred miles of trails in nearby Inyo National Forest.

Visitors have the opportunity to drive to a trailhead, venture up to the ridge and connect with the Pacific Crest Trail (PCT), and then use other cutoffs along the PCT to custom-route trips to remote lakes or streams, pristine meadows, mountaintops and canyons that seem touched by divine spirit. Elevations range from a low of 7,200 feet at trailheads to the peak at Mount Ritter at 13,157 feet. As you walk, you will understand why Muir called the Minaret range a "mountain temple," because it is one of the rare, special places on this planet.

Dozens and dozens of small lakes speckle the high mountain country, each of them created by glacial action and then filled each spring by melting drops of snow. All have trout jumping for hatching insects each evening and provide perfect campsites for people willing to hike to them. Access is best to the Ansel Adams Wilderness near Mammoth, via Highway 395.

The John Muir Wilderness, located about 20 miles to the south, is a true paradise of mountains, lakes and meadows. Mountaintops reaching 12,000 feet high poke holes into the heavens, and below are more than a hundred pristine lakes, including 25 that are home to rare golden trout. The high mountain meadows are filled with wildflowers, with violet-colored lupine the most common.

The longer you stay in these wilderness surroundings, the less important your everyday "real world" stresses will seem. Each day's hike is like taking a shower and washing off layers of urban dust caked on from the numbing routine of city life. After awhile, the experience will realign your senses, and you will suddenly understand what Muir meant by developing a oneness with your surroundings, because you will have done it.

"When one is alone at night in the depths of these woods . . . every leaf seems to speak," wrote Muir. "Perfect quietude is there, and freedom from every curable care."

Some people go to school to get history, and others go to church to get religion. With a good pair of boots, a backback, and inspiration, you can get both on the wilderness trail.

Access is best to the John Muir Wilderness from trailheads at lakes on the western slope of the Sierra, via Highway 168. There are many trailheads situated at lakes in the area that you can reach by car. They are set perfectly for a jump-off into the mountain wilderness. Here are four of the best:

Lake Mary

This is the largest of the 11 lakes in the Mammoth Lakes area, a good place to camp for the night before heading off on a hike the next morning. A trailhead is available on the east side of the lake. From there, the trail is routed along Mammoth Creek to Arrowhead Lake, Skeleton Lake, Barney Lake, and finally to Big Duck Lake. The Pacific Crest Trail looms just a mile yonder, where you can gain access to the wilderness interior.

Contact: Phone Inyo National Forest, (619) 934-2505; Crystal Crag Lodge, (619) 934-2436.

Convict Lake

This is one of the prettiest lakes in the world, fronted by conifers and framed by a back wall of wilderness mountain peaks. It is set at 7,583 feet. The trail on the north side of the lake heads up through a canyon along Convict Creek. In the space of five miles, it leads into the John Muir Wilderness and a series of nine lakes. The biggest is Bighorn Lake, originally a granite cirque sculpted by glacial action.

Contact: Phone Inyo National Forest, (619) 934-2505; Convict Lake Resort, (619) 934-3800.

Edison Lake

The lake is set at 7,650 feet, with a trail along the north side of the lake that is routed up Mono Creek and then connects to the Pacific Crest Trail. From there, you can head south up Bear Mountain, where the trail is routed through one of the West's most lush aspen groves, and beyond to Trout Creek. The other option is to travel north on the Pacific Crest Trail, heading toward Devil's Postpile National Monument and the crystal headwaters of the San Joaquin River.

Contact: Phone Sierra National Forest, (209) 841-3311.

Florence Lake

This is also a pretty lake, situated at 7,327 feet, with the Great Divide country providing a backdrop. From the inlet of the lake, a trail is routed up the South Fork San Joaquin River to the Pacific Crest Trail, about a five-mile trip. From there, you can continue southeast along the San Joaquin River (great evening trout fishing), turning into Evolution Valley. This was one of Muir's favorite areas and one of the prettiest meadows and woodlands in the entire high Sierra.

Contact: Phone Sierra National Forest, (209) 841-3311; Florence Lake Resort, (209) 966-3195.

2

Mammoth Lakes/ Eastern Sierra

In the southeastern Sierra Nevada

Children smile an average of 450 times a day, according to a new study, but adults only about 15 times. There's a unique place in California where the score can be evened.

In the southeastern Sierra Nevada, nature has carved out high mountain peaks and canyons, then sowed the West's most pristine lakes and streams, meadows and valleys. It is one of the few places in America where there are no limits to the scenic beauty and recreation opportunities. The area is Mammoth, named after the extinct mastodon of the Cro-Magnon age, and much of the surrounding area still retains the feel of ancient times. A hundred years ago, whenever John Muir wanted a change of scenery from Yosemite, this is where he came. Fifty years ago, Ansel Adams took many of his prized photographs here. Today, it still offers the public a place to make their own magic.

The greater Mammoth area has more than 100 lakes, most of them exquisite, including 20 you can drive to. There are 24 drive-to campgrounds, several near trailheads that provide jumpoff points into the Ansel Adams Wilderness, the Minarets and the John Muir Wilderness. The altitudes range to a 12,000-foot ridgeline, all granite and ice, and a bit lower, woods and water. It is in these mountains that Muir counseled with heaven.

The recreational opportunities include everything from fishing, hiking, boating and biking in the mountains to scenic tours in the nearby desert east of a ghost town (Bodie) and among the bizarre tufa spires at Mono Lake. Near Mammoth, there are rides on horseback, hot air balloons and gondolas at a ski area. Devil's Postpile National Monument, the world's best example of columnar-formed rock, is practically a sideshow.

You can rough it or you can go first-class. The town of Mammoth, population 5,000, has 50 restaurants, 80 rental condos, and 34 hotels and lodges. It is the gateway to the eastern Sierras, but it's a long way from any bustling metropolis, about a seven-hour drive from San Francisco.

What has the strongest impact on most visitors are the pristine waters, the excellent fishing and the mountain wildlands.

From the tiny drops of snowmelt, this is where the headwaters of the San Joaquin River are formed. It pours down a canyon—wild, untouched and absolutely pure, over boulders and into pools, so different from its pesticide-laden condition 200 miles downstream in the back Delta. From the campground at Devil's Postpile, I hiked upstream for a few miles on the John Muir Trail along the San Joaquin, then stopped to wade the river and cast with my fly rod, drifting a floating caddis into the pocket water.

The stream is not only pure, but it is vibrant with all matter of life, including brook trout, rainbow trout, and more rarely, a big brown trout, and in the high country, golden trout. When you cast a dry fly, watch it float downstream. The ensuing swirl of a hungry trout taking it down is a sight you'll never forget. In three hours, I caught and released 30 trout. The farther you walk upstream, the better it gets. But you do not need to walk in order to capture this experience.

In fact, you can drive right up to some of the prettiest sights of all, as well as some of the best fishing. Convict Lake, for instance, is a mountain shrine. It is set at 7,583 feet, always full to the brim with clear, blue water, and framed by a back wall of wilderness mountain peaks. There are so many others. You can reach Lake Mamie, Lake George, Lake Mary, Gull Lake, Silver Lake, Grant Lake and more than a dozen others by car. They are set in high mountain pockets, carved out by glaciers and then filled over time by snowmelt. Most now have boat ramps, marinas, campgrounds and the largest trout in the Sierra Nevada. Rainbow trout in the 20-inch class are caught every day at these lakes, and while most range from 10 to 12-inchers, there are also 10 to 12-pounders.

Many of these lakes also provide trailheads to hike into the backcountry. From Silver Lake at 7,600 feet, there is a trail along a stream that is routed up past Agnew Lake, Gem Lake and Waugh Lake to the headwaters of Rush Creek. It may be the prettiest stream in America, and the golden trout here are just as beautiful. Another trek departs at Convict Lake, and you hike up the trail adjacent to Convict Creek. It starts on the north side of the lake and in just five miles leads into the John Muir Wilderness and a series of nine lakes. The showpiece of them all is Bighorn Lake, which is even larger than Convict Lake.

After a few days out here, you begin shedding layers of civilization. Suddenly, money, honors and possessions seem irrelevant. That's because out in such a beautiful place, they are.

Directions: From the Bay Area, the best route is to take Highway 120 through Yosemite and over Tioga Pass to Highway 395, then drive south to the Mammoth Cutoff (Highway 203). Greyhound offers bus service seven days a week from San Francisco. A small airport is also available near Mammoth.

Weather: In the summer, temperatures average 80 degrees for a high and seldom get below 40 for a low. On the hottest days, short and spectacular thundershowers can occur in the afternoon.

Fishing information: Phone guide Gary Hooper or Rick's Sport Center at (619) 934-3416.

Horseback rides: Phone Red's Meadows at (619)934-2345.

Mountain biking course: Phone Mountain Adventure Connection at (619) 934-0606.

Hot air balloons: Phone High Sierra Ballooning at (619)934-7188.

Gondola rides: Phone Mammoth Ski Park at (619) 934-2571.

Golf: Phone Snow Creek Resort at (619) 934-6633.

Bodie Ghost Town: Phone (619) 647-6445.

Mono Lake Visitor's Center: Phone (619) 647-6572.

Road conditions: Phone (619) 873-6366.

Contact: For general information and a free travel packet, phone Mammoth Lakes Visitors Bureau at (800) 367-6572, or write to P.O. Box 48, Mammoth Lakes, CA 93546. Maps are available from Inyo National Forest, (619) 934-2505.

3
Yosemite

You know the stories about Yosemite. Too many people, right? Bears raid your food every night, right? A place where a vacation turns into an endurance test called You Against The World. That's what kept me away for 20 years.

Finally I was forced to go back. You see, some friends and I were hiking the entire John Muir Trail, all 211 miles of it, and from the trailhead at Mount Whitney it eventually pours right smack into Yosemite Valley. Either you hit Yosemite or you cancel the hike.

We decided to give it a few shrugs and take our chances. We headed to the park expecting congestion and confusion, just like many Bay Area residents who have delayed or never even made the trip. But it only took five minutes in Yosemite Valley to turn our attitudes around 180 degrees—leaving us completely under the spell of the world's greatest natural showpiece.

With a little homework, the people and bears can be dealt with easily enough; that's what this story is all about. But there is no preparation that will get you ready for your first look at Yosemite Valley.

As you drive into the park, you go through a tunnel and then, looking east, suddenly spot sections of high canyon walls. "Is this it?" It's just a start. You go around a bend and suddenly there is El Capitan, the Yosemite monolith, the largest single piece of granite in the world, rising straight up from the valley floor. Then the entire valley comes into view.

It looks as if it has been sculpted. The valley is framed by three-spired Cathedral Rocks and massive El Capitan, with the awesome Half Dome near the center. There is nothing like this sight anywhere. The canyon walls are crossed by long, silver-tasseled waterfalls, although sometimes they run a bit thin. On most afternoons, low-hanging clouds that look as if they were created by Ansel Adams will dot the sky from rim to rim.

Now don't think you should get in your car right now and head off for the park, although you can reach it from the Bay Area in three-and-a-half hours. That ambitious, sudden "Let's go!" is just what causes so many problems for people when they visit Yosemite. After paying the entrance fee, they suddenly find they don't have a campground or a place to stay, don't know where to turn, and are just as likely to wind up spending the night in a Markleeville hotel room as looking into a nice little campfire along Yosemite Lake.

Instead, first you should obtain a good map of Yosemite National Park, then spend a few evenings just gazing at it and planning your trip. The best park map is available from the Yosemite Association, P.O. Box 230, El Portal, CA 95318. Ask for the Yosemite National Park and Vicinity topographic map.

With that in hand, you can plan your vacation. Where are you sleeping? Your choices are developed campsites, wilderness camping and tent cabin rentals. Going for a walk? Choose between premium day hikes out of the valley and backpack trails in the high country. Fishing? The park has 300 lakes, but 60 percent of them don't even have fish in them. Horseback riding? Where? How much?

Or you could give up and just lay around. In fact, a lot of people do exactly that along the Merced River in Yosemite Valley. But even those folks rest easier if they know where they're spending the night.

The campgrounds in Yosemite Valley are filled by reservation only and are packed during the summer months. Well, the overpeopled valley is a nice place to visit but you probably wouldn't want to live there.

Options include 11 drive-in camps outside of Yosemite Valley that are filled on a first-come, first-served basis.

The largest of the camps is at Tuolumne Meadows, which has 325 sites available. This is also the farthest camp from the valley, and when all else fails, usually has a space available. As you enter the park, a sign noting campground availability is posted next to the entrance. It is wise to heed those words, go and secure a spot, then enjoy your trip. On summer weekends, finding a campsite can be a difficult task. Your effort can be eased greatly by arriving Thursday or Friday morning. Other options include reserving a tent cabin or staying at Yosemite Lodge.

Backpackers have an easier and far less expensive time of it. All you need is a free wilderness permit, a backpack and a trail to start walking.

To keep people pressure at a minimum, the park has set hiker quotas for each trailhead. Half of those quotas are filled by reservation through the mail (during the winter and spring)—the other half are available on a first-come, first-served basis. You can pick up your wilderness permit at one of four permit stations, located at Yosemite Valley, Tuolumne Meadows, Big Oak Flat and Wawona Ranger Station. With camping concerns taken care of, you can get on with the business of having a good time. Hiking, fishing and horseback riding provide the best of Yosemite.

The hikes starting in Yosemite Valley range from an easy half-mile jaunt to the base of Lower Yosemite Falls to a 17-mile grunt to the top of Half Dome with a near 5,000-foot climb, with plenty of other hikes in between.

When it comes to fishing, most anglers are terribly disappointed. I have a simple rule for Yosemite. If you can drive to it, don't expect to catch anything. The more difficult the access, the better the prospects.

A good primer is the 16-page booklet "Yosemite Trout Fishing," which rates the fishing at the park's 118 lakes that have trout. You see all kinds of crazy fishing methods being tried, but for the most part, you don't need anything complicated. Just use a light spinning rod and reel, and small lures such as the gold Z-Ray with red spots, black Panther Martin with yellow spots, blue/silver Kastmaster and yellow Roostertail.

My brother and I had a great time of it, catching as many as 30 trout apiece in one evening at Lyell Fork, with some to 14 inches at Emeric Lake. With a little homework, it can be done. Note that all trout stocks have been suspended and easy-to-reach lakes are getting fished out.

If you don't like to hike in the backcountry, you can rent a horse to take you there. Stables are located at four locations: Yosemite Valley, Wawona, White Wolf Camp and Tuolumne Meadows.

Of course, you might be perfectly content to sit in a different kind of saddle, the kind on the valley's sightseeing shuttle. To encourage visitors to park their cars, an open-air tour bus is available—along with a free valley bus shuttle around the valley floor.

The first explorer to see Yosemite had quite a different vantage point. It was Joe Walker, in 1833, whose team reached the valley floor by lowering their horses on ropes. Walker is considered by many to be the West's greatest trailblazer, yet his tombstone at his grave in Martinez reads simply: "Camped in Yosemite, November 13, 1833."

Since that date, millions of people from all over the world have visited the park. Ironically, its popularity is just the thing that keeps many Bay Area residents away from the park.

Haven't been to Yosemite in a while? Maybe not ever? It's the kind of place that's too spectacular not to visit.

Campsites

Yosemite National Park has some campgrounds that do not require reservations. Campsites are filled on a first-come, first-served basis. For best success, you should arrive before noon on weekday mornings to secure the best possible spot.

Wawona—Located along Highway 41 in Wawona at the southern end of the park, 27 miles from Yosemite

Valley. It has 100 campsites available.

Bridalveil Creek—Set along Glacier Point Road at 7,200 feet and 27 miles from Yosemite Valley. It has 110 campsites.

Crane Flat—Located along Highway 120 west near the Tioga Road turnoff at 6,200 feet elevation, 17 miles from Yosemite Valley. It has 169 campsites.

Tamarack Flat—Set along Highway 120 east at 6,300 feet, 23 miles from Yosemite Valley. It has 52 campsites.

White Wolf—A major camp along Highway 120 east at 8,000 feet, 31 miles from Yosemite Valley. It has 87 campsites.

Yosemite Creek—Set four miles from White Wolf, 35 miles from Yosemite Valley. It has 75 campsites.

Porcupine Flat—Also set along Highway 120 east, this one is 38 miles from Yosemite Valley. It has 52 campsites.

Hiking

Yosemite offers these ten good hikes:

Lower Yosemite Falls—Start at the shuttle stop for Yosemite Falls, and walk a half-mile round-trip. Easy.

Bridalveil Falls—Start at the Bridalveil Falls parking area, walk a half-mile round-trip. Easy.

Mirror Lake—Start at the shuttle stop for Mirror Lake and hike one mile to the lake. An option is a three-mile circle around the lake. Easy.

Upper Yosemite Falls—Start at Sunnyside Campground and hike 3.6 miles one-way, with a 2,700-foot elevation gain. Very strenuous, six to eight hours round-trip.

Vernal/Nevada Falls—Start at Happy Isles, a trailhead for the John Muir Trail. Vernal Falls is 1.5 miles with a 1,000-foot elevation gain, three hours round-trip. Nevada Falls is 3.4 miles one way with a 1,900 foot elevation gain. Very steep and strenuous, six to eight hours round-trip.

Half Dome—Start at Happy Isles and hike 8.5 miles to the top, including 500 feet on permanently mounted cables to make the summit. Very strenuous, 17 miles round-trip, 4,800-foot elevation gain, 10 to 12 hours round-trip. Plan to drink four quarts of water.

Panorama—Start at Glacier Point and hike to Yosemite Valley, 8.5 miles, with a 3,200-foot elevation loss. Moderate, four to five hours one way.

Four Mile Trail—Start at Southside Drive, road marker V18, and climb to Glacier Point in 4.8 miles, one way, with a 3,200-foot elevation gain. Strenuous, three to four hours one way.

Pohono Trail—Start at Glacier Point and hike 13 miles, with a moderate downgrade, 1,300-foot elevation loss, six to eight hours one way.

❖

Directions: The fastest route from the Bay Area is to take Highway 580 past Livermore, then take the Highway 205 cutoff to Highway 120. Past Oakdale, take the Yosemite turnoff and continue into the park.

Fee or Free: A national park access fee is charged; it includes a park map. Camping fees vary depending on type of site.

Map: Ask for the Yosemite National Park and Vicinity topographic map from the Yosemite Association, P.O. Box 230, El Portal, CA 95318; (209) 372-0200.

Valley Tent Camping: All campsites in Yosemite Valley are filled by reservation only. Phone Mistix at (800) 365-2267.

Outback Tent Camping: More remote campgrounds are available on a first-come, first-served basis. There are no guarantees that a site will be available; to increase your chance of success, get there before noon. For information, phone park headquarters at (209) 372-0200 or (209) 372-0302.

Wilderness Camping: A free Wilderness Permit must be in your party's possession. They can be obtained at permit stations located at Yosemite Valley, Tuolumne Meadows, Big Oak Flat and the Wawona Ranger Station. For more information, phone (209)372-0307 for a recording of conditions.

Tent Cabins/Lodging: Canvas tent cabins are available in Yosemite Valley and Tuolumne Meadows. Rooms are available at Yosemite

Lodge and the historic, first-class hotel, Ahwahnee. For information, phone (209) 252-4848.

Fishing: A 16-page booklet called "Yosemite Trout Fishing" is available by writing Yosemite Park and Curry Company, Yosemite National Park, CA 95389. Phone (209) 372-1445 for price information.

Horseback Riding: Horseback riding rentals are available from four locations: Yosemite Valley, Wawona, White Wolf Camp and Tuolumne Meadows. For information, phone (209)372-1248.

Roads/Weather: For a recorded message detailing road conditions, call (209) 445-5647.

Contact: For general information and a touch-tone menu selection, phone Yosemite National Park at (209) 372-0200.

Chapter 15

Activities & Adventures

44 Bay Area Lakes

Daybreak at San Pablo Reservoir brings one of the most heavenly pastoral scenes in the Bay Area: blues, greens, and placid water; small boats leaving fresh, white wakes; and happy anglers gathering about the lake, many with nice stringers of trout.

That unique combination of beauty and excitement makes San Pablo the Number One lake in my personal survey of the 44 recreational lakes in San Francisco, Santa Clara, Marin, Alameda, Contra Costa, Napa, Solano and Santa Cruz counties.

I rated the lakes from best to worst, considering a number of factors including boating, fishing, hiking, camping and scenic beauty. While San Pablo is the overall winner, other lakes won in individual categories.

Loch Lomond in the Santa Cruz Mountains is the prettiest in the Bay Area, just ahead of Alpine Lake in Marin County. Parkway Lake in Coyote has the highest catch rate for anglers. Bon Tempe Lake in San Anselmo offers the best hiking trails. Del Valle Reservoir south of Livermore provides the best campground and boating access. In addition, several lakes receive special bonus stocks of trophy-size trout: San Pablo, Lake Chabot, Del Valle, Merced North and South, Lafayette, Shadow Cliffs, Parkway and Isabel.

Also please note that several beautiful lakes don't make the list because public access is forbidden: Crystal Springs, Upper and Lower San Andreas, Pilarcitos, Felt, Searsville, Calaveras, San Antonio and Briones. I also consider Berryessa out of the Bay Area, so that lake is not rated either.

That leaves 44 lakes, far more than most people imagine. A good time can be had at any, regardless of their rating. Now, on with the show:

1—San Pablo Reservoir, northwest of Orinda

San Pablo provides a unique combination of beauty, excellent fishing, good access for boats, and a protected area for waterfowl. More trout are stocked here than in any lake in California, about 200,000 per year, joining resident bass, bluegill, and catfish. Boat rentals, a tackle shop and helpful employees make newcomers feel welcome.

Contact: Phone San Pablo Recreation Information Center at (510) 223-1661.

2—Loch Lomond Reservoir, near Ben Lomond

Loch Lomond is tucked in a canyon in the Santa Cruz Mountains and is circled by redwoods, creating a pristine setting which makes you feel far removed from civilization. On blue-sky days, the lake is often a deeper hue of blue than any other in the Bay Area. Trout stocks start every March, and a resident population of bass add to the prospects on summer evenings. Boat rentals, a launch, a shop and a picnic area are bonuses.

Contact: Phone Loch Lomond Reservoir at (408) 335-7424.

3—Lake Chabot, near Castro Valley

Chabot just plain "looks fishy," and it is, with abundant trout stocks and the biggest largemouth bass in the Bay Area. The largest bass in Bay Area history was documented here, 17 pounds and 2 ounces. Private boats are not permitted here, but rentals are available. Picnic sites, hiking trails and a nearby campground put Chabot right at the top of my list.

Contact: Phone Anthony Chabot Regional Park at (510) 881-1833 or East Bay Regional Parks at (510) 635-0135.

4—Del Valle Reservoir, south of Livermore

This long, narrow lake has a 100-site campground,

a boat launch for power boats and an adjacent park for picnics and hikes. The lake is well stocked with trout into early summer, and it also has bluegill for kids, smallmouth bass for know-hows, and some huge striped bass for the persistent few. It's often very hot and dry here in the summer months.

Contact: Phone Del Valle Regional Park at (510) 443-4110; Del Valle Boathouse, (510) 443-5201; East Bay Regional Parks, (510) 635-0135.

5—Lake Merced North, San Francisco coast

If you sit in a boat here along the tule-lined shore, you will feel like you are in a different world. That's because you are. This is a place of peace, with the fantastic bonus of a chance of catching a 10-pound rainbow trout. The tackle shop welcomes newcomers by providing a free tip sheet, rod-and-reel rentals, pre-tied leaders and boats with electric motors.

Contact: Phone Merced Bait Shop at (415) 753-1101.

6—Lafayette Reservoir, between Orinda and Lafayette

Because of its proximity to San Pablo Reservoir, Lafayette often gets missed by out-of-towners. But it shouldn't be overlooked, not with boat rentals, regular trout stocks and some huge but elusive largemouth bass. The catch rates here are quite good, with the best spot usually in the East Cove.

Contact: Phone Lafayette Lake Marina at (510) 284-9669.

7—Bon Tempe Lake, near San Anselmo

This is a pretty lake nestled on the northern slopes of Mount Tamalpais. It provides a starting point for some outstanding hiking trails, as well as some shoreline baitdunking areas for trout. No boats of any kind are allowed here, a big downer, but the plentiful trout stocks make up for that.

Contact: Phone the Marin Water District at (415) 924-4600; Sky Oaks Ranger Station at (415)459-5267.

8—Pinto Lake, near Watsonville

Little Pinto Lake is often overlooked, despite its being one of the few lakes in the Bay Area that provides both a campground and good fishing. Trout are stocked regularly into the summer, and then when the warm weather hits, a surprising crappie fishery takes over.

Contact: Phone Pinto Lake County Park at (408) 722-8129.

9—Lake Merced South, San Francisco coast

If you haven't seen Lake Merced lately, you will be surprised at the size and beauty of it. The lake is ringed by tules, provides decent trout fishing, and is best-known as an excellent spot to paddle a canoe, row a shell or sail a dinghy.

Contact: Phone Merced Bait Shop at (415) 753-1101.

10—Alpine Lake, in Fairfax foothills

The fishing is lousy, but the remarkable natural beauty of Alpine Lake, full to the brim and nestled below Mount Tamalpais, earns its ranking in the top 10. No boats or water contact are permitted, but the hiking and scenery make this a great destination. Park near the dam for a hike up the Cataract Trail, or at nearby Bon Tempe Lake, to hike along the far shore.

Contact: Phone the Marin Water District at (415) 924-4600.

11—Uvas Reservoir, west of San Martin

Uvas in one of the few lakes in Santa Clara County that usually has plenty of water in it, typically full to the brim in spring. It is regularly stocked with trout from February through April. From May on, it offers good shoreline bass fishing. A county campground is located nearby.

Contact: Phone Santa Clara Parks and Recreation at (408) 358-3741.

12—Lake Hennessey, north of Napa

Hennessey is a huge lake, 20,000 acres, 12 miles long and four miles wide. However, it is often lost in the shadow of Lake Berryessa to the east. It is an ideal lake for small boats, with no motors over 10 horsepower permitted. The lake is stocked with trout in the spring and offers fair bass fishing during the summer. Insider's note: The Hennessey Impoundment often has the best trout fishing.

Contact: Phone the Department of Parks and Recreation, Public Works and Water at (707) 257-9520.

13—Soulejule Reservoir, west of Petaluma

This little-known, hike-in lake (park at the base of the dam) provides some of the best shoreline fishing for crappie and bass in the Bay Area. Try it on a warm summer evening.

Contact: Phone the North Marin Water District at (415) 897-4133 or Western Boat at (415) 454-4177.

14—Calero Reservoir, southwest of Coyote

Calero has become so popular that you need a reservation to launch a boat. This is because the lake is usually kept full, and the catch-and-release fishing can be excellent for bass and crappie. Boating and hiking are at a premium here. The lake's appeal is only tainted by the health warning on eating any fish caught here; still, this remains a popular spot.

Contact: Phone Santa Clara Parks and Recreation, (408) 358-3741.

15—Arastradero Lake, Palo Alto foothills

A 20-minute hike through pretty foothill country will get you to this classic bass pond. No rafts or float tubes are allowed—a major error. This area is part of a 6,000-acre nature preserve, with lots of squirrels, chipmunks, and hawks.

Contact: Phone Foothills Park, (415) 329-2423.

16—Sandy Wool Lake, Milpitas foothills

Sandy Wool is a small lake, just 14 acres, but is surrounded by parkland with 16 miles of hiking trails. Boating without motors is ideal and fishing is decent for small planters after a trout stock.

Contact: Phone Ed Levin County Park at (408) 262-6980.

17—Chabot Reservoir, Vallejo

This lake is adjacent to Marine World, but you won't notice if you access it through Dan Foley Park. A prime spot for picnics, Chabot Reservoir is regularly stocked with trout.

Contact: Phone the Department of Fish and Game at (707) 944-5500.

18—Shadow Cliffs Lake, Pleasanton

Shadow Cliffs is a good idea that works. This is a water hole used to be a rock quarry but has been converted to a lake, providing boating and fishing for trout and catfish. At 143 acres, it is a decent-sized lake. It's not exactly pretty, rather like an ugly dog that you learn to love.

Contact: Phone Shadow Cliffs Regional Park at (510) 846-3000.

19—Don Castro Reservoir, Hayward foothills

Don Castro is the centerpiece of a regional park that doesn't get much attention. No boats are allowed and there are few trout, but prospects are fair during the summer for bass, catfish and bluegill.

Contact: Phone East Bay Regional Parks at (510) 635-0135, ext. 2200.

20—Cottonwood Lake, southeast San Jose

Cottonwood Lake is set in Hellyer Park, just a short hop off Highway 101. It is a favorite spot for windsurfing and sailing. It also has good picnic sites, six miles of bike trails, and is stocked with trout.

Contact: Phone Santa Clara Parks and Recreation at (408) 358-3741.

21—Lagunitas Lake, near San Anselmo

Lagunitas is a living science project, an attempt to recreate a wild trout fishery. The catch-and-release fishing rates are low, but the scenery is a high.

Contact: Phone the Marin Water District at (415) 924-4600; Sky Oaks Ranger Station at (415) 459-5267.

22—Parkway Lake, Coyote

The scenery at Parkway isn't so great, but trout and catfish are large and abundant. The high access fee pays for special stocks of trophy-sized trout.

Contact: Phone the lake's information recording at (408) 629-9111, or Coyote Discount Bait and Tackle at (408) 463-0711.

23—Stevens Creek Reservoir, near Cupertino

When full, Stevens Creek is quite pretty. It covers 95 acres, and it can fill quickly during a series of heavy rains. When that happens, the Department of Fish and Game always stocks it with rainbow trout, turning this lake into a respectable prospect. Boating speed limits are often enforced. Check with park headquarters for current regulations.

Contact: Phone park headquarters at (408) 867-3654 or Santa Clara Parks and Recreation at (408) 358-3741.

24—Lake Isabel, Pleasanton

This pay-to-fish water hole is heavily stocked with trout and catfish. Catches are high, but steep banks mar the scenery.

Contact: Phone Lake Isabel at (510) 462-1281.

25—Nicasio Lake, west of San Rafael

There are no picnic tables and no trees in the area. It's just this little lake in rolling foothill country. Summer evenings can be good for bass and crappie, but alas, no rafts or float tubes are permitted.

Contact: Phone the North Marin Water District at (415) 897-4133.

26—Contra Loma Reservoir, Antioch

No motors are permitted here, making Contra Loma ideal for rafts, prams and rowboats. The trout program is a winner, and striped bass always provide a reason to pray. Stark country.

Contact: Phone Contra Loma Reservoir at (510) 757-0404.

27—Lake Temescal, Oakland hills

Temescal is a little lake that responds quickly to trout stocks, but then, so do the cormorants. No boats are permitted. The lake was closed in the fall of '91 after the terrible Oakland fire scorched the adjacent hillside; rains washed high levels of silt into the lake. That problem is now solved.

Contact: Phone East Bay Regional Parks at (510) 635-0135.

28—Chesbro Dam, near Morgan Hill

When full, this reservoir covers 300 acres, and also provides some good-sized crappie prospects during the spring. The bass tend to be very, very small or absolutely giant with a case of lockjaw, so you end up either catching midgets or facing a monster. Visiting anglers often leave here amazed by a fish they saw, but rarely by a fish that they caught.

Contact: Phone Santa Clara County Parks and Recreation at (408) 358-3741.

29—Kent Lake, near Lagunitas in west Marin County

The hike to Kent Lake is a pretty one, almost like taking a walk through Tennessee woodlands. While this is a good spot for a picnic, it has no facilities, no boating and no fishing program. Scenic beauty alone gets it ranked in the top 30.

Contact: Phone Western Boat at (415) 454-4177.

30—Coyote Reservoir, near Gilroy

Years ago, this was the Bay Area's best bass lake, but water manipulations keep draining it. It can be full in spring, then empty by fall, and nobody seems to know what will happen from one year to the next. A campground along the edge of the lake is a redeeming quality, however.

Contact: Phone Coyote County Park at (408) 842-7800 or Santa Clara County Parks and Recreation at (408) 358-3741.

31—Phoenix Lake, near Ross

Improved facilities, access, parking, trout stocks, and boating access (even for rafts) are required before Phoenix Lake moves up the list. The Department of Fish and Game stocks it in late winter, providing fair shoreline fishing.

Contact: Phone Western Boat at (415) 454-4177.

32—Lake Anderson, Morgan Hill

This should be one of the top lakes in the Bay Area. It is big (1,000 acres), has crappie, bluegill, and bass, and a five-mile-per-hour speed limit that keeps the southern end of the lake quiet. Alas, the numbskulls that control the water level here are just as apt to drain it down to the bottom as to keep it full, and that prevents the implementation of any fishery programs, as well as preventing it from becoming a stable site for water sports.

Contact: Phone Santa Clara County Parks at (408) 358-3741.

33—Cull Canyon Reservoir, Castro Valley

This small lake in the hills gets little attention from fishermen, and it's easy to see why with only some dinky catfish to try for. The surrounding parkland gets it rated this high.

Contact: Phone East Bay Regional Parks at (510) 635-0135.

34—Campbell Percolation Pond, Campbell

Easy access is a bonus here; the lake is located just off Highway 17 at Camden Avenue. It's a mere dot of water, just five acres, but it is stocked regularly with trout.

Contact: Phone Santa Clara County Parks and Recreation at (408) 358-3741.

35—Cunningham Lake, San Jose

Trout fishing in an urban setting? That's what you get here. Cunningham Lake is located on Tully Road and Capitol, right next to Raging Waters waterslide. The lake covers 50 acres and is surrounded by a small park.

Contact: Phone the City of San Jose Parks Department at (408) 277-4661.

36—Merced Impoundment, San Francisco coast

Of the three lakes at Merced, this is the one that everybody forgets. It responds quickly to trout plants, but dies when not stocked. It is so small that during low water it can be afflicted with low oxygen levels and water temperatures, conditions that can cause all stocks to be stopped.

Contact: Phone Merced Bait Shop at (415) 753-1101.

37—Guadalupe Reservoir, southeast of Los Gatos

The fish are contaminated here, and the fact that nobody around these parts seems to care about it accounts for this poor rating. The lake itself covers 75 acres, a pretty setting in the spring in the foothills of the Sierra Azul Range. The bass fishing is fair, but don't eat 'em.

Contact: Phone Santa Clara Parks and Recreation at (408) 358-3741.

38—Lexington Reservoir, near Los Gatos

This can be a very pretty lake when it is full of water. Unfortunately that doesn't seem to happen often. In fact, even when it is full in spring, it has a way getting down to nearly nothing by late fall. But it's nice to dream. With more water, you get a quality reservoir with a boat ramp, trout plants and a picnic area. Without it, it's a mediocre skunk hole.

Contact: Phone Santa Clara Parks and Recreation at (408) 358-3741.

39—Lake Elizabeth, Fremont

During the hot summer in the East Bay flats, this is a relatively cool spot, set in Fremont's Central Park. Some small bass, bluegill and catfish provide a few longshot hopes.

Contact: Phone Central Park at (510) 791-4356.

40—Lake Vasona, Los Gatos

This is the kind of place you would go for a Sunday picnic, maybe to play softball. The lake is part of a 150-acre park near the Santa Cruz Mountains. Sailboating and rowing are options, but forget fishing.

Contact: Phone Santa Clara County Parks and Recreation at (408) 358-3741.

41—Lake Merritt, Oakland

The best thing about Lake Merritt is that you can rent a variety of boats, including canoes and paddleboats. You can even take sailing lessons here. It is also good for jogging, and birdwatching in the spring. Because the water is brackish, there are no resident fish.

Contact: Phone Lake Merritt Marina at (510) 444-3807.

42—Lake Almaden, San Jose foothills

The best thing going for Almaden, at 62 acres, is that a lot of folks bypass it, making it a good picnic site, particularly on weekdays. It is set in the foothill country near some abandoned mines, where mercury runoff has made all fish dangerous to eat.

Contact: Phone Santa Clara County Parks and Recreation at (408) 358-3741.

43—Shinn Pond, Niles

Once an old gravel pit, Shin Pond has been filled with water and stocked with bass and bluegill. The pond covers 23 acres, and the fishing is poor.

Contact: Phone East Bay Regional Parks at (510) 635-0135.

44—Lake Anza, Oakland hills

The lake itself, just 11 acres, doesn't offer much in the way of fishing, except for a few bluegill and small bass. You will find a nice sandy beach for a Sunday afternoon, however, and the pleasant surrounding parkland of Tilden Regional Park.

Contact: Phone East Bay Regional Parks at (510) 635-0135.

Camping by Bay Area Lakes

In my book, *California Camping*, which details 1,500 campgrounds in the state, we found 59 campgrounds in nine Bay Area counties. But of those, only seven are set beside lakes. Most people know of the campgrounds at Lake Berryessa, one of the most popular areas in California, but they haven't heard of the other six. Here's a capsule look at them:

Spring Lake

This is Santa Rosa's backyard fishing hole, but it is unknown to most people who don't live in the area. The lake is stocked with rainbow trout and has a resident population of bluegill and largemouth bass. It's located about five miles outside of Santa Rosa. The campground has 28 sites for tents or motor homes, and three spots for tents only. Although no reservations are taken, the campgrounds usually have space available. There's good fishing in the morning and evening, especially from March through early May.

Contact: Call Spring Lake County Park at (707) 539-8082.

Lake Chabot

This is the centerpiece of the East Bay Regional Park District, a pretty lake that was recently heavily stocked with rainbow trout and hard-to-catch largemouth bass that reach 10 pounds and up. Boat rentals are available here.

The park has 62 campsites for tents and 12 for motor homes. It is set four miles west of Castro Valley. On weekends, the camp either fills up or comes close to it.

Contact: Phone either the East Bay Regional Park District at (510) 635-0135 or Lake Chabot Park at (510) 881-1833.

Del Valle Reservoir

A lot of people have no idea that a big, cool lake is set in the golden hills south of Livermore. But Del Valle Reservoir is. It is stocked weekly with rainbow trout, supports populations of bluegill and smallmouth bass, and has some big striped bass as well. A full marina with boat rentals and a launch is available.

The campground has 110 sites for tents or motor homes, and 21 of the sites have full hookups available. The campground is typically full on weekends, but space is almost always available during the week.

Contact: Call either the East Bay Regional Park District at (510) 635-0135, or Del Valle Park at (510) 449-5201.

Uvas Reservoir

Set about 10 miles south of San Jose, this lake can provide good fishing for largemouth bass and crappie, and for trout after the late winter stocks. The best strategy is to sneak up on coves in the lake's backwaters during the evening, then cast a white crappie jig. Boating without motors is permitted.

The campground has 30 sites for tents and 15 spaces for tents or motor homes. All are provided on a first-come, first-served basis. Of the eight lakes in Santa Clara County, Uvas Reservoir has the best fishing.

Contact: Call either Uvas Canyon County Park at (408) 358-3751 or Coyote Discount Bait and Tackle at (408) 463-0711.

Coyote Reservoir

This is a long, narrow lake set in the oak and grass-covered hills east of Gilroy. Fishermen with boats can catch largemouth bass, primarily during the early morning and late evening.

The park has 74 campsites for tents or motor homes. No reservations are taken. A boat launch is set a quarter-mile from the campground.

Contact: Call either Lakeview Coyote Park at (408) 842-7800 or Coyote Discount Bait and Tackle at (408) 463-0711.

Pinto Lake

You say you never heard of Pinto Lake? Neither have a lot of folks. It is set just outside of Watsonville.

The lake is shaped like a horseshoe and it's good luck for fishing for rainbow trout, bluegill, catfish, and in some years, crappie.

There are two campgrounds; Marmo's Resort has 50 sites and Pinto Lake Park has 33 sites. Both areas permit tents and motor homes.

The lake is often full, but the campgrounds are often not, except on three-day weekends.

Contact: Call Pinto Lake at (408) 722-8129.

Chapter 15

Beach Camping

Beach camping can add up to the time of your life: cruising down the highway, watching ocean sunsets, fishing practically from your tent and playing hide-and-seek with all the little tidepool creatures. It goes on: waking up to the sound of the sea, playing tag with the waves, beachcombing at low tide and going on long walks with someone special.

But alas, if you are unprepared, just making it through a weekend can turn into an endurance test—you have about as much chance as enjoying yourself as trying to win a fight with an earthquake.

My first beach camping trip long ago was just like that. I arrived late one evening at a state beach in Monterey, with no reservations; the campground was full. So I had to strike out on my own, laying my sleeping bag down on a piece of secluded beach and going to sleep with the sound of waves in my ears.

Everything seemed great, right? Hey, the ocean was just waiting for me to pass into slumberland.

At about 4 a.m., a single thunderous wave cascaded over me. Are we having fun yet?

The following 10 hours were a disaster: turning into a human icicle in a wet sleeping bag; trying to sleep in the truck, a cold, foggy morning making the beach feel like the North Pole; eating a breakfast marinated in sand; getting hit in the arm with a sea gull dropping; and snagging up on every cast while trying to fish. By noon it was time to surrender.

Well, that was long ago. But you might have the same experience today if you head off unprepared.

For starters, camping reservations are a necessity. Coastal state beaches are among the most popular campgrounds in California, especially in the summer.

It is recommended that you call the campground of your choice to learn of projected availability, then call the Mistix toll-free reservation line to lock up a spot. The number is (800) 444-7275.

The next step is getting your gear together. Always have a list. At the very least, it will keep you from forgetting the toilet paper.

Then be prepared to deal with two key elements: the weather and the sand.

When many people across the country envision this coast, they think of warm, sun-swept days. The truth is that at Northern California beaches in the summer about half of the days are foggy and cold.

On warm days, inland damp fog will cloak the coast during the night—then break up by mid-morning. This fog brings with it a penetrating cold, the kind that goes right to the bones.

Therefore, a tent is mandatory. And if you plan to camp on sand, make sure you have the kind of tent that doesn't need stakes. The pegs usually won't hold. Guess how I know.

Also make certain that you have a warm sleeping bag, and with it, some kind of ground pad for insulation, either a light-weight Ensolite pad or a Therm-A-Rest. If you lay a sleeping bag directly on the ground or beach, the coldness of the ground will suck the warmth right out of you. By 2 a.m. you will feel like you are sleeping in a freezer, regardless of the air temperature.

Another key factor to an enjoyable trip is to concentrate on playing on the beach, rather than eating a good portion of it with every meal.

At state park beaches, picnic tables and food lockers are provided. Use them. If you are freelancing it in a remote area, this becomes more difficult.

One answer is to have all of your food in separate, air-tight containers. This will allow you to set your food down at your picnic site without worrying about it tipping over and filling with sand.

Of course, sometimes a disaster seems fated. One time I dropped a roasted hot dog on the beach, and it was so completely coated with sand that even my dog wouldn't eat it. Smart fellow.

For the most part, however, beach camping is a unique and fun experience. But do remember to bring a tide book. It just might keep you from getting a surprise dunking some night.

Sunset State Beach

Sunsets often look like they are imported from Hawaii at this park. Sunset State Beach, on the shore of south Monterey Bay near Watsonville, is a favorite for vacationers and a good alternative to Big Sur to the south. There are several good trails for short walks, and clamming can be good during low tides.

There are 90 spaces for tents or motor homes up to 31 feet long. Each comes with a picnic table.

Contact: For information, call Sunset State Beach at (408) 724-1266.

Half Moon Bay State Beach

A pretty and popular spot, Half Moon Bay State Beach offers tent campsites on a grassy area instead of sand. It is a prime spot for a long beach walk, especially during low tides. A bonus is the nearby Pillar Point Harbor, located seven miles to the north, with a boat launch, sportfishing operations and quality restaurants.

The park has 51 sites for tents or motor homes, with piped water and restrooms provided.

Contact: Call Half Moon Bay State Beach at (415) 726-8820.

Salt Point State Park

This is just far enough away from the Bay Area to give visitors a feeling of total separation from mass humanity. It is a great spot for abalone diving in season, beachcombing and quiet walks. Horses are available for riding.

The park has 110 campsites for tents or motor homes (up to 31 feet long) with all facilities provided at the park or in nearby Jenner.

Contact: Call Salt Point State Park in Jenner at (707) 847-3221.

Van Damme State Park

This park is at an ideal location for year-round adventures. You get an ocean frontage on one side and a forest on the other. In the winter, the nearby Noyo and Navarro rivers can provide steelhead fishing. The park has 70 campsites for tents or motor homes up to 35 feet long. All facilities are available at the park or nearby.

Contact: Call Van Damme State Park in Mendocino at (707) 937-5804.

Patrick's Point State Park

This is a real favorite, with campsites set amid Sitka spruce, trails that tunnel through thick fern vegetation, and an agate beach. There are several ocean lookouts where visitors can spot migrating whales. It's often foggy and damp here, but always beautiful.

There are 123 campsites for tents or motor homes up to 31 feet long, with picnic tables, fireplaces, and piped water provided. Restrooms are also available.

For more details on Patrick's Point State Park, see page 17.

Contact: Call Patrick's Point State Park in Trinidad at (707) 677-3570.

Birdwatching

Birds are light, airy, happy little fellows, and watching them can make you feel the same way.

That is why birdwatching has become one of the most popular activities in the Bay Area, as well as in many parts of the country. The Bay Area is an ideal place for the sport because the wide variety of habitats result in an equally wide variety of birds, including seabirds, songbirds, raptors, and waterfowl, both resident and migratory.

The sport has vastly changed in the past 20 years. In the good ol' days, birdwatchers all seemed to be nice little old ladies wearing giant rubber boots, with huge pairs of binoculars hanging from their necks. This was serious business, a mission, where they carefully noted every bird on their Audubon "Life List."

Well, these days birdwatchers look different. They are as apt to be bikers as little old ladies, and include everyone in between. The equipment has changed, too, with small, lightweight, high-optic binoculars, little backpacks to carry guide books, and new, high-tech waterproof hiking shoes.

The discovery has been made, you see, that this is really fun, a way to leave the weight of the daily grind behind and share in the world where all seems gentle and joyous. Most people get involved in the sport as a by-product of another adventure, whether walking, boating, fishing or hunting. You see the birds, watch them, and soon start wondering what they are. If you take the next step and find out, boom: you have become a birdwatcher.

Buying a home bird feeder is the next logical step, and Rubbermaid makes the widest variety of designs. Naturally, you then want to be able to identify the birds. *The Audubon Master Guide to Birding*, a three-part series of books that provides close-up photographs of each species, is the best available. If you then want to expand your search, *The Birders Guide to Northern California*, by Lolo and Jim Westrich, details 250 of the area's premium locations.

Another idea is to take part in a nature walk with an expert. These walks are offered most weekends at different locations in the Bay Area, and are listed in the *San Francisco Examiner's* Outdoor Calendar, which is published in Thursday's sports section. They include tours at Bothin Marsh north of Sausalito, Hawk Hill at the Marin Headlands, Palo Alto Baylands, Pescadero Marsh, Hayward Regional Shoreline, and San Francisco Bay Wildlife Refuge at both the Fremont and Alviso locations. A "Rare Bird Alert" is available on a recorded phone message at (510) 524-5592. (For more information about birdwatching around the San Francisco area, refer to the stories in Chapter 9.)

Avid birder Courtney Peddle contributed to this season-by-season synopsis of the best of Bay Area birdwatching:

Winter

Millions of shorebirds spend the winter on the Bay, and a variety of species can be seen on any mud flat, marshland or Bay tideland, and even on some lakes.

A personal favorite is the Hayward shoreline, always good for shorebirds with the bonus of peregrine falcons either hovering over the marsh, or perched on a power pylon. Sometimes, merlins can be seen there. An added bonus is a flock of up to 200 American white pelicans.

Another good spot in the East Bay is Arrowhead Marsh (Martin Luther King Regional Shoreline) in Oakland. Some 30 species live there. Several pair of blue-winged teal winter there, uncommon in the Bay waters. At high tide, this area is also a top spot to see rails, which are typically elusive and more often heard than seen.

Nearby is the Elsie Roemer Shoreline, located on Alameda's south shore, which is also an excellent area for rails during high tides. This habitat is ideal for dowitchers and rare red knots; the ratio is about 300 dowitchers to one knot. Lake Merritt is always good in the winter, with about 10 species of waterfowl, including plenty of Barrow's goldeneyes, rarely spotted elsewhere. Mergansers and scaups are more common, and sometimes you can spot tufted ducks as well.

Spring

The Bay's mud flats have an abundance of seabirds, but the real spectacles take place during late April and May at Pigeon Point Lighthouse on the San Mateo County coast.

On a good day, you can see 200,000 (that's right, 200,000) loons, scoters, brants, gulls and terns heading north. On a lucky day, you might see a million shearwaters, literally enough to speckle the ocean black for 15 miles, and plenty of fulmars and kittiwakes, too. There are many other good areas. Point Reyes and Bodega Bay are among the best, particularly in the vicinity of fishing docks for migrating seabirds. In fact, the coastline is alive with shorebirds gaining glorious breeding plumage before they head north.

A favorite spot in May is Mitchell Canyon on the northeast side of Mount Diablo for rare migrants, including rufous, calliope and costa's hummingbirds, along with hammond's and willow flycatchers and many warblers.

Summer

During the first week of July, squadrons of endangered brown pelicans arrive to the coast. Sometimes, they stop to circle and feed on anchovies; otherwise, they fly low-lying lines along the ocean swells, eventually entering San Francisco Bay and visiting the Fisherman's Wharf area. Another real show is out at sea, where thousands and thousands of murres congregate in the vicinity of the Farallon Islands, the murres' breeding area. They are joined by a number of well-traveled seabirds.

At Audubon Canyon Ranch on the Marin Coast, up through early July, huge herons kick their young out of the nest, and you can watch the juveniles experience their first attempts at flight. There are an additional 60 species of birds here. The saltwater marshes of the Bay also attract several species of herons, along with egrets, cormorants, and the inevitable coot. (For more details on Audubon Canyon Ranch, see the story on page 130.)

Fall

The Point Reyes National Seashore is the feature point in the fall. Arriving here is a huge variety of both migrating small birds and larger shorebirds. The best spots are the groves of cypress, upland pastures, and ranch feedlots between Pierce Ranch and the Point Reyes Lighthouse. Another option is the long, uninterrupted shore for viewing very special shorebirds. (For more details on Point Reyes National Seashore, see the story on page 86.)

Clam Digging

Clamming is an ideal family adventure, because everyone's on equal terms, youngsters and adults alike. Techniques vary widely. On a single beach, one might see such tools as garden hoes, shovels and cultivators, or long, narrow clammer's shovels and clam guns. I've even seen kids use a piece of abalone shell to dig for cockles, and after finding one, look at their dad as if they were the king of the world.

But if you don't know when to go, you won't find clams, only lots of sand. During minus outgoing tides, the prime clamming grounds up and down the coast are unveiled. With a little preparation, you can be ready.

Horseneck and Washington clams are available for the taking, depending on where you go. Don't expect to find clams on long, exposed stretches of sandy beach. Clams need protection. Such ideal clam habitats are available at certain parts of Bodega Bay, Tomales Bay, Half Moon Bay, south of Pigeon Point, and in Elkhorn Slough at Moss Landing.

Cockles are my favorite, and are especially popular in Tomales Bay, Half Moon Bay and Ano Nuevo. These little fellows will bury themselves in a rock and sand mix, usually just three or four inches below the surface. A three-pronged garden cultivator, used as if one were weeding a patch of lettuce, can produce the limit of 50 on a good day. Children prefer using a small hand shovel and the hands-and-knees technique. The minimum size cockle legally taken is one-and-a-half inches in diameter, and participants must have a measuring device and state fishing license in their possession when digging.

Cockles are choice morsels when steamed and dipped in garlic butter sauce, a simple preparation. Horseneck and Washington clams, on the other hand, require a fairly extensive beating to soften them up for eating. But their size makes up for the work. They get big, though state law requires any horseneck or Washington clam dug must be kept until the bag limit is reached, regardless of size or broken condition.

To find horsenecks, you should be out during the minus tide, scanning the tidal flats, searching for the telltale sign of a small siphon hole in the sand. The hole is actually the neck hole for the clams, through which they feed. If you spot the bubbling hole, dig and dig fast. The clam will withdraw its long neck, leaving no sign of its whereabouts. But rest assured, somewhere below where that small hole appeared will be a clam.

The favored tool for these larger specimens is the clammer's shovel, a long slender device engineered to dig a narrow yet deep hole in the least amount of time possible.

Though adults may savor the tranquility of a day on the coast, youngsters want action. Clamming is one way to make sure that everybody gets what they want.

Where to go clamming

Bodega Bay: During a minus tide, the harbor will completely drain except for the channel, leaving acres of prime spots, particularly on the western side. Horseneck clams are most abundant. Call Tides Wharf at (707) 875-3554.

Tomales Bay: This long, thin waterway offers more than 10 miles of prime clamming just 45 miles from San Francisco. Your best bet is on the western shoreline in the Tomales Bay State Park. Call Tomales Bay State Park at (415) 669-1140.

Half Moon Bay: Just inside both the south and north ends of the harbor, or rock jetty, are popular spots for locals and tourists alike. Call Hilltop Store at (415) 726-4950.

Ano Nuevo: The rock and sand mix cockles need is abundant in this area, but be careful not to actually dig on the Ano Nuevo State Reserve, where it is prohibited. You can dig between Pigeon Point and Franklin Point. To make sure of the boundaries in Ano Nuevo, call Ano Nuevo Reserve at (415) 879-2025.

Elkhorn Slough: Located just 20 miles south of Santa Cruz at Moss Landing, this area has a legendary reputation for its Horseneck and Washington clams. For information, call the Department of Fish and Game at (408) 649-2870.

Deep Sea Fishing

There's a nearby mountain range that is constructed something like the Sierra Nevada, but you won't find it on any road map. It's buried beneath miles of sea water. Tucked below the ocean surface along the Bay Area coast is rock ridgeline, complete with craggy peaks and canyons that drop thousands of feet. Just like the Sierra is a home for wildlife, this underwater range is perfect for fish.

A huge variety of big rockfish live here along with cabezone and lingcod, up to 50 pounds. The best time of the year is in September and October, when the big lings here emerge from the depths of the canyon bottoms to spawn along many of the mountain tops. But the fishing is good as long as the ocean is calm enough to allow it.

The highest peak is 25 miles west of San Francisco, where the Farallon Islands break the surface. The ridgeline extends for about 100 miles, to just north of Bodega Bay. Reefs (south to north) such as the Farallones, Soap Bank, Fanny Shoals and Cordell Bank attract vast schools of rockfish year-round, and big lingcod every fall.

Fishing for them is a lot of fun for newcomers and experienced hands alike. In any case, you are likely to fill up your freezer. It is common for anglers to bring home burlap bags filled with 15-fish limits often weighing 75 to 85 pounds, on trips to these spots. The best lingcod spots are at Soap Bank, which is just south of Cordell Bank, and just offshore of the South Farallon Islands.

The *Sea Angler* from Bodega Bay ventures to Cordell Bank daily when seas allow it. On a typical trip in the fall, boat loads of 25 to 35 fishermen will catch 30 to 60 lingcod, in addition to the limits of 15 rockfish per rod.

The Soap Bank, a rarely fished spot due to its distance from sportfishing ports, can offer even better action. Lingcod up to 50 pounds are caught every fall. The only sportfishing vessel fast enough to reach the Soap Bank is the *Cobra* out of Richmond Marina, a 96-footer with three engines that hits this spot daily. In many cases, the boat ride takes longer than it does for fishermen to limit out.

The rigging is quite simple. Most people buy a shrimpfly rig, that is, a pre-tied leader with three red/yellow shrimpflies. Small strips of squid are baited on the hooks, then dropped to the ocean bottom—usually 200 to 450 feet deep.

The boat does not anchor, but drifts over the reefs, and the speed of the drift is controlled by the intensity of the wind. In turn, this is the variable that decides how much sinker weight is required. It can vary from eight ounces to two pounds, though one-pound weights usually do the job. Instead of lead sinkers, you can add some excitement to your trip by trying a 16-ounce, chrome-plated Diamond jig or Yo Ho jig for a sinker. A chrome jig dangled near the sea bottom is the ticket for big lingcod, which will often smash into it in order to protect the territory they have staked out.

The problem is that these jigs, complete with large treble hooks, can snag up so fast on the bottom that it can seem like the rocks are biting better than the fish. On calm autumn days, when the boat drift is slight and fishermen have plenty of time to dangle baits over the reef, it is common for everybody aboard to catch two or three fish at a time.

On one trip to the Farallon Islands, a gent shouted for the gaff—which usually means a big fish is on the line. But when *Sea Angler* skipper Rick Powers looked over the side, he instead saw what looked like a stringer of 15 fish.

"What the heck are you doing using a stringer," Powers said. "This is the ocean. We put them in a burlap bag out here. You put them on a stringer and all you're going to do is attract a bunch of sharks."

The fishermen just grinned. "Look closer," he said.

We all did. It turned out that the man had a custom-tied leader with 15 baits on at once—and he had caught the 15-fish limit in one drop.

Deep Sea Selections

Cordell Bank: The *Sea Angler* makes trips daily out of Tides Wharf in Bodega Bay. Call (707) 875-3495.

Soap Bank and Fanny Shoal: The *Cobra*, the fastest sportfishing vessel in the Bay Area, hits Soap Bank regularly out of Sausalito. Call (510) 283-6773.

Farallon Islands: *C-Gull* and *New Donna D* out of Emeryville make regular trips; call (510) 654-6040. *Capt. John* from Princeton also makes the run; call (415) 726-2913.

Deep Reef: This is the favorite spot for the *Blue Horizon* from Princeton in Half Moon Bay; call (415) 726-2913. Also try the *Queen of Hearts* at (415) 726-7133.

New Year Island: Stagnaro's Fishing Charters sends boats here from Santa Cruz. Call (408) 425-7003.

Capitola: Fishing the edge of inshore kelp beds in shallow water can be productive. Skiff rentals are available at Capitola Wharf. Call (408) 462-2208.

Monterey: The *Holiday* works the Monterey underwater canyon. Call (408) 372-0577.

Fort Bragg: The *Trek II* out of Noyo Harbor runs Friday through Sundays to local reefs. Call (707) 964-4550.

Eureka: The *Moku* makes two half-day trips out of Easy Landing to Table Rock, or in Humboldt Bay. Call (707) 442-3474.

Bald Eagle Watching

Dark sky, silent flight. The sight of a bald eagle lifting off at sunrise from a treetop always makes you aware of what true greatness is.

The power from just a few wingbeats can propel a bald eagle for hundreds of yards, gliding on its six-foot wingspan while keeping a razor-sharp watch for prey. Morning light makes its white head and tail feathers glisten. It's the kind of scene that can stir your spirit.

It is also the kind of scene that is not so quite so rare anymore, especially in California. As winter arrives and the jet stream sends arctic weather into the Pacific Northwest and Canada, the eagles head south, with more wintering in the Golden State than anywhere else in the lower 48.

They have their favorite spots, and that's where you come in. From December through March, taking an eagle watching trip can be a uniquely rewarding adventure. On such a tour, it has become typical to see 10 to 20 bald eagles, often more, along with golden eagles and osprey. For most people, the trip provides a rare look at the best the world has to offer.

The best areas for sighting bald eagles in California are at Lake San Antonio in Monterey County, and in the Klamath Basin National Wildlife Refuge in the northeastern part of the state. During the winter, there are usually close to 1,000 eagles in the Klamath Basin, and about 60 at Lake San Antonio, a significant increase in the past 15 years.

While eagles are still not as abundant as the ones on the backs of quarters, it is rare not to see the great bird at these two habitats.

Other areas offering good opportunities to see eagles include Eagle Lake (62 eagles) near Susanville and Shasta Lake (14 eagles) north of Redding. Eagles can also be spotted at Trinity Lake north of Weaverville and at Lake Britton near Burney. In the Bay Area, the foothill country of remote Alameda and Contra Costa counties provides enough habitat and open space for a few resident bald eagles, though sightings can be rare.

Terry Davis of the Monterey County Parks Department helps direct the organized eagle tours at Lake San Antonio, the only place in California where such a trip is available. (At the Klamath Basin, it's a do-it-yourself proposition.)

"The increase at Lake San Antonio coupled with reports of increases in other parts of the country is a positive indication that the eagle population is again on the rise," said Davis. "Through research, education, restrictions on the use of chemicals, and the establishment of alternative habitats, environmentalists have made a valuable effort to maintain and increase the eagle population."

The tours at Lake San Antonio provide the chance for anybody, regardless of their experience in the outdoors, to see bald eagles, and lots of them. Lake San Antonio is located in central California near King City. There is a year-round campground, motor home hookups, and cabin rentals at the lake, with hotels available in King City and Paso Robles.

The eagle tours have become quite popular and reservations are advised. The trip starts with a 30-minute slide presentation, which will put you in the right frame of mind. Then you board the *Eagle One*, a 56-foot tour boat on pontoons, and you are provided with binoculars by park assistants. There is a seat for everybody, but when the eagles start getting spotted, most people get too excited to stay put. The trip is two hours long; the brunch trip runs three hours.

It is a big lake which is subject to great fluctuations, but even when at minimum pool, it still has more than five miles of water to the dam. In addition, the lake rises very quickly in winter. That is because the water comes all at once, rather than over the course of several months from the snowmelt in late spring and early summer.

Up in the Klamath Basin, it's a different world.

Modoc County covers an area as large as the Bay Area's nine counties, yet has a population of only 8,600, not counting dogs. Its remoteness is part of the attraction for visitors, as are the eagles, which typically number 950 during the winter. It is an ideal locale for eagles because they have an abundance of waterfowl to feed on. In fact, preying eagles are nature's way of cropping out the ducks that are in less-than-perfect health.

No organized eagle watching trips are available here. Instead, you create your own self-guided tour, with rangers providing tips on the best areas to see eagles.

Two keys here are to come prepared for cold weather, and to plan to stay overnight in a hotel, not in a tent. The temperature can hover between 15 and 30 degrees through most of the winter, sometimes colder, and unless you plan on hibernating, you're better off in a hotel room for the night than in a sleeping bag.

That done, you can enjoy your days watching the most majestic of American birds, and keep your toots warm at night. It's an experience that will stay with you for a long time.

Lake Antonio Tours: For information, write Eagle Tours, Monterey County Parks, P.O. Box 5279, Salinas, CA 93915-5279. Reservations: call (408) 755-4899.

Klamath Basin: For a free brochure, write the Klamath Basin National Wildlife Refuge, Route 1, Box 74, Tule Lake, CA 96134. Information: call (916) 667-2237. For lodging information, write Shasta Cascade, 1250 Parkview Avenue, Redding, CA 96001, or phone (800) 326-6944.

Fee or Free: A modest fee is charged for tours at Lake San Antonio. Low group rates are available, which inspires schools, senior organizations and environmental clubs to make the trip. Special weekend morning brunch tours are also available.

Firewood Gathering

You bring the great outdoors indoors every time you light a match to firewood that you have cut and split yourself. Part of the appeal is the sweet smell. As your fire burns, the mountain scent of acres of pines, firs, cedars and madrones is recaptured in your living room. Then you notice a different kind of heat than you get from a thermostat, a penetrating warmth that gives your home the feel of a cozy log cabin.

You toss another log on the fire and you get the satisfaction of seeing and feeling the results of your own labor, from that nice stack of wood out back to a quiet night in front of the fireplace.

From forest to fireplace, cutting your own firewood can be easy, fun and save you hundreds of dollars in the process. It can also add a special dimension to a weekend camping/fishing trip, even if you just spend a few hours at it, like in the middle of the day when the fishing goes flat. You end up bringing home a nice stack of firewood as well as memories of your good times.

The price and time is right. It costs only $10 to $20 to buy a firewood permit from the U.S. Forest Service, which allows you to cut two cords of wood from trees that are dead or down. Fall is an ideal time to cut, because timber companies are putting the wraps on summer logging operations. This means there are plenty of slash piles—logs judged unusable by timber operations—where you can cut a load of firewood.

It all makes for time well spent in the miles of mountain country that comprise our national forests.

In California, there are 95 ranger districts in the national forests—mountain land that is owned and used by the public.

These forests are far different than national parks, such as Yosemite. A national park is considered something of a nature preserve, while a national forest is there to be used—to be fished, hunted, hiked, and to some extent, logged.

The national forests closest to the Bay Area are Mendocino (east of Ukiah), Tahoe (east of Marysville), Eldorado (east of Placerville) and Stanislaus (east of Sonora). They are close enough that you can combine a weekend camping trip with a session of firewood cutting and come up a winner.

If you plan on visiting more distant national forests, such as Shasta-Trinity or Klamath, it is wise to finagle an extra day or two for your trip. Otherwise, you'll spend too much time driving and not enough time in the forest. Instead of fun, it will seem like work.

You should take your time, decide which national forest you want to visit, then buy a map for it. For maps, write to the U.S. Forest Service, Office of Information, 630 Sansome Street, San Francisco, CA 94111. These maps detail all backcountry roads, as well as hiking trails, streams and lakes that you previously may not have known even existed.

The next step is to call the district office and ask about firewood availability. In areas where a timber sale has been completed, dead and downed logs are often lying around, waiting to be cut up. In other spots, it can be slim pickings.

You must show up at the district office in person to purchase your firewood permit. While you're at it, the information officer will usually tell you precisely where to go. On the firewood trips I've taken, the Forest Service even provided free locator maps to pinpoint the best spots.

On one trip, it took little over an hour to fill my pickup truck, which left plenty of time to hike, fish and explore the area.

If you don't have a pickup truck, you'll have to team up with somebody who does, rent one or limit the size of your load. Occasionally, some Bay Area neighbors share in the cost of renting a large flatbed truck, head to the mountains as a team and pool their permits, then cut, split and stack enough wood for everyone involved.

Wood is measured by the "cord," which describes a well-staked pile that measures four-by-four-by-eight feet. You can fit a cord of wood in a standard-size pickup truck bed, but only if it is carefully stacked. Most people will settle for about half a cord, since a cord can weigh a lot, especially if it's wet.

With a wood-burning stove or fireplace insert, two to three cords is usually enough to get you through a winter in the Bay Area. People living in mountain areas use about six cords per year.

The savings? Your permit will get you two cords of firewood—which would cost you anywhere from $250 to $450 in the Bay Area. In mountain areas, the price is about half that. The cost of hardwoods, such as oak or madrone, is usually 25 percent higher than softwoods, like pine or cedar, because hardwoods burn hotter and longer. Mixing hardwoods and softwoods can make for the ideal fire—the pine will keep your flame, but the oak will throw off more heat, and burn all night long.

You don't need much equipment, but you'll be lost without a few essentials. A good chainsaw, of course, is a prerequisite, and most cost in the $200 range. Some rental companies have them available. My preference is for a chainsaw with a 20 to 24-inch bar. Smaller ones, the chainsaws with 12 to 14-inch bars, are designed for limbing, not logging. The 36-inch saws are heavy and powerful, designed for professional tree fallers, and can be dangerous in the hands of a novice.

Homelite, McCulloch, Stihl, Echo and Husquavama are the most popular brands. I own two different kinds, and members of my family own two other brands. All have performed well. *Consumer Reports* has completed an excellent safety study on them, describing how manufacturers have changed design to virtually eliminate kickback.

By state law, you must have a fire extinguisher and shovel, and it is also wise to wear heavy boots and leather gloves. A few wedges and a maul or sledge can be critical if you get your chainsaw stuck in a log. They can also be used by a friend to split the logs which you're cutting rounds off of a fallen tree.

The most important safety factor always is to make the trip with a friend, and to alternate cutting and loading. Otherwise, fatigue gradually sets in, and the cutter becomes vulnerable to a serious accident.

The most common error, which increases as fatigue sets in, is to look directly down at your cut. If the saw were to jam on a knot or kick back, your face would be directly in the path of the chain. Instead, always keep your head out of the plane of the chainsaw. This is where a companion, watching for any errors, can keep the cutter out of trouble. Alone, you may not even be aware of the mistake.

Kickback, which occurs when a dull saw hits a tough spot or knot, is the most dangerous element of woodcutting. The best prevention for that type of accident is to keep your chainsaw razor sharp.

Your logs should be split either with a maul, or a sledge and wedge, so the wood will dry and make a perfect-sized package for your fireplace. Cedar, pine and fir can often be split with one swing of the maul, with no wedge necessary. After being split, the wood will be cured as soon as two to four months, but burns best after sitting for a year. If the tree has been dead and down for a considerable amount of time, the wood may be ready to burn immediately.

It's a good project for teamwork—with one person cutting, another splitting and another loading. In only an hour, you can have enough firewood cut, split and stacked for many nights of warm fires.

Cutting with a group will also simplify your trip. Instead of problems, you will have solutions. Instead of work, getting a load of firewood will be a fun diversion on a weekend camping trip.

Sources for Firewood

Eldorado National Forest, east of Placerville: Write 100 Forni Road, Placerville, CA 95667, or phone (916) 622-5061.

Klamath National Forest, west of Yreka: Write 1312 Fairlane, Yreka, CA 96097, or phone (916) 842-6131.

Lassen National Forest, east of Redding: Write 55 South Sacramento Street, Susanville, CA 96130, or phone (916) 257-2151.

Los Padres National Forest, south of Monterey: Write 6144 Calle Real, Goleta, CA 93111, or phone (805) 683-6711.

Mendocino National Forest, northeast of Ukiah: Write 420 Laurel Street, Willows, CA 95988, or phone (916) 934-3316.

Modoc National Forest, in the northeastern corner of the state: Write 441 North Main Street, Alturas, CA 96101, or phone (916) 233-5811.

Plumas National Forest, northwest of Lake Tahoe: Write P.O. Box 11500, Quincy, CA 95971, or phone (916) 283-2050.

Shasta-Trinity National Forest, north and west of Redding: Write 2400 Washington Avenue, Redding, CA 96001, or phone (916) 246-5222.

Sierra National Forest, south of Yosemite National Park: Write 1600 Tollhouse Road, Clovis, CA 93611, or phone (209) 487-5155.

Six Rivers National Forest, between Eureka and Crescent City: Write 1330 Bayshore Way, Eureka, CA 95501, or phone (707) 442-1721.

Stanislaus National Forest, east of Sonora: Write 19777 Greenley Road, Sonora, CA 95370, or phone (209) 532-3671.

Tahoe National Forest, northwest of Lake Tahoe: Write Highway 49 and Coyote Street, Nevada City, CA 95959, or phone (916) 265-4531.

How to Get Started: Get the U.S. Forest Service brochure on firewood cutting by writing the U.S. Forest Service, Office of Information, 630 Sansome Street, San Francisco, CA 94111, or phone (415) 705-2874.

How to Get a Map: You can obtain a detailed map of the national forest you want by writing the Office of Information, 630 Sansome Street, San Francisco, CA 94111. Phone (415) 705-2874 for the price.

How to Know Where to Cut: Stop in at the district office, purchase a cutting permit, then receive directions pinpointing areas to cut your firewood.

What to Bring: A chainsaw, gas, a can of two-cycle oil, 30-weight oil for the chain, sturdy boots, gloves, a fire extinguisher and a shovel are mandatory. If your chainsaw gets jammed in a tree, a maul and a few wedges can get you free. If you flood the engine, a spark-plug wrench can come in handy.

Law of the Land: Cut only trees that are dead and down.

Fishing with Kids

Youngsters don't just want to do; they want to do well. Thus fishing becomes quite a challenge, a sport which requires logic, persistence and timing, because the idea isn't just to fish, it's to catch fish.

Which reminds me of a youngster named Justin Stienstra of Palo Alto, my brother's stepson. Justin has had his share of success, with good grades in school and All-Star play on the baseball field, and he tries just as hard with a fishing rod. But over a three-year period in which he made 10 fishing trips, the results did not equal his efforts.

"In that time, I caught two fish," he confided to me. "Make that three, but one got off."

That's all changed now, though.

Many youngsters, and adults too, can empathize, and many quit the sport out of frustration. So the mission of every newcomer to fishing should be to have an adventure where you are going to catch fish, lots of them, one after another, no matter what size, and get a glimpse of the excitement that is possible.

So Justin, my brother Rambob, and I embarked on a crusade in Northern California to catch fish. Not just a few. Dozens of them. There are hundreds of lakes, streams and coastal areas where this is possible.

For example, Clear Lake, along the tules outside of Clear Lake State Park, is an excellent spot to catch bluegill. For yellow perch, try your luck at Copco Lake in Siskiyou County. You can't go wrong.

For a wilderness adventure, hike in to Coit Lake in Henry W. Coe State Park in the Gavilan Mountains and you'll find plenty of bass. Hike in at Rae Lakes in the

John Muir Wilderness, and also at Sapphire Lake in the Trinity Alps Wilderness, and you'll get plenty of trout.

There are several streams where you'll be able to catch a lot of fish. The Upper San Joaquin River, upstream of Devil's Postpile, is a winner for trout, as is Kings River near Road's End in Kings Canyon National Park. Juvenile steelhead are plentiful near Orleans on the Klamath River in September.

Along the coast, you can find rockfish at shallow-water kelp beds at San Simeon as well as at the Farallon Islands and at the shallow water reefs along the San Mateo County coast.

At any of these spots, and dozens of others, you can really haul them in. That chance is all the motivation one requires, and exactly what Justin Stienstra needed to discover.

Our trip took us far north, right to the Oregon border, to Copco Lake, where the yellow perch bite like piranhas. On his first cast, Justin caught two perch, one on each hook. In the next three hours, he caught dozens and dozens of them—there's no limit—and the three of us caught close to a hundred. No secret how: all it takes is a little piece of worm, or red yarn, near the boat ramp.

"I never realized this could happen," Justin said.

Well, it can. All you have to supply to make it happen is the do.

Copco Lake: Phone Shasta Cascade Wonderland Association, (800) 326-6944.

Clear Lake: Phone Clear Lake State Park, (707) 279-4293; Ferndale Marina, (707) 279-4866.

Coit Lake: Phone Henry W. Coe State Park, (408) 779-2728.

Rae Lakes/John Muir Wilderness: Phone Sierra National Forest (209) 487-4155.

Sapphire Lake/Trinity Alps Wilderness: Phone Shasta-Trinity National Forest, (916) 246-5222.

Upper San Joaquin River: Phone Inyo National Forest, (619) 647-6525.

Kings River: Phone Kings Canyon National Park, (209) 565-3341.

Klamath River: Phone Shasta Cascade Wonderland Association, (800) 326-6944.

San Simeon kelp beds: Phone San Simeon Landing, (800) 347-9717.

Farallon Islands: Phone Huck Finn Sportfishing, Princeton, (415) 726-7133; *Capt. John's*, Princeton, (415) 726-2913; the *Cobra*, Sausalito, (510) 283-6773.

Chapter 15

Flying Lessons

I looked down the runway and discovered I could barely breathe. I was just too excited. I thought I heard cannons going off in the cockpit, then I realized it was just my heart pounding.

"Push the throttle forward all the way, and then when I tell you, pull back on the yoke."

It was flight instructor Rusty Ballinger assigned to my "orientation flight," where newcomers to aviation are provided with a demonstration flight in small airplanes in the hope that they will be tempted to try for a private pilot's license.

"Go ahead," Ballinger said with a smile. "Do it now."

I did as directed. The engine roared and the airplane began moving down the runway at San Carlos Airport, slowly at first, then faster and faster. I noticed how easy it seemed to use the rudder pedals to keep the plane pointed down the center line. But for a moment, it looked as though the runway wasn't long enough. The cannons fired again in my chest. Then suddenly it seemed the airplane started flying all by itself. We lifted off, and in seconds we were above the jammed traffic on US 101.

By now, I couldn't breathe at all. Breathe? Hey, I was gripping the yoke too hard to worry about breathing.

"See, the airplane wants to fly," Ballinger said. "It's not so difficult. Let it climb up to 800 feet, then head on over toward the Dumbarton Bridge."

"Take control, take control," I ordered Ballinger.

"Why?" he asked. "What's the matter?"

"I have to breathe."

Finally, with Ballinger flying the plane, I took my first genuine breath of air since climbing into the cockpit. I looked at my hands and there were large, red creases in each from the death grip I had on the yoke. But then, after a few deep breaths, I gazed down over the South Bay, and it didn't seem so dangerous after all. Within a few minutes, I was breathing almost normally and took the yoke again.

"You see, flying gives you a new perspective on the world and it's safe," Ballinger said. "I have over 12,000 hours in the air. The most dangerous part of flying is driving to the airport."

Orientation flights such as this are offered at several general aviation airports around the Bay Area as a way to introduce newcomers to flying. The flight generally lasts about an hour, costs around $35 and is available at small airports in San Carlos, Palo Alto, Novato, Hayward and Livermore.

Anybody can do it by simply making a phone call and setting up an appointment. Even if you decide not to continue on toward a pilot's license, that first flight is an exhilarating experience.

A week later, participants often find that they are telling so many people about it that they decide to do it again. And again. And again. Until suddenly they discover they are reading flight books, studying aviation law, scanning charts, and dreaming of flight destinations. That's what happened to me. A year after my orientation flight, I was handed my private pilot's certificate after passing written and oral tests and a flight check with an inspector from the Federal Aviation Administration.

The cost of flying can be very expensive or very cheap, depending on how you go about it. To get a private license often requires $3,000 to $4,000 in plane-rental fees, and an additional $1,000 in private tutoring fees. But it can cost a lot less. The most economical way is to take a "ground class" in flying at a community college, available in evening sessions once a week. In these courses, the final exam is the FAA written test. That done, when you start flying you won't be paying top-dollar fees to learn basics that are covered in the low-cost college ground school.

The plane-rental fee can also be reduced to next to

nothing. Instead of renting a plane for $40 to $50 an hour, it's become increasingly common for several student aviators to pool their funds and buy a small trainer for $12,000 to $18,000. After getting their licenses, they sell the plane to another pool of students for the same price, and get their entire investment back.

Those who take a ground-school course at a community college, and join forces with other students to buy a trainer, can earn a pilot's license for just over $1,000 in instructor (no solos until checked off) and insurance fees.

In return, you get a wonderful view of the world and a fast way to travel. From a pilot's seat, the Bay Area looks like a band of connected cities on the flats, surrounded by mountain wilderness. Lakes are everywhere—there are over 60—including at least a dozen large, beautiful reservoirs that are off-limits to visitors. The Bay itself looks like the Mediterranean Sea, speckled with half a dozen little islands.

And fast? From San Carlos, you can fly to Livermore in just 15 minutes. It's worth the trip just to look down on the traffic jams on Interstate 580 as you sail by at 120 knots. And get this: even in the slowest plane, you can reach Monterey in about 45 minutes.

To keep it safe, student pilots are only allowed to perform skills they have mastered with an instructor aboard, and they also must demonstrate a knowledge of aviation law and associated subjects before they move on to each successive step in the process.

On my first flight, we flew out over the East Bay hills, checking the water levels at Del Valle, Calaveras, and San Antonio reservoirs. Then we practiced a few basic turning maneuvers, a meager attempt to coordinate aileron and rudder control. Finally, we headed back over the Bay, getting clearance from the San Carlos control tower to put the plane in sequence in the landing patter.

"Do you want to land her?" asked instructor Ballinger.

"What? Me? Land a plane?" I was flabbergasted.

"Sure. I'll help you."

Well, that plane made it down all right, and to this day I'm not too sure how responsible I was for it. But after turning off the runway, and clearing our taxi route with San Carlos ground control, Ballinger could sense I was hooked.

"Tell me, " Ballinger said, "isn't flying the greatest feeling in the world?"

"Well, not really," I replied. "It's actually the second greatest feeling in the world."

"Then what's the first?" he asked.

"That's easy," I answered. "Landing."

❖

Fee or Free: Cost for a one-hour orientation flight is in the $35 range.

Contact: For information on orientation flights, call any of the following numbers: Golden Gate Aviation, San Carlos Airport, (415) 592-2550; Palo Alto Flying Club, Palo Alto Airport, (415) 494-6946; Marin Air Services, Gnoss Field, Novato, (415) 897-7101; Aero Financial, Livermore Airport, (510) 443-5500.

Gold Panning

Money doesn't grow on trees, but it does sprout like weeds, however, in many California streams. This doesn't mean that you can take out a garden hoe and start digging up bags of $100 bills. But with a gold pan and skilled hands, you can find yourself 25 to 100 flakes of gold per hour. If you pluck a gold nugget, even a small one, you'll be laughing your way to the bank.

A lot people believe that most of the earth's gold has already been taken from nature's grasp by wily miners. But in California, gold seekers have literally only scratched the surface. Envision the earth's core as a pressurized molten mass, emerging where it can find cracks and fissures in the surface. The gold often rises to the earth's surface where it can find these weak spots—and the Mother Lode gold belt is so famous for this that California is known worldwide as the Golden State. The gold rises out of the bowels of the earth on these veins and stringers, and winter storms and spring snowmelt rob the gold from the bedrock and bring it to existing river canyons and feeder streams. From Mariposa up to Downieville, streams such as the Feather, American, Yuba, Mokelumne, Tuolumne and Stanislaus all cross the gold belt.

One fellow who developed remarkable expertise in the search for gold is the late Jim Martin, a long-time panner and sluice boxer who wrote the book *Recreational Gold Prospecting*.

"You can be walking along a trout stream fishing, and suddenly see a small gold nugget and you'll be hooked on it for life," Martin told me. "Gold fever is contagious. I have been up in the mountains since the 1950s; gold intrigues me. It's a lot like fishing. If you don't get anything, then it's time to try a new spot. You never know when you're going to get the big one."

You need a little equipment to get started. A gold

pan, a shovel, a magnifying glass, a toothpick, tweezers, and a bottle to put your gold in is all that is needed.

But that doesn't make it easy. The key elements to successful gold panning are knowing how to separate the silt and worthless fool's gold from the genuine gold—and exactly where to ply this art. Master that and you have better make an appointment with the assayer at Wells Fargo.

"The thing to do is to sit on the edge of a stream on a comfortable log or rock, and to keep the pan underwater while swishing it from side to side," Martin said. "You need to let the flow of water carry the lighter stuff out of the pan."

After about five minutes, you will have reduced the contents of your pan to nothing but jet black sand and gold flecks. Put a bit of water in your pan and swirl it in a circular direction. This will bring to light the flecks of gold—those shiny little rascals you're in search of.

"If you see anything big, pick it out with your tweezers," Martin continued. "We call those 'picker outers.' Usually you just see the flecks. Take a toothpick, moisten the tip, then pick out the gold and put it in your bottle. With a magnifying glass, this is no problem."

Some gold seekers use mercury to separate the gold, but this can be quite dangerous to your health if the liquid enters your system through a nick on one of your fingers, or through other cuts. "Don't fiddle with mercury," advised Martin. Others will not attempt to separate the gold from the black sand while at streamside, but instead collect it, and do the fine, intensive work under a bright light at home. "The real key is processing a lot of material," Martin acknowledged.

To start your search, you need to select one of the rivers along the gold-bearing belt. Rarely will you find gold above 4,500 feet. Nature makes the rules, and you have to play by them.

Traces of past gold activity are usually best tipped off by piles along the stream. These are called tailing piles, where miners removed rocks as they were trying to search out a hot spot. The remains of abandoned cabins and any semblance of a man-made tunnel or cave are tip-offs as well.

"I have a spot on a tributary to the Feather River where you can pick out one hundred flakes of gold per hour," Martin said. "It's all in tiny flecks. I have another spot where you find these little nuggets. They're harder to find. You have to get right down in the bedrock, get in where nobody else has been. The average person might find a pocket where you find several nuggets, then go a number of days without finding any. You just never know."

Hiking the Peninsula

The Peninsula is one of California's classic paradoxes. It has some of the state's prettiest parkland and open space, yet it also has that hellish commuter trap, Highway 101, one of the ugliest roads anywhere.

Because of the latter, many folks forget about the former. But there are refuges available on the Peninsula that are set in landscapes that seem very distant from the highway's stream of brake lights. If you haven't made a visit lately, you might be surprised not only by the beauty, but by the lack of people and sense of peace in many of these areas.

There are many spots like this, yet they typically have relatively few visitors, especially on weekdays. Here is a synopsis of five of my favorite areas:

1—Skyline Trail, Woodside

Huddart and Wunderlich Parks are two of the Peninsula's prettiest redwood parks. (For more on Huddart, see page 185; for Wunderlich, see page 191.) This trail connects them, a one-way distance of about seven miles. The trail is ideal for a shuttle, and since most people don't like taking that trouble, you've got a beautiful trail with few folks on it.

Your best bet is to start at the north entrance at Huddart County Park at Kings Mountain Road, then hike south to Wunderlich, losing about 1,000 feet in elevation in the process. The trail generally parallels Highway 35, but you will feel very far from any road.

Information: Phone the San Mateo County Parks Department, (415) 363-4020; Huddart Park or Wunderlich Park, both at (415) 851-1210.

2—Sweeney Ridge, San Bruno

Everybody's heard of Sweeney Ridge, right? Well, you might think so until you actually get out and hike it. Often, you won't see another soul. The trailhead from the south parking lot at Skyline College is routed up to the Bay Discovery Site, about a 45-minute walk. From there, you get some of the best views anywhere, the Pacific Ocean on one side, and the South Bay on the other. (For more information on Sweeney Ridge, see the story on page 164.)

Information: Phone the Golden Gate National Recreation Area, (415) 556-0560.

3—Mills Canyon Park, Burlingame

City and county parks frequently get overlooked by out-of-towners, and such is the case here. Mills Canyon is a 40-acre city park set just east of Skyline Boulevard off of Arguello. The feature is Mills Creek, a pretty stream with pools and short cascade drops. Figure about an hour to hike the loop trail along the creek. It is a wildlife refuge, with no formal park headquarters, entrance station, or even telephone.

Information: Phone Burlingame City Parks, trail map available, (415) 696-7245.

4—Purisima Creek Redwoods, Skyline

This area is set along Highway 35 (Skyline Boulevard), four miles south of the junction with Highway 92. Here you will find untouched wildlands with redwoods and ferns, ocean views, and if you hike it, a beautiful little stream. It is an open space preserve, a do-it-yourself special, not a developed park. The best trailhead is near Skyline Road mile marker SM 16.65, where you can make a four-mile downhill trip amid redwoods. With a companion, you can park another vehicle at the trail's end (at Higgins Canyon Road near Half Moon Bay), giving you a one-way hike with no uphill grunt. (For more on Purisima Creek Redwoods, see page 182.)

Information: Phone the Midpeninsula Regional Open Space District, (415) 691-1200. A trail map is available.

5—Arastradero Lake Trail, Palo Alto foothills

It is about a 10 or 15-minute walk from the parking area to reach the lake, and it is always a refreshing sight to top the rise and see this nice little pond. It is usually full, ringed by tules, with ducks and coots paddling about. There are also ground squirrels, rabbits, hawks and owls in the surrounding hills. The park covers about 600 acres; a trail map is available at the parking area. There is no formal entrance station or telephone, but the rangers at nearby Foothills Park manage the preserve.

It is easy to reach off of Highway 280. Take the Page Mill Road exit, then turn right at Arastradero Road. The parking area is just two miles up the road on the right side.

Information: Phone Foothills Park, (415) 329-2423; Palo Alto Parks and Recreation Department, (415) 329-2487.

Houseboating

Just turn the key, let the engine rumble to life, then point the houseboat out toward the open water. That is about as difficult as it gets. The rest of your vacation can seem like it is on automatic pilot.

Houseboats are available for rent at four of the state's largest lakes, Shasta, Trinity, Oroville and Don Pedro, as well as at the San Joaquin Delta. A houseboat is a floating RV where you can barbecue from your front porch, fish from your back deck, camp anywhere, and get sun, water and a complete getaway from working. For many, nothing could be better,

The prices vary greatly according to the size of the boat, how many days rented, whether it includes a weekend, and if it's peak season. In the Delta, for instance, a houseboat that sleeps four costs $495 for three days, Friday afternoon through Sunday evening. At Shasta Lake for a week, it can be nearly $2,000.

Even on the high end, however, the cost can be whittled down by sharing it with a group of people. At Holiday Harbor at Shasta Lake, for instance, a houseboat that sleeps 12 rents for $1,925 for a week (in the summer), which is equivalent to $23 per day, per person. That is why it is one of the favorite types of vacations for groups of college students.

Or for anybody else. It is safe, easy and fun.

Here is a capsule of the destinations where houseboats are available:

The San Joaquin Delta

The Delta is a vast mosaic of waterways, covering more than 1,000 miles of navigable waters. You can scan a map and dream of where you want to go, then spend a week at it and not even see a fraction of it. There is just so much water. Most of the houseboat rentals are in the back Delta near King Island (generally near Stockton). This area has many quiet sloughs where you can park the boat for the night, fish for catfish, or just sit there and do absolutely nothing except look at the water. Sounds good to me.

Information: Phone Herman and Helen's, (209) 951-4634; Paradise Point Marina, (209) 952-1000; King Island Houseboats (209) 956-5209.

Lake Oroville

When the drought ended, Oroville filled with water. This created a beautiful sight, astounding to some who had become accustomed to seeing it nearly empty. The reservoir covers some 15,000 acres, including extensive lake arms, each of which is like a separate lake. Since it is set at 900 feet in the foothill country, warm weather arrives here earlier than at lakes farther north. The fishing for trout and bass is very good from April through early June, and then when the water warms up from July through early fall, it becomes a great lake for waterskiing and swimming.

Information: Phone Bidwell Marina, (916) 589-3165; Lime Saddle Marina, (916) 877-2414.

Don Pedro Reservoir

The last time you drove to Yosemite, you probably drove right past Don Pedro, that big lake with the extended lake arms, located right along Highway 49 in the gold country. It's worth a look, especially in the spring, when it's fullest. The lake can cover 13,000 surface acres and 160 miles of shoreline. The far-reaching lake arms provide secluded haunts, both for parking the boat for the night or fishing for bass, bluegill and catfish. It is set at 800 feet in the foothills 30 miles east of Modesto, so the weather is very hot in the summer.

Information: Phone Don Pedro Marina, (209) 852-2369; Moccasin Point Marina, (209) 989-2383.

Shasta Lake

This is the houseboating capital of the West. Giant Shasta has 1,000 houseboat rentals and plenty of water for them, 365 miles of shoreline in all. It's one of the few places where there is enough room for everybody: anglers, waterskiers, swimmers and all kinds of boats. With five major lake arms, there are many little secret spots that can be explored only by boat. The fishing is often excellent in the spring and early summer, with abundant numbers of trout and bass.

Information: For the complete list and prices of the seven marinas with houseboat rentals, write Shasta Cascade, 1250 Parkview, Redding, CA 96001, or phone (800) 326-6944.

Trinity Lake

Trinity Lake is located in the mountains of Northern California north of Weaverville, set at the foot of the Trinity Alps.

Because of its location, summer and warmer temperatures do not arrive here until mid-June, and that means reservations are easier to come by than at other houseboat destinations. It's a big reservoir, 175 miles of beautiful shoreline, surrounded by national forest. In the cool spring months, fishing for trout and smallmouth bass is often excellent; the state record for smallmouth was caught here. Because it is such a long drive from the Bay Area, there are far fewer vacationers here than at the other spots listed.

Information: Phone Cedar Stock Resort, (916) 286-2225; Estrellita Marina, (916) 286-2215; Trinity Alps Marina, (916) 286-2282.

Lakes with Cabin Rentals

When all you do is do, then maybe it's time to just do nothing.

Take a seat in front of a cabin set alongside a lake, gaze out at the water, maybe sip a drink, and just enjoy breathing again. Maybe take a boat out and cruise around a little, maybe fish a little, but for the most part, do nothing.

In my travels across Northern California, I've found 19 lakes where you can do just that, lakes where you can rent a little self-contained cabin, or a unit overlooking the water. They range from upscale cottages beside Davis Lake in the Sierra Nevada to cabins with lookouts of Trinity Lake in Northern California.

Here's a selection of the possibilities:

Lake Almanor, Plumas County

Almanor, a big lake with 52 miles of shoreline, has offerings ranging from exclusive lakeside cabins on the Almanor Peninsula to rustic cabins and motels with individual units. (For more details on Plumas County, see page 73.)

Contact: Write the Plumas County of Chamber of Commerce, P.O. Box 11018, Quincy, CA 95971, or phone (800) 326-2247.

Bear River Reservoir, Amador County

Bear River Lodge offers lakeside units, including a few with very nice views. The lake is set at 5,800 feet along Highway 88 in the Sierra Nevada, and receives bonus stocks of trophy-size trout in the summer.

Contact: Write Bear River Resort, 40800 Highway 88, Pioneer, CA 95666, or phone (209) 295-4868.

Lake Berryessa, Napa County

This is the Bay Area's backyard lake, offering a close-to-home spot for boating, waterskiing and good trout fishing for those who troll deep enough. There are several lakeside resorts, including Putah Creek, which has cabins at the north end of the lake, and Steele Park, which has apartments overlooking a lake arm.

Contact: Write the Berryessa Chamber of Commerce, P.O. Box 9164, Spanish Flat Station, Napa, CA 94558, or phone (800) 726-1256, or (707) 966-2347.

Blue Lakes, Lake County

Four resorts sit aside this pretty lake that is often lost in the shadow of its nearby big brother, Clear Lake. If you want bass, go to Clear Lake. If you want trout in a quiet setting, try Blue Lakes.

Contact: Write Lake County Visitor Information, 875 Lakeport Boulevard, Lakeport, CA 95451, or phone (800) 525-3743.

Bucks Lake, Plumas County

This lake is known as one of the best places to catch trout in Northern California. There are two lodges with cabins, but note that each has only a few units with lake views.

Contact: Write the Plumas County Chamber of Commerce, P.O. Box 11018, Quincy, CA 95971, or phone at (800) 326-2247.

Camanche Lake, Amador/Calaveras Counties

About 20 cottages are available on this lake located in the Mother Lode. The bass fishing is excellent in the spring; the weather gets hot in July and August.

Contact: Write Camanche Recreation, 2000 Camanche Road, Ione, CA 95640, or phone (209) 763-5121.

Clear Lake, Lake County

Dozens of privately operated resorts offer units with lake views. This is one of the West's best fishing lakes for bass and catfish. As a natural lake, not a reservoir, the lake levels stay near full through summer. (For more details on Clear Lake, see page 107.)

Contact: Write Lake County Visitor Information, 875 Lakeport Boulevard, Lakeport, CA 95453, or phone (800) 525-3743.

Davis Lake, Plumas County

Davis Lake, located north of Truckee, has several upscale cabins set within walking distance of the lake. This is favorite spot for evening trout rises near creek inlets.

Contact: Write the Plumas County Chamber of Commerce, P.O. Box 11018, Quincy, CA 95971, or phone (800) 326-2247.

Eagle Lake, Lassen County

This is a huge lake that is known for its giant cutthroat trout, stark beauty and spring winds. Eagle Lake is set in distant Lassen County, where there are only a couple of stoplights in the entire county. Lakeview Inn offers lakeside accommodations, and there are also cabin rentals at Spalding Tract.

Contact: Phone the Lakeview Inn at (916) 825-3223; write the Lassen County Chamber of Commerce, 36 South Lassen Street, P.O. Box 338, Susanville, CA 96130, or phone at (916) 257-4323.

Gold Lakes Basin

This is one of the more beautiful areas you can drive to in California, complete with mirror-like lake settings in the northern end of the Sierra. Cabins are available at Salmon Lake, Packer Lake, Gold Lake and Sardine Lake.

Contact: Write the Plumas County Chamber of Commerce, P.O. Box 11018, Quincy, CA 95971, or phone (800) 326-2247. For fishing information, call the Sportsmen's Den at (916) 283-2733.

Lewiston Lake, Trinity County

This is a jewel of a lake set below Trinity Lake and surrounded by the Shasta-Trinity National Forest. Units are available near some of the lake's best trout fishing.

Contact: Write Lakeview Terrace Resort, Star Route Box 250, Lewiston, CA 96052, or phone (916) 778-3803.

Lake Pillsbury, Lake County

Pillsbury is set in the Mendocino National Forest northeast of Ukiah. Evening trout fishing is often good. Lake Pillsbury Resort, the only resort on the lake, offers lakeside lodging and a small marina.

Contact: Write Lake Pillsbury Resort, P.O. Box 37 Potter Valley, CA 95469, or phone at (707) 743-1581.

Shasta Lake, Shasta County

This is the big daddy of Northern California lakes with 365 miles of shoreline. Each lake arm is like a separate lake. There are four lakeside resorts that offer cabins or rooms with a view of the lake.

Contact: Write Shasta Cascade, 1250 Parkview, Redding, CA 96001, or phone (800) 326-6944.

Lake Shastina, Siskiyou County

This lake is set just north of Mount Shasta near Weed and has townhouses and chalets overlooking the lake.

Contact: Write Carol Richardson, Lake Shastina Accommodations, 6030 Lake Shastina Drive, Weed, CA 96094, or phone (916) 938-4111.

Trinity Lake, Trinity County

Cedar Stock Resort offers cabins that overlook this giant reservoir. At 2,300 feet, the lake is set at the gateway to the Trinity Alps; summer arrives here around July.

Contact: Write Cedar Stock Resort, Star Route 510, Lewiston, CA 96052, or phone (916) 286-2225.

Lake Tahoe, El Dorado County

You name it and it's here, from do-it-yourself private cabins to resorts that provide everything for you.

Contact: Write Lake Tahoe Visitor's Authority, P.O. Box 16299, South Lake Tahoe, CA 96151, or phone the Tahoe Visitor's Bureau at (800) 288-2463, press 0, then ask for "Tahoe Travel Planner."

Mountain Biking

I hate mountain bikes and I love mountain bikes. I hate them because when I go hiking, they always seem to be running over me. I love them, because they're so much fun when used in the right place.

Michael Hodgson can empathize with this paradox, as well as provide Bay Area bikers with tips on the best places for their sport. He's both an editor of *Backpacker* magazine, the bible for hikers, as well as the author of two books on mountain biking. That's a strange combination, because usually the two don't mix.

"A pedal-powered vehicle that can go virtually anywhere is enough to thrill many outdoor adventurers," Hodgson says. "Yet at the same time it can send chills down the spine of many hikers and wilderness purists. It's not hard for anyone to understand a hiker's anger at being startled out of a peaceful, contemplative state by an out-of-control, mach-speed mountain biker. Yet it is also not hard to imagine the joy of quietly pedaling along a mountain ridge by way of a jeep trail bathed in early morning light."

Hodgson's goal is to make peace between hikers and bikers, and that mission is well underway with the publishing of his two books, one a guidebook to Bay Area biking, the other a humorous analysis of the sport. The guidebook, *Mountain Biking in the Bay Area: A Nearly Complete Guide* (published by Western Tanager Press in Santa Cruz), details the Bay Area's 50 best mountain biking trails, whereas *Mountain Biking For Mere Mortals* provides glimpses into the sport, covering topics such as "how to surgically remove an implanted bike," "how to repair your bike with a mallet," and "the safe load limit for lycra riding pants."

The key to quality biking in the Bay Area is to use the old, abandoned ranch roads that have been converted to trails in so many parks.

"There are places where mountain bikes don't belong," Hodgson says. "That starts with trails that are signed as closed to mountain bikers, trails that are open but too wet to ride on, and trails where proven and potential trail-use conflicts are unresolvable and hazardous to all users." He also agrees with rangers that mountain bikes have absolutely no place in a designated wilderness area.

However, Hodgson does suggest alternatives. In his guidebooks, he details rides where bikers of all abilities will have fun, including many back roads in remote parklands. Here is a capsule look at quality rides in the Bay Area:

Samuel P. Taylor State Park, Marin County

This redwood paradise is a great place to take the family, particularly for weekend trips based out of the park's campground. The finest mountain biking in the North Bay can be accessed from here. That includes nearby Bolinas Ridge, several rides on ranch roads at Point Reyes, and two pleasant rides within park boundaries—one to Devil's Gulch, the other a paved route along Papermill Creek.

Contact: Phone Samuel P. Taylor State Park at (415) 488-9897.

Briones Regional Park, Contra Costa County

Beautiful Briones Lake is the centerpiece of this park, which covers 5,300 acres of rolling grasslands and oak woodlands. A challenging loop ride is a route that goes from the Homestead Valley Trail to Sindicich Lagoon, around Briones Peak and back. Sure, this one is a puffer, but the view from the peak is well worth the grind.

Contact: Phone Briones Regional Park at (510) 229-3020.

Annadel State Park, Sonoma County

This park, located just off Highway 12 southeast of Santa Rosa, provides a myriad selection of ranch roads. They crisscross 5,000 acres of rocky terrain, including a route that takes you to a backcountry bass lake. "You can easily spend a full day riding at Annadel," Hodgson says. (His favorite destinations are Ledson Marsh and the trail towards Lake Ilsanjo, the Rough Go Trail and the Spring Creek Trail. (For more details on Annadel State Park, see page 97.)

Contact: Phone Annadel State Park at (707) 539-3911.

Montebello Open Space Preserve, Santa Clara County

This region provides some of the best riding areas on the Peninsula. A bonus is that the routes connect to adjacent greenbelts, including Long Ridge Open Space Preserve, Saratoga Gap Open Space Preserve, Stevens Creek County Park and Skyline Open Space Preserve. "If you are truly gonzo," Hodgson said, "it is possible to connect one continuous loop encompassing all of these parks."

Contact: Phone the Midpeninsula Regional Open Space District at (415) 691-1200.

Wilder Ranch, Santa Cruz

This state park is located two miles north of Santa Cruz, adjacent to Highway 1. It is an historical preserve, but hidden beyond the ranch are several excellent mountain biking trails (mostly jeep roads). The trail system is ideal for beginners, yet still fun for advanced riders.

Contact: Phone Wilder Ranch at (408) 426-0505.

Nordic Skiing

Cross-country skiing is inexpensive, adventurous, peaceful—it can even be slow, if you want it to be. It is relatively easy to learn and one of the few outdoor sports where females outnumber males, 53 to 47 percent.

"Cross-country skiing is just so very peaceful," said Jacqui James at Royal Gorge. "It's also an escape, getting away from the crowds, faxes and phones. I've done it for three years and I love it. I tried downhill once or twice, but it wasn't for me. I much prefer cross-country. You can set your own pace."

You also don't have to look over your shoulder, something that can be frustrating for downhill skiers on crowded slopes. In fact, the differences between downhill and cross-country skiing are amazing, with no lines, no stress and no alpine hot doggers. It's also a lot safer. Note, for instance, that there are usually no ambulances waiting at the end of the trail.

California has about 25 cross-country ski areas, as well as dozens of other locations where this sport is popular. At nordic centers, the groomed ski trails have two grooves, one for each ski. You set each ski in a groove, and you're off. You push along in a walking motion, and enjoy the glide. Instead of strapping your boots into a fixed binding, as with downhill skis, you are attached to your skis by just the tips of your boots. Cross-country skis are also longer and narrower than downhill skis, and have no cutting edges. After all, the idea is to glide, not to race and make cuts.

In most cases, newcomers can ski quite a bit of terrain with just a few friendly pointers from a companion. With a lesson and a little practice, you can enjoy most runs in any nordic center. As for expense, rental of boots, skis and poles is usually about $15 a day, and a ski pass goes for about the same. Package deals can usually be found in the $25 to $30 range.

For instance, one of best deals anywhere is at Royal Gorge, the capital of cross-country skiing in the West, located at Soda Springs along Interstate 80 in Sierra Nevada. For $30 to $40, you get rental skis, boots, poles, a 90-minute group lesson and a full-day trail pass. For information, phone (916) 426-3871.

Royal Gorge has more than 80 trails that span over 300 kilometers of set tracks, far more than any other cross-country ski area in the West. Other quality areas include Kirkwood, Tahoe-Donner and Tahoe Nordic, all with 65 to 70 kilometers of set track trails. The trails are usually marked by ribbons tied off of trees poking up through the snow. At the big cross-country areas, the network of tracks can make it look like an elaborate miniature railroad has taken over the area for winter.

The quiet is something else. You will find that once you get used to it, you may never again want to put up with lines, noise and high prices at one of the big downhill ski parks.

When you first start, cross-country skiing seems to require little physical effort. But after even 20 minutes, you will realize that this is an aerobic workout, great exercise. After a day or two at it, the sport will hone your body like a knife blade on a whet stone. After a few weekends, you will glow from the exhilaration.

Tahoe Area

Tahoe Paradise Sports, near the airport in South Lake Tahoe, (916) 577-2121.

Bijou Cross-Country Ski Area, in South Lake Tahoe, (916) 541-4611.

Spooner Lake Cross-Country Ski Area, south of Incline Village, (702) 749-5349.

Clair Tappaan Lodge, near Soda Springs off Interstate 80, (916) 426-3632.

Incline Cross-Country Ski Area, north of Tahoe off Highway 28, (702) 831-6500.

Kirkwood Cross-Country Ski Area, south of Tahoe off Highway 88, (209) 258-6000.

Northstar Cross-Country Ski Area, north of Tahoe off Highway 267, (916) 562-1010.

Royal Gorge Cross-Country Ski Area, near Soda Springs off Highway 80, (916) 426-3871.

Squaw Valley Nordic, northwest of Tahoe off Highway 89, (916) 581-6637.

Strawberry Touring Company, eight miles east of Kyburz off Highway 50, (916) 659-7200.

Tahoe Nordic, two miles east of Tahoe City off Highway 28, (916) 583-0484.

Central Sierra

Bear Valley, located 55 miles east of Angels Camp on Highway 4, (209) 753-2834.

Leland Meadows, 37 miles east of Sonora on Highway 4, (209) 965-4389.

Yosemite Mountaineering, based in Yosemite Valley, (209) 372-1244.

Northern California

Childs Meadows, nine miles southeast of Lassen Park on Highway 36, (916) 595-4411.

Mount Shasta Nordic Center, northeast of Redding on Highway 89, (916) 926-8610.

Fifth Season, at Mount Shasta, (916) 926-3606.

Lassen Ski Touring, at the southwest entrance to Lassen Park on Highway 36, (916) 595-3376.

Orienteering

"I've never been lost," Davy Crockett is said to have told Jim Bowie in 1831, "just been confused a few times."

Well, some 160 years later, hikers still tell the same joke about getting "confused" when out in the woods. Lost? Never. Of course not. Just confused.

But now there is a new Bay Area monthly event that can teach you how to keep from getting "confused" on your weekend adventures. You may not meet Davy Crockett, but you will discover the skills of woodsmanship, visit some beautiful wild places all around the Bay Area, as well as meet other hikers who are learning how to find their way. It is called "orienteering," and each month there is a meet in a different area where participants track a course using a map and compass. The cost of one of these orienteering meets depends on the level of difficulty of the course attended, but it is typically quite low.

"I love maps. I love the challenge of reading a map to figure out where you are," said Scott Bohle, who helps direct the Bay Area Orienteering Club. "It is a thinking sport. You are not following anybody. The object of our meets is to keep track of where you are and move as quickly as possible through an unknown area."

Even legends happen to get lost now and then. In the 1840s, explorer and U.S. Army Captain John C. Fremont was supposed to lead an army division into Northern California as part of a multiflank attack to claim the area as U.S. territory. Instead, as the story goes, Fremont directed his troops in circles for a week in Oregon and missed out on the conquest (though still he has towns, schools, and streets named after him).

Fremont probably insisted that he was not lost. "Just a little confused." Well, the Bay Area Orienteering

Club is dedicated to helping people get unconfused.

Many people have no sense of direction. Ironically, many who admit this become the most proficient in using a map and compass. Because they realize that they cannot trust their instincts, they accept that they must trust their instruments. After all, a compass never lies. The end result is a confident edge in any weekend outing.

The key factors in getting lost and staying lost are unfamiliarity with an area, weather (fog, snow), darkness (no flashlight and a moonless sky)—and of course, having navigation instruments but not knowing how to use them, or not even having them at all.

In a forested park, a good map and a compass can keep you on track. In a wilderness area, a topographical map, that is, one that has gradient lines showing elevation changes and an altimeter (which measures altitude), can get you nearly anywhere.

You see, it has always been easy to get lost, or confused a little. What you can discover, however, is that it can be just as easy to stay found.

Contact: Phone the Bay Area Orienteering Club at (415) 383-4429 or (415) 365-4275. All club meets are publicized in the Outdoors calendars in the *San Francisco Examiner* and the *San Francisco Chronicle.*

Pacific Crest Trail

The Pacific Crest Trail is America's greatest hike, crossing a land spiked by 13,000-foot granite spires, untouched sapphire lakes filled with trout, and canyons that drop as if they were at the edge of the earth.

Every day you are surrounded by the ultimate natural beauty the world can offer: the sound of bubbling, crystal mountain streams. Their symphony recharges both you and the mountain with energy. The high meadows are flooded with wildflowers, mostly violet-colored lupine, their stalks bending to a light breeze. Deer, bears and marmots are your companions, and you are just a temporary visitor to their wilderness home.

After a few weeks, you'll cast off concerns about the physical challenge of the hike and surrender to the natural untouched beauty of the high country wilderness.

The Pacific Crest Trail spans 2,627 miles, starting at the California/Mexico border and routing north through the Sierra Nevada and Cascade ranges, finally ending at the Canadian border.

The trail has 1,682 miles in California, 441 miles in Oregon, and 504 miles in Washington. The lowest point is at 400 feet near Palm Springs and the highest is at 13,180 feet at Forester Pass in the southern Sierra Nevada. In addition, a short, steep cutoff trail is available that takes hikers to Whitney Summit, a 14,496-foot elevation, the highest point in the lower 48.

If hikers do not have the time, energy or equipment to complete the entire trail, hundreds of connector links to the Pacific Crest Trail are available that allow hikers to customize shorter trips. The trail passes through 24 national forests, seven national parks, three Bureau of Land Management districts and five state parks. All of these provide easy access links to the trail. In fact, according to a survey by the Forest Service, only one percent of the people hiking the Pacific Crest Trail manage to complete it in a single summer. But members of the 99 percent club keep coming back.

While the route has been established for years, always known simply as the "PCT," the trail was officially completed just a few years ago when the Bureau of Land Management designated the final link across a stretch of Southern California desert. Its completion has helped to inspire the proposal of the American Discovery Trail, a byway crossing America from west to east. Along with the 2,109-mile Appalachian Trail, they are the world's most ambitious hikes.

Hikers from across America are attracted by the glacial-cut high Sierra range, volcano-sprouted mountains of the Cascades, and lakes and streams filled with the purest water in the world. Most visitors traverse a 50 or 60-mile section of it in a week, only rarely covering the entire length. The complete hike is a five-month trip requiring exceptional physical stamina, complicated logistics of stashing food bags at key locations, and most importantly, the time to do it.

My longest hike on the PCT was a 250-mile thump, including sidetrips, from Mount Whitney to Yosemite Valley. It took 20 days, more than half of which were spent at elevations over 10,000 feet. I have also explored several different sections in Northern California, Oregon and Washington. In the process, I have met hikers from all parts of the country, all out for the same reasons, to experience pristine beauty, to accept the physical challenge, and to walk in the footsteps of legends.

Jim Penkusky and Susan Day of Columbia, Maryland, both in their mid-20s, completed the entire route, leaving Mexico in March and arriving at the Canadian border in mid-October. I met them at Little Gladys Lake near Devil's Postpile National Monument.

"The rangers in northern Washington said that

they usually get their first big snow before or after the first week of November," Penkusky said. "We're aiming to finish a little ahead of that. That's when the weather window shuts down."

"Why do it?"

"I feel like I've been called to these mountains for years."

The diversity of habitat is the trail's most striking feature. You get it all: mountain peaks carved by glacial action; hardened volcanic flumes; seas of conifers in dense, forested valleys; untouched meadows and wetlands; and austere deserts sprinkled with tiny wildflowers.

The natural beauty can be overwhelming for newcomers. From Mount Whitney looking north, you can see rows of mountain peaks spanning nearly 100 miles, all of them 11,000 to 14,000 feet high. In the Sisters Wilderness in central Oregon, there are divine freestone streams and small emerald green lakes. The Pasayten Wilderness in Okanogan Forest in northern Washington has sections of forest and vegetation so thick that they are virtually impenetrable.

The longer you stay out in these surroundings, the greater your sense of oneness with the natural beauty around you. Eventually, this feeling bonds all hikers.

But even in perfect beauty you must confront some frustration, sometimes danger. This is true on the PCT as well and it comes in the form of icy passes. Between Whitney and Yosemite alone there are 10 passes, all situated at over 11,000 feet. The optimal time to brave these passes is in early July or August. If you time this portion of your trip too early in the season, like late May or early June, or after a big winter of snow, they can be loaded with miles of snow and ice. The worst is Forester Pass, at 13,180 feet, located in Southern California east of Sequoia National Park.

The best strategy for traversing these high mountain passes is to camp at the base of them the night before. Then climb them in the morning, fresh from a night's rest. After just a few ascending steps, the thin air at such a high altitude forces you into a rhythmic cadence, as if you were running a marathon. Steep trails at high altitudes can do that to you quick.

The ice field at Forester can stop you even quicker. Its steep slope can make it a formidable crossing, and in the morning, when temperatures are still cold, its surface is slick and hard. You try to dig your boot into the ice for grip, but there is little grip available. Some hikers bring ice axes; most others are prisoners of hope, where hiking becomes an act of faith. Slowly, with the caution of a surgeon, you work your way across the iced slope, positioning each step in the frozen bootprints of past hikers. Finally, you make it safely to the top. Maybe not completely sane, but on top.

Trail experience, you discover, often has less to do with intelligence than with your ability to learn a lessons. The same can also be true of fishing, of course, but those lessons can come quite a bit more easily.

At one pool along the Kern River where I dunked a sore ankle, a trout actually bit me in the foot. At Rae Lakes, located just north of Glen Pass (11,978 feet), I caught 10 trout in 20 minutes using a bare hook—the only problem was the fish kept hitting the split-shot sinker instead of the hook. In 75 nights of camping on the Pacific Crest Trail, I've never gone a night without trout for dinner (that will probably jinx me on my next trip).

Rainbow and brook trout are abundant at thousands of lakes set along the PCT, brown trout are big but rare, and in the high-elevation lakes in the southern Sierra, golden trout are a special prize. The golden may be the most beautiful of all trout, with a crimson stripe and many dark discs in a line along the side, a bright gold band along the belly, and the top of its body lightly spotted.

The hundreds of streams along the way are fresh with pure, cold oxygenated water, healthy native trout, and an evening bite that makes for a lifetime of memories.

Wildlife viewing is also exceptional. This is because relatively few roads provide direct access to the trail, which means visitors must first hike in on a connecting link before hooking up with the PCT. The final result is that hunting pressure during the fall season is low in many areas, since such a demanding hike is required to reach the high country.

So deer, bears, marmots, squirrels and other little furry things are abundant and unafraid. One evening while I was camping in the Marble Mountain Wilderness in Northern California, three deer, including a magnificent four-point buck in velvet, sauntered right through camp. It was the perfect end to a day in the mountain wilds.

All along the Pacific Crest Trail, you'll find pristine spots. Near Tawny Point in the high plateau country north of Whitney, for instance, there are acres of wildflowers, what John Muir called "bee pastures," and being among them can make you feel remarkably content.

The lookouts are the best in America, with 100-mile vistas common along any ridge, offering everything from views of snow-covered volcano tops to canyons that drop 7,000 feet. Sometimes you'll find yourself sitting in a vibrant meadow above a lake, scanning the scenery while nibbling on a stick of beef jerky. It is something you never forget.

Then there is the good tired feeling you get at the end of each day's hike, a feeling that you have asked the best from your body and received it.

At the end of every trip is a certainty that some part of you belongs in this wilderness.

❖

Contact: For a free brochure called *The Pacific Crest Trail—Washington, Oregon, California*, write the Office of Information, USDA-Forest Service, 630 Sansome Street, San Francisco, CA 94111, or call (415) 705-2874.

Rivers to Raft

If you have ever wondered what it feels like to get shot out of a cannon, you should try rafting the Upper Klamath River and tumbling through Hell's Corner Gorge. Rapids like Satan's Gate, Scarface and Ambush can make you feel like a human cannonball.

If you don't want to join the circus, consider a canoe or raft trip down the Middle Klamath, from Horse Creek on downriver. There's just enough white water to make the trip exciting, but it's still tame enough to make a family outing of it.

If you have never taken a raft or canoe trip, you may be curious about why people get excited about the sport. On the Upper Klamath, you can find the answer. I recommend it, either for curiosity seekers going solo, experts looking for a challenge or for a family outing.

One spring, when the Klamath was near flood stage, six of us in three rafts challenged the entire river from its headwaters in Oregon all the way to the Pacific Ocean. We did it in six days, covering as many as 50 miles per day, and tumbled through more than a thousand rapids in the process.

The whole idea about rafting is to get out there on the "edge." The Klamath can get you there. The first rapid you face in the Hell's Corner Gorge is called Caldera. We were roaring downriver when the nose of the raft headed straight into a big wave, the boat completely disappearing underwater. Moments later, the raft popped up in the air, surging forward—and right then a crosswave hit us from the right and flipped us. I went flying out of the raft like a piece of popcorn.

I went floating down the rapids, the hydraulics of the river pulling me under water, and then I popped to the surface. The life-saving equipment makes sure of that. You just time your breathing as you go bobbing along until you eventually come to an eddy, where you can paddle over to gain safety.

A lot of people never flip, but to most, it's kind of like a badge of honor. "Yeah, I rafted Hell's Corner Gorge and Branding Iron got us good."

River rapids are rated on a scale of Class I to VI, with Class I being a piece of cake and Class VI being suicide. The Upper Klamath has Class IV and V whitewater, and the mid-Klamath Class II, sprinkled with some Class III.

So if you want more of a family-oriented trip, the Middle Klamath provides it. By raft or canoe, it's a fun trip.

My preference on the Middle Klamath is to go by canoe. You get more speed, faster cuts, faster decisions and alas, faster flips.

Many rivers on the slopes of the Sierra Nevada run low in the summer. The Klamath provides the answer all summer long.

Here's a river-by-river guide, listed from north to south:

Easy to Moderate

Lower Klamath River

Beginners are advised to put in below Weitchpec, as the river broadens here and the rapids are not as menacing. Above Weitchpec, particularly near Happy Camp, rafting experience is necessary to safely navigate the dangerous rapids called the Ikes. Ishi Pishi Falls, however, should be avoided at any cost. It is Class VI and cannot be attempted without risking your life.

Contact: For more information, call the U.S. Forest Service at (916) 842-6131 or Whitewater Voyages at (800) 488-7238.

Trinity River

The 16-mile stretch from Lewiston to Douglas City is a good weekend trip. From Big Sur to South Fork Junction is 21 miles. It's okay for intermediates.

Contact: For more information, call the U.S. Forest Service at (916) 623-6106 or Kimtu Adventures at (800) 562-8475.

Sacramento River

With 400 miles of river to choose from, there's something for everybody. Above Shasta Dam, the river is difficult, especially for canoeists. Downstream of Redding, the only real tough spot is Iron Canyon Rapids. From Red Bluff on down there are 100 miles of easy paddling.

Contact: For more information, call Shasta-Cascade at (800) 326-6944 or Turtle River Rafting at (800) 726-3223.

Eel River

The section from Dos Rios to Alderpoint (50 miles) is for advanced rafters only and you should be wary of the waterfall beyond the sharp turn at Island Mountain. From Alderpoint to the South Fork (32 miles), however, is an easy paddle and it's an ideal first trip.

Contact: For more information, call Turtle River Rafting at (800) 726-3223.

Middle Fork of the Eel River

This is a beautiful run, siting high in the mountains with picture-postcard scenery. This river is rarely in good shape past June.

Contact: For more information, call Tributary Whitewater at (916) 346-6812.

Cache Creek

Here's a six-mile, one-day run that is ideal for the Bay Area rafter—put-in is upstream of Rumsey. The river is little more than 100 miles from San Francisco. One note: Please remember to pick up your trash. (For details on Cache Creek, see page 101.)

Contact: For a brochure or more information, phone Upper Cache and American River Rafting Trips at (707) 255-0761.

South Fork of the American River

A good put-in is at the Route 193 Bridge and take-out is at either the picnic area beyond the State Historical Park (six miles) or the short road off Route 49. Warning: Do not try to run from Peavine Ridge Road to El Dorado Powerhouse—it's a death trip!

Contact: For more information, call Adventure Connection, (800)556-6060.

East Fork of the Carson River

The river has many good campsites in the 20 miles from Markleeville to Gardnerville. There's one bad set of rapids about halfway through the run. The beauty of this mountain river run is one to remember. By the way, the casino in Gardnerville is a killer.

Contact: For more information, call Ahwahnee Whitewater at (800) 359-9790.

Stanislaus River

This was the second most popular stretch of water in America until it was flooded by the backwaters of the New Melones Reservoir. What's left is a moderate stretch of water with some small rapids from Knights Ferry to Oakdale Bridge (13 miles).

Contact: For more information, call the U.S. Forest Service at (916) 985-4474 or OARS at (800) 446-RAFT.

Kings River

The nine miles of river from Upper Kings Campground to Kirch Flat Campground are okay for intermediates. Warning: only advanced rafters should try the stretch from Pine Flat Dam to Centerville. It's beautiful water, but lives have been lost here.

Contact: For more information, call the U.S. Forest Service at (209) 855-8321 or (209) 787-2589 or Zephyr Whitewater at (800) 431-3636.

Difficult

Upper Klamath River

The Upper Klamath starts in Oregon and tumbles its way into Copco Lake, with exciting rapids along the way. It's runnable throughout the year because flows are regulated by releases from the John C. Boyle Reservoir in Oregon.

Contact: For more information, phone Wilderness Adventures at (800) 323-7238.

Salmon River

Here's a favorite for experts. Many short, quick rapids run from the forks of the Salmon on downstream to where it pours into the Klamath. The scenery is outstanding with high canyon walls bordering the river.

Contact: For more information, phone Wilderness Adventures at (800) 323-7238.

South Fork of the Eel River

A good put-in is at Richardson Grove State Park where you can float 40 miles through redwoods to Weott, a good run that takes three or four days. Warning: portage around the low-level bridge before Benbow Lake.

Contact: Call Tributary Whitewater at (916) 346-6812.

North Fork of the Yuba River

The preferred stretch of water is the lower portion from Goodyear's Bar to the Route 20 bridge, but portage around the 10-foot dropoff near Route 49. Warning: do not try the four miles from Downieville to Goodyear's Bar; it is unrunnable.

Contact: Call Tributary Whitewater at (916) 346-6812.

North Fork of the American River

This is a very popular run from Colfax to the North Fork Dam (18 miles), but dangerous at a few spots. It is advisable to scout rapids before attempting to run. Warning: Do not try the Giant Gap Run below the dam—it's suicide.

Contact: Call California River Trips at (916) 626-8006.

Main Tuolumne River

Here's a real heart thumper. From Lumsden Campground to Ward Ferry Bridge is 18 miles of wild beauty. Until flows drop in mid-summer, this stretch of water is almost continuous rapids.

Contact: For more information, call the U.S. Forest Service at (916) 985-4474 or Sierra Mac River Trips at (800) 457-2580.

Merced River

The best water here is from Briceburg to Bagby, 15 miles of Class III and IV rapids. When you portage around the 20-foot waterfall, look out for poison oak. The rapids ease greatly beyond the waterfall.

Contact: For more information, call the U.S. Forest Service at (916) 985-4474 or Mariah Wilderness at (800) 4-MARIAH.

Upper Kern River

The prized section on this river is from Kernville to Lake Isabella, a half-day, five-mile run for advanced paddlers only. Very scenic. Avoid the river above the bridge, which is a very tough run.

Contact: For more information, call Kern River Tours at (619) 379-4646.

Salmon Fishing Beyond the Golden Gate

The richest marine region from Mexico to Alaska is along the San Francisco Bay coast, a unique area that provides the longest ocean season anywhere for salmon fishing. It is called the Gulf of the Farallones, an underwater shelf that extends 25 miles out to sea until dropping off to Never-Never land. The plankton-rich waters here attract shrimp, squid, anchovies and herring, and they, in turn, attract hordes of feeding salmon. It means that on any given day of the nine-month season, a fisherman has the chance to head out on the briny deep and tangle with the king of the coast.

The salmon typically range from four to eight pounds, but there are enough in the 15 to 25-pound class to keep fishermen on edge. The limit is two, with a minimum-size limit of 20 inches, and there are several periods every season when every angler aboard every boat limit out.

One key is finding the baitfish. Do that and you find the salmon. The most popular method of fishing is trolling, which allows anglers to cover the maximum amount of water in the minimum amount of time. The big sportfishing vessels from Bay Area ports fan out across the Gulf of the Farallones like spokes in a turning wheel. When one finds the fish, the skipper alerts the rest of the fleet and everybody catches fish.

If the baitfish are shallow, tightly schooled and easy to locate, as is common in mid-summer and early fall, a number of anglers will abandon trolling. Instead they drift mooch, using light tackle, anchovy-baited

Shim jigs, and set the hook on each fish. This technique produces lower catch rates, but the average size of the salmon is much larger.

If you are new to the game, learning how is as easy as tumbling out of bed in time for the 6 a.m. boat departure. A list of the full-time sportfishing vessels is included with this adventure to get you pointed in the right direction. Trips include bait, instruction and a heck of a boat ride under the Golden Gate Bridge. Rod rentals are available along with leaders, sinker releases and sinkers. You should bring a lunch, drinks, warm clothing and, if you're vulnerable, seasick pills.

Before heading out to sea, the skippers provide brief instructional lessons. They explain that the strategy is to locate a school of anchovies, which are a favorite baitfish for salmon. To attract the salmon, each fisherman trolls an anchovy as the boat cruises slowly amid the school. A two or three-pound cannonball sinker is used to get the bait down, and is attached to a sinker release. The universal rigging is to tie the sinker release to your fishing line, then to use three to six feet of leader from the sinker release to the bait. If you need help, the deckhand will tie your rig for you.

After the cruise to the fishing grounds, the fishermen aboard drop the baits overboard and the trolling begins. Most often, the rods are put in holders, and the angler stations himself nearby. When a salmon strikes, the sinker is released and drops to the ocean floor—and the tip of the pole starts bouncing.

This is where the excitement starts. You grab the rod and immediately sense the weight of the salmon. I've caught hundreds of salmon, and it still gets to me every time.

The first key is keeping your drag set light, particularly at the beginning of the fight. Many salmon escape in the first few seconds after taking the bait, when the excited angler clamps down too hard on the line. Well, salmon are too strong for that. Slam the brakes on them, and the hook will pull out in a flash.

Instead, take your time and enjoy the fight. Keep a bend in the rod. Give them no slack, but don't muscle them either. It takes an "in-between" touch to land big salmon. Not too tight, not too loose.

When you eventually lead the salmon alongside the boat, the deckhand will provide the crowning touch with the net. If you own your own boat, this should be done with a single, knife-like up-and-down motion. Don't try to reach, scoop or chase the fish with the net—if you hit the line, it will be "adios."

You can maximize trolling results with a number of additional inside tricks which are particularly effective on private boats. Many people experiment with use of downriggers, plastic planers, dodgers, flashers and mixing the use of Krocodile and Andy Reeker spoons, hoochies, anchovies clasped in Salmon Rotary Killers, and probing from the surface to the ocean bottom. On a party boat, however, the techniques are straightforward and the catch rates typically high.

Another technique that is gaining in popularity is mooching. Instead of trolling, the skipper turns the engine off, and lets the boat drift in the current. Instead of putting the rods in holders, you keep it in your hands. Instead of a heavy sinker and an anchovy, you use a half-ounce Shim jig and a small chunk of anchovy. My experience with the big salmon is that the best rigging is to fillet an anchovy from its dorsal fin on back to the tail, including the tail in the fillet—then to hook it near the front of the fillet on the jig. You let the line out as the boat drifts.

With rod in hand, you feel every nibble, twitch and bite. Don't jig it, but keep it steady; the sway of the boat will do the work. You might catch rockfish, kingfish, jacksmelt, mackerel and even perch along the way, particularly if working inshore reef areas. With the engine off, the ocean is peaceful and quiet. That ends abruptly when a salmon attacks.

When a salmon grabs the bait, there is no doubt about it, and you must be ready for it. Underwater filming of attacking salmon by my pal Dick Pool shows that they arrive at full velocity from the underside of the bait. As a result, when you get a strike while mooching, you get some immediate slack in the line. If you do not reel down to the fish immediately and remove that slack, that salmon will be one long-gone desperado before you can regain your composure.

Good tackle can help, both for trolling and mooching. For trolling, I like a seven-foot rod with a tip strong enough to withstand the weight of trolling the cannonball sinker. The rod should be matched with a medium-weight, revolving spool saltwater reel with 20-pound test line.

For drift mooching, you need lighter, more sensitive tips, since you are using just a quarter-ounce or half-ounce weight. One of my favorites is a shorter graphite rod with a stiffer tip, like the LCI 7.5-foot GBB764. Ed Migale of San Francisco Custom Tackle specializes in making personalized rods built specifically for mooching and trolling. Level-wind reels make good companions for mooching rods, with 10 to 16-pound lines.

Make certain you have your reels filled with fresh, premium line. Salmon, particularly the big ones, can bulldog you and run in erratic spurts. All it takes is one nick on some old line and it breaks. If you rent a rod-and-reel combination on the boat and the line is low and old, demand something better. You deserve it.

Spring is a unique time in the Gulf of the Farallones, because it marks a switch in the feeding pattern of the salmon. In March, salmon feed primarily on shrimp. But with the arrival of April and May comes the migration of huge schools of anchovies from southern waters into the area. The salmon will chase down the baitfish like Jesse James running down a stagecoach.

During this time of year, the schools of bait will often move to inshore areas, along the Marin coast and also San Mateo County coast near Daly City, Pacifica and Half Moon Bay. The salmon will follow them.

This is your chance. The fish are out there waiting for you. All it takes is a boat ride, a fishing rod and your bait—and by the end of the day, you will likely be telling the tale of tangling with salmon, king of the Golden Gate fish.

Where to Book a Boat for King Salmon Trips

The following list of sport vessels that run daily trips for salmon is provided by the Golden Gate Fisherman's Association.

San Francisco

Butchie B, (415) 457-8388

Chucky's Pride, (415) 564-5515

Edibob, (415) 564-2706

Ketchikan, (415) 981-6269

Lovely Martha, (415) 621-1691

Miss Farallones, (415) 352-5708

New Easy Rider, (415) 285-2000

New Florie S, (415) 878-4644

New Holiday IV, (415) 924-5575

Quite A Lady, (415) 821-3838

Viking, (415) 566-2916

Wacky Jacky, (415) 586-9800

Sausalito

Flying Fish, (415) 898-6610

Ginnie C II, (415) 454-3191

Louellen, (415) 668-9607

Mr. Bill, (415) 892-9153

Endigo, (415) 332-4903

New Merrimac, (415) 388-5351

New Rayann, (415) 924-6851

Pacific Queen, (415) 479-1322

Salty Lady, (415) 348-2107

Stardust, (415) 924-1367

Berkeley

El Dorado I and II, (510) 223-7878 or (510) 849-2727

Emeryville

New Fisherman III, (510) 837-5113

Huck Finn, Salmon Queen, New Donna D and Rapid Transit, (510) 654-6040

Jubilee (510) 881-7622

Half Moon Bay

Capt. John, (415) 726-2913

Huck Finn, (415) 726-7133

New Capt. Pete, (415) 726-7133

Outlaw, (415) 726-7133

Red Baron, (415) 726-2525

Bodega Bay

Jaws, New Sea Angler, (707) 875-3495

Merry Jane, New Florie S, Sea Dog III, (707) 875-3344

Challenger, (707) 875-2474

Santa Cruz

New Stagnaro, (408) 425-7003

Sea Dancer, New Holiday, (408) 476-2648

Monterey

Holiday, New Holiday, Checkmate, Tornado, (408) 375-5951

Capt. Randy, Sur Randy, Randy I, Randy II, (408) 372-7440

Point Sur Clipper, Star of Monterey, Miss Monterey, (408) 372-0577

Top Gun, Magnum Force, Blazer, (408) 372-2203

San Francisco Bay Fishing Potluck

Thousands of tourists, one after another every summer day, pay $15 a pop to take a 45-minute boat tour of San Francisco Bay, cruising around the Golden Gate Bridge and Alcatraz. The views might not be so bad, but the tourists are passing right over the best the Bay has to offer with nary a clue. If only they knew . . .

If only they knew, that is, that just below them in the Bay's emerald green waters are striped bass, halibut, salmon, lingcod, cabezone, sharks and several species of rockfish. Together they make up such a smorgasbord of fishing that Bay trips are called "potluck," and like Friday night church specials, they give anglers a place to practice their own religion. They bring their offerings, then take their pick at the table.

You're invited, too. All the while you are in the center of the most beautiful metropolitan area in the world, ringed by the San Francisco skyline, the Golden Gate Bridge, Mount Tamalpais in Marin, Alcatraz, Angel Island and the Bay Bridge. It is stunning, even for locals who take such sights for granted. However, it is the fishing, not the views, that provides the excitement.

You send a live anchovy down to the bottom, then start wondering what will grab it. Sometimes you can't even guess. On one trip, I thought I was fishing for striped bass, and in back-to-back drifts, I caught a 17-pound salmon and a 23-pound halibut. Another time, we thought we were fishing for halibut, and my partner Jeff Patty caught the two-fish limit of striped bass on two straight drops to the bottom.

Then there's skipper Chuck "The Wizard" Louie, owner of *Chucky's Pride*. On a recreational trip with his pals, where he got a chance to fish instead of captain his boat, he caught a striper, halibut, salmon, lingcod, cabezone, china rockfish, blue rockfish, bolinas cod, flounder and shark. That's right, he landed 10 species of fish on one trip. Count 'em.

The season starts in May, when the Bay's first schools of striped bass, or what I call "scout fish," start arriving from the Delta, a prelude to the summer fun. Shortly thereafter, halibut start moving in from the ocean. Those two species, striped bass and halibut, join a resident population of rockfish, lingcod and sharks. June and July are the peak months, and after a short hiatus in August when most of the fish migrate out to the Bay Area coast, they are right back in September, but this time joined by salmon migrating upstream through the Bay.

"Every day is different, and wondering what will happen next has always kept it fresh for me," said skipper Cliff Anfinson, who has spent 7,500 days on the Bay as captain of the *Bass-Tub*. Every summer, the stripers and halibut are attracted to San Francisco Bay by hordes of anchovies and pods of shiner perch. But unlike in the ocean, where the anchovies roam freely, in the Bay they often find themselves trapped by tidal action against ledges, rockpiles and huge pillars. Right then the sportsfish, especially striped bass, arrive at these key spots and attack en masse. Aha! Right then the potluck boats also move into position, drifting over the key habitats, with the anglers aboard dangling live anchovies in front of the fish. It is an offer they can't refuse.

This doesn't mean, however, that all you have to do is toss out a bait, set the hook and hang on for the ride. It isn't that simple. There are times when you don't get a bite for hours, swear there isn't a fish in the entire Bay, then suddenly start catching everything but Moby Dick. Then there are days when you need a Jaws of Life to pry the fishes' mouths open.

Why the crazy fluctuations? The key is that all of

the Bay's feeding activity is tidal oriented. When the tides are wrong, you might as well pretend you're on a tourist boat and gaze at Coit Tower, or maybe wait for someone to jump off the bridge. Even on the good days, when the tides are right, there is usually plenty of slack time broken by two-hour periods when the fish go on the bite.

I remember one late June day where I arrived at Fisherman's Wharf in San Francisco at 4 p.m., getting ready for a twilight trip. After all, the tides were projected to be perfect between 5:30 p.m. and 7 p.m., right under the Golden Gate Bridge. Well, just as I arrived, a boat returned for the day, and the 18 anglers aboard were mighty glum, having caught only three striped bass between them.

One of the departing unfortunates recognized me, then asked why I was going out. "After all," he said, "there's no fish."

"I guess we'll just have to hope for the best," I responded. But inside, I knew that all the key factors—tides, baitfish, fish migrations and weather—were perfectly aligned and that evening would bring the chance for greatness.

It turned out to be the best evening of fishing I have ever had in the Bay, catching and releasing striper after striper. At one point, I had landed 13 striped bass, bulldogs all. As we fished under the Golden Gate Bridge, it became a magical setting: the fog moved in, the golden lights of the bridge cast a glow, the old foghorn blared away, and the 15 anglers aboard shared a little piece of striper heaven.

So the first lesson is that you must match the tides to the spots, or be in close touch with one of the Bay's potluck skippers who are already expert at it. The latter is easy enough, just a phone call away; see the adjoining list of each harbor's potluck boats.

Here are a few rules for the wise:

1—The best fishing for striped bass is during strong incoming tides at the rockpiles between Alcatraz and the Golden Gate Bridge, and during

slow to moderate outgoing tides at the south tower of the Golden Gate Bridge, Lime Point and Yellow Bluff.
2—The best fishing for halibut is during slow to moderate tides, especially just after the high tide tops out, at the southwest side of Angel Island, along the western shore of Alcatraz, and offshore San Francisco's Crissy Field and Baker Beach.
3—The best fishing for salmon in the Bay is always during the first two hours of the outgoing tide, just after a high tide of five-and-a-half feet or higher has topped out, near Belvedere Point and Raccoon Strait.
4—During moderate tides, it is possible to catch the most species.
5—Bay fishing is always lousy when there are minus low tides.
6—The striper bite dies during slack water or slow tides.
7—The halibut bite dies when tides are very strong.

In addition to this information, you must be able to figure whether a tide is weak or strong, and that is easy enough. You simply calculate the difference between two consecutive tides. In the Bay Area, a tidal swing of 4.5 feet or more is a moderate to strong tide, and a tidal swing of 4.5 feet or less is considered a moderate to weak tide. For instance, when a low tide of 0.2 feet is followed by a high tide of 6.6 feet, there is a tidal swing of 6.4 feet, equivalent to a strong incoming tide for San Francisco Bay.

This is critical knowledge because it can allow anglers to plan trips far in advance. All you need is a tide book. But without one, it is like planning a trip with a blindfold on.

Because the tides key the bites, there is usually no reason for the trip to start in the middle of the night. That is why Bay potluck trips leave dock fairly late by West Coast standards, usually around 7 a.m. Often there is no rush to reach the fishing grounds either, especially if the skipper has analyzed the tides and knows that the day's bite will start at 10 a.m.

The trip opens with a short instructional lesson and safety review. If you are new to the game, don't be shy about it; it seems many newcomers are aboard every trip, including tourists from all parts of the country.

The skipper starts by demonstrating the tackle. My favorite setup is the Fenwick 847 rod, the Penn Jigmaster 2/0 reel, with fresh 20-pound monofilament. Then the skipper will explain the three-way swivel concept. It is simple enough. You tie your fishing line from one of the swivels. Then you tie off your sinker from another, using about eight inches of leader for rocky areas, one inch for sandy areas. From the remaining swivel, you tie on three feet of leader to a short-shanked 2/0 live bait hook. The skippers sell pre-tied rigs for a small fee.

Live anchovies and shiner perch are the baits of choice. Anchovies are hooked through the nose vertically, shiners through the nose horizontally.

Once on the Bay, the skipper will position his boat at the foot of an underwater ledge, then with the motor still chugging and the tide running past, will allow the boat to move in a controlled drift toward the ledge. Anglers will keep their sinkers near the bottom, then reel in a bit to "walk" the live anchovy up the ledge. This is when you get bit—the tidal action will trap anchovies against the ledge, and sure enough, the striped bass, halibut and other fish will arrive for a picnic.

Except in the end, it is you who has the real smorgasbord. On one such trip, I remember a nice, old gent, Ron Brawn of San Francisco, who was having a great day of it, catching a good-sized halibut and several rockfish. He was a unique fellow, with an old Calcutta fishing rod, the kind that were so popular in the 1950s but are rarely seen anymore.

Then on a drift just north of the Golden Gate Bridge off the Marin coast, the old guy hooked something huge. That old rod bent and strained, and the battle went on. Suddenly, the rod snapped right in two. This was one fight it looked like the fish was going to win. There was this nice old guy with half a rod and a giant fish on it.

But Ron wouldn't give up. He struggled away, trying to get leverage with the little stub that was left, and after another five minutes, it was the fish that was beat, not Ron. It was a real beauty, a striped bass that was well over 20 pounds.

Meanwhile, just a few hundred yards away, there was a tourist cruise boat making the rounds. A few tourists had binoculars aboard that boat, and apparently they had witnessed the battle.

With binoculars of my own, I watched them as they tried to explain what they had seen to the other tourists, yet they got little response.

I just smiled. You see, most folks just don't understand what is possible on the Bay. If only they knew . . .

Boats, Ramps and Bait

San Francisco: *Bass-Tub*, (415) 456-9055; *Chucky's Pride*, (415) 564-5515.

Berkeley: *Happy Hooker*, (510) 223-5388. Excellent boat ramp available at Berkeley Marina.

Emeryville: *Huck Finn* and *New Mary S*, (510) 654-6040; *New Donna D*, (510) 222-4158. Excellent boat ramp available at Emery Cove Marina.

Point San Pablo: *New Keesa*, (510) 787-1720.

San Rafael: *Superfish*, (415) 898-6989. Decent boat ramp available at Loch Lomond Marina.

Live bait: Live shiners are available at Loch Lomond Live Bait at Dock A at Loch Lomond Harbor in San Rafael, (415) 456-0321; Live anchovies are available at J&P/Meatball Bait at Fisherman's Wharf, (415) 441-0111.

Secluded Camping

If you want solitude, your best bet is getting on Highway 5, kicking it up north for five hours, and setting in at an unimproved Forest Service campground. In my book *California Camping*, we discovered 240 campgrounds in some of the state's most remote areas—Shasta (56), Siskiyou (42), Trinity (48), Modoc (14), Lassen (19), Tehama (16) and Del Norte (45) counties. Here are 10 choices to start with:

Shasta—Deadlun

Most people have never heard of Iron Canyon Reservoir. Go to Deadlun Camp and you'll get a good taste of it, with good swimming and boating by day and fishing in the early morning and late evening. The campground has 30 spots with no fee charged. It's located at 2,750 feet, surrounded by Shasta-Trinity National Forest.

Directions: The camp is seven miles northwest of Big Bend on a Forest Service Road. The turnoff is marked on Highway 299.

Contact: For more information, call the Shasta Ranger District at (916) 275-1587.

Madrone

This camp is out there in the boondocks, between nothing and nothing, and set in a forest of fir and pine. It's adjacent to Squaw Creek, which is okay for swimming, trout fishing, too, if you walk upstream a ways. The camp has 13 campsites and no fee is charged. It is set at a 1,500-foot elevation, located about 50 miles northwest of Redding.

Directions: From Redding, take Highway 299 east for 40 miles, then take the Fenders Ferry Road, a gravel road, west for 20 miles.

Contact: For more information, call the Shasta Ranger District at (916) 275-1587.

Siskiyou—Trail Creek

Here's a beautiful spot away from everything. It's set between Callahan and Cecilville near the Salmon River at a 4,700-foot elevation. You can hear the gurgling of Trail Creek nearby as you sleep. The campground has 15 units.

Directions: To get there, turn west at Callahan off State Route 3 and drive about 15 miles.

Contact: For more information, call the Scott River Ranger District at (916) 468-5351.

Shadow Creek

This is a good alternative to Trail Creek, located five miles west of the Trail Creek Camp. It has space for 10 campers. It's a peaceful, away-from-everything spot with good swimming in the South Fork of the Salmon River. The closest amenities are in Cecilville, population 25, about five miles away. For hiking trails, a map of the Klamath Forest details the possibilities.

Directions: Turn west at Callahan on State Route 3 and drive about 20 miles.

Contact: For more information, call the Scott River Ranger District at (916) 468-5351.

Trinity—Jackass Springs

Here's an isolated campground that gets very little attention, yet is set right along one of California's favorite reservoirs—Trinity Lake. The camp has 21 campsites and is free. Just show up with your gear. It is set at a 2,500-foot elevation, beneath the towering Trinity Alps. You can camp right along the east shore of Trinity Lake.

Directions: It is located five miles off Trinity Mountain Road, an unpaved access road.

Contact: For more information, call the Weaverville Ranger District, (916) 623-2121.

Big Flat

The South Fork of the Salmon River and Coffee Creek provide a beautiful setting for this little-known spot. It is right on the edge of the Trinity Alps Wilderness, and is a premium jump-off spot to the Caribou Lakes (a nine-mile hike) for a backpacking trip.

Directions: The camp is at a 5,000-foot elevation, located 20 miles west of Coffee Creek Road off State Route 3.

Contact: For more information, call the Weaverville Ranger District at (916) 623-2121.

Modoc—Cave Lake

Here's a spot out in the sticks. This lake is located very near the Oregon border in northeastern California, and adjoining Lily Lake, providing a double-barreled fishing opportunity. Both have eastern brook trout and rainbow trout. The campground has six spots, with no fee charged (heck, if they charged, somebody would have to hang out for a couple of years to collect enough money just to pay for one dinner).

Directions: The drive includes a nine-mile climb on a gravel road, leaving Highway 395 and taking Pine Creek Road to the lake at a 6,600-foot elevation.

Contact: For more information, call the Warner Ranger District at (916) 279-6116.

Lassen—Crater Lake

And you thought Crater Lake was in Oregon? Well, there's another Crater Lake that nobody's heard of on the eastern side of Mount Lassen. It has pretty good fishing, primarily for rainbow trout and brook trout, but don't expect anything huge. An option is to take a piece of bacon or chicken on a hook and get yourself a pot full of crawdads. There are 16 campsites.

Directions: To get there, drive nine miles east on a dirt road from Bogard Ranger Station, turning off State Route 44.

Contact: For more information, call the Eagle Lake Ranger District at (916) 257-2151.

Tehama—Beegum Gorge

Here's a hidden, obscure spot with just three campsites, but it's free, quiet and there's some fair evening trout fishing on nearby Beegum Creek. It's set at 2,200 feet and overlooked by the Yolla Bolla Mountains. Expect hot weather and bring all your own supplies.

Directions: The campground is located 6.5 miles southwest of Platina off State Route 36, west of Red Bluff.

Contact: For more information, call the Yolla Bolla Ranger District at (916) 352-4211.

Del Norte—Big Flat

This is a nice little spot set along Hurdy Gurdy Creek, close to the South Fork of the Smith River. I have had some good trout fishing success here, searching out spots on the river where rapids tumble into pools, and then casting a blue/silver Kastmaster into the whitewater. The fish bite where the water flattens out. There are 16 campsites and piped water is available.

Directions: To get there, turn off Highway 199 just east of Gasquet and then turn south on South Fork Road and drive 25 miles.

Contact: For more information, call the Gasquet Ranger District at (707) 457-3131.

Skiing for Kids

What do you do with your small children when you go skiing? Leave them with a babysitter? Spend your day on the Bunny Hill?

An alternative for parents is to enroll youngsters in a carefully-designed kids ski program. For kids, it is easy and fun, and it has worked so well for families that many ski areas are offering some form of an all-day program for young children, ages 6 to 12.

The program is called the "Ski Wee" at some ski areas, "Junior Program" at others, but regardless of the name, it allows both parents and their children to enjoy a day of skiing on their own, out of each other's way. In the process, many problems are solved.

Youngsters often perform much better without pressure from their parents. They'll enjoy being in a class with other children around their age and level of experience. Parents can have a much better day of skiing without worrying about their children. The program is all day and includes lunch.

It is part of a national instructional program formatted by *Ski Magazine.* Some 50 ski resorts are taking part in the program across the country, including four in the Sierra.

The nearest to the Bay Area is the Dodge Ridge Ski Area, located east of Sonora on Highway 108. Heavenly Valley at South Tahoe, Sierra Summit south of Yosemite, and June Mountain in the southeast Sierra also feature the program. A number of other ski resorts have junior programs, but they do not follow the format designed by *Ski Magazine.* At Dodge Ridge, the program costs $50 per day and includes ski rentals, instruction, full-time supervision, lunch and snacks. If you supply the skis, the price is $43.

The junior ski class starts at 10 a.m. when the youngsters are placed in groups of six, all grouped according to age and skiing ability. Most of the instructors are young women with professional experience in teaching children.

First the youngsters are taught how to put on skis and walk on snow. They are then shown some basic skiing techniques. Instead of a traumatic test in front of their parents, any mistakes just become good fun with a group of friends, all of whom are likely making the same mistakes. By the end of the day, the kids will know how to get on and off rope tows and lifts, how to make a straight downhill run, and how to fall down.

For young children, the most difficult part of the lesson is not how to ski, but how to stop. Some just fall down and consider the mission accomplished.

However, with a little practice, kids can learn to "snow plow." The position slows the skier on a downhill run.

When parents return at 4 p.m., the kids are given a progress card, a bag of treats and a list of ski pointers.

A lot of people think skiing is just for adults. This program is proving that just isn't true. In addition, it solves two problems at once: It frees adults for a day of skiing, and it allows children to learn the sport in a fun, pressure-free environment.

Ski Instruction: Ski resorts that feature *Ski Magazine's* instructional program:

Dodge Ridge Ski Area. Located on Highway 108, 32 miles east of Sonora. For information, call (209) 965-3474. A brochure is available by writing P.O. Box 1188, Pinecrest, CA 95364.

Heavenly Valley: Located near Lake Tahoe on Highway 50. For information, call (916) 541-1330 or write P.O. Box 2180, Stateline, NV 89449.

Sierra Summit: Located just south of Yosemite National Park along Highway 168. For information, call (209) 893-3316, or write P.O. Box 236, Lakeshore, CA 93634.

June Mountain: Located near Bishop in East Sierra off Highway 395. For information, call (619) 934-2571 or write, P.O. Box 24, Mammoth Lake, CA 93546

Chapter 15

Sno Parks

When you're young, there is nothing quite so enjoyable as throwing a light, fluffy snowball at the back of your brother's head.

Unless, that is, you're taking a flying leap into a 10-foot mound of light, dry powder snow, and are then mistaken for the Abominable Snowman. Or sailing down a snowbank on a metal saucer. Or maybe taking a little adventure on cross-country skis into a forested wonderland.

On second thought, nothing can top nailing your brother with a snowball. Guess how I know?

The towering snowfalls of winter in the Sierra Nevada have inspired many a well-aimed throw. They have also inspired many a family to head up to the snow country to play in the stuff, praying they wind up in a good spot. The answer to the prayer method is provided by a dozen "Sno Parks," offshoots of California State Parks.

These Sno Parks are actually snow-cleared parking lots, with direct access to snow playing areas, cross-country skiing and in a few cases, snowmobiling. They are ideal for families who want winter recreation, yet don't want to pay the high price of outfitting a family for downhill skiing. You pay a few bucks for a parking permit, which is then used to pay for snowplowing to keep the parking area clear.

To obtain a permit, phone (916) 653-8569, or write Sno-Park Program Manager, P.O. Box 942896, Sacramento, CA 94296-0001. It is a $75 fine to park without a permit. Note that all parking is on a first-come, first-served basis, and having a parking permit does not guarantee you a spot. The most popular areas are at Donner Summit, Carson Pass and Lake Alpine, which fill nearly every weekend morning in the winter.

Thus, you need some strategy in selecting your

destination. Here is an area-by-area guide to assist in your approach:

Cisco Grove

Located on the north side of Interstate 80 at Cisco, Nevada County, at the entrance to Thousand Trails Campground. Notes: Small snow play area, good area for snowmobiling. No overnight parking. Guided snowmobile tours are available at Thousand Trails Campground. Capacity: 50 cars.

Contact: Phone the park at (916) 426-3362.

Yuba Gap

Located on the south side of Interstate 80 at Yuba Gap, Nevada County, on the adjacent frontage road. Notes: Excellent for cross-country skiing, with marked trails. Guided snowmobile tours also available. Sno Park permits available at Snow Flower grocery store. Capacity: 50 cars.

Contact: Phone the park at (916) 389-9614.

Donner Summit

Located on the south side of Interstate 80 just beyond Boreal Inn, Nevada County, Castle Peak exit. Notes: Very popular cross-country skiing area, can be crowded on weekends, often filled to capacity early on weekend mornings. No snow playing allowed. Bordered by private property. On steeper slopes in backcountry, beware of avalanche danger after heavy snowfall. Capacity: 70 cars.

Contact: Phone the Sno-Park Program Manager at (916) 653-8569.

Donner Lake

Located on the south side of Interstate 80 at Donner Lake, Nevada County, at Donner Lake State Park, Donner Lake exit. Notes: Limited snow play area (no sledding), but restrictions against snowmobiles keep things quiet. No overnight parking. Capacity: 35 cars.

Contact: Phone the Sno-Park Program Manager at (916) 653-8569.

Blackwood Canyon

Located on the west side of Highway 89, three miles south of Tahoe City, Placer County. Notes: Decent snow play area for North Tahoe visitors. Cross-country skiers should avoid the steeper terrain on the north side of Blackwood Canyon, as there is serious avalanche danger here. Capacity: 30 cars.

Contact: Phone the Sno-Park Program Manager at (916) 653-8569.

Taylor Creek

Located on the west side of Highway 89 near Fallen Leaf Lake in South Tahoe, El Dorado County, near Camp Richardson. Notes: Great cross-country ski trips available here to Fallen Leaf Lake. Snow play area, no snowmobiles allowed. Capacity: 30 cars.

Contact: Phone the Sno-Park Program Manager at (916) 653-8569.

Lake Tahoe

Located on the northeast side of Highway 89, just north of the junction with Highway 50, El Dorado County, at Forest Service Visitor Center along Lake Tahoe. Notes: Set along Lake Tahoe's south shore, excellent snow play area, but no sledding. A great option is cross-country skiing along the lake's edge. Capacity: 30 cars.

Contact: Phone the Sno-Park Program Manager at (916) 653-8569.

Echo Summit

Located on the south side of Highway 50 at Echo Summit, El Dorado County. Notes: One of the best snow play areas anywhere, but it's no secret and very popular. No snowmobiles allowed, some cross-country skiing in the area. Capacity: 100 cars.

Contact: Phone the Sno-Park Program Manager at (916) 653-8569.

Echo Lake

Located on the road to Echo Lake off Highway 50, El Dorado County, one mile west of Echo Summit. Notes: Excellent for cross-country skiing, poor for snow playing. No snowmobiles allowed. Capacity: 100 cars.

Contact: Phone the Sno-Park Program Manager at (916) 653-8569.

Iron Mountain

On Iron Mountain Road (past Iron Mountain Ski Area) off Highway 88, El Dorado County. Notes: Popular snowmobile area, loud and fast. Get the picture? Capacity: 30 cars.

Contact: Phone the Sno-Park Program Manager at (916) 653-8569.

Carson Pass

Two locations on Highway 88 at Carson Pass, 60 miles east of Jackson, or 25 miles south of Lake Tahoe. One parking lot is at Carson Pass on the south side of the highway; there is a second parking lot one-quarter mile west of Carson Pass on the north side of highway. Notes: Outstanding cross-country ski area, small snow play area (rated poor); no snowmobiles allowed, a plus. Often fills early on weekends. Capacity: 100 cars.

Contact: Phone the Sno-Park Program Manager at (916) 653-8569.

Lake Alpine

On Highway 4, 50 miles east of Angels Camp, just past the turnoff to Mount Reba Ski Area. Notes: Beautiful setting, excellent snow play area, but popular, and often crowded. Usually fills up on weekends.

Contact: Phone the Sno-Park Program Manager at (916) 653-8569.

Walking in San Francisco

The most spectacular easy strolls anywhere are in San Francisco, along trails that are routed along the Bay, the mouth of the Golden Gate, and the Pacific Ocean.

There are four excellent starting points, each providing many sidetrip options, and near-flat terrain for easy adventures and great views.

1—Bay Promenade

This is a paved trail along the Bay's shoreline from Marina Green to Fort Point. It is virtually flat, yet the views are magnificent, with the backdrop of the Golden Gate Bridge, Alcatraz, Tiburon and Sausalito. The entire trail is popular for joggers and walkers. For people looking for a fitness workout, an option here is one of the Bay Area's most popular par courses, located along the route at Marina Green.

Sidetrips include visiting the Presidio, which runs alongside much of the route, and the old Muni Pier. Fishing for kingfish and jacksmelt can be very good there.

Directions: From Highway 101, take the Marina Boulevard exit near the southern foot of the Golden Gate Bridge, and drive on Marina Boulevard toward Fisherman's Wharf. Parking lots are available off Marina Boulevard at Fort Mason, Marina Green, Crissy Field and near the St. Francis Yacht Club.

2—Golden Gate Bridge

This is the Number One tourist walk in the world, but surprisingly few locals ever get around to trying it out. After one trip here, I came to the conclusion that my dog could understand English better than the folks out walking that day.

The view is incomparable, of course. If you look eastward from the center of the bridge, you see Alcatraz, Angel Island and the Bay framed by the San Francisco waterfront and the East Bay hills. On weekends, the pathway on the eastern side of the bridge is for walkers only, while the pathway on the west side of the bridge is reserved for bicyclists.

Directions: Parking is available at either the north end of the bridge at Vista Point, or at the south end of the bridge, just west of the toll stations. At the latter, to reach the bridge, after parking you walk under a short tunnel that runs under Highway 101, then loop up to the pathway entrance.

3—Land's End Bluffs

The Coastal Trail provides one of San Francisco's greatest lookouts. The trailhead is at Land's End (near the Cliff House Restaurant), and from there you meander eastward.

It is a dirt trail sprinkled with pine needles, set near bluffs topped with cypress trees. In one glance, you take in the mouth of the Bay, crashing breakers, the Golden Gate Bridge and the Marin Headlands in the foreground, and the Pacific, the Farallon Islands and Point Reyes in the background.

Directions: From the south, take Skyline Boulevard (The Great Highway) north past Lake Merced and continue to the Cliff House Restaurant. From the east, take Geary until it deadends at the ocean and Cliff House Restaurant. Parking is available along Geary, Skyline and in a dirt lot across from Louis' Restaurant.

4—Ocean Beach

San Francisco has a unique stretch of beach that provides a wide variety of hiking and jogging trails. Ocean Beach is set along the coast's Great Highway, of course, and here you will discover a long expanse of beach, a paved jogging trail and miniature parks at Fort Funston and Thornton Beach.

The beach ranges about three miles, and its huge expanse makes it popular for jogging on the hard-packed sand at low tide. A paved jogging trail is located just east of the Great Highway.

Fort Funston has trails along ocean bluffs, including the coast's first wheelchair accessible trail on the three-quarter-mile Sunset Trail. A bonus in this area is the most popular hang gliding spot in the Bay Area, and those daredevils are something else to watch. Thornton Beach is located less than a mile to the south of Fort Funston, and offers a beach where sand dollars seem abundant, as well as a protected valley for hiking and picnics.

Directions: Parking is available on the west side of the Great Highway at the intersections with Fulton or Sloat, and also at Fort Funston at Thornton Beach along Highway 35.

For more information on these walks, phone the Golden Gate National Recreation Area at (415) 556-0560.

Whale Watching

At first, all you see is what looks like a little puff of smoke on the ocean surface. Out of the corner of your eye you spot it, and your attention becomes riveted to the spot like a magnet on steel. A closer look—and there it is again—but it quickly disappears.

You watch, waiting, but the sea is quiet. A row of cormorants glides past, a dozen murres are paddling around, and for a moment you forget why you're out here on the briny blue. Then your daydreams are popped by a giant tail, the size of a lifeboat, breaking the sea surface.

A moment later, the head and back of a gray whale surge into view.

After you have seen a whale—a real, live friendly sea monster—you will never again look at the ocean in quite the same way. When you see a whale, you often regain the feeling that this world of ours is still a place where great things are possible. Because a whale is just one of those things.

And there are 18,000 of them swimming along the California coast, cruising 50 to 100 miles per day within the range of charter boats and many shoreline lookouts. Seeing one not only makes you feel special, but can instill the kind of excitement that will stay with you for many years. Every time you look at the ocean, you will remember it.

These giant air-breathing creatures average more than 40 feet long and can weigh more than 30 tons. They will often keep pace alongside a boat, spouting, occasionally emerging to show their backs. As they gain confidence, they may fin you, give you a tail salute, and if you're particularly lucky, do a half breech in your full view. In one spectacular 20-minute sequence off the Half Moon Bay coast, I saw 10 or 15 humpback whales leaping completely out of the water in full 180-degree pirouettes. They landed in gigantic splashes on their backs beside the boat, perhaps trying to clean off the barnacles. Now and then, a pair would even criss-cross like Wilkinson Sword Blades in front of our path. This occurred while on a fishing trip, and it was simply luck that we ran into the rare humpbacks.

However, there is little luck involved in spotting gray whales. The gray whale migration is a 5,000-mile rip from Arctic waters to Baja, a migratory route that brings them along the Bay Area coast from January through April. You don't need a boat to see them, but it can help.

Since the whales cruise along the surface, you can see the little "puffs of smoke," their spouts, as in, "Thar she blows."

Some whales seem attracted by the big boats and will play tag with you on the southern route, disappearing and reappearing several times over the course of an hour.

Skippers have learned that most gray whales will follow a migratory course from Point Reyes on southward past the Farallon Islands near the continental shelf. Most skippers will start the day by heading south, hoping to pick up some whales and cruise parallel to them for many miles.

Before boarding a large vessel for an ocean cruise, you'd be well advised to take a seasick preventative.

An option is to skip the boat ride and drive to a lookout along the coast. However, don't expect to see much of the whales. You will see whales from considerable distances blowing their steam. Still, even from a distance, it's an exciting affair. From the San Mateo County coast at Pigeon Point, I have seen as many as 200 whale spouts before I stopped counting.

The best lookouts are from the bluffs at Davenport in Santa Cruz County; Pigeon Point, San Gregorio; or the tip of Point Reyes in Marin County. Binoculars and a clear day can do wonders.

Contact: For general information, phone the Oceanic Society in San Francisco, (415) 441-1106.

Berkeley: Phone Dolphin Charters, (510) 527-9622.

San Francisco: Phone the Oceanic Society, (415) 441-1106. From December through April, they offer full-day whale watching excursions from San Francisco and half-day trips from Half Moon Bay.

Monterey: Phone Sam's Charters in Monterey (408) 372-0577.

Half Moon Bay: Phone the *Huck Finn*, (415) 726-7133 or the *Capt. John,* (415) 726-2913.

Fisherman's Wharf: Phone the *Wacky Jacky*, (415) 586-9800; the *Butchie B*, (415) 457-8388; or the *Easy Rider*, (415) 285-2000.

Sausalito: Phone the *Salty Lady*, (415) 348-2107; or the *New Rayann*, (415) 584-1498.

Bodega Bay: Phone the *Challenger*, (707) 875-2474.

Wildlife Watching

Almost everybody gets a thrill out of seeing large furry things, providing they don't take a bite out of you. Little furry things, too.

I'm not talking about seeing Bigfoot, or Littlefoot either. Rather I mean spotting elk, bear, deer, antelope, rabbits or squirrels, and in some spots along the coast, even otters and elephant seals. You may even see a marten, bobcat or mountain lion. As for Bigfoot, I haven't seen him myself, so far.

But California does have plenty of critters, large and small, in a wide variety of habitats across the state. Seeing them can add a new dimension to adventure travel. On a trip to Point Reyes, for instance, I once spotted 13 elk, six deer, three rabbits and a fox, all in just two hours between Pierce Ranch and Tomales Point. A trip like that can lift your spirits for weeks.

In my travels across California, part of my mission has been to search out and find the best places to see lots of big furry things. Here is my list:

Elk

There are three really exceptional habitats to see elk, two in the Bay Area and another along the north coast. They are Point Reyes National Seashore (trailhead at Pierce Ranch), Grizzly Island Wildlife Area south of Fairfield and Prairie Creek Redwood State Park along Highway 101, north of Eureka.

At Point Reyes and Grizzly Island, you'll find tule elk, and Roosevelt elk at Prairie Creek. These elk are monstrous critters that can stand five feet at the shoulder with antlers tall enough to poke holes in the clouds. They are not difficult to track, spot with binoculars, and then stalk to within 125 yards for a close look. Keep your distance, keep the wind in your face, and stay out of sight on your approach so that you don't scare them off.

Contact: Phone Point Reyes National Seashore, (415) 663-1092; Grizzly Island Wildlife Area, (707) 425-3828; Prairie Creek Redwoods State Park, (707) 488-2171.

Bears

Yosemite National Park has become the bear capital of the world. They are not as interested in you as in your food, and if you can stay awake long enough at night during a campout, you are destined to meet Yogi and Boo-Boo. Smarter than your average bears. In the summer months, the most likely areas to see bears are at the hike-in camps at Lyell Fork (five miles in from Tuolumne Meadows), Emeric Lake (two days in, near Vogelsang Pass) and Little Yosemite (on the trail from Yosemite Valley to Half Dome). Bears are so abundant at Lyell Fork and Little Yosemite that the park provides hang wires or metal lockers to keep your food out of their reach.

One time at Emeric Lake, I had three bears in my camp at once, all prowling around as quietly as possible, trying not to wake me. Right then, on the other side of the lake, a lady started banging a pot and shouting. Those three bears in my camp immediately took off in that direction, and by the time I got around the lake to see what all the commotion was about, there were seven bears going through two giant ice chests. It turns out that banging on a pot is like ringing the dinner bell.

Contact: Phone Yosemite National Park, (209) 372-0200.

Deer

Many of the most famous deer photographs ever taken in California, the classic giant bucks guarding their does, were taken at Lava Beds National Monument in early winter. The park is located in Siskiyou County, covers 70 square miles, and is best known for its lava tubes, its caves and its remoteness. But it is also at Lava Beds where so many giant deer spend the winter.

Heavy snow will drive deer to lower elevations, so the best spots to explore are regions where there is about an inch of snow or less. Expect very cold weather, dress for it, and plan to stay at a hotel either at Dorris or Tule Lake, rather than camping.

Another spot not far from Lava Beds to see lots of deer is Timber Mountain, just west of Highway 395 (the turnoff is just north of the California Highway Inspection Station). In past Decembers, I have seen several hundred deer here in just a few hours. It's best to park at the top of the mountain (actually a large hill), then creep to the rim and peer over the side.

Contact: Phone Lava Beds National Monument, (916) 667-2282; Shasta Cascade Wonderland Association, (800) 326-6944.

Sea otters

These are lovable little critters, popping up around kelp beds in the Big Sur area, often nibbling on a sea urchin or an abalone. Otters have a lot of personality, always happy, frolicking in the kelp shallows or playing peek-a-boo with beach visitors.

One of the best spots to see otters is at Andrew Molera State Park. After parking, it's about a one-mile walk to the beach, with the trail routing through a few cypress trees and then entering an expansive half-moon shaped beach. At times, you can sit back and watch the little guys for hours as they play, ducking in and out of the water. The game never ends. The rangers will provide a list of the best otter viewing areas.

Otters can be found at nearly any of the kelp beds in Big Sur from Carmel Bay to Julia Pfeiffer-Burns State Park.

Contact: Phone Andrew Molera State Park, (408) 667-2315.

Elephant seals

Every winter, these massive creatures arrive at Ano Nuevo State Reserve, 20 miles south of Pescadero, to fight, mate and get plenty of sleep. For viewing, tours are routed along roped-off paths, and it has become so popular that reservations are required through Mistix.

Sea elephants grow up to 20 feet and 5,000 pounds, and the big bulls will slam their open jaws into the necks of competing males and try to scare them off. All the males are scarred, whether from neck bites in a fight or from a quick chomp from a Great White shark. When they move, they squirm like giant slugs.

A typical tour takes about two hours to cover about two miles, during which time you are apt to see dozens and dozens of the giant blobs of flesh, lolling around, making weird clucking sounds and occasionally rising up for a challenge. (For more details on Ano Nuevo, see page 216.)

Fee or Free: A minimal fee is charge for tours at Ano Nuevo. There is also a parking fee.

Contact: Phone Ano Nuevo State Park, (415) 879-0852; Mistix reservation line, (800) 444-7275.

Chapter 15

Windsurfing

What starts out simply as a curiosity can sometimes turn into a lifelong passion. That's just what often happens with windsurfing.

A newcomer's interest is often kindled by the sight of a windsurfer cutting across San Francisco Bay, maybe through ocean breakers, or across Lake Merced; it looks effortless, fast and exciting. The vision has a way of sticking in your mind, and before long, you say to yourself, "I'd like to try that."

Then comes the awakening. While windsurfing can be fast and exciting, it's anything but easy, and it can even be downright humiliating the first time out. But with practice, you can bridge that gap between your initial vision and the reality. Instruction, equipment rental and quality waters are available in San Francisco. The San Francisco School of Windsurfing offers a package deal for newcomers that includes an eight-hour course and equipment rental. They offer beginner courses at Lake Merced South, and intermediate and advanced courses at Candlestick Point State Park.

Those with previous experience who do not want a lesson can rent a sailboard and wet suit at Lake Merced. Advanced-level boards are available at Candlestick. "We have good equipment and there is somebody watching out for you all the time," said Jeff Craft of the School of Windsurfing.

A large number of windsurfers can be seen most afternoons clipping across the water near Candlestick. It's an ideal spot with strong winds yet calm water, and the area is a lot better suited for windsurfing than baseball. Yet for experts, one of the ultimate experiences in windsurfing is cutting across San Francisco Bay near Chrissy Field on a clear summer evening, mastering the wind out of the northwest, whipping across the water like a surface torpedo.

Intermediate-level windsurfers can cruise at 15 to 20 miles-per-hour with no problem. If the water is choppy, they'll sail along in the wakes of ferry boats to get a smooth, free ride. Advanced-level windsurfers can rip at 30 to 35 miles-per-hour, and some are now passing the magic 40-miles-per-hour speed.

It takes practice to reach that level of performance, of course. The first time on the board can be humbling, especially for skilled athletes who come to the sport with high expectations. It usually takes two or three tries before you can manage a decent ride across a lake or lagoon. Once that's accomplished, it's usually exciting enough to encourage participants to take the sport a step further. Eventually many even decide to buy their own equipment.

"You have to be a sharp buyer," Craft said. "You can usually get something good quality for $400 or $500. It's very important to get a good, thick wet suit, because the water is cold in San Francisco Bay."

Once you own the equipment, you're only limited by the conditions nature provides and the skills you've mastered.

Over a summer, you can learn all the tricks of the trade, from squeezing out every bit of push from a light breeze to learning how to cut a gale down to manageable proportions. In time, you will be able to cut through high breakers and rip from Crissy Field in San Francisco to Sausalito in 10 minutes, averaging 30 to 35 miles-per-hour.

You can also venture to many other areas, near and far, to enjoy the sport. San Francisco Bay and Maui are among the most glamorous windsurfing spots in the country, for example, and Lake Tahoe in the summer may be the most beautiful. The Delta is a hot spot; so is Del Valle Reservoir. Other popular spots in the Bay Area include Pillar Point Harbor in Half Moon Bay, Lake Merced South, Foster City Lagoon, Larkspur Landing, Coyote Point, and Sunnyvale Baylands Park. There are many others.

All you need are decent wind and water, things which California has in abundance. One of the peculiarities of California weather causes 60-degree temperatures, fog and low barometric pressure on the coast, but 100-degree temperatures and high barometric pressure in the Central Valley. That change from cold to hot creates wind blowing out of the west, and in turn, guarantees the ideal conditions for this sport in the Bay Area.

If you daydream of a sport where you can be free like the wind, this is the one for you. It's quite a vision: you're cutting across the water's surface, skipping over boat wakes like a flying fish, and hanging on for the ride while the wind takes you yonder.

The fantasy is enough to inspire the curious. After all, someday that just might be you sailing across the Bay.

❖

Contact: Phone the San Francisco School of Windsurfing, (415) 750-0412 or (415) 753-3235; Events West in Mill Valley, (415) 383-9378; the American Boardsailing Institute in Fairfax, Marin County, (415) 454-1448. A free brochure that includes a list of windsurfing schools is available by phoning (800) 333-2242.

Chapter 16

Top Adventure Listings

Top Adventures

10 Bay Area Backroads

The thing people hate most about driving in the Bay Area is that their speed always seems to be set by the cars around them.

You know how that goes. The driver behind you is rarely patient, but the one ahead of you has all the time in the world. After awhile, you may even feel like giving up, especially if the horizon is filled with brake lights. In the process, you may even remember a time years ago when there weren't so many cars on the highways, when driving in the Bay Area was actually a pleasure.

You say you don't remember that? Well, believe me, it used to be that way. And it still is that way in some special places, 10 of them in all, the best of the Bay Area's backroads.

You see, one of the best things about the Bay Area is that in an hour or less, you can be driving down a beautiful backroad where you can set whatever pace you want, and enjoy a ride in a quiet country setting. When you put your foot on the brake, it is because you want to slow down and take in the surrounding beauty, not because some cretin just cut in front of you.

These roads come in all varieties, but by any name, place or setting, slow always beats fast. Here are 10 favorite secluded backroads. Several of these trips can be routed so that they connect to each other:

San Mateo County

Old Stage Road—This is an old two-laner that connects Pescadero to San Gregorio, about a 20-minute drive through coastal hills and ranches. There is one section where giant eucalyptus trees perfectly frame a straight, 100-yard stretch of road with a beautiful old home at the end, a classic piece of Americana.

Directions: Take Highway 1 south about 20 miles past Half Moon Bay. Turn east on Pescadero Road and drive three miles to Pescadero, then turn left on Old Stage Road.

Kings Mountain Road/Tunitas Creek Road—Kings Mountain Road departs from Woodside on the Peninsula, then winds like a pretzel up and over Skyline Boulevard, then down the other side (where it becomes Tunitas Creek Road) eventually to Highway 1 and the ocean. In the process, it passes through redwoods, mountain lookouts, travels along a stream, rolling grasslands, and eventually leads to the coast. It is narrow, twisty and slow. In other words, it's perfect.

Directions: From Highway 280 on the Peninsula, take the Highway 84 exit and drive west into Woodside. Continue through Woodside, then turn right on Kings Mountain Road and you're on your way.

Santa Clara County

Page Mill Road/Alpine Road/Pescadero Road—Just add some twists and you lose the crowds. That is what this route does, with some beautiful scenery. It climbs out of the Palo Alto foothills, providing some great vistas of the South Bay and passing several parklands, then crosses Skyline Boulevard and passes through a series of redwood forests. At times in the early summer, usually in the evening, the fog buries the coastal foothills, and this road provides a dramatic lookout above them looking westward. Eventually, the road connects to Pescadero, where you can take Old Stage Road (see previous page).

Directions: From Highway 280 in Palo Alto, take the Page Mill Road exit and drive west.

Mount Hamilton Road—This is the twistiest road in California, built that way on purpose so that the grade would be easy enough for horses towing wagons to make it up to the top. And the top is the highest point in the Bay Area: Mount Hamilton, east of San Jose. At 4,062 feet, it provides a fantastic lookout over both the Santa Clara Valley to the west and miles of wildlands to the east. Once you reach the top, you can extend the trip by heading east on San Antonio Valley Road then continuing (it becomes Mines Road in Alameda County) all the way to Livermore.

Directions: Head south on Highway 101 into San Jose, then take the Alum Rock turnoff and drive east through San Jose (I know, a real bummer). Turn right on Mount Hamilton Road (Highway 130) and continue for 22 miles to the peak and beyond.

Alameda County

Mines Road—If this road feels like it is out in the middle of nowhere, that's because it is. It is routed south out of Livermore, running in a valley between Crane Ridge to the east and Cedar Mountain Ridge to the west; much of it runs along Arroyo Mocho Creek. It is wild, untouched country, and the farther you go, the wilder it gets. When the road crosses into Santa Clara County, it becomes San Antonio Valley Road and is routed all the way to Mount Hamilton (see above). You may even see a herd of elk way out here.

Directions: Drive on Highway 580 to Livermore, then take the North Livermore Avenue exit, and drive south into town. Continue on North Livermore Avenue, which becomes South Livermore Avenue, and as you leave town, Tesla Road. Shortly after it becomes Tesla Road, turn right on Mines Road and continue south for 15 miles into San Antonio Valley.

Contra Costa County

Clayton Road/Marsh Creek Road/Morgan Territory Road—This trip is a microcosm of the Bay Area, from hell to heaven in one easy lesson. You start by driving from Concord to Clayton on Clayton Road, and amid the traffic, you may wonder what the heck you are doing here. In Clayton, turn right on Marsh Creek Road and you will find out. The road is routed from the base of the northeastern flank of Mount Diablo to some of the most remote sections of the county. From here, turn south on Morgan Territory Road, where it is routed for nearly 20 miles through wildlands, leading eventually to Livermore and Highway 580.

Directions: From Highway 680 in Concord, take the Concord Avenue exit and drive east into Concord, where the road becomes Clayton Road. Drive southeast into Clayton, then turn right on Marsh Road. Drive about four miles, then turn right on Morgan Territory Road and take off for yonder.

Sonoma County

Petaluma to Bodega Bay—If you don't like to drive slow, here is a 50-miles-per-hour option where you can feel like you are visiting the rolling dairylands of the Midwest. Shortly after departing Petaluma, you drive west through old-style country, complete with Jersey cows. The road meanders its way along, then you climb a hill, pop over the ridge, and find a great view of Bodega Bay.

Directions: From Highway 101 at Petaluma, turn west on Bodega Avenue (signed turnoff), drive through Petaluma and continue west for about eight miles. Turn north (right) on Valley Ford Road, then continue west on the Valley Ford Cutoff/Highway 1 to Bodega Bay.

Solano County

Birds Landing/Rio Vista—On a trip out to Rio Vista, my brother made a wrong turn and we found this backroad by accident. Since much of the area borders the Grizzly Island Wildlife Area, there is a chance to see all kinds of critters, and in half an hour, we saw pheasant, heron, ducks, hawks and ground squirrels, but no Bigfoot. Highway 12 to Rio Vista gently climbs and falls with the foothills, and then the road to Rio Vista is flat as you explore rural farm country. It feels like you are thousands of miles away from the Bay Area, not just 35 miles from Vallejo.

Directions: From Highway 80 in Fairfield, take Highway 12 south to Rio Vista, and turn right, driving down Main Street, which deadends at the Sacramento River. Turn right (west) on Montezuma Hills Road and drive about eight miles to Landing Road. Turn left, drive to Birds Landing, then turn right on Collinsville Road and drive one mile. At the Y, veer to the left and take Shiloh Road back to Highway 12.

Marin County

Lucas Valley Road/Sir Francis Drake Loop—Marin isn't all condos, yuppies and BMWs, and this trip proves it. Lucas Valley Road is a pretty route that heads west through woodlands, over a hill and down along Nicasio Creek to Nicasio Reservoir. It deadends at Petaluma Road, where you turn left, cross the lake and travel through foothill country—choosing to either head farther out, all the way to Point Reyes if you want, or back south to the metropolis.

Directions: From Highway 101 north of San Rafael, take Lucas Valley Road west, all the way to Nicasio Reservoir, where the road deadends at Petaluma Road. Turn left and drive over the bridge at the lake and continue to a Y. To go to Point Reyes, veer right on Point Reyes Road. To return to civilization, turn right on Platform Road, which later turns into Sir Francis Drake Boulevard and runs all the way to Highway 101.

Bolinas/Fairfax Road—If you like to mix in a hike with a drive, this is the best choice in the Bay Area, with access to 15 trailheads for secluded hikes and three lakes. The road leaves Fairfax and climbs a hill, passing a golf course, a series of trailheads, and then traces above Alpine Lake, one of the prettiest lakes in the Bay Area. If you take the Sky Oaks turnoff, you can also get access to Bon Tempe and Lagunitas lakes. After crossing the dam at Alpine Lake, the road has several hairpin turns (these usually keep the speeders away) and will lead you into the remote western flank of Mount Tamalpais.

Directions: From Highway 101 in Corte Madera, take the Sir Francis Drake Boulevard exit and drive west into Fairfax. Then turn left on Bolinas/Fairfax Road.

10 Great Redwood Forests

Redwood forests are sanctuaries for both peace and adventure, and the Bay Area is the only metropolitan area in the world that has them.

Ten great redwood forests remain in the Bay Area, all of them areas of pristine beauty, ideal for weekend getaways. They are perfect for hiking, picnics and some even for camping. Or you can just sit against one of these ancient trees and let the beauty of the surroundings sink in.

The Bay Area has nearly 125 parks, and it is the redwood parks that are the most loved. Unlike Yosemite, they are not being loved to death. Of all the Bay Area parks, it is at these where you will find the least litter, the fewest trail violations by outlaw mountain bikers, and the visitors with the most reverent state of mind. Redwoods do that to you.

The redwoods themselves are some of nature's most awesome living things, often hundreds of years old and giant. The big trees form a massive canopy, shielding the forest floor from direct sunlight, creating perfect settings for lush fern beds, cool mornings, and soft dirt hiking paths. It's like taking a walk through an outdoor cathedral.

Here are the Bay Area's top 10 redwood parks:

Big Basin State Park, Felton

This is California's oldest state park, and by far still the Bay Area's most beautiful. It covers thousands of acres of giant redwoods, some of the trees 2,000 years old, has a 70-foot waterfall in a canyon lined with ferns, and 80 miles of hiking trails. The best is a 12-miler that runs from park headquarters, past the waterfall, then along Waddell Creek to the Pacific

Ocean. Some 150 campgrounds are provided at the park. (For more details on Big Basin, see page 213.)

Contact: Phone park headquarters, (408)338-6132.

Butano State Park, Pescadero

This is my favorite place in the Bay Area for a Sunday walk. It's not too remote (10 miles from Pescadero), yet it is detached from civilization. It includes a great 11-mile loop trail that cuts through redwoods and around a mountain rim with lookouts over the ocean. Cutoff trails link up with the loop trail, providing the opportunity to customize a shorter trip. The interior of the park is a quiet and protected redwood and stream setting, with lots of deer and squirrels. About 40 campsites are available here.

For more details on Butano, see page 207.

Contact: Phone park headquarters, (408)879-0173.

Memorial County Park, La Honda

Memorial Park is tucked in a redwood pocket between the tiny towns of La Honda and Loma Mar. There are 50 miles of trails available that cut in and out of redwoods and chaparral. One is routed along Pescadero Creek down to adjacent Sam McDonald County Park. It is a great network of trails. In addition, six miles of trails are wheelchair accessible. The pools of the creek have what appear to be little trout in them, but they're not. They are actually baby steelhead, and catching them is prohibited. About 135 campsites are available.

Contact: Phone park headquarters, (415)879-0212. If the phone is unattended, call (415)363-4020.

Muir Woods National Monument, Marin

This is the most visited redwood park in the world, and is such a popular destination that the loop trail along Redwood Creek on the valley floor is paved for the weekly Sunday parade of tourists. But there are other options, such as hiking off onto one of the cutoff trails (Panoramic Trail, Dipsea Trail) which are routed up and out of the crowded valley. These will give you the quiet paradise you desire, as well as an aerobic workout. At the top of the Panoramic Trail (a three-mile hike), you clear the tree tops and get a lookout over the entire valley, a virtual sea of conifers. No campsites are available.

For more details on Muir Woods, see page 134.

Contact: Phone park headquarters, (415)388-2596.

Samuel P. Taylor State Park, Marin

As you enter the park, you will notice immediately that it is the classic woods and water setting, with redwoods, a stream and a campground with 60 sites. That makes it a paradise for family visits, particularly for weekend trips based out of the park's camp. However, it is also a popular jump-off spot for mountain biking, with old ranch roads that are ideal for bikes; hikers wanting to stay clear of them should keep on the narrow track trails. A bonus is that a paved, wheelchair accessible trail is available along Papermill (Lagunitas) Creek.

Contact: Phone park headquarters, (415)488-9897.

Portola State Park, La Honda

This park is known for its hiking, camping and communing with quiet the prime attractions. There are 14 miles of trails routed through varied settings amid redwoods, along a creek, and into chaparral. For the Bay Area, the park feels quite remote. That enhances the camping experience here; about 50 campsites are available. The road in is twisty, and that keeps the unambitious out. (For more details on Portola State Park, see pages 211-212.)

Contact: Phone park headquarters at (415)948-9098.

Redwood Regional Park, Oakland

Parks in the East Bay are best known for their spectacular views of the Bay, but if it is beautiful surroundings you want, Redwood Regional Park has them. The park has a surprising grove of redwoods, with a trout stream (no fishing permitted) running through the valley floor. The trail here (Stream Trail) is one of the prettiest hikes in the East Bay Regional Parks, and it has been peaceful, too, since they kicked out the mountain bikers (who were careening downhill, plowing uphill hikers). You could also try the East Ridge Trail, the French Trail or the West Ridge Trail (part of the East Bay National Skyline Trail), which is more remote, but which heads up and above the wooded valley. No camping is permitted.

Contact: Phone the East Bay Regional Park District at (510)635-0135, then ask for extension 2578.

Huddart County Park, Woodside

This is Woodside's backyard playland, with 1,000 acres of redwoods, tan oak and madrones. The trails vary in difficulty, some as easy as a short, nearly flat loop past some large trees and a creek, others as difficult as a climb to nearly 2,000 feet. It is the best hiking park on the Peninsula, with all manner of cutoffs and links to other trails, including a newly completed connector to nearby Wunderlich Park. No camping is permitted.

For more details on Huddart, see page 185.

Contact: Phone (415)851-0326 (park headquarters), or if the phone is unattended, (415)363-4020.

Wunderlich County Park, Woodside

Wunderlich has a magic sense of remoteness, while actually being very close to a lot of people. There are 25 miles of secluded trails, a good hiking network with many intersections, providing a chance to customize your own outing. The trails are routed through lush ravines and tall redwoods, and if you are ambitious, they can take you on a climb of nearly 2,000 feet in 10 miles (a five-hour hike) to the Skyline Ridge. In return, you get lookouts over the South Bay. No camping is permitted.

For more details on Wunderlich, see page 191.

Contact: Phone park headquarters at (415)851-7570. If the phone is unattended, call (415)363-4020.

Purisima Creek Redwoods, Half Moon Bay

This is a vast, primitive area, 2,500 acres in all, that spans from the Skyline Ridge on westward to the foothills near Half Moon Bay. In between is a beautiful parkland with redwood forests, wild berries and wildflowers, and also great views of the Pacific Ocean. It feels like Big Sur, Mount Tamalpais and the Humboldt Coast all in one. There are three access points, two on Skyline (Highway 35) and one southeast of Half Moon Bay; a map is absolutely essential. No camping is permitted.

For more details on Purisima, see page 182.

Contact: Phone the Midpeninsula Open Space District at (415)691-1200.

Best 10 Hikes

You don't have to be the second coming of John Muir to have a John Muir-like experience. At least not on my 10 favorite hikes in California, each of which provides a divine experience in a unique, pristine land.

None of these hikes require backpacking or wilderness camping, but all are one-day walks, including a few that take just 20 minutes to an hour. Regardless, all will take you into untouched, natural landscapes, nature's shrines, where you can escape civilization and refresh yourself among pure surroundings.

These trails will lead you to the finest panoramas California can offer. They include the grandest waterfall, lookout and beach in the Bay Area, truly secluded redwood forests, a fern-walled canyon on the north coast, and high Sierra lakes.

What you invest is a little time and a little energy, walking to a place where machines are not allowed. In return, you get an experience that will stay with you for a long time. It is what some people call "the power of place." It's difficult to explain, but you know it when you feel it. And when you feel it, you don't forget it.

Here is a synopsis of 10 of my favorite places where you can capture that feeling:

Berry Falls, Big Basin State Park

A two-hour walk from park headquarters takes you through giant redwoods, over the Big Basin rim, down into a canyon, and ultimately to a fern-lined gorge that frames a 70-foot waterfall. It is a mountain cathedral, with refracted sunlight making the waterfall's mist droplets look like floating crystals. If you hike onward, you come upon another series of cascading falls, particularly spectacular the day after a hard rain.

For more details on Big Basin, see page 213.

Hiking Time: Figure five hours for the round-trip, including a one-hour lunch at the falls; add more than an hour for the return trip if you take an optional loop route.

Location: In the Santa Cruz Mountains, about 20 miles from Santa Cruz.

Contact: Big Basin State Park, (408)338-6132.

Tenaya Lake, Yosemite National Park

One of the prettiest lakes anywhere in the world, this is where Muir got religion. Tenaya Lake is set in Yosemite's high country, at 8,163 feet, where the granite surroundings are glacier carved and polished. Polly Dome plunges right into the lake, where it is mirrored on calm, blue-sky days. There's a parking area and picnic area near the lake, and from there, you can meander on trails around the lake, or the ambitious can climb up the back side of Polly Dome for one of Yosemite's most awesome, yet lesser-known, views. The Tuolumne Meadows Campground is nine miles away.

Hiking time: As little as 20 minutes, as much as half a day, depending on your desires.

Location: In Yosemite National Park, nine miles west of Tuolumne Meadows.

Contact: Yosemite National Park, (209)372-0200.

Convict Lake, Inyo National Forest

This beautiful lake has a backdrop of wilderness mountain peaks, and is fronted by a sprinkling of conifers, an incredible sight at 7,583 feet. Easy to reach off Highway 395, it has an excellent trail network that starts near the campground. The hike is routed on the north side of Convict Lake, heading west, then up through a canyon along Convict Creek. In the space of five miles, it leads into the John Muir Wilderness and nine other lakes including Bighorn Lake, a huge mountain pool.

Hiking time: An hour will get you past Convict Lake and up to Convict Creek. All day will get you up to the adjacent lakes and back down again.

Location: In the eastern Sierra, north of Bishop off Highway 395.

Contact: Inyo National Forest, (619)934-2505.

Saddlebag Lake, Inyo National Forest

Saddlebag Lake, set at 10,087 feet, is the highest lake you can drive to in California. It is stark and beautiful, absolutely pristine, with trails that head into a high granite wilderness where the lakes are rock bowls carved by glacial action. The trail loops around the eastern side of the lake, then splits into two wilderness routes. The easier hike of the two is the left fork, which will take you to Greenstone, Wasco and Steelhead lakes, close enough to reach on a morning hike.

Hiking time: Taking the left fork, the hike will take five to six hours.

Location: West of Lee Vining off Highway 120.

Contact: Inyo National Forest, (916)647-6525.

Edison Lake, Sierra National Forest

The trail out of Edison Lake is overlooked by most hikers, yet it provides easy access to the Pacific Crest Trail, an outstanding wilderness trout stream (Mono Creek), and a look at Bear Mountain to the south. Edison Lake, at 7,650 feet, is where the trip starts. Take the trail on the north side of the Edison Lake and hike up toward the inlet, then along Mono Creek. Shortly thereafter, it connects to the Pacific Crest Trail, where a steep, 40-minute climb up Bear Mountain will have you perched in the most wondrous grove of aspens anywhere on the planet.

Hiking time: Best done overnight, camping at the junction of Mono Creek and the Pacific Crest Trail. It's a 14-mile round-trip.

Location: About 80 miles northeast of Fresno.

Contact: Sierra National Forest, (209)841-3311.

East Peak, Mount Tamalpais

Mount Tam, Marin County's old sentinel, was John Muir's favorite winter hiking spot. There is no better place to see the Bay Area than from the East Peak Lookout at 2,571 feet. You can drive to a parking area set just below the summit, then with a short (typically 20-minute) but steep walk, claim a perch on this mountain peak. Sunsets to the west, particularly with a fog layer below, are incredible. So are sunrises to the east, when the entire Bay Area seems enveloped in an orange hue.

For more information on Mount Tamalpais, see page 125.

Hiking time: About 20 to 25 minutes up, then about 15 minutes back down.

Location: Marin County.

Contact: Mount Tamalpais State Park, (415)388-2070.

"Otter Beach," Andrew Molera State Park

I named this beach myself, so don't ask the rangers where Otter Beach is. The beach is like a fantasy, where sea otters play hide-and-seek with you as they duck up and down in nearby kelp beds. The ocean laps against a huge sand expanse, protected and calm, creating a setting that is the essence of peace. From the parking area along Highway 1, it's about a 30-minute walk to the beach. The rangers will give you a one page handout of the best places to see otters.

Hiking time: About an hour, round-trip.

Location: Big Sur, south of Monterey, west of Highway 1.

Contact: Andrew Molera State Park, (408)667-2315.

Fern Canyon, Prairie Creek Redwoods

This is one of the most unique settings in California. You start at Gold Bluff Beach, an enormous wilderness beach, then hike inland along a creek into Fern Canyon. In the canyon, you are bordered by vertical walls that are covered with huge, lush ferns, topped by redwood trees that create a massive forest canopy. There is wet greenness everywhere, the sound of water, and the magical sense that here amid the giant fern walls you are protected and safe. The trail is routed east through the bottom of Fern Canyon, then up to the canyon rim. Finally it loops back through redwoods, eventually breaking through to the beach expanse. There is nothing like it anywhere else.

Hiking time: About an hour, more if you linger in the canyon or stroll on the beach.

Location: Prairie Creek Redwoods State Park, near Orick (north of Eureka) on the north coast.

Contact: Prairie Creek Redwoods State Park, (707) 488-2171 or (707)445-6547.

Stout Grove, Jedediah Smith State Park

When you visit the sacred old redwoods, you want it quiet, as if you were entering a forest church. That's what you get at Stout Grove, set near the Smith River in an obscure section of Jedediah Smith State Park, far removed from the parade of tourists in the redwoods along Highway 101. The centerpiece here is the Stout Tree, measuring 340 feet tall and 20 feet in diameter. The easily walkable, soft dirt trail is routed through this forest, a classic setting, with big trees and giants beds of ferns—yet no one around. It is like a walk back in time. (For more details on Jedediah Smith State Park, see page 15).

Hiking time: Three hours for a full exploration of the grove by trail, can be shortened to as little as a half-hour to the Stout Tree and back.

Location: Park entrance is on Highway 199 northeast of Crescent City.

Contact: Jedediah Smith State Park, (707)458-3310 or (707)464-9533.

Lassen Summit, Lassen Volcanic Park

So you want to feel like you are standing on top of the world? The hike up to Lassen Summit, set at 10,457 feet, will get you pretty close. It is the easiest major mountain to climb in California, about a two-hour hike to the top, covering two-and-a-half miles. As a reward, you get an incredible view of Mount Shasta to the north, about 250,000 acres of wildlands to the east, and the Sacramento Valley plunging westward. The mountaintop itself can be explored for hours, having all sorts of strange volcanic flumes, crags and hideouts. A sure winner, especially for families. (For more details on Lassen National Park, see page 60.)

Hiking time: Four hours round-trip, longer if you plan to have lunch, enjoy the view, or explore the hardened volcanic flumes on top.

Location: East of Red Bluff.

Contact: Lassen Volcanic National Park, (916)595-4444.

Top 25 Lakes

Most people have no idea of the number, diversity and quality of lakes in California that are ideal for summer vacations—camping, boating, fishing and hiking. In a survey I completed for my books *California Camping* and *California Fishing*, I counted 373 lakes you can drive to, 483 lakes you can hike to, 185 streams, and 1,531 campgrounds.

On a county-by-county basis, here is capsule look at 25 of the best lakes you can reach by car. Note that many of them have numerous other lakes and streams in close proximity to provide additional options.

Sanger Lake, Del Norte County

A small, hidden and beautiful little lake, set below Sanger Peak (5,862 feet) in Six Rivers National Forest. Primitive camping is available, with fair fishing for small brook trout. A circuitous drive on mountain roads keeps many visitors away.

Contact: Six Rivers National Forest, (707)442-1721.

Stone Lagoon, Humboldt County

Of the three freshwater lagoons along Highway 101 north of Eureka, Stone Lagoon is the best. An ideal site for canoe campers, with a boat-in campsite at Ryan's Camp. Some large cutthroat trout are a bonus.

Contact: Department of Fish & Game, Eureka, (707)445-6499.

Kangaroo Lake, Siskiyou County

This small lake is literally nestled in Scott Mountain, at a 6,000-foot elevation. Fishing for brook trout is often excellent, and it is wheelchair accessible with a paved trail right to the lake. Trails out of camp connect to the Pacific Crest Trail.

Contact: Klamath National Forest, (916)842-6131.

Lewiston Lake, Trinity County

One of the prettiest lakes in California, with shoreline camping at Mary Smith Camp and a low-key lakeside resort at Lakeview Terrace. Set at the foot of the Trinities, with 15 miles of shoreline. Fishing is good for trout below Trinity Dam.

Contact: Shasta-Trinity National Forest, (916) 623-6106; Brady's Sportshop in Weaverville , (916)623-3121; Lakeview Terrace, (916)778-3791.

Lily Lake, Modoc County

Set out in No Man's Land, at this lake you get guaranteed solitude, free drive-in camping and a high desert setting with a few conifers sprinkled about. If the brook trout here don't bite, try nearby Cave Lake. No motors are allowed on the lake.

Contact: Modoc National Forest, (916)233-5811.

Cleone Lake, Mendocino County

This is the centerpiece of MacKerricher State Park, located just north of Fort Bragg, an outstanding layover when touring Highway 1. A lot of park visitors are surprised to find this little lake, which provides good trout fishing and fair bass fishing. No motors are allowed. Camping reservations are advised.

Contact: MacKerricher State Park Headquarters, (707)937-5804.

Iron Canyon Reservoir, Shasta County

This lake is shaded, emerald green, and has a resident bald eagle and a nearby campground nestled in a forest. It has a boat ramp, good trout fishing, and is just hard enough to reach that it gets bypassed by the Winnebago set.

Contact: Shasta-Trinity National Forest, (916)275-1587.

Manzanita Lake, Lassen County

This is the jewel of Lassen Volcanic National Park, with the park's largest campground nearby, offering easy access to a premium wild trout fishery (two-fish limit, with all fish over 10 inches to be released). No motors are allowed, but the lake is ideal for a canoe or pram.

Contact: Lassen Volcanic National Park, (916) 595-4444.

Bucks Lake, Plumas County

This is no secret spot, not with several campgrounds set near the lake, and not with the highest catch rates for trout in the north Sierra. It is a premium spot, set at 5,150 feet near Quincy, with a full service marina with boat rentals.

Contact: Sportsmen's Den, (916)283-2733; Plumas National Forest, (916)283-2050.

Lake Sonoma, Sonoma County

The anglers versus waterskiers war has been resolved here with specific areas set up for each. Good boat-in camping is available on the north arm. The bass and bluegill fishing can be excellent; field scout Clyde "The Wrench" Gibbs and his family once caught and released 50 fish in one day here.

Contact: U.S. Corps of Engineers, (707)433-9483.

Blue Lakes, Lake County

You get lakeside cabins (and campsites), decent fishing, yet it's not a killer drive to get here. The lakes are long and narrow, and are overlooked because of their nearby proximity to Clear Lake, just 10 miles away.

Contact: Le Trianon Resort, (707)275-2262; Pine Acres, (707)275-2811.

Lake Solano, Solano County

This small, quiet lake sits just below the dam of Lake Berryessa (where all hell breaks loose every weekend). No motors are allowed, making it good for canoes, rafts and rowboats. A county park campground adds a nice touch.

Contact: Lake Solano County Park, (916)795-2990.

Lake Berryessa, Napa County

This is the Bay Area's backyard fishing hole, with 750 campsites and 165 miles of shoreline, and everybody knows about it, right? What you may not know is that cabin and condo rentals are available at Putah Creek Resort and Steele Park.

Contact: Putah Creek Resort, (707)966-2116; Steele Park, (707)966-2330; Markley Cove, (707)966-2134.

Bullards Bar Reservoir, Yuba County

One of the prettier reservoirs in the Central Valley foothill country, set at a 2,300-foot elevation, with 55 miles of shoreline, several campgrounds and good fishing. Good boat-in camps are located near French Point and upstream at Madrone Cove.

Contact: Emerald Cove Resort, (916)692-2166.

Stampede Reservoir, Sierra County

A classic Sierra lake in the granite high country, at 6,000 feet, good-sized at 3,400 acres, yet easy to reach and with an extended boat ramp and a half dozen campgrounds. Fishing is good for trout, rarely including some giant mackinaw trout.

Contact: Tahoe National Forest, (916)587-3558.

Bowman Lake, Nevada County

A sapphire jewel set at 5,568 feet near Emigrant Gap, with a primitive campground and the area's best fishery for brown trout. There are many other lakes nearby.

Contact: Tahoe National Forest, (916)265-4531.

Hell Hole Reservoir, Placer County

An awesome sight, with high granite walls framing a deep blue lake in the high Sierra. The drive in is long and winding, you need a boat to fish it right (for mackinaws and browns), and there are no camps directly on the lake. Regardless, the beauty makes up for it.

Contact: Eldorado National Forest, (916)333-4312.

Lake Tahoe, El Dorado County

The prettiest state park campground is at Emerald Bay. And what need be said about Tahoe? Always an inspiring sight, 22 miles long, 1,645 feet deep, clear enough to see a dinner plate 75 feet deep. Dozens of lakes within 20 miles to the west provide side-trip options.

Contact: Tahoe Basin Management, (916)573-2600; Emerald Bay State Park, (916)541-3030.

Silver Lake, Amador County

Set in a classic granite cirque at 7,200-feet, it was created from the flows of the Silver Fork American River. Two camps and a boat ramp make it easy; fishing for trout (rainbows, browns, mackinaws) crowns it.

Contact: Eldorado National Forest, (209)295-4251.

Blue Lakes (Upper and Lower), Alpine County

These lakes are often lost in the shadow of giant Tahoe to the north, but still shine for visitors. Blue Lakes are set in the high country, at 8,200 feet, with several camps in the vicinity. Lower Blue has the best trout fishing, by boat at the north end, just at the underwater dropoff.

Contact: Toiyabe National Forest, (702)882-2766.

Lake Alpine, Calaveras County

Here's the prettiest sight on Highway 4, at 7,320 feet. It has good fishing during the evening rise, developed camps, and good hiking in the area. Once scarcely known, it has become popular lately. Little Mosquito Lake farther up Highway 4 is a good side trip.

Contact: Stanislaus National Forest, (209)795-1381.

Cherry Lake, Tuolumne County

Located just outside the northwest border of Yosemite National Park, at a 4,700-foot elevation, with a campground, boat ramp, and jump-off points for backpackers. Trails are routed north into Emigrant Wilderness, or east into Yosemite, providing access to dozens of backcountry lakes.

Contact: Stanislaus National Forest, (209)962-7825.

O'Neill Forebay, Merced County

The state record striped bass was caught here, 67 pounds, and 20-pounders are caught almost daily, though little guys are lot more likely to fill five-fish limits. Nearby Basalt Camp at San Luis Reservoir provides a spot to overnight it. During the summer, expect hot weather, and high winds in the afternoon.

Contact: San Luis Recreation Area, (209)826-1196.

Tenaya Lake, Mariposa County

This is one of the prettiest lakes in the world, a showpiece of the Yosemite National Park high country. Walk-in picnic sites are available, and nearby Tuolumne Meadows provides a camping option. The only downer is the fishing, which is lousy. No boats are allowed.

Contact: Yosemite National Park, (209)372-0200.

Convict Lake, Mono County

The lake is framed by a back wall of wilderness mountain peaks, fronted by a conifer-lined shore, set at 7,583 feet. Sounds beautiful? It is. You'll find good fishing, wilderness trailheads, and all facilities available at the lake.

Contact: Inyo National Forest, (619)934-2505; Convict Lake Resort, (619)934-3803.

Three Peaks

Some places seem to have a quality to them, something you feel rather than see.

Tenaya Lake, tucked in granite in Yosemite's high country, is one of the few places that has it. Lake Berryessa does not. An ancient redwood forest on the north coast? Like a sacred cathedral. A few oaks in the foothill grasslands? Sorry, they don't seem to have the magic. The Klamath River? Yep. The much bigger Columbia? Nope.

California's three best known mountains all qualify—they have it. Whitney, Shasta and Lassen. There is something of mystery and challenge, of fire and ice, giant rocks and hidden spirits. Sure, you can enjoy them by simply looking. Whitney at 14,497 feet, Shasta at 14,162 feet, and Lassen at 10,457 feet stand apart from surrounding ranges. In the western hemisphere, there are only a scarce few places that can project the power of these mountains.

But you can share that power by taking it a step further and climbing one. Maybe even all three.

"What? Me? I've never climbed anything in my life. I don't even like climbing a ladder. I'd never do that."

Well, you'd be surprised at where you might walk after you start taking a few steps. My brother Rambob and I, for instance, never figured to climb any to mountaintops. Then, in 1985, we climbed Whitney because it is the official start of the 211-mile John Muir Trail. Up on top, we felt the power of the high country and were drawn to it. We climbed Shasta a year later and had the kind of special feeling that stays with you for months. The following year, we climbed Shasta again, then a day later, Lassen. Now it's in our blood.

Newcomers can make the climb, too. My research editor, Robyn Schlueter, had never climbed mountains before and she made it to the top. Once you get started, the steps come easier than you might think, and the reward is something that lasts.

Mount Lassen—10,457 feet

This is a good introduction to mountain climbing. The summit climb is a two-and-a-half-mile zigzag of a hike that just about anybody with a quart of water can handle, yet provides one of the most spectacular peaks anywhere.

In Lassen Volcanic National Park, 50 miles east of Red Bluff, you can drive to the trailhead at the base of the mountain. The trail surface is hard and flat, so you can get into a nice hiking rhythm, and with a 15 percent grade, it isn't a killer. Most people take under two hours to reach the top, about a 2,000-foot elevation gain. In the process, though, newcomers often ask themselves, "Why am I doing this?" When they reach the crest, they find out.

The view is superb, with the awesome Mount Shasta 100 miles north appearing close enough to reach out and grab a hunk of. To the east are hundreds of miles of forests and lakes, with Lake Almanor a surprise jewel, and to the west, the land drops off to several small volcanic cones and the Central Valley.

The peak itself is the top of a huge volcanic flume and you can spend hours probing several craters and hardened lava flows. Lassen last blew its top in a series of eruptions from 1914 to 1921, which in geologic time is like a few minutes ago.

It's a prime first mountain experience. We met people of all ages and in all kinds of physical shape. If you bring water, something which a number of hikers curiously forget, you'll make it. It's that simple.

Directions: Take Interstate 80 north to Interstate 505, then proceed to Interstate 5. Drive approximately 95 miles north to Red Bluff and take the Highway 36/Lassen Park exit. Continue east for 47 miles to the Highway 89 cutoff, then turn north and proceed to the park entrance.

Key notes: Bring at least a quart of water, a windbreaker, sunglasses, sunscreen and a hat, and get an early start to beat the heat.

Contact: For a map and general information, phone Lassen National Park at (916)595-4444.

Mount Whitney—14,496.8 feet

This is the Big Daddy, the highest point in America's lower 48. It's a long, steep hike from the trailhead at Whitney Portal, climbing 6,100 feet in 10 miles. But a decent trail takes you to the top, so no mountaineering equipment in necessary.

Whitney is located in the southern Sierra at the foot of Lone Pine on Highway 395. It's a giant rock cut by glaciers, not formed from a volcano like Shasta and Lassen, and the peak reflects it—sheer rock outcrops on the edge of dramatic, plunging canyons.

Nothing can prepare you for the lookout. It is absolutely astonishing. To the west is the entire Western Divide, to the north are rows of 11,000 to 13,000-foot peaks, and eastward, the mountain drops straight down—11,000 feet down in just 15 miles—to the Owens Valley. The top itself is oval with a jagged edge, with a little rock house constructed to protect hikers from storms.

The hike is a genuine heart-thumper, yet inspiring at the same time. It includes 100 switchbacks to climb Wotan's Throne, and in the final miles, the ridge is cut by notch windows in the rock. You look through and the bottom drops thousands of feet at your boot tips. Some people try the 20-mile round-trip in one day, but that makes it an exhausting rush. A better strategy is to hike in and set up a base camp at 10,000 feet, getting acclimated to the altitude. The next day, you can hit the top and return, carrying a minimum of equipment for the ascent.

Directions: There are several possible routes, but the most direct is to head east to Sacramento, then turn south on Highway 99 and drive 48 miles to Highway 88. Turn east and proceed 120 miles to the junction of Highway 88 and U.S. 395 at Minden, Nevada. Turn south and drive approximately 200 miles to the town of Lone Pine. Turn west on Whitney Portal Road and drive 13 miles to the trailhead and campgrounds.

Notes: Bring pain reliever for high altitude headaches, good hiking boots, warm weather gear in a daypack, along with plenty of water, high energy snacks, sunglasses, sunscreen and a hat. A wilderness permit is required to climb, and can be obtained at the ranger station in Lone Pine.

Contact: The Inyo National Forest Mount Whitney Ranger District in Lone Pine can provide maps and information; phone (619)876-5542.

Mount Shasta—14,162 feet

This is the true king of California mountains, the giant volcano that rises alone 10,000 feet above the surrounding hills in Northern California. Along with Mount Rainier in Washington and McKinley in Alaska, it is among the most majestic and powerful mountains in the western hemisphere.

You feel that power every step of the way to the top. But to get there, you must have the right equipment, and that means crampons on your boots and an ice axe, which makes hiking up the glacier fields enjoyable rather than slip-and-slide. The more snow there is, the easier and more fun the climb.

The hike is a scramble of a trail across small rocks, then when you hit snow, it becomes an easier walk with the help of crampons. The ice axe becomes important when you reach Red Banks, a steep, ice-bordered, massive rock outcrop at 11,500 feet. You can either climb the Red Banks Chute, a rock and ice-laden crevice, or circle around it.

The peak is astounding, a relatively small volcanic flume which you can climb on top of. On clear days, you feel like you are on top of the earth, with hundreds of miles visible in all directions. Steaming sulphur vents at the foot of the final 300-foot summit climb give rise to the memory of John Muir, who spent an icy night trapped on the peak, hugging a vent to keep warm.

Shasta is also a mountain of mystery, with tales of Lemurians and Yaktavians, elfin creatures said to live in its interior. Even its creation is legend: in Indian lore, Shasta is said to have been created when gods stuck a hole through the clouds and built a giant teepee with the broken pieces.

The best strategy is to hike in to treeline at 8,000 feet and set up a base camp at Horse Camp, where a natural spring provides unlimited water. The next morning, start walking by 4:30 a.m. and figure seven to eight hours to the top. It's a seven-mile trip, rising more than 6,000 feet in the process. Every step can be a memorable one.

Directions: Take Interstate 80 north to Interstate 505, then proceed north to Interstate 5. Drive approximately 180 miles north to the town of Mount Shasta. Take the Central Mount Shasta exit and head west on Lake Street, which turns into Everett Memorial Highway, and drive about 15 miles to the parking lot at Bunny Flat. It's about an hour hike from there to Horse Camp.

Notes: In addition to the equipment listed for Whitney, bring crampons, an ice axe, warm clothing and at least two quarts of water. The Forest Service requests that all climbing parties obtain a wilderness permit and sign a register prior to their trip; this can be accomplished at the ranger station in Mount Shasta.

Contact: For equipment rental and weather information, phone The Fifth Season, (916)926-3606, or House of Ski, (916)926-2359. For maps and general information, phone the Shasta Cascade Wonderland Association, (800)326-6944, or the Shasta-Trinity National Forest Mount Shasta Ranger District at (916)926-4511.

Best Five Bike Rides

The Bay Area is the most beautiful metropolitan area in the world, and if you don't believe that, try seeing it on a bicycle.

The five best bike routes mix the sensational with the divine, with both lookouts and pristine surroundings. Some of these routes are well-known, some are not, but all are safe, suitable for a family, group or solo riders, and are easily accessed for great half-day adventures.

Because of the Bay Area's temperate climate, any month is good for biking. November is my favorite, with fall colors, ideal temperatures, and often no wind at all (between storms). It's key for cyclists to pick a roadway or byway where they won't mix with many cars or hikers, because both are incompatible with bikes. These five bike tours provide that, as well as great natural beauty:

1—Golden Gate Bridge to Sausalito

This is the classic ride in the Bay Area. You ride north right across the Golden Gate Bridge (the lane on the west side is reserved for bikes on weekends), then upon reaching land, take the loop under the bridge, ride down to Fort Baker, and from there, head right into Sausalito for eats. A good side trip includes poking around Fort Baker, where there is a great view of the Golden Gate from Yellow Bluff.

Insider's note: Park your vehicle at the southern foot of the Golden Gate Bridge, just west of the toll plaza. If you want to extend this into a longer trip, see Bike Trip #4 on page 437.

2—Dumbarton Bridge to Coyote Hills

The view from the highest point on the Dumbarton Bridge makes you feel like you could reach out and touch all of the Bay Area's highest peaks: Mount Hamilton, Mount Diablo, Mount Tamalpais and Montara Mountain. You are also circled by the South Bay's tidelands and an open expanse of water, all quite sensational. The Bay is the highlight, with the Dumbarton Bridge providing a bike path that separates cyclists from car traffic with a cement barrier.

Insider's note: The best place to park your vehicle is at the eastern foot of the Dumbarton Bridge. From there, the trip can be extended on either side of the South Bay. At Newark, you can explore the San Francisco Bay National Wildlife Refuge or head farther north to Coyote Hills Regional Park. At East Palo Alto, a paved bike trail is routed south to the Palo Alto Baylands, and beyond (just south of Ming's Restaurant) to a bike trail that extends all the way to the Shoreline Regional Park in Mountain View.

Contact: Phone the U.S. Fish and Wildlife Service, Newark, (510) 792-0222.

3—Inspiration Point to San Pablo Ridge

This is one of the Bay Area's great family bicycle trips, the trail being routed four miles right along the crest of San Pablo Ridge, the East Bay's best vista. The "trail" is actually a small paved road with a dividing line that is off-limits to cars. The views are beautiful in all directions, especially to the west of San Francisco Bay and the city skyline, and also to the east to Briones Lake. The route is shared by walkers and joggers, but it works out fine, with most of the foot traffic staying just off the paved portion of the trail.

Insider's note: There are no restrooms available on the trail, and just a few benches and picnic tables.

Directions: From San Francisco, drive across the Bay Bridge and take Highway 24 into the East Bay hills. Drive through the Caldecott Tunnel and then take the Moraga Way exit. At the bottom of the off ramp, turn left at Moraga Way (it goes under the freeway and becomes Camino Pablo). Continue on Camino Pablo for two miles, then turn left on Wildcat Canyon Road. Drive about two miles on the winding road, and look for the Inspiration Point parking area at the top of the hill on the right.

Contact: Phone (510)635-0135, ext. 2200.

4—Marin Byway, Sausalito to Bothin Marsh

A superb biking/jogging/walking path is available from Sausalito on northward to San Quentin Prison. Park in Sausalito and start pedaling north, where you will pass under the Highway 101 overpass, then continue on the trail through Bothin Marsh Open Space Preserve. It borders Richardson Bay, and is quite pretty and varied, crossing small bridges over tidal waterways. The area is beautiful both at high tide, when the bay is full of water and vibrant with life, and at low tide as well, when little sandpipers and migratory birds poke around the mud.

Insider's note: It is possible to route a trip from the Golden Gate Bridge all the way to San Quentin Prison on this path, with the route interrupted by town streets on only a few occasions.

5—Peninsula's Byway, San Mateo to Woodside

Canada Road is the centerpiece of this trek, a backroad in the beautiful Peninsula foothills. The road borders the San Francisco Fish and Wildlife Refuge, Crystal Springs Reservoir, the Pulgas Water Temple, the Phleger Estate, and goes all the way to Woodside, where you can find lunch. An excellent parking area is available along Highway 92 near its junction with Highway 280. This trip is easy, pretty, and who knows, you might even see a herd of deer on the adjacent wildlands.

Insider's note: "Canada" Road, by the way, is pronounced so it rhymes with Mexican "pinata," not the country. On the first and third Sundays of each month from March through October, the road is closed to all motor vehicle traffic from Highway 92 to Edgewood Road.

Waterfalls of the Bay Area

Many people would like to know what heaven is like, but they aren't real eager to make the trip.

Visiting the Bay Area's waterfalls can solve that. Each seems divine, yet to enjoy the experience all you have to do is take part of a day, drive to the trailhead, and hike a little.

The Bay Area has several hidden waterfalls that make perfect destinations for walks. Any time from early winter through early summer is the time to visit, when winter rains turn creeks from trickles to fountains.

The best of them is Berry Creek Falls in Big Basin, and its nearby cousin, Cascade Falls, located a mile uphill and upstream. Many smaller ones can be searched out in Marin County on the flanks of Mount Tamalpais, with Cataract Falls and Carson Falls my personal favorites. Alamere Falls at Point Reyes, which runs into the ocean, is the most unique.

In the East Bay, there are two good falls and lots of little ones. The largest is Joaquin Murietta Falls (100 feet high in the Ohlone Regional Wilderness), and also Abriego Falls in Briones Regional Park. There are numerous other little seasonal falls tumbling down the centers of small canyons throughout the East Bay system, such as in Little Yosemite at Sunol Regional Wilderness, and also in Wildcat Canyon and Tilden regional parks.

Here are descriptions of my favorites:

1—Berry Creek Falls, Big Basin

This is set deep in a redwood forest in Big Basin State Park, about a two-hour walk (sometimes a bit longer) from headquarters on the Skyline-to-the-Sea Trail. See the story on page 213 for more details.

You hike past giant redwoods, making the short climb to the rim of Big Basin, then walk westward, downhill along an easy grade, surrounded by lush forest. Eventually, you come around a bend to the waterfall, which is 70-feet high and framed perfectly in a fern-lined canyon. It looks like a scene out of an Ansel Adams' photograph.

Information: Big Basin State Park, (408) 338-6132.

2—Cascade Falls, Big Basin

The Cascade Falls are named after a series of short, steep and vibrant waterfalls located a mile upstream of Berry Creek Falls in Big Basin. The trail is very steep, actually stepped in staircase fashion, paralleling the falls. At one spot, you can dip your head into the falling water without getting the rest of you wet.

Information: Big Basin State Park, (408) 338-6132.

3—Cataract Falls, Mount Tamalpais

Cataract Falls are located on the creek that feeds Alpine Lake on the northern flank of Mount Tam. The trailhead is at a hairpin turn on Bolinas-Fairfax Road at the dam. From there, you hike up, up, up—a steep but short climb, and well worth it.

Information: Sky Oaks Ranger Station, (415) 459-5267.

4—Carson Falls, Mount Tamalpais

This is a small, seasonal waterfall that tumbles from rocky chutes into pools. Eventually, the creek pours into giant Kent Lake less than a mile downstream. The trailhead is at Liberty Gulch, the first deep cove at Alpine Lake that drivers reach coming west on Bolinas-Fairfax Road. The hike is routed up Old Sled Trail, crossing the ridge at Oat Hill Road, then down to the falls on Old Spool Trail.

Information: Sky Oaks Ranger Station, (415) 459-5267. The best map available is "Trails of Mount Tamalpais," which is available for $5.95 at park interpretive centers or by mail from Olmsted Brothers, P.O. Box 5351, Berkeley, CA 94705.

5—Alamere Falls, Point Reyes

Alamere is a unique and surprising waterfall, tumbling 40 feet from a bluff right down to the beach. The "stream" then runs a short distance right into the ocean, one of the few places anywhere which does so. There are several routes to reach it, the shortest requiring a 5.6-mile hike from the Palomarin Trailhead, located north of Bolinas.

Information: Point Reyes Visitor Center, (415) 663-1092. For a free map of the Point Reyes area, write to Map, Point Reyes National Seashore, Point Reyes, CA 94956.

6—Murietta Falls, Sunol Regional Wilderness

A free-flowing creek runs through a rocky gorge, then plunges 100 feet over a cliff, landing in the rocks below. Upstream of Murietta Falls, there are an additional series of small pools and cascades. Why do so few people know about it? Because is it a long, hard 13-mile walk to get there, and in addition, this creek goes dry in the summer.

Information: Sunol Regional Wilderness, (510)862-2244; or Regional Park Headquarters, (510) 635-0135.

7—Abriego Falls, Briones Regional Park

This waterfall is set in a heavily-vegetated ravine, just up the trail from Wee-Ta-Chi Camp as you climb toward the Briones Ridge. It's a small waterfall, narrow and cascading, just a trickle in the summer. Over the years, its flows have hollowed out the rock face, giving it a shallow cave-like appearance. It is unusual and worth seeing.

Information: Briones Park, (510) 229-3020, or Regional Park Headquarters, (510) 635-0135, ext. 2200.

Appendices

Parks and Recreation Areas

East Bay Regional Park District

The East Bay Regional Park District manages more than 50 parks that cover 75,000 acres in Alameda and Contra Costa counties. There are more than 1,000 miles of trails that cut through all kinds of settings, and an additional 100 miles of trails that connect the parklands.

Contact: For information and free maps, phone (510) 531-9300, ext. 2208, or write the East Bay Regional Park District, 11500 Skyline Boulevard, Oakland, CA 94619.

Golden Gate National Recreation Area

Redwood forests, grassy hillsides and ocean bluffs make this a spectacular attraction in Marin County. Some of the best spots are Muir Woods, Tennessee Valley, the Marin Headlands and Mount Tamalpais. A network of trails connects the different parks.

Contact: For a free map and brochures, call the Golden Gate National Recreation Area at (415) 556-0560, or write the National Park Service, Building 201, Fort Mason, San Francisco, CA 94123.

Midpeninsula Regional Open Space District

This is one of the best-kept secrets on the San Francisco Peninsula, with 25,000 acres of open land sprawling across more than 300 preserves—most of them set along the Peninsula ridgeline at Skyline Boulevard. Access is free.

Contact: For maps, phone the Midpeninsula Regional Open Space District office at (415) 691-1200, or write 330 Distel Circle, Los Altos, CA 94022.

Point Reyes National Seashore

This is a diverse place where you can see tule elks, a waterfall that flows onto the beach, and whale spouts on the ocean, all in one day. The terrain varies from grasslands and chaparral ridges to ocean bluffs and forest.

Contact: For information and a free brochure, call (415) 663-1092, or write Point Reyes National Seashore, Point Reyes, CA 94956.

California State Parks

The greater Bay Area has close to 20 state parks that provide hiking opportunities, along with 15 state beaches. The parks range from Angel Island in the center of San Francisco Bay to the redwood forests of Big Basin, Butano and Henry Cowell parks in the Santa Cruz Mountains.

Contact: For a brochure, write to the Publications Office, Department of Parks and Recreation, P.O. Box 942896, Sacramento, CA 94296-0001.

Other Options

Many Bay Area counties also manage their own parks, and you can obtain information by calling them directly. To obtain maps for prime hikes outside of the Bay Area, contact the U.S. Forest Service, which manages 16 national forests in California.

Contact: A guide sheet to National Forests is free by writing USDA-Forest Service, Office of Information, Pacific Southwest Region, 630 Sansome Street, San Francisco, CA 94111. Maps of individual forests, which detail all hiking trails and lakes, cost $2 from the same address. For information, call (415) 705-2874.

Nature Preserves

The quiet America—it is land unencumbered by concrete, stop lights and miles of cars and people. It is a delicate place, where you can retain the belief that you, one person in a vast world, are still important. It is a retreat where you can slink away from the masses and focus on the life immediately around you.

An organization called The Nature Conservancy is committed to preserving habitats in their natural state. In Northern California alone, more than 10 areas have been bought by or donated to the Conservancy—which offers free access to all. Each preserve offers something special, like the mystical attraction of Bishop Pine Reserve near Inverness.

The number of people allowed on a preserve varies from as low as two people per day to as many as 30, depending on the fragility of the area. Access is free, but you must make a reservation—which is easily arranged by calling the Conservancy at (415) 777-0487. Camping is not allowed on the preserves themselves, but campgrounds are situated near every area.

The goal of The Nature Conservancy is to preserve rare and threatened areas. The Conservancy does not take political stands like other environmental organizations, but works by acquiring lands and offering a special and quiet place to be enjoyed by all. A reservation is your only requirement.

The Conservancy is a nationwide organization that owns more than 1.5 million acres, operates 670 preserves and has projects in all 50 states.

Exploring remote areas has become so popular in this state that no matter where you go, it's often difficult not to come upon a party of hikers. On a preserve, your solitude is guaranteed—call it The Quiet America.

Here's a breakdown of the preserves available in Northern California:

Spindrift Point Preserve

Spindrift serves as a viewing area for the migrating gray whales that breach as they pass by the rocks at the tip of the point. The preserve is graced with meadows that provide elaborate wildflower displays and are home for a variety of wildlife.

It's a summer haven for kingfishers, hawks, gulls and the California brown pelican, among many other birds. It's located along the Marin Coast near the community of Muir Beach, just a short drive from San Francisco. Camping is available at the Point Reyes National Seashore. Access is limited to five people per day.

Bishop Pine Preserve

Bishop Pine is a 400-acre area in Marin County about 35 miles north of San Francisco. It sits on the Point Reyes Peninsula, overlooking Tomales Bay near Inverness. The Samuel P. Taylor State Park and the Point Reyes National Seashore offer nearby camping.

The preserve is named after its stand of Bishop pines, which exists within the dense growths of a mixed evergreen forest. This is home for deer, coyote, squirrels, chipmunks and bobcats. A spring-fed stream flows through the center of the preserve and empties into Tomales Bay at Willow Point.

Fairfield Osborn Preserve

Fairfield Osborn consists of 150 acres of oak, evergreen forest, fresh water marsh, ponds and streams high on the slopes of the Sonoma Mountains, 60 miles north of San Francisco.

Copeland Creek crosses the preserve which helps support deer, foxes, weasels, quail and owls. As many as 20 people per day are allowed on the preserve. Camping is allowed at Sugar Loaf Ridge and Sonoma Coast State Beach.

Boggs Lake Preserve

Boggs Lake is nestled in the mountains between Kelseyville and Cobb Valley in Lake County, just eight miles south of Clear Lake, where camping sites are plentiful.

It offers an unusual combination of vernal pool and pond that sit in a basin of volcanic rock. As the lake dries in the summer, wildflowers bloom in concentric rings in the shallow water. The animal life consists of the common natives of the area: deer, raccoons, skunks and an occasional bobcat, mountain lion or fox. Five to ten people per day are allowed access to this area.

Northern California Coast Range Preserve

This is the oldest and largest preserve in Northern California, where some 8,000 acres were protected in 1958. Black bears, deer, mountain lions and other mammals are still found in a wild state here, unaccustomed to the presence of man. Virgin Douglas fir forests in Northern California have been cut extensively for wood products. But here, in one of the few remaining stands, you can still experience the tranquil life that has been unchanged for centuries.

It is situated between Laytonville on Highway 101 and Westport on Highway 1. Camping is offered on the coast at Russian Gulch and Van Damme State Park.

Lanphere-Christensen Dunes Preserve

Just a few people per day are allowed in this fragile area, which is situated along the Pacific Ocean just north of Humboldt Bay near Eureka.

The dunes were formed by the accumulation of sand washed onshore by waves, then blown inland by sea winds. A beach pine forest is found farther inland, where dense stands of trees tower over ferns and mosses and offer an undisturbed home for the wild.

Camping is allowed at Patrick's Point, Prairie Creek and Redwood State Park, where trails are like tunnels through lush vegetation.

McCloud River Preserve

Here's your chance, flyfishers. Rainbow and brown trout are native to this river, where catch-and-release with flies and lures with single, barbless hooks is the rule.

Ten rods per day are allowed on the preserve, five by reservation.

McCloud sits in a steep, forest-lined canyon that's home for ringtail cats, black bears, mountain lions and blacktail deer. More than 85 species of birds, including bald eagles, have been seen on the preserve.

Sacramento National Wildlife Preserve

John Muir described these woodlands as "forests of tropical luxuriance." The dense foliage of oaks, cottonwoods, ash and willows provide habitat for a wide variety of wildlife, such as beavers, mule deer, river otters, ringtail cats, mink and wildcats. No other terrestrial habitat in the state supports so large a number of bird species, including the very rare yellow-billed cuckoo.

The preserve is located near the Sacramento River southwest of Chico and nearby camping is available at Woodson Bridge State Recreation Area and Colusa Sacramento River State Recreation Area.

Elkhorn Slough Preserve

Elkhorn Slough is the second largest salt marsh in California, and is one of the last major undisturbed estuaries on the coast.

It opens into Moss Landing, between Santa Cruz and Monterey, and contains a seven-mile tidal channel. The preserve contains 441 acres.

Some excellent clamming is available on low tides (in the minus one-foot range) just west of the preserve. Camping is available at Fremont Peak.

Big Creek Preserve

Big Creek is located about 45 miles south of Carmel and, at sea level, includes nearly four miles of rock coast centered in the California Sea Otter Refuge. The reserve land rises from the ocean to an elevation of 4,000 feet at its eastern boundary with Santa Lucia Mountain.

The preserve is home to mountain lions, black-tailed deer, bobcats and endangered sea otters. Plus 125 bird species have been observed, including hawks, owls and a myriad number of shorebirds.

Big Creek is also one of the last central coastal areas that supports a vigorous run of steelhead.

Camping is available at Julia Pfeiffer-Big Sur State Park and Andrew Molera State Park. The preserve will allow 20 people access per day.

Midpeninsula Regional Open Space District

The public is a lot smarter than some people (er, politicians) think. For one thing, the public had the wisdom to create the Midpeninsula Regional Open Space District.

The District was established in a ballot vote in 1972, which also provided for annual funding to purchase open space lands on the Peninsula. There are now 23 preserves covering more than 35,000 acres, much of it among the most pristine hiking areas in the Bay Area.

This is part of a trend that has attracted the attention of metropolitan centers across the country. Question: how do you preserve the Bay Area's natural aura from urban sprawl? Answer: you buy open space, then preserve it forever.

That has been the answer in the East Bay with the East Bay Regional Park District, in the North Bay with the Marin Water District and Golden Gate National Recreation Area, and more recently, on the Peninsula.

The first preserve the Midpeninsula Regional Open Space District bought was the Foothill Preserve, 210 acres located adjacent to Page Mill Road in the Palo Alto foothills. That was in June of 1974, and since then, more than 35,000 acres have been purchased, preserved and opened to the public with free access. They are located in San Mateo County, Santa Clara County, and in a small portion of Santa Cruz County.

The following is a synopsis of them:

Fremont Older Open Space Preserve

An historical home is the centerpiece, surrounded by 4.5 miles of trails.

Notes: 740 acres, located in the Cupertino foothills.

Los Trancos

It features the San Andreas Fault Trail, which traces an earthquake faultline for more than a mile.

Notes: 270 acres, located on Page Mill Road near Skyline above Palo Alto.

Montebello

Great hiking is available here, 13 miles of trails in all, including the three-mile loop hike on the Stevens Creek Nature Trail.

Notes: 2,600 acres, located on Page Mill Road, opposite Los Trancos Preserve.

Purisima Creek Redwoods

This is a gorgeous area with redwoods and superb views of the coastal foothills and ocean. Wheelchair access is available, along with rugged hiking.

Notes: 2,500 acres, located on Highway 35 south of Highway 92.

Rancho San Antonio

Deer Hollow Farm is the main attraction, a small working demonstration farm, including animals.

Notes: 970 acres, located in Cupertino foothills.

Saratoga Gap

You get exceptional views of the Santa Clara Valley here, along with good hiking with lots of rock outcrops.

Notes: 615 acres, located on Highway 35 and Highway 9.

Windy Hill

There are panoramic views of the Peninsula, with a parking area along the road at the lookout, and 10 miles of hiking trails.

Notes: 1,130 acres, located on Skyline north of Alpine Road.

Coal Creek

This preserve is known for its rolling meadows, historic barn, and in the spring, blooming wildflowers.

Notes: 490 acres, located on Skyline Boulevard, north of Page Mill Road.

El Corte de Madera Creek

13 miles of trails make for excellent hiking, with the area heavily forested. There are also fascinating sandstone formations.

Notes: 2,800 acres, located on Skyline Boulevard, south of Kings Mountain Road.

El Sereno

This is primarily chaparral foothill country, but with exceptional views of Lexington Reservoir and the South Bay.

Notes: 1,080 acres, located in Saratoga/Los Gatos foothills.

Foothills

Here is the oldest preserve in the system, featuring woodlands and ravines, knolls and lookouts.

Notes: 210 acres, located on Page Mill Road in Palo Alto foothills.

La Honda Creek

This area is made up of open grasslands with hilltops, offering spectacular views of the San Mateo County coast, and lots of wildlife. Permit required for access.

Notes: 840 acres, near La Honda.

Long Ridge

You get views of the coastal redwoods, with an excellent 7.5-mile loop hike available that includes connections to Montebello Preserve and Skyline County Park.

Notes: 980 acres, on Skyline, just north of the intersection with Highway 9.

Pulgas Ridge

A new favorite, with cool canyons and ridgetop views of the adjacent San Francisco watershed lands and its lakes.

Notes: 290 acres, located off Highway 280 and Edgewood Road.

Ravenswood

This is set along South San Francisco Bay, with tidelands, marshlands and lots of birds. Trail construction is planned for the future.

Notes: 370 acres, located adjacent to East Palo Alto.

Russian Ridge

This is one of the best, with a 2,500-foot lookout summit, providing views of Monterey Bay to the west and Mount Diablo to the east; also offers six miles of trails.

Notes: 1,500 acres, located on Alpine Road, near Skyline Boulevard.

Sierra Azul I

This includes densely wooded canyons, old orchards, and a 3.5-mile trail routed through both.

Notes: 1,310 acres, located east of Highway 17, near Kennedy Road.

Sierra Azul II

Mount Umunhum and other classic peaks are the highlights, though public access is currently sharply limited. High hopes for the future.

Notes: 6,000 acres, located above Los Gatos, south of Highway 17.

Skyline Ridge

Highlighted by eight miles of trail, two beautiful farm ponds with lots of wildlife and birds, and access to the adjacent Russian Ridge Preserve.

Notes: 1,250 acres, located on Skyline Boulevard, south of Alpine Road.

Stevens Creek Shoreline

This is a nature study area along the South Bay, a birder's paradise, with waterfowl, shorebirds and trails along a levee.

Notes: 55 acres, located in Mountain View, off Highway 101 on Shoreline Boulevard.

St. Joseph's Hill

A prime spot for hiking and horseback riding, with meadows, wildflowers and the remains of an old vineyard.

Notes: 360 acres, located south of Los Gatos, near Lexington Reservoir.

Teague Hill

Just recently bought and protected as a wildlife habitat, with public access planned for the future. It overlooks Woodside.

Notes: 630 acres, located in the Woodside foothills.

Thornewood

An historic house and grounds are the centerpiece, with docent tours available by reservation.

Notes: 140 acres, located on La Honda Road near Portola Valley.

Note—To obtain a visitor's guide or a trail map for any of the preserves, write the Midpeninsula Regional Open Space District office, 330 Distel Circle, Los Altos, CA 94022, or phone (415) 691-1200.

Index

A

C

D

H

P

S

Y

Z

About the Author

Tom Stienstra is the outdoors writer for the *San Francisco Examiner*, which distributes his column nationally on the Scripps News Service. He was named California Outdoor Writer of the Year in 1990 and 1992, and elected as a director of the Outdoor Writers Association in 1992. He lives "out in the woods" in Northern California, and continually explores North America's wild outdoors as a hiker, boater and pilot.

Other books by Tom Stienstra include:
California Fishing: The Complete Guide
California Camping: The Complete Guide
Pacific Northwest Camping: The Complete Guide
Rocky Mountain Camping: The Complete Guide
Careers in the Outdoors